Governing Security under the Rule of Law?

Governing Security under the Rule of Law?

Edited by:

J. Blad
M. Hildebrandt
K. Rozemond
M. Schuilenburg
P. Van Calster

Eleven International Publishing
The Hague
2010

Published, sold and distributed by Eleven International Publishing
P.O. Box 85576
2508 CG The Hague
The Netherlands
Tel.: +31 70 33 070 33
Fax: +31 70 33 070 30
Website: www.elevenpub.com

Eleven International Publishing is an imprint of Boom uitgevers Den Haag.

ISBN 978-90-8974-409-8

Preface

This volume nourishes on the international conference held on 23 April 2010 in Hotel New York, Rotterdam. The conference, on 'Governing Security Under the Rule of Law?', was organised by the Research School Safety and Justice (OMV).[1] It was in fact the concrete result of the Advanced PhD Course on Safety, Security and Justice.

From 2000 until 2011 the OMV has been a platform of collaboration for a set of research institutes in the Netherlands,[2] focused on social science and legal research of issues in safety and justice. This entailed interdisciplinary exchanges and cooperation across institutional boundaries, thus generating a network of senior and junior legal and social science researchers. The main function of the OMV was to provide an educational environment for PhD students, starting from the idea that safety and justice should not be studied from a mono-disciplinary perspective. The courses and seminars meant to introduce PhD students to the relevant criminological, sociological, psychological en legal approaches, sensitizing young researchers to the tensions between various types of safety, security and the role of policing, legal certainty and democratic government. In the OMV Educational Program the Advanced Course on Safety, Security and Justice was introduced as follows:

> 'The safety and security of citizens will be explained as the "raison d'être" of the state, while at the same time the state should provide the means to contest its own authority as it may itself threaten the security of its citizens. This is commonly called the paradox of the "Rechtsstaat": saved by the state and saved from the state (by the state). The tension between protection of citizens against each other (crime) and protection against unjustified state intervention forms the core of joint research between lawyers and criminologists. The aim is not to resolve this tension or to deny it, but to sustain it and to investigate the actual problems it raises and their possible solutions.'

---

1 The Dutch name of the Research School is 'Onderzoeksschool Maatschappelijke Veiligheid' (OMV). Since 2009 the official English name has been Research School Safety and Justice, to emphasize that safety and justice should not compete for priority, even if their co-existence requires.

2 Members were as of 1999 Erasmus University Rotterdam (EUR), University Amsterdam (VU), Leiden University (UL), Netherlands Institute for the Study of Crime and Law Enforcement (NSCR), University of Twente (UT), Addiction Research Institute Rotterdam (IVO), Research and Documentation Centre (WODC), Knowledge for business (TNO), Institute for Safety, Security and Crisis Management (COT). Recently TNO and COT have left the School, while the VU extended its participation by the Security Lab.

In the Course Materials the more concrete content of the Advanced Course was described as:

> 'The central theme of this course is the role played by the (criminal) law in securing both safety and justice. Instead of presenting a coherent argument that explains how we can reduce risk by introducing novel policy measures or novel legislation, students will be confronted with three different approaches to the issue of governing security. Following Ulrich Beck's call for attention in his text on *Risk Society Revisited: Theory, Politics, Critiques and Research Programmes*, the idea will be to challenge overly general approaches to both risk and its remedies. Instead of developing grand theories or reductive quantitative models the course will invite students to rethink the issue of security in context and to re-evaluate the role played by the criminal law. The course will start with a rational reconstruction of one of the core texts on the Classical School of Criminal Law Philosophy: Beccaria's *On Crimes and Punishments* by Klaas Rozemond. His point will be to raise the question of whether a moderate penal climate that puts constraints on the operation of the State's ius puniendi is in fact an effective instrument to secure both safety and justice, as Beccaria claimed. In their *Governing Security*, Johnston and Shearing claim that reality has proved Beccaria's dream of a criminal law that is both effective and just to be an illusion. The second part of the course will develop the notion of restorative justice as an alternative procedure to deal with criminal offenses, especially those that involve identifiable victims. John Blad will argue that some specific harms can be addressed without punishing the offender, claiming this to be a more effective intervention than the use of the ius puniendi. He will, however, raise the question of how this approach can be made compatible with the protective and instrumental aspects of the criminal law. Finally, in the third part of the course, Beck's appeal to contextualise risk will be taken up in a different approach to the study of risk. Marc Schuilenburg and Patrick Van Calster will explore how actual networks of things, people, policies etc. form 'assemblages' that aim to reduce risks in particular contexts, depending on the interactions between stabilized patterns of behaviour (e.g. the criminal law, the police, retail shops) and all kinds of actants (e.g. consumers, surveillance cameras, architectures, service providers, lamp posts, dogs, coffee shops etc.). They will make visible how the governance of security sometimes operates in function of a logic that is at odds with core principles of the criminal law, and raise the question of how we could understand the protective and instrumental functions of the criminal law, without falling prey to either a lame idealism or a cynical "Realpolitik".'

Following up on the Advanced Course the Dean of Education, the teaching staff and several of the PhD students prepared a conference on this theme by inviting international keynote speakers, notably Adam Crawford and Philip Stenning, and disseminating a call for papers. The topic of the conference evolved from the contents of the Course and was described as follows:

> 'The central theme of this working conference is the role played by the (criminal) law in securing both safety and justice. Instead of attempting to produce a coherent argument that explains how we can reduce risk by introducing novel policy measures or novel legislation, participants are asked to confront three different approaches to the issue of governing security. Following Ulrich Beck's call for attention in his text

> on *Risk Society Revisited: Theory, Politics, Critiques and Research Programmes*, the idea will be to challenge overly general approaches to both risk and its remedies. Instead of developing grand theories or reductive quantitative models the conference aims to rethink the issue of security *in context* and to re-evaluate the role played by the criminal law.'

The teaching staff wrote three introductory papers around the three core texts by Beccaria, Beck and Johnston & Shearing. This formed the backbone of the three parts of this volume, which brings together criminal law scholars, criminologists, scholars of public administration and legal philosophers from within and without the OMV. We think that in presenting this volume the OMV has come up with a topical contribution to the debate over the political, legal and scientific implications of the shift from government to governance and from top-down to nodal models of governing security.

Due to changes in the national research 'climate' the board of the OMV decided to end the collaboration, at least in its present form. Luckily the topic has taken root rather firmly, since as off October 2010 we have a Minister of Safety and Justice. Whether this indicates their willingness to take the findings of this Research School to heart we cannot assume. Renaming one's Ministry after 'safety' could point in the direction of a further entrenchment of 'the culture of fear', discussed in another English volume recently published by the OMV. Let's hope this 'Etiquetten-schwindel' merely confirms the duty of the state to warrant the safety of its citizens *in a way that* safeguards their fundamental rights and liberties.

Anyway, this volume will be the last of an interesting series of publications in the OMV-series on the topic of 'safety and justice', thus closing the ranks of a productive undertaking. We hope and expect that similar interdisciplinary and interuniversity crossbreeding will continue in other forms, notably enriching the Graduate Schools that are presently taking over.

Mireille Hildebrandt
Dean of Education of the Research School Safety and Justice

Table of Contents

1. Introduction

René van Swaaningen

Over the last couple of years, the PhD Research School OMV has at various occasions engaged with the tensions new models of crime control pose to the Rule of Law. The 'Culture of Fear' that incites ever more intrusive security measures, or the precautionary logic that is based on risk assessments, have been scrutinised in previous OMV-volumes (Hildebrandt et al., 2009; Hildebrandt and Pieterman, 2010). Now we will examine what questions new forms of 'nodal governance' pose to the idea of the *Rechtsstaat*, the continental European embodiment of ideas on good governance ruled by written law. The development of this classical model of criminal law is often seen to have started with Césare Beccaria's famous book *Dei Delitti e delle Pene* (On Crimes and Punishments) from 1767. A number of the contributions gathered in the first part of this latest OMV-book discuss what the current value is of Beccaria's postulate of a legal system that regulates the right to punish – the so-called *ius puniendi* – and offers citizens guarantees against arbitrary (State) intervention. To what extend is Beccaria's dream of an effective and legitimate criminal law still alive?

Today, both the States' *ius puniendi* and the guarantees against arbitrary intervention seem to be under siege. The idea that the right to punish would be under attack needs some explanation in an era that is mostly characterised as very punitive; and this new punitiveness is, moreover, informed by 'penal populism' rather than any rational expert knowledge on effectiveness or proportionality (Downes and Van Swaaningen, 2007). The times that abolitionists and other penal reformers argued for a less punitive approach to crime seem long gone. But, in the increasingly influential 'restorative justice' movement, that is notably inspired by the works of John Braithwaite, the notion that 'reintegrative shaming' is a more effective means of crime control than sheer punishment has in a way taken its position – albeit in a less radical appearance. Yet, the question can be posed to what extend a more informal model of restorative justice would undermine the protective or instrumental aspects of the criminal law. In a second part of this book the pros and cons of ways of sidestepping the punitive system will be discussed.

Two people who have straightforwardly concluded that Beccaria's dream of a criminal law that is both effective and just is an illusion are Les Johnston and Clifford Shearing – in their book *Governing Security* from 2003. The new 'dream' of effectiveness lies in risk assessment, calculability, precautionary intervention, in numerous networks of 'things', people and organisations who form 'assemblages' that are meant to reduce risks in a certain context and in all kinds of other 'agents of social control' – varying from fellow citizens to surveillance cameras to architecture to lamp posts to service providers, etc. In one way or another the word 'just' seems to have disappeared from the dream. In the third part of this book these new ways of 'governing security' are examined. The question how this counter-logic to Beccaria's dream affects both safety and justice plays a key role in this respect.

Ideas on risk-led policy and actuarial justice hark back on Ulrich Beck's work on the risk society of the early 1990s. It has been applied to new developments in criminal justice by Malcolm Feely and Jonathan Simon (1994). In 1997, Richard Ericson and Kevin Haggerty have argued that the role of the police in a risk society changes into that of information brokers. Feeley and Simon point at new preventative rationales behind sanctioning and practices of screening, profiling and selective incapacitation based on somebody's estimated risk of mainly recidivism. Ericson and Haggerty build their argument on the internal system-logic and the alleged inevitability of technological developments. It is, they argue, unlikely that relatively new and complex crimes – ranging from e.g. radicalisation to transnational organised crime – will be discovered by coincidence or by traditional police investigation methods. New techniques are simply needed to create an effective criminal justice system. And if new information or biometric techniques are available, they will also be used; regardless of any normative considerations.

Today we can do hardly anything else but conclude that ever since a risk-based rationale has permeated the whole criminal justice system. Characteristics of the logic of risk-thinking, such as the desire to predict and control risks, the paradoxical relation towards the 'expert' – who is both needed to assess the risks and mistrusted because he does not talk the language of 'ordinary people' – and 'fear' as the motor behind the current obsession with security and the introduction of a wide array of security measures are but all too visible. In his contribution to this OMV-book, Adam Crawford has pointed at the fact that, whilst risk-management presupposes a rational approach of problems, the politics of fear behind it is based in the irrational. In this way, policy-choices that are as such irrational – i.e. not in line with research findings – are rationalised with a discourse of 'evidence based best practices', 'precaution' or 'risk management' to make it seem *as if* things were manageable.

In an earlier publication, I have indicated where actuarial practices conflict with some longstanding principles of criminal law (Van Swaaningen, 1997). Are we still presuming innocence? The least we can say is that a risk-profile takes an advance on the determination of guilt. Can we still speak of 'equality before the law' if we argue that certain individuals or groups have high criminogenic risk? To what extent is the 'concrete suspicion', needed to treat somebody as a 'suspect' in a criminal law context, created beforehand by proactive policing? And if the risk of recidivism becomes so dominant in the attribution of punishment, to what extend does the principle of proportionality still hold? Do crime control practices need to be brought back under the Rule of Law, or are our classical legal principles in need of revision in the light of the new developments? This discussion is taken further in the first part of this book.

1. Part I Beccaria's Dream of an Effective and Legitimate Criminal Law

In his opening chapter Adam Crawford gives an overview of recent developments of 'governing security' in Britain. Since the Dutch authorities often take their policy examples from the UK, it is worthwhile reading Crawford's critical account of most notably the Anti-Social Behaviour Orders (ASBOs), that are to be introduced in the Netherlands, whilst in Britain an increasing number of practitioners (and indeed also politicans) wants to get rid of them. According to Crawford, the common rationale behind many of these new measures is that risks are being individualised, 'good behaviour' is seen as something that can and should be enforced, 'regulation' takes the place of traditional law enforcement, and uncertainties are met by an precautionary logic.

This rationale of crime control does obviously not echo Beccaria's dream – although Crawford discusses this just in passing. In his next chapter, Klaas Rozemond seems to accept Johnston and Shearing's thesis that Beccaria's dream has not come true if we look at current crime control practices. But, Rozemond's answer is a rational reconstruction of Beccaria's theory, mining it for explanatory indicators that are highly relevant for today's security programmes. The advice to take care of one's own security because the State cannot do that can, however, hardly called 'new': the advice in the 17th Century Nightwatcher's State was rather similar. That only changed with Beccaria's 'dream of rationality'.

Tineke Cleiren offers an interesting perspective on the challenges nodal governance poses to the Dutch criminal justice system, specifically because it is based in the continental idea of the *Rechtsstaat* rather than the Anglo-Saxon notion of the Rule of Law. Cleiren argues that the State has become a player, rather than the keeper or the leader it traditionally was. She links the emergence of increasingly intrusive crime policies to the disappearance of many welfare arrangements. Especially because the judiciary has become more dependent on other actors – such as the police, forensic experts, the child protection council – and are more bound by policy-guidelines, Ard Schoep stresses the necessity of an independent judiciary in order to prevent an increasing instrumentalisation of criminal justice. It is quite telling in this respect that under the new Right-wing Dutch government the name of the Ministry of Justice is changed into Ministry of Security and Justice – with Security first. Finally, in his chapter, Jean-Marc Piret demonstrates how the discussion on terrorism is used as a trigger to lift legal guarantees. By calling terrorism suspects 'unlawful enemy combatants' and torture 'moderate physical pressure' war-talk is introduced to neutralise criminal law's guarantees against arbitrary intervention. Exceptions to normal criminal procedure and the introduction of all kind of emergency measures tend to be expanded to other areas and form thereby a very slippery slope for Beccaria's dream.

2. Part II Sidestepping the Punitive System

Phillip Stenning kicks off the second part of this book with a critical account of restorative justice. He poses the question whether conflicts really (only) belong to the parties directly involved – as famously argued by Nils Christie in his classic 'Conflicts as Property' from 1977. Moreover, Stenning argues that the assumption that victims and communities are willing to be made responsible for the settlement of (their) disputes is debatable. He also challenges the claim that restorative justice has a substantial impact, and argues that it only offers an alternative for one of the many functions of criminal justice.

John Blad answers that many of the proclaimed functions of criminal law (e.g. deterrence) do not hold in an empirical sense either, whereas this has never been an argument to abolish criminal law. One of the things that can be avoided by restorative justice is the 'production of criminal identities' as is the negative side-effect of the penal labelling process. We accept criminal law, and the dispersal and growth of quasi-penal arrangements through 'nodal governance', so easily, not because they 'work', but because we hold them for normal and indispensible, without seriously posing the question what this idea is based on. In an interesting, rather detailed exposé of Beccaria's work Hendrik Kaptein argues that restorative justice is quite compatible with Beccaria's dream: notions about compensation and even shaming can be traced back in *Dei Delitti e delle Pene*. Kaptein describes restorative justice as a civilised form of retribution.

In yet again a very different way Abiola Makinwa shows that proximate settlements can be more effective than distant, penal sanctions. She applies a private law transaction approach to the problem of international corruption. Such an approach could well be more effective than penal sanctions because it implies more interaction; a logic that remains closer to the origins of corruption. Hereby she challenges the idea that restorative approaches are only suited for small-scale individual problems in a local setting.

3. Part III A Close-Up of 'Governance of Security' Practices

Patrick Van Calster and Marc Schuilenburg open the third part of the book with a philosophical exposé of the so-called 'molecular', the unpredictable elements that are always in a state of flux, that ultimately determines the 'molar', the solid and 'controllable' reality. This 'molecular' reality is an addition to the formal description of institutions and phenomena that needs to be taken into account in our analyses. It sheds light on the question of what happens *beyond* the rules and official lines and on the role acceptance and customs play in this respect.

In the next chapter, Monica den Boer and Jelle van Buuren focus on concrete 'surveillance nodes' on the level of the European Union. The EU is in the process of developing itself into a super-node, which is tentacled by smaller but powerful nodes that interlink public and private actors in the member states through surveillance systems. The expansion of surveillance assemblages is intimately connected with the growing popularity of precautionary logic. Many of the new regulations on the use of information and biometric techniques or on data exchange between different systems are actually conflicting with national law, but because the 'security argument' is effectively played out against legal principles and civil rights there is, as Den Boer and Van Buuren call it, an 'absence of controversy'.

In the next chapter both the empirical and the normative claims of the new governance of security are challenged. Tobias Arnoldussen argues that all these risk-assessments, calculations and estimations only offer merely quasi-certainty. In an interesting way he links the new knowledge claims of 'measuring is knowing' positivists with Michel Foucault's theory of the power-knowledge relation and speaks of 'governance by numbers'. Human rights and justice resist quantification, Arnoldussen argues.

In the last chapter Barbara van Caem approaches ideas on proximity and distance in communities, which is also implicit in the debate on restorative justice, from an empirical angle. She concludes that the success of a community-based governance of security varies strongly from one neighbourhood to another. Active citizen participation in a more general sense is the key to a success of such an approach; if that is absent community-based policy also falls flat.

References

Downes, D., & Swaaningen, R. van (2007). The Road to Dystopia? Changes in the Penal Climate of the Netherlands. In: M. Tonry & C. Bijleveld (Eds.), *Crime and Justice in the Netherlands* (pp. 31-72). Chicago: The University of Chicago Press.

Ericson, R.V., & Haggerty, K.D. (1997). *Policing the Risk Society*. Oxford: Clarendon.

Feeley, M., & Simon, J. (1994). Actuarial Justice: The Emerging New Criminal Law. In D. Nelken (Ed.), *The Futures of Criminology* (pp. 173-201). London, etc.: Sage.

Hildebrandt, M., Makinwa, A. & Oehmichen, A. (Eds.) (2009). *Controlling Security in a Culture of Fear*. The Hague: Boom Juridische uitgevers.

Hildebrandt, M., & Pieterman, R. (Eds.) (2010). *Zorg om voorzorg*. The Hague: Boom Juridische uitgevers.

Swaaningen, R. van (1997). Beginselen van strafrecht in een risicomaatschappij. In J.R. Blad & P.A.M. Mevis (red.), *Het gelijkheidsbeginsel* (pp. 53-68). Deventer: Gouda Quint.

Part I: Beccaria's Dream under Reconstruction

2. Regulating Civility, Governing Security and Policing (Dis)order under Conditions of Uncertainty

Adam Crawford

> 'Can we know the risks we face, now or in the future? No, we cannot: but yes, we must act as if we do.' (Douglas and Wildavsky 1982: 1)

As historians correctly remind us, we live in what are undoubtedly the most secure, orderly and civil times in the history of humanity, in Europe in particular. The dangers threatening our lives and our person are fewer and further between than in the past. We live longer and generally are more prosperous. Ironically, however, as Bauman (2006: 130) notes, it is here and at this time, 'that the addiction to fear and the securitarian obsession have made the most spectacular careers in the recent years. Contrary to the objective evidence, it is the people who live in the greatest comfort on record, more cosseted and pampered than any other people in history, who feel more threatened, insecure and frightened, more inclined to panic, and more passionate about everything related to security and safety than people in most other societies, past and present'. It is against this paradoxical backdrop, in which the scope of personal freedom and individual autonomy have apparently expanded, that the obsessive quest on the part of governments and citizenry alike for security, order and civility increasingly inform and infuse diverse aspects of everyday life and its contemporary governance. Despite the relative safety to body and possessions and the declining aggregate crime rates experienced across many western jurisdictions in recent decades (at least since the mid-1990s), governing threats to personal safety and local social order have become major governmental preoccupations. They have become a focal point for attention, activities and actions. Consequently, the fears born and fed by subjective and existential insecurities have become very real in their consequences. They have become self-stimulating and aggrandising. In that they prompt defensive actions and breathe life into institutional quests for (unattainable total) security, they tend to scatter tangible reminds of our vulnerabilities and anxieties, and, in so doing, give credibility and immediacy to the threats from which fears over safety are deemed to emanate. Bauman once more notes: 'It is our response to anxiety that recasts somber premonition as daily reality, giving a flesh-and-blood body to a spectre' (*ibid.*: 133).

The aim of this paper is deliberately wide-ranging as it attempts to draw connections and linkages between some of the specific themes engaged with in this collection of essays. I intend to illustrate the manner in which regulatory ideas and practices have: (i) challenged criminal law responses to crime and disorder; (ii) blurred traditional distinctions between crime/incivility, criminal/civil law and formal/informal responses; and (iii) been appropriated in an assault on principles of criminal justice – notably proportionality, due process and protections for young people. Furthermore, I hope to demonstrate how under conditions of uncertainty, novel regulatory ideas have fostered precaution, prevention and pre-emption that prompt more intensive, more extensive and earlier interventions. In presenting these arguments, I will draw primarily on examples from the UK, but with the implication or inference that the themes to which I refer have resonance and salience beyond the UK in other parts of Europe, notably in the Netherlands, albeit that these are likely to take specific forms, influenced by differing constitutional arrangements, local cultures and political traditions.

In this paper, I highlight the convergence of four inter-related thematic trends that collectively influence and go some way to help explain the scope and nature of contemporary security governance and the politics of urban safety. The first of these has been described as the 'individualisation of risk' (Beck *et al.* 1994; Beck and Beck-Gernsheim 2001; Bauman 2001a), a conceptualisation that foregrounds the manner in which human identity is progressively transformed from a fixed 'given' to a malleable 'task', whereby individuals are charged with responsibility for choosing and performing that task and for the consequences or their performance. Second, and allied to this, is the 'politics of behaviour' (Field 2003), whereby governments have increasingly re-focused their energies on governing individual behaviour, incivilities and local social disorder. The third trend has seen a shift in modes of governance from law to 'regulation' (Braithwaite 2008); from traditional 'command and control' style government to forms of governance 'at a distance' through 'regulated self-regulation'. The final trend concerns the manner in which 'risk' and 'risk assessment' as organising narratives of governance have been augmented and supplanted by conditions of 'uncertainty' which have placed an emphasis on precaution as an organised response. In conclusion, I draw these strands together to suggest that in the search for security, civility and order and in a context of uncertainty, a precautionary logic has increasingly come to the fore. As a result, the threshold for intervention and the grounds for pre-emptive action have become dramatically refigured and lowered such that mere suspicion, the subjective perceptions of others and fears about what might occur – infused by worst-case scenarios – come to constitute sufficient grounds for governmental actions. Moreover, these interventions have significant implications in that they infringe liberties and restrict freedoms of those deemed 'dangerous', 'awkward' or 'different' as much for what they might do as for what they have done.

1. The 'Individualisation of Risk'

Ulrich Beck's 'Risk Society' thesis has influenced and informed much recent thinking in the social sciences. In essence, he argues that the 'risk society' constitutes a new stage of modernity, which has seen the production of new risks that lie beyond the control of nation states with potential impact that transcends national territories. Global warming is the archetypical example of such risk. In the process, it is argued, managing hazards has become a central preoccupation of contemporary societies. As 'risk' thinking has spread and risk assessment technologies have proliferated, so individuals and institutions have become heavily dependent on expert advisors; to provide guidance as to what is healthy and what is safe. However, in response to such questions, scientific experts frequently provide conflicting information, facts and opinions. Science in this light is shown to be fallible. Beck notes: 'Science becomes indispensable, and at the same time devoid of its original validity claims' (1992: 165). This fallibility of scientific advice engenders uncertainty and anxiety among a wary public. Moreover, in the subsequent public debate, risk professionals no longer monopolise risk-talk nor do they exclusively influence policy-formation. This both democratises debate – in that the radio chat shows' conclusions and the views of ordinary members of the public may be as valid as those of the 'experts' – and simultaneously renders policy debate more volatile.

This argument has obvious implications for governments' limited capacity to manage and assert sovereign control over contemporary risks, notably in the face of global forces – as illustrated by the recent financial crisis. So too, it has implications for individuals. The break-up of the welfare state and the onset of neo-liberal reforms have served to proliferate and disperse risks once deemed the responsibility of the nation-state. Where previously contained through social insurance – public welfare provisions – risks have increasingly become individualised. In this light, a defining feature of contemporary living is the institutionalised need, on behalf of individuals, to construct and invent one's own 'self' and actively shape one's future in the face of contemporary risks. According to Bauman: 'Modernity replaces determination of social standing with compulsive and obligatory self-determination' (2001b: xv); individuals' life trajectories become 'elective'. Here 'choice' becomes not only a meta-narrative and defining condition, but also a requirement. How one lives becomes a 'biographical solution to systemic contradictions' (Beck 1992). Whilst, risks continue to be socially produced, it is the responsibility and the necessity of coping with them that have become increasingly individualised. Failure, too, is internalised as the product of one's own doings. Social problems are thereby recast as personal faults and individual deficiencies. Public issues are redefined as private and personal troubles:

> 'Living your own life therefore entails taking responsibility for personal misfortunes and unanticipated events. Typically, this is not only an individual perception, but a culturally binding mode of attribution. It corresponds to an image of society in which

> individuals are not passive reflections of circumstances but active shapers of their own lives, within varying degrees of limitation.' (Beck and Beck-Gernsheim 2001: 24)

'Individualisation' exhibits both a positive face and a dark side. 'Creating the self' generates self-determination with democratic potential, whereby individuals can escape from fate and social conventions to play a greater part in public life, particularly evident in the increased range of apparent choices and wider public participation available to girls (Arnot 2008). However, the flip-side of this obligation to actively shape one's future destiny is personal blame for failure: 'Your own life – your own failure' (Beck and Beck-Gernsheim 2001: 24). Consequently, causes are detached from wider structural or societal dynamics and become fastened to individual responsibility; bad outcomes are the result of bad choices as well as the incapacity of individuals to respond to opportunities and actively shape events. In this regard, binding traditions, social institutions and long-term commitments have been replaced by diverse forms of institutional guidance. This guidance focuses more evidently on influencing people's choice rather than the circumstance in which choices are made or people's capacities to realise their preferences. As a consequence, individualisation produces vastly different effects where there are institutional resources (welfare, education, health, human rights, etc.) which people can draw upon in coping with the contradictions of modern personal biographies.

Some time ago, Catherine Villeneuve-Gokalp (1981) noted that 'when the age of choice arrives' – *quand vient l'âge des choix* – it has particular ramifications for young people in transitions to adulthood. Young people are literally charged with making their own bed and lying in it! Yet, the overwhelming evidence, from Britain at least, is that despite the institutionalisation of individual choice, the scope for youth social mobility has narrowed over recent decades. A recent IPPR report – aptly entitled *Freedom's Orphans* - that provides an overview of the evidence in relation to youth attainment concluded: 'Family background is becoming a more important determinant of outcomes across the board' (Margo *et al.* 2006: 47). Furthermore, whilst the measures of youth attainment are improving for the majority of young people, for the most disadvantaged groups many indicators are getting worse. Social class remains the most powerful explanation of outcomes and behaviour. Consequently, 'the current conception of what young people need in order to succeed in life (exercising their own "agency") and the role of the state in supporting them is increasingly anachronistic' (*ibid.*: vii). Not only are young people burdened with greater responsibility to construct their own 'do-it-yourself' biographies, but so too this apparent freedom (albeit trapped within the strictures of social and structural constraints) carries a latent anxiety-generating threat for on-looking adult populations as they recoil at the perceived implications for traditional social mores and values. Moreover, under contemporary conditions, young people appear less reliant on adults for access to information, goods and services in a consumerist society, in which rapid developments in technology often serve to undermine paternalistic social relations and traditional practices as young people are more adept at adjusting to and exploiting technological innovations. These pressures on intergenerational relations present common dilemmas and questions about youth across Europe (Lagrée 2002). They express themselves in concerns about 'the disappearance of childhood' (Postman 1982), 'toxic childhood' (Palmer 2006) and a 'crisis in child well-being' (Layard and Dunn 2009) as well as in fears about young people as harbingers of social decline. Nowhere is this more evident than in the UK which was placed bottom of a league table of 21 rich countries on diverse indicators of child well-being (UNICEF 2007). The American *Time* magazine aptly captured the mood with its April 2008 cover story: 'Unhappy, unloved and out of control: An epidemic of violence, crime and drunkenness has made Britain scared of its young'. Consequently, as Beck and Beck-Gernsheim assert: 'the talk of a "decline of values" contains something else, namely the fear of freedom, including the fear of freedom's children, who must struggle with new and different types of problems raised by **internalised** freedom' (2001: 158, emphasis in original). In this context, the youth population is easily viewed as fear-inducing and incomprehensible to older generations in a way that is both novel but simultaneously reinforces longstanding and recurring themes regarding the manner in which one generation bemoans declining standards and projects concerns about moral decay on its youth (Pearson 1983).

2. The 'Politics of Behaviour'

It is this 'fear of freedom' and more specifically the 'fear of freedom's children' which in large part animates the second trend to which I now turn. In his book *Neighbours from Hell: The Politics of Behaviour*, Frank Field (2003) – an influential member of Tony Blair's first New Labour government in 1997 – argues that the foremost issue facing governments is the collapse in social virtues and common decencies. For Field, the 'politics of behaviour' has replaced the historic 'politics of class' that structured traditional political divisions and was instrumental in moulding respectability and decency in Britain during the nineteenth and twentieth centuries. This decline in standards of civility, according to Field, finds its most clear expression in the perceived rise in 'anti-social behaviour' (ASB). Crucial to Field's analysis is the belief that the type of ASB that blights social relations is novel, hence, it demands new modes of response: 'because it is new, effective means of dealing with it have generally still to be devised' (*ibid*.: 44). For Field, the distinguishing mark of ASB is that each incident, by itself, does not warrant legal response, but it is in its regularity and repetitiveness that ASB 'wields its destructive force' (*ibid*.: 45). Central also to Field's analysis is the focus on 'public space'. Politics, he argues, needs to reconnect with questions about 'the kinds of people we want as citizens'. He is keen to stress that intervention should not encroach on the private sphere. However, once private opinions and the 'values that determine conduct' operate in the public domain 'they cease to be a private concern only, and become part of the stuff of politics (...). If the new politics can be said to be about anything, it is on how best to challenge the private views and values which are impacting so adversely on public conduct' (*ibid.*: 55).

Field's analysis is pertinent for our purposes, not only because his diagnosis of contemporary problems of behaviour chimes with, and has informed, the resultant anti-social behaviour (and 'Respect') agenda which has been a prominent facet of British government policy in the last decade, but also because of the solutions that he proffers. He articulates the need for a politics that seeks to rebuild 'a shared sense of common decencies' through the construction of a new 'social highway code' (*ibid.*: 137) in which conditionality is a defining element:

> 'the best way of doing this is to begin forging a series of contracts which cover the behaviour of all of us as we negotiate the public realm (...). These contracts need to cater for each key stage in our life, at birth, at school, in work, in drawing welfare and at retirement. If the tide is to be turned and anti-social behaviour put to flight, the task is nothing less than the forging of a series of public contracts on behaviour (...) to help shape behaviour these contracts have to be built up, taught and enforced.' (*ibid.*: 82).

Ultimately, what Field is calling for is a fundamental reworking and re-writing of the (implicit) social contract in the shape of a multitude of formal micro-social contracts setting out social responsibilities, obligations, duties and commitments as well as rights and benefits. This is what Tony Blair's government evocatively termed the 'something for something society' (Home Office 2003); whereby access to public services, resource and social insurance are conditional upon conduct and behaviour. Importantly, the form of the 'contract' (or rather quasi-legal contract) is identified, here, as the appropriate regulatory tool rather than the penal or criminal law (Crawford 2003; 2009b). Not only is the former the archetypical mode of neo-liberal control but it also accords well within a market-based regime of choice, in treating its prime agents as autonomous rational choice actors.

But it is in his diagnosis of the fundamental social malaise as lying in the degradation of local order (and insecurity) due to individual behaviour that Field's analysis resonates so vibrantly with contemporary shifts in governance. Whilst what Field describes as the 'politics of behaviour' has taken different forms across divergent jurisdictions – from 'zero tolerance policing' to concerns with 'quality of life' and 'community cohesion' – what they all reflect is a fundamental narrowing and re-sighting of the preoccupations of governing to focus on public displays of individual behaviour as the crucible in which the fortunes of governments are forged. Responding to, and assuaging, public perceptions via the regulation of uncivil behaviour has become an increasingly prominent governmental *raison d'être*. These concerns dovetail (albeit ambiguously) with the 'individualisation of risk' thesis. Whereas Field sees private values polluting the public domain as the source of contemporary social ills, by contrast Beck implies that public issues are redefined as private matters, to be resolved internally. It is the blurring and transgression of the boundary between private and public – between the individual and the social – and the legitimate role and expectations of the citizen and the state which have been rendered so problematic.

What both perspectives point to is the limited capacity of the state to effect change, in the face of uncontrollable flows of capital, goods, people and risks, and the renewed focus on the management of public displays of personal behaviour. The internal world of the individual is seen as the site where societal problems are raised and, consequently, where apparently they must be resolved. Hence, micro-management is gradually replacing the tasks of macro-government. The appropriate role of government has shifted to that of steering, persuading, monitoring and correcting people's life-style 'choices'. In this, aside from offering institutional guidance, increasingly, the role of the state is reduced to one of mopping up market failures and market excesses – from the social consequences of the meltdown in the banking system, via the alcohol-fuelled excesses of the night-time economy (so evident across most British towns and cities), to the socially marginalised 'flawed consumers' of a market economy (Crawford and Flint 2009).

The particular – and somewhat peculiar – governmental form that this has taken in the UK has been the 'anti-social behaviour' (and Respect) agenda, which has stimulated an unprecedented period of intensive hyper-activity and frenetic reform. ASB has come to comprise a distinctive, if capacious, policy field around which consecutive New Labour governments have introduced a plethora of hybrid tools that blur traditional distinctions between civil and criminal processes and challenge established assumptions about due process, proportionality and the threshold for intervention (Burney 2009). The broad definition of ASB extends to a wide range of activities, misdemeanours, incivilities and crimes. In legislation it is defined as behaviour that 'causes or is likely to cause harassment, alarm or distress' to others. This characterisation is both subjective and context-specific as it rests on public perceptions. Above all else, the ASB agenda is concerned with governing 'youth' and it is in response to perceptions of youthful behaviour that much government energy has been targeted.[3]

[3] One of the key measurements of ASB incorporated into the British Crime Survey since 1992 has been the extent to which 'teenagers hanging around on the streets' are deemed to constitute a problem. In the decade between 1992 and 2002 the percentage of respondents who perceived this to be a 'big' problem increased by nearly two-thirds from 20% to 33%.

The array of new hybrid powers includes, *inter alia*, acceptable behaviour contracts (ABCs), anti-social behaviour orders (ASBOs), parenting orders, parenting contracts, tenancy demotion orders, anti-social behaviour housing injunctions, 'crack-house' closure orders, designated public places orders, dispersal orders and penalty notices for disorder. Collectively and individually, many of these modes of control represent a shifting orientation towards forms of governance and behavioural regulation that focus less on knowing and accounting for past incidences than disrupting, reordering and steering possible futures. They seek to regulate crime and disorder through their consequences for, and interconnections with, wider notions of community well-being and public reassurance. Simultaneously, they reflect an individualisation of control, in which responses are tailored around personal and contextual characteristics. In the process, there has been a subtle shift from due process requirements and proportionality as defining ideals of justice to security and public perceptions as predominant overarching preoccupations (Crawford 2009a).

The most noteworthy of the new powers is the ASBO, a civil order which results in criminal sanctions if breached. This has generated significant concern that civil proceedings are being used as a way of evading higher standards of proof and evidentiary burdens associated with the criminal justice process. For instance, the manner in which civil proceedings allow forms of hearsay evidence, not admissible in the criminal court, has been central to securing successful ASBO applications. Furthermore, the ASBO – in the name of effectiveness (Home Office 2005) – permits publicity which in the case of young people has eroded the traditional right to anonymity in civil and criminal proceedings (Cobb 2007). In common with some other new powers – such as dispersal (Crawford 2008) and parenting orders – ASBOs constitute what Simester and von Hirsch (2006) term 'two-step prohibitions', whereby the possibility of criminal sanctions arise only in respect of future conduct, not in relation to the conduct that gave rise to the order in the first place. The conditions imposed at the fist step create something tantamount to what the European Commissioner for Human Rights described as 'personalised penal codes, where noncriminal behaviour becomes criminal for individuals who have incurred the wrath of the community' (Gil-Robles 2005: 34). The conduct that breaches the order, under all other circumstances, may constitute legal behaviour and there need be no direct relationship between the ultimate punishment and the original behaviour. Consequently, ASBOs criminalise conduct which otherwise might have been lawful – such as visiting certain places (from which the person is excluded), meeting certain people (from whom the person has been directed not to associate) or wearing certain items of clothes (which have been prohibited). The hybrid and civil preventive model introduced by the ASBO has been subsequently adapted and transplanted to the regulation of risks in other realms, such as the alcohol-related 'drinking banning order' (Violent Crime Reduction Act 2006), the terrorism-inspired 'control order' (Prevention of Terrorism Act 2005) and the organised crime-associated 'serious crime prevention order' (Serious Crime Act 2007) (see Macdonald 2007; Zedner 2007b).

The wide-ranging nature of the grounds that may trigger an ASBO, ABC, parenting or dispersal order affronts the 'principle of maximum certainty' and the requirements of 'predictability' and 'fair warning' (Ashworth 2006: 74), as it is not clear that the application of the law is knowable in advance. This undoubtedly offends the principles and spirit of Beccaria's 'dream' of an effective and legitimate criminal law and weakens legal constraint on the operation of the state's *ius puniendi*. Ramsay (2009: 135-6) notes how the lack of 'fair warning' evident in much ASB legislation may mean 'it is ultimately impossible to be sure that you have acted cautiously enough in the face of the uncertainties involved and that the problem of insecurity is therefore created by the law rather than solved by it'. Furthermore, in the 'two-step' process, principles of proportionality are decoupled from structuring the relationship between past acts and future constraints. This use of ASB powers is evidence of what Ericson refers to as 'counter-law' whereby: 'New laws are enacted and new uses of existing law are invented to erode or eliminate traditional principles, standards, and procedures of criminal law that get in the way of pre-empting imagined sources of harm' (2007: 27). In this light, 'the counter-law of security is designed to trump law that seeks to protect citizens from excesses of security' (*ibid*.: 163).

3. Regulation

The innovations intrinsic to many of the new powers and technologies spawned in recent years accord with the third trend, namely an apparent shift from command-and-control style legal forms of control to hybrid modes of regulated 'self-regulation'. According to some commentators, we now live in an age of 'regulatory capitalism' (Braithwaite 2008). A defining feature is the expansion in novel mechanisms of regulatory activity that seeks to control, direct or influence behaviour and the flow of events. Increasingly, regulation operates through plural auspices straddling traditional distinctions between corporations, the state and civil society (Scott 2004). From this perspective, regulation not only highlights diverse strategies to foster compliance that lie between punishment and persuasion but also enlists wider actors including the subjects of regulation themselves. Consequently, as I have argued elsewhere (Crawford 2006), regulatory theories connect closely with arguments about 'networked' or 'nodal governance' (Johnston and Shearing 2003; Burris *et al*. 2005). The latter notions seek to provide a conceptual map of the unfolding terrain of governance understood as 'the property of networks rather than as the product of any single centre of action' (Johnston and Shearing 2003: 148), in which the state is accorded no particular conceptual priority in order to highlight the range of governmental nodes that exist and the relationships between them – notably the actual points where knowledge and capacity are mobilised for transmission across networks. Regulatory theories, by contrast, provide normative accounts of good governance through novel forms of regulation (Black 2001). Importantly, this perspective challenges us to think critically about the distinctiveness or uniqueness of state action within contemporary governance.

In contrast to traditional mechanisms that have been associated with sovereign state-centred rule, regulation is said to become 'responsive' where regulators recognise and respond to the conduct of those they seek to regulate in ways that are sensitive to the conditions in which regulation occurs and the capacity of the regulated for self-regulation (Braithwaite 2002: 29). Such responsiveness, it is argued, is likely to produce more legitimate and more effective regulatory outcomes. Implicit in models of regulation, therefore, are diverse assumptions about the motivations and competencies of regulated individuals and groups, as well as different theories of compliance that inform these. The vexed question with which regulatory theorists and practitioners must grapple is which regulatory tools to deploy under specific conditions; when to punish and went to persuade (Braithwaite 2008: 88).

In this vein, a hugely influential paper on *Personal Responsibility and Changing Behaviour* written for the Prime Minister's Strategy Unit (Halpern *et al.* 2004) argued for ways in which government can act as a more effective 'persuader' in changing behaviour in a manner that enhances personal responsibility. It highlights the limits of top-down (command-and-control) regulatory strategies and illustrates how governments can 'help people to help themselves'. Consequently, ideas of 'regulatory justice' have increasingly come to inform British policy debates about reform of the sanctioning system and the role of criminal justice therein. As a result reforms have been designed to 'modernise sanctioning toolkits across the regulatory system, reflecting the risk-based approach to regulation and the broader regulatory reform agenda' (Macrory 2006a: 6). Importantly, the concern is with a wide-scale canvas of public risk in which criminal prosecution is understood as a cluster of 'sanctioning tools' within a much larger framework of regulation.

From a regulatory perspective, in practice however, questions of effectiveness often come to trump normative principles of due process and proportionality. As such, the vernacular of regulation has been used frequently by politicians as a conceptual stick with which to attack the perceived failings of established criminal procedures. In many senses, an abiding legacy of the ASB agenda has been to deploy the language of regulation – particularly in its benevolently clothed terminology of 'better' and 'responsive' regulation – to legitimise forms of state interventionism and control that challenge and circumvent traditional principles and values of (criminal) justice. By fusing civil and criminal processes, hybrid prohibitions have fostered 'new variations of liability' designed specifically to evade established safeguards that themselves have been redefined as troublesome obstacles to effective regulation (Ashworth 2004: 265). This much was explicitly acknowledged by Tony Blair, whilst Prime Minister: '[T]he whole purpose of the antisocial behaviour legislation is to change the terms of trade if you like, change the rules of the game, make sure that when we need to act quickly, we are able to act quickly'.[4] Legal principles of due process and proportionality were too often seen as getting in the way of 'action' through effective social regulation (Ashworth and Zedner 2008).

In the 'politics of behaviour', the language of regulation is particularly attractive in that it not only provides a critique of hierarchical command-and-control style rule of law (and normative principles associated with it) but also because: it conforms with, and advances, an epochal argument that 'new times' demand new responses (in keeping with Field's arguments); it fosters an 'individualisation of control' tailored to the demands of particular circumstances rather than in accord with universal principles; it permits an intensification of control through notions of 'regulatory pluralism' (Gunningham and Grabosky 1998) that advocate the deployment of a mixture of regulatory instruments; its preoccupation with the effectiveness tends to dominate over normative issues (or principles of 'parsimony' that commentators like Braithwaite emphasise); it predominantly treats the subjects of regulation as rational, motivated and capable subjects; and its primary focus is on 'governing the future' rather than normatively re-ordering the past (Crawford 2009a). An abiding concern with the appropriation of the language of regulation in the context of governing crime, disorder and incivility has been the latent capacity for 'regulatory spirals' to develop against a background of public anxieties about insecurity and a pervasive risk-averse 'culture of fear' (Furedi 2002). The Better Regulation Commission astutely outlined the dangers of such an inadvertent regulatory response to perceived risks:

> 'The perception of a risk emerges (...). A public debate follows, often based around headlines and incomplete or biased information, resulting in a call for "something to be done", which is amplified by the media. Instinctively, the public looks to the Government to manage the risk. Responding to this public pressure, the government makes ambitious claims that it can solve the problem and steps in with a regulatory response, rarely considering the tradeoffs involved. As a result, the role of the Government as risk manager is reinforced. When the regulations are implemented, they inevitably fail to solve all the problems and also bring with them unintended consequences. With good implementation, some hazards are prevented, but this does not make news. Other hazards are not prevented and problems persist, leading to calls for more government action. As a result of more regulation, people complain that liberties and enterprise are diminished and criticise the "nanny state". Governments are blamed for interfering and acting unreasonably and, as a result, the national level of frustration shifts up a notch. (If we are not careful), governments

4 Speech at the Meridian Community Centre in Watford, 2 September 2005. See: http://www.number10.gov.uk/Page8123 (last accessed 4.6.2010).

> may seek to address issues of frustration and disengagement through more regulation.' (2006: 7-9)

This narrative of 'regulatory creep' and interference with civil liberties aptly captures many of the key facets of the ASB agenda and the impact of regulatory ideas caught up in the complex 'politics of behaviour' over the past decade in which public (mis)perceptions play a vital role. Ironically, all the talk of 'better regulation' has not diminished the resort to the criminal law and criminalisation as central governmental tools for fostering social compliance. The last decade in Britain has seen the proliferation in the number and range of new criminal laws[5] and has seen the continued expansion in the numbers of people incarcerated within the prison system.[6] Thus, whilst the criminal legal process, one moment, is lambasted as a 'lost cause' (Ashworth 2000) for its incapacity to regulate behaviour, the next moment it is resurrected as a vital and expanding component of regulation. Despite assertions to the contrary, assumptions that 'regulatory justice' necessitates 'an extended toolkit' and a 'richer range of sanctioning tools' (Macrory 2006b: 8, 17) are likely to presage greater interventionism, reinforced communication of government as sovereign risk manager and an extend role of punishment.

4. Conditions of Uncertainty and Precaution

This brings us to the final theme namely the allied notions of uncertainty and precaution that have come to the fore in policy debate and political initiatives. The contemporary focus on governing future risks has raised questions about the robustness and fallibility of risk assessments. To prevent, pre-empt and manage future risks and insecurities demands 'bringing the future into the present'. By necessity, it relies upon knowledge derived from the past. Risk-based (actuarial) thinking involves prediction based on past events and probabilities of the possible loss, injury or other adverse circumstances projected into the future. It treats the future as knowable, based on rational scientific knowledge. Whilst the science of 'prediction' has significantly influenced the world of governing crime and insecurity in the form of 'actuarial justice' (Feeley and Simon 1992); profiling and targeted policing (Harcourt 2007) as well as risk-focused prevention (Farrington 2007), the scientific-base for prevention and pre-emption remains highly indecisive and ambiguous. In governing the future, uncertainty prevails. Determining where risks arise from and who presents a risk test the limits of our ability to predict the future. The limitations of knowledge merely

5 It is estimated that between 1997 and mid-2006, some 3,200 new criminal offences were created, over 1,000 of which were introduced by primary legislation (Morris 2006). During the same period, the Home Office produced some 60 crime-related bills.

6 Since the beginning of 1993 the prison population in England and Wales has more than doubled, rising from 41,600 to over 85,000 by June 2010.

magnify uncertainty. Furthermore, they question the extent to which the individualisation of risk is realised in practice or alternatively, takes the form of 'categorisation' whereby, individuals 'are grasped not as coherent subjects, whether understood as moral, psychological or economic agents, but as members of particular subpopulations and the intersection of various categorical indicators' (Feeley and Simon 1994: 178). My own assessment of these debates (as I hope to demonstrate) is that in the context of security, criminal justice practices that infuse the language of risk still retain notions of individual need (O'Malley 2004), whilst the lack of robust and un-contentious scientific knowledge has weakened the claims of risk prevention through actuarial justice.

In the context of (internal) security threats, the attacks in the US on 11 September 2001 poignantly highlighted the problems of foresight, raised questions about established methodologies for generating actionable intelligence and challenged certain assumptions about the appropriate threshold for intervention. As such, 9/11 influenced much security debate regarding risk assessment, managing insecurities and how formal systems of control are enacted under conditions of uncertainty. In a European context, this was given further salience in the light of the subsequent bombings in Madrid in 2004 and London in 2005. In a much-quoted statement, the former US Secretary of Defence, Donald Rumsfeld speaking in early 2002, assessed the so-called 'new' terrorist threats in the light of the 9/11 attacks and the failure to predict or prevent them, in the following memorable turn of phrase:

> 'Reports that say that something hasn't happened are always interesting to me, because as we know, there are known knowns; there are things we know we know. We also know there are known unknowns; that is to say we know there are some things we do not know. But there are also unknown unknowns – the ones we don't know we don't know.'[7]

Whilst his comments were much derided at the time, Rumsfeld intimated a deeper set of concerns and (by implication) challenges for governments in responding to perceptions of crime and insecurity (notably those associated with terrorist violence). He drew attention to the changing shape and source of contemporary threats to societies, highlighting the limits of expert knowledge about risks, underscoring the unknowability of the future and raising questions about how to govern under conditions of uncertainty. By implication, it is the 'known unknowns' and the 'unknown unknowns' – not simply the 'known knowns' that should be the focus of our concern and hence that we should fear.[8]

---

[7] US Department of Defense News Transcript, 12 February 2002: <http://www.defenselink.mil/transcripts/transcript.aspx?transcriptid=2636> (last accessed 4.6.2010).

[8] Interestingly, Rumsfeld omitted to mention a fourth category of 'unknown knowns'; the things we know but do not admit to knowing! This is the 'silent evidence' (Taleb 2007) that governments ignore, discard, shade from view or lock away. This reminds us of the political nature of knowledge claims and the uses of knowledge.

Crucially, the challenge for governments is how to respond to these 'unknowns'. What is inferred is the need for intervention and action before a threat or risk becomes a 'known'. It is a clarion call for early intervention – for pre-emptive governance – even before risks have expressed themselves or become acknowledged. It proclaims the need to anticipate and forestall potential harms. Massumi notes,

> 'rather than acting in the present to avoid an occurrence in the future, pre-emption brings the future into the present. It makes present the future consequences of an eventuality that may or may not occur, indifferent to its actual occurrence.' (2005: 7–8)

Under conditions of uncertainty a pre-emptive and preventive logic implies a precautionary approach. The 'precautionary principle' has an established role in policy decisions concerning environmental protection and management. In some legal systems, such as in laws of the European Union, the precautionary principle is a general and compulsory legal principle (European Commission 2000). It imposes upon public bodies a duty to act to avert serious or irreversible damage (Sunstein 2005; Wiener *et al.* 2010). It implies a responsibility to intervene and protect the public from exposure to harm where scientific investigation is insufficient, inconclusive or uncertain but where there are indications of possible adverse effects or plausible risks. Protections should be relaxed only if further evidence emerges that supports an alternative explanation. It is applied in circumstances where there are reasonable grounds for concern that an activity is, or could, cause harm but where there is uncertainty about the probability of the risk and the degree of harm (Ewald 2002).

Table 1: The lens of 'risk' and of 'uncertainty'

Risk	**Uncertainty**
• Knowledge is reliable • Analysis based on evidence • Risk assessment • Evidence-based policy • Actuarial techniques/tools • 'Science of prediction' • Categorisation of dangerous populations • Profiling, targeted policing and surveillance	• Knowledge is unreliable • Separation of evidence/ analysis from action/ response • 'What if?'; Worst-case scenarios • Pre-emption, prevention • Early intervention • Suspicion – 'actionable intelligence' • 'Pre-crime' – *incivilities, anti-social behavior, 'radicalisation'*

In the resultant 'war on terror', the precautionary principle took the form of the 'one per cent doctrine'. Ex-vice President Dick Cheney articulated this as follows: 'If there is a one per cent chance (...) we have to treat it as a certainty in terms of our response (...). It's not about our analysis or finding a preponderance of evidence. It's about our response' (cited in Suskind 2006: 62). Importantly, this approach to precaution in the face of uncertainty saw the separation of evidence and analysis from action and response. The bar for intervention was to be reset at a radically lower level, and the basis for action was to be 'as if' it were a certainty. Interestingly, whilst the Bush administration eschewed the precautionary principle in relation to health and environmental regulation, it embraced it in the context of security.9 Whereas placing the burden of proof on demonstrating safety was seen to be problematic in the context of the environment and health (such as GM food for example, see Levidow 2001) because it might stifle innovation and produce damaging effects of institutionalised fear, this was not deemed relevant in relation to security.

Anticipating and forestalling potential crime and behaviour-related harms, in a risk-averse 'culture of fear' where a 'politics of behaviour' prevails, will frequently imply erring on the side of caution. From this perspective, people are to be judged in terms of what they *might* do. Zedner notes, 'precaution places uncertainty – not knowledge – centre stage' (2009: 37). In contemporary quests for security, it is 'uncertainty' that comes to constitute an increasingly dominant 'justification for governmental action (...). It is now our not knowing, our inability to know, or unwillingness to prove what we think we know that provides the reason to act before that unknown threat makes itself known' (*ibid.*: 58). What Rumsfeld is highlighting is a subtle shift from 'risk' analysis to 'uncertainty' as the lens through which state's construct the social problems they seek to govern (see Table 1). Zedner notes:

> 'Whereas risk-thinking stimulated the development of profiling, targeted surveillance, categorisation of suspect populations and other actuarial techniques for managing high-risk populations, uncertainty promotes a different set of techniques geared at requiring public officials to act preemptively to avert potentially grave harms using undifferentiated measures that target everyone.' (2009: 45)

Whilst risk assessments seek to predict the future on the basis of knowledge about how people performed and events unfolded in the past, the logic of security decisions under uncertainty focuses on the questions 'what might be?' or 'what if?' (Walklate and Mythen 2008). This prompts the identification of 'worst-case scenarios' and potential catastrophic consequences without a clear understanding of the likelihood that such outcomes will occur (Sunstein 2007). Given the emotions and affective sentiments that crime, disorder and threats to

---

9 A White House official in charge of vetting regulations is quoted as having told the *New York Times* in 2003 that the Bush administration considered the precautionary principle 'to be a mythical concept, perhaps like the unicorn' (cited in Gardner 2008: 319). On the divergent and selective application of precaution to particular risks in Europe and the US see Wiener *et al.* (2010).

security generate, such premonitions are liable to dampen public attention to questions of probability and proportionality of response. In this light, uncertainty and not knowing, rather than being constructed as a cause for fatalistic inertia, are invested with the urgent need for vital and potent pre-emptive measures, as well as a radical rethinking of the legitimate grounds for early interventions (Dershowitz 2006). Uncertainty privileges security and provokes preventive action before risks express themselves (O'Malley 2004).

Governing under conditions of uncertainty has significant implications for traditional principles of criminal justice, notably the presumption of innocence, due process protections and proportionality. Mythen and Walklate note: 'Once one assumes a projective 'What if?' position, presumption of innocence metamorphoses into presumption of guilt' (2008: 234). In defending the decision to go to war with Iraq, Tony Blair gave an illustrative summation of the logical perils of governing by posing the question 'what if?':

> 'Here is the intelligence. Here is the advice. Do you ignore it? But, of course intelligence is precisely that: intelligence. It is not hard fact. It has its limitations (…). But in making that judgement, would you prefer us to act, even if it turns out to be wrong? Or not to act and hope it's OK? And suppose we don't act and the intelligence turns out to be right, how forgiving will people be?'[10]

The larger the scale of the risk and the more harmful its consequences might be, the more indefensible inaction becomes. In such circumstances, the question 'what if?' prompts action 'just in case'. Uncertainty, by demanding precaution, invokes action even in situations where it is not possible to know the precise nature or extent of the potential threat that is posed. This is where decision-making about security is facilitated, 'not in a context of certainty, nor even of available knowledge, but of doubt, premonition, foreboding, mistrust, fear and anxiety' (Ewald 2002: 294).

Yet as Zedner (2009) notes, 'uncertainty' does not displace 'risk'. Rather, they co-exist at the evident boundaries of knowledge. The contemporary governance of risk – in contrast to the assertions of some criminologist (Feeley and Simon 1994) – is not dominated by the logic of actuarialism (least of all in the field of crime and insecurity), and contrary to Knight's (1921) distinction, risk and uncertainty are not different classes of object. Risk management, Power (2007) proposes, has taken the form of 'organised uncertainty'. He traces the shift from risk analysis to risk governance and argues that much of what today we call risk management is in fact 'uncertainty management' – i.e. 'efforts to manage "risk objects" for which probability and outcome data are, at a point in time, unavailable or defective' (*ibid.*: 26). Yet 'risk' retains an important place, for

[10] http://webarchive.nationalarchives.gov.uk/+/http://www.number10.gov.uk/Page5461 (last accessed 4.6.2010).

risk unlike uncertainty, always demands action. It implies the need to make decisions about the future and the allied allocation of responsibility for decisions taken. It insinuates the decidability and management of danger and hence raises expectations about its governance. Power goes on to argue: 'Uncertainty is therefore transformed into risk when it becomes an object of management, regardless of the extent of information about probability' (2007: 6). Rumsfeld's 'unknown unknowns' and Cheney's 'one per cent doctrine' are both attempts to 'organise uncertainty' as if it was manageable. In so doing, the management of uncertainty creates expectations and distributes responsibilities. Most notably, the public are drawn into this web of expectations over future governance, especially in relation to risks over which they have some responsibility and which impact most acutely on their perceptions of security and safety. In the politics of risk management as in the politics of policing and insecurity, public perceptions matter. This enmeshing of the public in risk governance, however, generates its own dilemmas:

> 'Public perceptions of risk are not simply a new factor in more intelligent risk analysis, they are a source of risk themselves. So, the shift from risk analysis to risk governance is in part a strategy to govern unruly perceptions and to maintain the production of legitimacy in the face of these perceptions' (Power 2007: 21)

However, Wynne (1993) warns against any simplistic assumption that laypeople are essentially defensive, risk- and uncertainty-averse, and unreflexive whilst science, on the other hand, is assumed to be the epitome of reflexive self-criticism. Rather, he shows that laypeople display considerable reflexive negotiation of their identity in relationships to science and scientific institutions. Related claims in the context of crime and security 'talk' have recently been voiced by Loader and Sparks (2010).

Whilst not knowing can be a powerful justification for intervention, so too, risk assessments allow the narrowing of risk pools such that the inconveniences of universal precautions can be displaced onto certain (often marginal) groups alone. Hence, whilst uncertainty might license 'undifferentiated measures that target everyone', as Zedner (2009: 45) argues, and the targets of surveillance are increasingly arbitrary, there are strong political incentives and economic imperatives to reduce this burden to the most 'risky' groups in society. The pressures to target resources and minimise the burdens of security to the general public are likely to result in the sacrifice of 'other people's' freedoms to make 'us' (the dominant majority) feel more secure. In legitimising and informing the process of targeting, knowledge (or a least certain knowledge claims) about risk remains vital. As Ericson astutely notes, 'risk assessment is rarely based on perfect knowledge, and typically frays into uncertainty' (2005: 659). Whilst we all might be inconvenienced at airports by the routine (post-9/11) security checks, these have not displaced more targeted forms of screening nor the quest for 'fast-track' procedures for less risky groups – for example, on the basis that they buy into schemes that require the provision of personal and biometric data (such as a fingerprint and/or an iris scan).[11] Rather than sidelining knowledge, responding to conditions of uncertainty prompts the search for and legitimises imperfect and less robust knowledge claims. Thus, subjective perceptions (rather than objective risks) become more important in informing reassurance strategies (Crawford 2007). The quest for novel sources of information upon which strategies can be constructed prompts a host of precursory identifiers of 'potential risk' and categorisations of 'suspect populations' – or what Zedner (2007a) aptly terms 'pre-crime'.[12] This highlights various forms of behaviour or activities which come to be seen as 'troublesome' and hence 'criminalisable' not in and of themselves (i.e. because they are directly harmful to others *per se*) but because of the way in which they are conceived – from a developmental and temporal perspective – as in someway precursors to criminal behaviour. This includes behaviour that is not-yet-criminal but which is deemed to be an indicator of likely or potential future criminal conduct. 'Anti-social behaviour' is an exemplary illustration of 'pre-crime'; heralding earlier intervention. Likewise the contemporary focus on 'failing' families and 'inadequate' parenting in relation to youth crime has been justified by reference to the likely consequences of non-intervention. To this end, in 2006 Tony Blair announced targeting families and screening for risk of future criminality to prevent problems developing when children grow older. He justified this by articulating a classic precautionary approach: 'If we are not prepared to predict and intervene far more early, children are going to grow up in families that we know perfectly well are completely dysfunctional'.[13]

In the context of terrorism, indicators of 'radicalisation' have become the 'pre-crime' equivalent. In the process, policy preoccupations with 'radicalisation' establish a significantly lower threshold for intervention, as set out both in the

---

[11] For example, Frankfurt airport started a biometric scheme in February 2004 as part of the EU's Border Check initiative and Heathrow announced the establishment of such a scheme in Terminal 3 in late 2006. America's Transportation Security Administration – set up to improve security after 9/11 – launched its Registered Traveler Pilot Program at five airports in 2004 (Frary 2004).

[12] Pre-crime 'shifts the temporal perspective to anticipate and forestall that which has not yet occurred and may never do so (...). The shift is not only temporal but also sectoral; spreading out form the State to embrace pre-emptive endeavours only remotely related to crime' (Zedner 2007a: 262).

[13] Despite Blair's apparent certainty and confidence in the predictive capacity of developmental criminology's risk-focused prevention in relation to juvenile criminality, a government scientific report a few years earlier had arrived at a very different conclusion:

> '[A]ny notion that better screening can enable policy makers to identify young children destined to join the 5 per cent of offenders responsible for 50-60 per cent of crime is fanciful. Even if there were no ethical objections to putting "potential delinquent" labels round the necks of young children, there would continue to be statistical barriers... [Research] shows substantial flows out of as well as in to the pool of children who develop chronic conduct problems. As such [there are] dangers of assuming that anti-social five-year olds are the criminals or drug abusers of tomorrow...' (Utting 2004: 99)

UK's counter-terrorism 'Prevent' agenda (HM Government 2009) and the analogous European strategy (European Union 2005). Aradau and van Munster are therefore correct to assert that 'the war on terror displays an insatiable quest for knowledge: profiling populations, surveillance, intelligence, knowledge about catastrophe management, prevention, etc.' (2007: 91). Risk here is reconceptualised as 'precautionary risk', which 'has given birth to new configurations of risk that require that the catastrophic prospects of the future be avoided at all costs' (*ibid.*). Here, suspicion becomes actionable intelligence. Intelligence, after all, is simply information with value-added analysis (Walker 2007: 1455). It is 'information that has been processed to provide foresight – a predictive capacity about how to act at some point in the future to achieve particular objectives given certain conditions' (Innes 2006: 229). But the robustness of the predictive capacity may be weak or highly contingent.

What is evident is the manner in which counter-terrorism responses have come to inform, and be informed by, developments and trends in neighbourhood policing, border controls and community cohesion more generally. In the process the precautionary principle, traditionally associated with serious, irreversible damage and environmental catastrophe, has leaked into the regulation of low-level social disorder, incivilities and disruptions to quality of life. It is increasingly argued that the demands of contemporary policing in the context of uncertainty necessitate the better integration of community intelligence through neighbourhood policing with counter-terrorism activities: 'Community intelligence applied to counter-terrorism is precisely the type of data that might help police to circumvent the intelligence gaps and blind spots that seemingly inhere in their established methods' (Innes 2006: 230). Regardless of its merits in generating 'actionable intelligence', such a vision of policing presages both a pervasive extension of 'the subtle indicators of suspicion' (*ibid.*: 224) and an intertwining of 'high' and 'low' policing as well as a blurring of sources of insecurity and types of harm.

As such, uncertainty and precaution demand the voracious collection of diverse sources of information, to enable analysts to 'join up the dots'. This has prompted greater investment in the use of data pools, the storing of DNA records and risk profiling. Information and personal data collection, searching and sifting are at the forefront of 'organising uncertainty' and 'managing risk'. Personal data drawn from official and public records and from consumer activities are increasingly used by commercial interests and governments to differentiate and classify customers, citizens and aliens alike through algorithmic profiles. On the one hand, 'categorical seduction' informs the corporate wooing of prized consumers. On the other hand, 'categorical suspicion' attends to certain groups of potential offenders and 'dangerous types' (Lyon 2007: 103). Here, information provides the basis for social sorting. However partial the profiles generated, their capacity to respond to the demands for organising uncertainty, stimulate quests for additional sources of information upon which categories of suspicion might be constructed, despite the vast quantities of 'false positives' that such data trawling, by necessity, generates. Collectively, the increasing combination of disparate data pools allows for the construction of a 'surveillance assemblage' (Haggerty and Ericson 2000) with added dimensions of social sorting potential, but also considerable scope for friction, failure and information overload.

5. Contested Expertise and Evidence

The pathology of insecurity lies not only in the limitations of knowledge on which to construct predictive interventions but also in the manner in which knowledge and expertise are contested. Knowledge, as Ericson notes is both an 'object and instrument of suspicion' (2007: 204). Not only may there be deeply held distrust on the part of the public of expert judgements of risk but so too for politicians the language of risk may not sit well with requirement for action. This is particularly evident in relation to the sensitivities of crime and victimisation where demands for certainty abound. As Ewald notes, 'this does not mean that scientific expertise is useless, but that it will not release the politician from the sovereignty of his or her decision' (2000: 77). Managing uncertainty means that politicians are selective in their tolerance of potentially harmful activities.

Witness, for example, the furore in Britain in early 2009 when Professor David Nutt, the Chair of the Advisory Council on the Misuse of Drugs (ACMD), in an editorial in the *Journal of Psychopharmacology* suggested that the risk of death from the drug Ecstasy is lower than the risk of death from horse-riding – an addiction he tongue-in-cheek termed 'Equasy' (Nutt 2009a). He used the comparisons of risks to highlight the need for a 'more relevant harm assessment process' and concluded: 'The use of rational evidence for the assessment of the harms of drugs will be one step forward to the development of a credible drugs strategy' (*ibid.*: 5). In an enlightening response to such a 'scientific claim', the British Home Secretary at the time, Jacqui Smith, demanded that he apologise and told MPs: 'I felt his comments went beyond the scientific advice that I expect from him as chair of the ACMD (…). He apologised to me for his comments, and I have asked him to apologise to the families of the victims of ecstasy, too'.[14] This highlights the political and cultural salience of certain risks and harms as against others, as well as the manner in which public perceptions once enmeshed in risk governance generate their own dilemmas that can serve to undermine a rational harm assessment debate.

[14] Hansard, House of Commons 9 Feb 2009: Column 1093.

However, the matter did not rest there. In October 2009 Professor Nutt was sacked from his government advisory post by the subsequent Home Secretary, Alan Johnson. Professor Nutt's subsequent crime was to give a lecture (which was later published) on the relative risks of various drugs in which he argued that Jacqui Smith's use of the 'precautionary principle' in reversing a decision to downgrade the classification of cannabis, could do more harm than good. An extract that particularly wrangled with the government is worth quoting at length:

> 'To repeat what the former Home Secretary said, "*We must err on the side of caution and protect the public*." As this is protection from the known unknowns, at first sight it might seem the obvious decision – why wouldn't you take the precautionary principle? We know that drugs are harmful and that you can never evaluate a drug over the lifetime of a whole population, so we can never know whether, at some point in the future, a drug might lead to or cause more harm than it did early in its use. The precautionary principle (...) may end up doing more harm than one might assume (...). More important, I think, the precautionary principle misleads. It starts to distort the value of evidence and therefore I think it could, and probably does, devalue evidence. This leads us to a position where people really don't know what the evidence is. They see the classification, they hear about evidence and they get mixed messages. There's quite a lot of anecdotal evidence that public confidence in the scientific probity of government has been undermined in this kind of way (...). Making all drugs class A would be a logical conclusion of the precautionary principle, but would be a supreme mistake.' (Nutt 2009b: 8, emphasis in original).

This incident highlighted not only the manner in which – under conditions of uncertainty – expert advice becomes contested, but also the way in which a precautionary logic diminishes the value of evidence and decouples it from directly conditioning the nature of the response. In its place, worst-case scenarios, 'what if?' questions and suspicion fill the void. Managing risk perceptions squeezes out and supplants rational risk analysis.

6. Concluding Thoughts

Contemporary security threats from terrorist violence, through 'ordinary' crime to acts of disorder and anti-social behaviour, undoubtedly present real and pressing challenges for governments, businesses and citizens alike. But there are evident dangers that in the way in which we both interpret risk and 'unknown dangers' and respond to them, we may be undermining some of the core values and principles of democratic societies, whilst eroding relations of social trust and mutual toleration. As a consequence, the balance between security and freedom has become possibly the most prominent contemporary challenge for European polities. The demand for security in societies where individuals have come to experience ever greater 'freedom' is a vexed one. The concern is that it frequently means sacrificing 'other people's' freedoms to make 'us' feel more secure. This has adverse implications for marginal and marginalised groups within societies, those upon whom dominant groups project their fears and anxieties. Hence, the questions 'whose fears?', 'whose security?' and 'whose freedoms?' are particularly salient albeit often less evident in debates about threats of terrorism and political violence as well as other contemporary fears and responses to them. In the political confrontation between fear and liberty, where necessary, actions that infringe liberties are more evidently justifiable if those who support the actions are burdened by them and their impacts are not restricted to members of identifiable minority groups – whether implicitly or through differential implementation.

In governmental responses to perceptions of crime and insecurity, notably terrorism, precaution is becoming a key driver, in a way that licenses early interventions before our 'unknown unknowns' express themselves. In a context of uncertainty and in the search for (an unattainable absolute) security, mere suspicion, the perceptions of others, the appearance of potentially risky behaviour and worst-case scenarios may be sufficient grounds for pre-emptive action. There is a need to consider and challenge the evidence and assess the different courses of action available. As Sunstein asserts: 'Democratic governments care about facts as well as fears… they take careful steps to ensure that laws and policies reduce, and do not replicate, the errors to which fearful people are prone' (2005: 226). In 'governance through precaution', we may be in the process of discarding cherished civil liberties and legal principles in order to intervene at the earliest possible stage to stop our unknown demons surfacing. In so doing, we are in the process of widening our apparatuses of control and overloading these with information from diverse data-banks, in the hope that this will allow us to 'join up the dots' to identify potential risks and pre-empt the future. Whilst deliberate inaction in the face of evidence of possible serious and irreversible harm is understandably hazardous, so too over-reaction can at times present greater dangers, particularly where this generates unintended consequences and results in the consumption of resources that might have been deployed in more beneficial endeavours.

References

Aradua, C., & Munster, R. van (2007). Governing Terrorism Through Risk: Taking Precautions, (un)Knowing the Future. *European Journal of International Relations, 13(1)*, 89-115.

Arnot, M. (2008). *Educating the Gendered Citizen*. London: Routledge.

Ashworth, A. (2000). Is the Criminal Law a Lost Cause? *Law Quarterly Review, 116*, 225-56.

Ashworth, A. (2004). Social Control and Anti-Social Behaviour: The Subversion of Human Rights. *Law Quarterly Review, 120*, 263-291.

Ashworth, A. (2006). Four Threats to the Presumption of Innocence. *South African Law Journal, 123,* 62-96.

Ashworth, A., & Zedner, L. (2008). Defending the Criminal Law: Reflections on the Changing Character of Crime, Procedure, and Sanctions. *Journal of Criminal Law and Philosophy, 2*, 21-51.

Bauman, Z. (2001a). *The Individualized Society*. Cambridge: Polity.

Bauman, Z. (2001b). Individually, Together: Foreword. In U. Beck & E. Beck-Gernsheim (Eds.), *Individualization*. Cambridge: Polity.

Bauman, Z. (2006). *Liquid Fear*. Cambridge: Polity.

Beck, U. (1992). *The Risk Society*. Cambridge: Polity.

Beck, U., & Beck-Gernsheim, E. (2001). *Individualization*. Cambridge: Polity.

Beck, U., Giddens, A., & Lash, S. (1994). *Reflexive Modernization*. Cambridge: Polity.

Better Regulation Commission (2006). *Risk, Responsibility and Regulation – Whose risk is it anyway?* London: Better Regulation Commission.

Black, J. (2001). Decentring Regulation: The Role of Regulation and Self-Regulation in a 'Post-Regulatory' World. *Current Legal Problems, 54*, 103-146.

Braithwaite, J. (2002). *Restorative Justice and Responsive Regulation*. Oxford: Oxford University Press.

Braithwaite, J. (2008). *Regulatory Capitalism*. Cheltenham: Edward Elgar.

Burney, E. (2009). *Making People Behave*. Cullompton: Willan.

Burris, S., Drahos, P., & Shearing, C. (2005). Nodal Governance. *Australian Journal of Legal Philosophy, 30*, 30-58.

Cobb, N. (2007). Governance through Publicity: ASBOs, Young People, and the Problematization of the Right to Anonymity. *Journal of Law and Society, 34(3)*, 342-73.

Crawford, A. (2003). Contractual Governance of Deviant Behaviour. *Journal of Law and Society, 30(4)*, 479-505.

Crawford, A. (2006). Networked Governance and the Post-Regulatory State? *Theoretical Criminology, 10(4)*, 449-79.

Crawford, A. (2007). Reassurance Policing: Feeling is Believing. In A. Henry, & D.J. Smith (Eds.), *Transformations Of Policing*. Aldershot: Ashgate.

Crawford, A. (2008). Dispersal Powers and the Symbolic Role of Anti-Social Behaviour Legislation. *Modern Law Review, 71(5)*, 753-84.

Crawford, A. (2009a). Governing through Anti-Social Behaviour: Regulatory Challenges to Criminal Justice. *British Journal of Criminology, 49(6)*, 810-31.

Crawford, A. (2009b). Restorative Justice and Anti-Social Behaviour Interventions as Contractual Governance. In P. Knepper, J. Shapland, & J. Doak (Eds.), *Urban Crime Prevention, Surveillance, and Restorative Justice: Effects of Social Technologies*. London: Taylor & Francis.

Crawford A., & Flint, J. (2009). Urban Safety, Anti-Social Behaviour and the Night-Time Economy. *Criminology and Criminal Justice*, *9(4)*, 403-14.

Dershowitz, A.M. (2006). *Preemption: A Knife that Cuts Both Ways*. New York: Norton.

Douglas, M., & Wildavsky, A. (1982). *Risk and Culture: An Essay on the Selection of Technological and Environmental Dangers*. Berkeley: University of California Press.

Ericson, R. (2005). Governing through Risk and Uncertainty. *Economy and Society*, *34(4)*, 659-72.

Ericson, R. (2007). *Crime in an Insecure World*. Cambridge: Polity.

European Commission (2000). *Communication from the Commission on the Precautionary Principle*. 2 February. Brussels: European Commission.

European Union (2005). *The European Union Strategy for Combating Radicalisation and Recruitment to Terrorism*. 14781/1/05. Brussels: Council of the European Union.

Ewald, F. (2000). Risk in Contemporary Society. *Connecticut Insurance Law Journal*, *6*, 365-79.

Ewald, F. (2002). The Return of Descartes's Malicious Demon: An Outline of a Philosophy of Precaution. In T. Baker, & J. Simon (Eds.), *Embracing Risk*. Chicago: University of Chicago Press.

Farrington, D.P. (2007). Childhood Risk Factors and Risk-Focused Prevention. In M. Maguire, R. Morgan, & R. Reiner (Eds.), *The Oxford Handbook of Criminology*. Oxford: Oxford University Press.

Feeley, M., & Simon, J. (1992). The New Penology. *Criminology*, *30*, 449-74.

Feeley, M., & Simon, J. (1994). Actuarial Justice: The Emerging New Criminal Law. In D. Nelken (Ed.), *The Futures of Criminology*. London: Sage.

Field, F. (2003). *Neighbours from Hell: The Politics of Behaviour*. London: Politico's.

Frary, M. (2004). Fast Track? You Must Be Joking. *Times Online*, available at: <http://www.timesonline.co.uk/tol/travel/business/article455482.ece>

Furedi, F. (2002). *Culture of Fear*. London: Continuum.

Gardner, D. (2008). *Risk: The Science and Politics of Fear*. London: Virgin Books.

Gil-Robles, A. (2005). *Report by the Commissioner for Human Rights on his Visit to the United Kingdom*, 4-12 November 2004. Strasburg: Council of Europe.

Gunningham, N., & Grabosky, P. (1998). *Smart Regulation*. Oxford: Oxford University Press.

Haggerty, K., & Ericson, E. (2000). The Surveillant Assemblage. *British Journal of Sociology, 51(4)*, 605-22.

Halpern, D., Bates, C., Mulgan, G., & Aldridge, S., with Beales, G., & Heathfield, A. (2004). *Personal Responsibility and Changing Behaviour: The State of Knowledge and its Implications for Policy.* London: Cabinet Office.

Harcourt, B. (2007). *Against Prediction: Profiling, Policing and Punishing in an Actuarial Age.* Chicago: University of Chicago Press.

HM Government (2009). *United Kingdom's Strategy for Countering International Terrorism*, Cm. 7547. London: The Stationery Office.

Home Office (2003). *Respect and Responsibility – Taking a Stand Against Anti-Social Behaviour*, Cm 5778. London: Home Office.

Home Office (2005). *Guidance on Publicising Anti-Social Behaviour Orders.* London: Home Office.

Innes, M. (2006). Policing Uncertainty: Countering Terror through Community Intelligence and Democratic Policing. *Annals, AAPSS, 605*, 222-41.

Johnston, L., & Shearing, C. (2003). *Governing Security.* London: Routledge.

Knight, F. (1921). *Risk, Uncertainty and Profit.* Boston: Houghton Mifflin.

Lagrée, J.-C. (Ed.) (2002). *Rolling Youth, Rocking Society Youth Take Part in the Post-Modern Debate on Globalization.* Paris: UNESCO.

Layard, R., & Dunn, J. (2009). *A Good Childhood: Searching for Values in a Competitive Age.* London: Penguin.

Levidow, L. (2001). Precautionary Uncertainty: Regulating GM Crops in Europe. *Social Studies of Science, 31(6)*, 845-78.

Loader, I., & Sparks, R. (2010). *Public Criminology?* London: Routledge.

Lyon, D. (2007). *Surveillance Studies: An Overview.* Cambridge: Polity Press.

Macdonald, S. (2007). ASBOs and Control Orders: Two Recurring Themes, Two Apparent Contradictions. *Parliamentary Affairs, 60(4)*, 601-24.

Macrory, R. (2006a). *Regulatory Justice: Sanctioning in a post-Hampton World.* London: Better Regulation Executive.

Macrory, R. (2006b). *Regulatory Justice: Making Sanctions Effective.* London: Better Regulation Executive.

Margo, J., & Dixon, M., with Pearce, N., & Reed, H. (2006). *Freedom's Orphans, Raising Youth in a Changing World.* London: IPPR.

Massumi, B. (2005). P*arables for the Virtual.* Durham NC: Duke University Press.

Morris, N. (2006). Blair's 'Frenzied Law Making'. *The Independent*, 16 August.

Mythen, G., & Walklate, S. (2008). Terrorism, Risk and International Security: The Perils of Asking What if? *Security Dialogue, 39(2-3)*, 221-42.

Nutt, D. (2009a). Equasy – An Overlooked Addiction with Implications for the Current Debate on Drug Harms. *Journal of Psychopharmacology, 32(1)*, 3-5.

Nutt, D. (2009b). *Estimating Drug Harms: A Risky Business*. Briefing 10, London: Centre for Crime and Justice Studies. Available at: <http://www.crimeandjustice.org.uk/opus1714/Estimating_drug_harms.pdf>

O'Malley, P. (2004). *Risk, Uncertainty and Government*. London: Glasshouse Press.

Palmer, S. (2006). *Toxic Childhood*. London: Orion.

Pearson, G. (1983). *Hooligan: A history of Respectable Fears*. Houndmills, Bassingstoke: Macmillan.

Postman, N. (1982). *The Disappearance of Childhood*. New York: Vintage.

Power, M. (2007). *Organized Uncertainty: Deigning a World of Risk Management*. Oxford: Oxford University Press.

Ramsay, P. (2009). The Theory of Vulnerable Autonomy and the Legitimacy of the Civil Preventive Order. In B. McSherry, A. Norrie, & S. Bronitt (Eds.), *Regulating Deviance: The Redirection of Criminalisation and the Futures of Criminal Law*. Oxford: Hart Publishing.

Scott, C. (2004). Regulation in the Age of Governance: The Rise of the Post-Regulatory State. In J. Jordana, & D. Levi-Faur (Eds.), *The Politics of Regulation in the Age of Governance*. Cheltenham: Edward Elgar.

Simester, A.P., & Hirsch, A. von (2006). Regulating Offensive Conduct through Two-Step Prohibitions. In A. von Hirsch, & A.P. Simester (Eds.), *Incivilities: Regulating Offensive Behaviour*. Oxford: Hart Publishing.

Sunstein, C. (2005). *Laws of Fear: Beyond the Precautionary Principle*. Cambridge: Cambridge University Press.

Sunstein, C. (2007). *Worst-Case Scenarios*. Cambridge, Massachusetts: Harvard University Press.

Suskind, R. (2006). *The One Percent Doctrine: Deep Inside America's Pursuit of Its Enemies Since 9/11*. London: Simon & Schuster.

Taleb, N.N. (2007). *The Black Swan: The Impact of the Highly Improbable*. London: Penguin Books.

UNICEF (2007). A*n Overview of Child Well-Being in Rich Countries*. Florence: UNICEF.

Utting, D. (2004). Overview and Conclusion. In C. Sutton, D. Utting, & D. Farrington (Eds.), *Support from the Start: Working with Young Children and their Families to Reduce the Risks of Crime and Anti-Social Behaviour*. London: DfES.

Villeneuve-Gokalp, C. (1981). *Quand vient l'âge des choix*. Paris: PUF.

Walker, C. (2007). Keeping Control of Terrorists without Losing Control of Constitutionalism. *Stanford Law Review, 59(5)*, 1395-463.

Walklate, S., & Mythen, G. (2008). How Scared are We? *British Journal of Criminology, 48(2*), 209-25.

Wiener, J.B., Rogers, M.D., Hammitt, J.K., & Sand, P.H. (Eds.) (2010). *The Reality of Precaution: Comparing Risk Regulation in the United States and Europe*. London: RFF Press.

Wynne, B. (1993). Public Uptake of Science: A Case for Institutional Reflexivity. *Public Understanding of Science*, *2(4)*, 321-37.

Zedner, L. (2007a). Pre-Crime and Post-Criminology. *Theoretical Criminology*, *11(2)*, 261-81.

Zedner, L. (2007b). Preventive Justice or Pre-Punishment? The Case of Control Orders. *Current Legal Problems*, *60*, 174-203.

Zedner, L. (2009). Fixing the Future? The Pre-Emptive Turn in Criminal Justice. In B. McSherry, A. Norrie, & S. Bronitt (Eds.), *Regulating Deviance: The Redirection of Criminalisation and the Futures of Criminal Law*. Oxford: Hart Publishing.

3. Beccaria's Dream on Criminal Law and Nodal Governance

Klaas Rozemond

1. Introduction

Cesare Beccaria had a dream: a rationally constructed criminal law system would prevent citizens from harmful conduct and would create 'the greatest happiness shared among the greater number' (Beccaria 1995: 7). Through clear laws and proportionate punishments this dream would come true. Unknown crimes, unfair trials and cruel punishments would belong to the past. Beccaria dreamt his dream in the 18th century, when Enlightenment had reached its highest point. Since that century, his rational desires are partially realized in many legal systems by means of statutory crimes, fair trials and sentencing practices based on principles which have developed over the past two centuries.

Yet his dream did not come true. In recent criminological literature it is argued that the state has lost its monopoly on the 'governance of security'. Private companies, organizations and citizens try to protect their own security through 'networked governance' or 'nodal governance' (Johnston and Shearing 2003, Wood and Dupont 2006, Wood and Shearing 2007). The state is just a knot or 'node' in the social network of the governance of security and the criminal law is no more than one of many instruments to protect the security of citizens and companies. Participants in the nodal governance are relatively less interested in the punishment of past conduct. The governance of security is mainly directed at reducing the risks of harmful conduct in the future. The punishment of crimes from the past can only be considered as an important state activity as long as it reduces the risks of future crimes.

The main reason Beccaria's dream did not come true may be found in the failure of the criminal law based on the rational principles of Beccaria's theory. The official publications of criminal laws and the proportionate punishments of crimes are not enough to protect the security of all citizens in an effective way. In the risk society, individuals and companies demand much more security than the state can offer by means of the criminal law. Therefore, they look for alternative means for the failing state. Companies hire their own security personnel or they contract security companies to protect their security in so called 'mass private properties' (sport stadiums, amusement parks, shopping malls, office buildings), they cooperate to protect their security in 'business improvement districts' and they hire specialized companies or create special departments to reduce harmful conduct like fraud and theft by personnel and clients. Citizens who can afford it, withdraw themselves in 'gated communities' with private security provisions, or they develop their own strategies to protect security without the support of the state, for instance by surveillances of neighborhood watches and private alarms in their homes.

These social developments raise the question: what is left of Beccaria's dream? Are citizens still equally protected by the law and by fair trials and proportionate punishments? Beccaria's dream was founded on principles of equality, legality and proportionality. Are these principles still effectively in force under the nodal governance of security? Beccaria's dream was also based on an instrumental theory of the effects of the criminal law: the concentration of power in the state monopoly on the criminal law is the most effective way to protect the security of all citizens in a fair and equal way. When these principles are abandoned, the effectivity and normativity of the governance of security become problematic: are the alternative arrangements of nodal governance capable of offering equal security to all citizens and are these arrangements effective in the sense that citizens are better protected than under the criminal law?

In this article I will presuppose that the shift from the state monopoly on the governance of security to the nodal governance of security indeed has taken place as some authors have argued, although this view has been met with criticism in criminological literature (Crawford 2006, Loader and Walker 2006, Loader and Walker 2007). I will investigate which consequences this shift can have for the Beccarian ideals concerning the effectivity and normativity of the criminal law. I will analyze the main points of the Beccarian theory on the normative foundations of the criminal law and the effectivity of the state monopoly on the governance of security by means of the criminal law.

Before I will go into Beccaria's dream, I will summarize the theory of Les Johnston and Clifford Shearing on the fall of the state monopoly and the rise of the nodal governance of security. Johnston and Shearing consider Beccaria as the representative theorist of the classical criminal law which has lost its monopoly on the governance of security. According to Johnston and Shearing, Beccaria's dream represents the punitive mentality of the classical criminal law, while the nodal governance of security is the expression of a risk mentality, which means that the nodal governance of security is mainly aimed at risk reduction and not at punishment of crime. Johnston and Shearing consider the punishing of past behavior as an instrument to reduce the risk of harm that is one of the many instruments of the risk society. They are aware of the normative and instrumental problems of the wavering of the state monopoly. Therefore, they are looking for effective alternatives which will satisfy certain normative demands.

Beccaria's dream can be used in the search for alternatives, because his dream contains the ideals of a just and effective governance of security. The classical state monopoly on the governance of security can only be lifted when the nodal alternatives meet the ideals of the Beccarian dream. In that sense his dream is still valid, though it cannot be fully realized by the criminal law. The alternative arrangements of nodal governance can be critically tested on the basis of Beccarian principles. When these arrangements cannot satisfy this critical test, that could be a reason to look for a more prominent place of the state in the governance of security to guarantee the Beccarian principles of equality, legality and proportionality.

2. Nodal Governance

In their book *Governing Security* Les Johnston and Clifford Shearing argue that the state monopoly on the governance of security has been replaced by forms of networked governance in which the state, private companies and citizens work together to protect security. In the networks of governance the distinction between public and private forms of governance is blurred. The state itself is using forms of cooperation in which the state hires private security companies to execute its tasks in protecting security. Citizens and companies use the services of the state, sometimes on a commercial basis, but these services have lost their privileged status in the sense that police activities are no longer considered as the main instruments to protect security. These activities are part of larger networks in which citizens and companies use a diversity of security instruments to protect themselves. They do not want to rely exclusively on state protection, but they want to organize their own governance of security. The state also uses a range of instruments and strategies which are primarily aimed at reducing security risks. The punishment of criminals is no longer the main instrument to protect the security of citizens and companies (Johnston and Shearing 2003: 13-18, 31-36; Shearing 2006).

Johnston and Shearing describe these developments in terms of security programmes. They make a distinction between the classical punitive program in which the criminal law has a central position and the modern risk program of nodal governance in which the state has lost its monopoly. According to Johnston and Shearing, a security program can be analyzed in terms of order, authority, institution, instrument, mentality and practice. A security program contains an order which determines what safe and unsafe conduct is. This order can be defined by an authority which has the power to announce the rules of order. Certain institutions execute the security program and use specific security instruments to enforce the rules of the program. From the definition of order by an authority and from the institutional enforcement of order a certain mentality can be deduced which is expressed in a practice of security governance (Johnston and Shearing 2003: 6-9).

The idea of a security program fits very well with the practice of the criminal law. According to Johnston and Shearing, this practice is the expression of a punitive mentality which can be deduced from the order of the criminal law en from institutions (police, prosecution, judiciary) which enforce the criminal law. The main instrument of these institutions is punishment (imprisonment, fine) which is executed in cases of crimes and misdemeanors. The punitive mentality is directed at behavior from the past. Criminal law institutions are mainly occupied with the investigation, prosecution and punishment of crimes which already have been committed. Punishment is determined by the seriousness of the crime and the personality of the perpetrator. Preventive considerations also play a part in the determination of punishment, and in that sense the punitive mentality is aimed at the future, but the main aspect of the criminal law is the fact that the institutions involved are handling crimes which have been committed and are in need of a state response (Johnston and Shearing 2003: 15, 24, 41, 48, 54, 95).

In contrast with the punitive program of classical criminal law the risk program of nodal governance is not primarily directed at the past, but mainly at the future: the reduction of harm risks. The criminal law can play a part in this reduction of risk, but the risk mentality of nodal governance implies that punishment is always too late, because the harm of crime already has occurred at the moment of punishment. Nodal governance is aimed at the reduction of harm and therefore risk instruments are aimed at prevention, for instance by way of exclusion of risk groups from certain city areas or the exclusion of these groups from certain services. Exclusion is one of the most important risk instruments expressing the risk mentality. The closed gate (with a camera to observe the person who wants admission) is the main instrument to control risk in buildings, business districts and gated communities. In a more abstract form the exclusion from services is another means to control risk without the direct aid of the state (Johnston and Shearing 2003: 81-84).

Risk programmes are more hybrid than the classical punitive program, because of the lack of a clear order and a central authority which defines the rules, and because the main institutions and instruments of risk programmes are more difficult to identify in society. Citizens, companies and state organizations use a diversity of security instruments to reduce the risk of harm, without central authorities or binding rules which govern all the instruments used, like 'risk taxation' or 'risk management' as it is developed by private companies which have been growing in recent years and use these instruments to control the risk of harm. Private security companies have become the main competitors to the state in the governance of security (Johnston and Shearing 2003: 84-92).

Specific strategies are being presented by the state as classical forms of governance, for instance the strategy of *Zero Tolerance Policing* which is aimed at providing security in city areas. The state claims its successes with *Zero Tolerance Policing* on the basis of classical policing instruments like surveillance, but Johnston and Shearing argue that *Zero Tolerance Policing* is a form of cooperation between the state, private companies and citizens in which the state applies strategies aimed at risk reduction (Johnston and Shearing 2003: 98-116). *Zero Tolerance Policing* is not only directed at suspects of crimes, but also uses instruments like anti-social behavior orders and forms of preventive bodily searches. These instruments create the risk that innocent persons are the target of state interventions to reduce the risk of crime. The 'anti-social behavior' is more broadly defined than the classical crimes of the criminal law and specific forms of surveillance can be used against persons belonging to risk groups without a formally defined suspicion that these persons have committed crimes.

Johnston and Shearing are aware of these problems, but they also analyze the positive effects of the loss of the state monopoly on the governance of security. They argue that as a consequence of this loss citizens can provide for their own security with the use of local knowledge and capacities. Johnston and Shearing give the South African Peace Committees as an example of these positive effects. This form of 'local capacity policing' can be considered as the expression of a democratic ideal which holds that local conflicts are to be solved with local means and capacities and not with the use of state force (Johnston and Shearing 2003: 151-160).

3. Beccarian Rationality

Johnston and Shearing mention the theory of Cesare Beccaria on the criminal law as an example of the punitive mentality which fits the classical monopoly of the state on the governance of security (Johnston and Shearing 2003: 42-45). According to Beccaria, punishment by the state is the main instrument to provide security. Beccaria was an Enlightenment thinker who developed his theory on crime and punishment as a protest against the abuse of the criminal law by the ruling sovereigns who furthered their own interests with state power and often acted against the interest of its citizens (Beccaria 1995: 3, 7-8, 9). Beccaria also protested against cruel treatment of suspects, unfair trials and harsh punishments. In his book *Dei delitte e delle pene (On Crimes and Punishments)*, published in Livorno (Italy) in 1764, Beccaria argued that persons have to transfer part of their natural freedom to the state in the interest of their security. The state could determine what the crimes are by clearly formulated laws. When violations of the laws would be met by proportional punishments, the security of all citizens would be better protected than in a state of nature in which persons have to take care of their own security.

Beccaria followed Thomas Hobbes in his opinion that the state of nature is a state of war of all against all (Hobbes 1996). Persons in the state of nature can end this war by means of a social contract on the transfer of freedom to the sovereign who will protect their security with the power that has been transferred to him (Beccaria 1995: 9, 11, 12). Beccaria disagreed with Hobbes on the amount of freedom which has to be transferred in order to end the war in the state of nature. According to Hobbes, persons have to transfer all their freedom, except for the natural right to self defense. Beccaria did not want to go that far. According to him, persons only had to transfer as much of their natural freedom as is necessary to protect their security. Beccaria also had a different opinion on the powers of the sovereign which are unlimited in Hobbes' political philosophy. Beccaria followed Montesquieu in the idea that the right of the sovereign to punish would not go further than is necessary to protect the security of all citizens. Beccaria also was of the opinion that a separation of powers was necessary to limit the power of the sovereign (Beccaria 1995: 10, 12-13).

Beccaria's book is especially well known for its protest against torture (Beccaria 1995: 39-44), its criticism of the death penalty (Beccaria 1995: 66-72), its arguments for publicly known laws which clearly state the crimes, and its reasoning in favor of proportionate punishments (Beccaria 1995: 19-21) and fair trials (Beccaria 1995: 97-98). Beccaria was an important propagandist for the modernization of the criminal law on the basis of Enlightenment principles. Beccaria also tried to improve the theory of the criminal law by arguing for a specific relation between rationality and normativity. He wanted to show that persons transfer a part of their natural freedom to the state to further their interest in security. The rationality of this transfer demands that individuals do not transfer more freedom than is necessary for the protection of their security.

Beccaria's arguments in favour of the rationality of the criminal law and the social contract relate to several levels of human reasoning. The first level concerns the human capacity to search for pleasure and to avoid pain. Certain crimes can give pleasure to the perpetrator and therefore the punishment of the crime has to cause more pain than the pleasure of the crime (Beccaria 1995: 9, 21). People are motivated to act on direct impulses of their senses and therefore prompt punishment would be the most effective instrument against crime. Individuals are also capable of weighing the short term pleasure of crime against the long term pain of future punishment. The time between the direct pleasure of crime and the pain of future punishment cannot last too long, because otherwise individuals would not make a psychological association between crimes and punishments (Beccaria 1995: 49). This is a second level of reasoning in Beccaria's theory. Beccaria added a third level of rationality to the first two levels. Individuals can reason on a higher level of abstraction when they make decisions on the basis of written laws which determine what are the crimes and punishments. This third level can only function when the laws are clearly stated and publicly known (Beccaria 1995: 17-18). To this third level of reasoning a fourth level can be added which Beccaria himself did not mention explicitly. It is only possible to understand the meaning of the law when a person understands the political and legal system of which the law is a part. A person has to know the meaning and function of the sovereign, the laws, the crimes, the prosecution and the judiciary within the system in order to be able to weigh the pleasure of crime against the pain of punishment.

With the social contract, Beccaria added a fifth level of rationality to his theory. The social contract presupposes the ability of individuals to rationally compare the state of nature with the state under the rule of the sovereign. According to Beccaria, individuals will make this comparison on the basis of their rational self-interest and they will be able to measure the amount of freedom they will have to transfer to the sovereign in order to protect their security in an effective way. This fifth level of rationality raises certain problems, because Beccaria not only formulated a social contract theory, but he also used utilitarian criteria to evaluate the acts of the sovereign. Beccaria thought that individuals in the state of nature or under the rule of the sovereign will not reason on the basis of the utilitarian principle to promote 'the greatest happiness shared among the greater number' (Beccaria 1995: 7). They will only act on the basis of self-interest. This raises the problem that on the basis of their own interest, individuals may not comply with the law, while at the same time it is in their own interest that everybody else does (Beccaria 1995: 10). A possible solution to this problem is rational self binding through the social contract and the criminal law of the sovereign. The punishment of individuals who do not comply with the criminal law gives everybody a reason not to commit crimes. Parties to the social contract should be able to see the rationality of this reasoning and also should be able to limit their freedom on the basis of this reasoning. This adds a sixth level of reasoning to the five levels mentioned before. The sixth level is the theoretical level on which individuals are able to formulate a solution to the problem of the contradiction between contractual self interest and utilitarian common good[1].

On the basis of Beccaria's theory, individuals can be divided in six categories. Some individuals can only reason on the first level of rationality in reaction to direct forms of pleasure and pain. Other individuals can reason on a second level and compare direct forms of pleasure and pain with future ones. A third category consists of individuals who are able to reason on the basis of the laws defining crimes and punishments. On a fourth level of abstraction, individuals can understand the political and legal system of which the laws and the punishment are a part. Some individuals are able to compare the state of nature with the state of the sovereign and the ability to make this comparison is the fifth form of rationality. The highest level of rational abstraction consists of reasoning to solve the contradiction between self interest and social utility. A person who is able to reason on the six levels of rationality has strong reasons not to commit crimes. According to the theory of Beccaria, a society of individuals with the ability to reason on all six levels of rationality will be a society with maximum security and maximum freedom, provided that the state will function effectively and will promptly and proportionally punish transgressions of the criminal law.

4. Beccarian Explanations of Crime

Beccaria's theory on the rationality of individuals can explain why a rationally constructed criminal law would be effective when the criminal law system would comply with principles of equality, legality and proportionality. When all citizens are capable of reasoning on the six levels of rationality, and when all crimes are clearly defined by the law and are promptly and proportionally punished by the state, the criminal law would make Beccaria's dream on

[1] The complex relation between social contract theory and utilitarianism in Beccaria's theory is analyzed by Young 1983. On a more general level this relation is the subject of Hudson 2003.

effectivity and normativity come true. The Enlightenment ideal of Beccaria was that all citizens can reach the six levels of rationality by upbringing and education (Beccaria 1995: 110, 105-107). According to the Enlightenment dream, the criminal law can provide security for all rational citizens, while the citizens transfer no more freedom than is necessary to protect their security. Punishment would infringe the freedom of citizens no more than is necessary, including the freedom of the perpetrators who would be punished proportionally. When citizens can reach all six levels of rationality, limitations on freedom by punishments will only be necessary in exceptional cases. The need of those limitations will increase when citizens cannot reach all six levels, but can only reason on the lower levels.

Beccaria's theory can explain why the criminal law would not effectively protect security in certain circumstances. The explanation can be found in a failing state which cannot react promptly with proportionate punishments on all committed crimes. Because of this failure, an essential part of Beccaria's theory of the social contract would become inoperative: even the most rational citizen will only comply with the criminal law when the threat of punishment effectively wipes out the pleasure of the crime. When punishment does not follow promptly after the crime, a reason to comply with the criminal law disappears, although it cannot be excluded that a fully rational person would comply to the law even when he knows that punishment will not follow promptly.[2]

The explanation of crime can also be found in the failed reasoning of citizens who are not capable to react adequately on punishments of crimes and the threat of punishments in the criminal laws. When these two explanations are combined, the criminal law could end in a complete failure according to Beccaria's theory. When the state cannot react promptly to crime with proportionate punishment and citizens are not capable of reasoning rationally – even on the lower levels of rationality – crime rates would rise and society would degenerate towards a state of nature. The failing rationality of individuals could be caused by inadequate education or by social or psychological problems of perpetrators. This could be handled by other instruments than the criminal law, for instance programmes of reintegration based on social and psychological knowledge and therapeutic treatment.[3] The failure of the state could be repaired by improving the criminal law system and its effectivity by punishing promptly to provide security for all citizens.

It is also possible that Beccaria's theory is ill-founded or incomplete and that other explanations can be given for the rising crime rates and the failing criminal

[2] For instance a person with the rationality of Socrates who realizes that he himself suffers the most harm of the crimes he will commit (Plato 1994: 46 e.f. and 78 e.f.).

[3] Johnston and Shearing point out that after Beccaria the punitive program was adapted in the 'neoclassical compromise' of criminal punishment and therapeutic reintegration (Johnston and Shearing 2003: 45-48). David Garland has called this adaption 'penal welfarism' (Garland 2001: 27 e.f.).

law system: political, economic and cultural explanations such as those given by David Garland in his book *The Culture of Control* (Garland 2001). These explanations are based on more general developments in society. The social and economic equality or inequality can be an explanation for the crime rates of a society. In her book *The Prisoner's Dilemma*, Nicola Lacey argues that egalitarian societies react less harshly towards crime than societies with great economic differences without social welfare. A causal relationship may exist between crime rates and the equal or unequal distribution of wealth (Lacey 2008).

Perhaps it is possible to amend Beccaria's theory on crime and punishment which can be considered as an incomplete theory. Beccaria's theory only deals with the distribution of freedom and security. A complete theory of crime would also deal with the distribution of other primary social goods and the relation of this distribution with the criminal law system. A starting point of such a criminal law theory could be *A Theory of Justice* in which John Rawls defends a general theory of the social contract (Rawls 1999). In a society that is just according to the Rawlsian principles of justice, citizens would not have a reason to commit crimes to further their own interests.[4] When a society does not meet up completely with the Rawlsian principles of justice, individuals would have more reason to commit crime, especially when they are the victims of injustice. Crime rates could be explained by the *relative deprivation* of individuals who are the worst off in a relatively unjust society, as Jock Young has argued in his book *The Exclusive Society* (Young 1999). Punishment of crime would have the effect of strengthening the feeling of injustice of those who are being punished when the primary social goods are unequally and unfairly distributed in society. This explanation would add a seventh level of rationality to Beccaria's theory.[5]

It is possible that Beccaria's theory, amended with a seventh level of rationality, does not give the correct explanation of crime rates, because his theory does not correspond with the way human beings take decisions on committing crimes and the way punishments have an effect on these decisions. It may be possible that individuals generally do not decide to commit crimes after reasoning according to Beccarian models of rationality (or more modern theories of rational choice). Other personal and social factors determine the crimes people commit and the way society reacts to those crimes, for instance emotional and cultural factors which fall outside the scope of rational reasoning. I will not raise further doubts on Beccaria's theory on rationality. My purpose in this article is to look for Beccarian explanations of crime and punishment and Beccarian explanations of alternatives to the criminal law, such as the rules, authorities, institutions, instruments, mentalities and practices of nodal governance. The next step would be to test these explanations empirically, but to

4 See on the complex relation between rationality and justice Rawls 1999: 450 e.f.

5 See on the moral problem of crime and punishment in an unjust society Reiman 2007 with references to Rawls and to Hobbes and Locke who according to Reiman defend opposing conclusions on the moral status of crime in an unjust society. This explains the ambivalence in the title of his article.

be able to do that, it must be shown that nodal governance does not necessarily presume a completely different theory in comparison to Beccaria's theory of the criminal law.

5. Beccarian Explanations of Nodal Governance

When the state fails to provide the necessary security for all, individuals to a certain extent fall back into a state of nature in which they have to provide for their own security. Therefore, the rise of nodal governance could be explained and justified by the Beccarian theory that the social contract is only effective and binding when everybody's security is better protected under the criminal law than in the state of nature. When individuals are worse off under the criminal law, they can use other social and legal instruments to protect their own security as an alternative or an amendment to the Beccarian social contract.

This would mean that individuals can reason according to the six or seven levels of Beccarian rationality in relation to the institutions and instruments of nodal governance. Beccarian reasoning would lead to the conclusion that individuals cannot completely depend on the criminal law of the state to provide their security. According Beccaria's social contract theory, individuals do not transfer all their freedom to the state. They transfer no more freedom than is necessary for the protection of their security. When the transfer of freedom does not have the desired effect, the Beccarian social contract allows for individuals to withhold a part of their freedom in order to protect their own security with legal and social instruments other than the criminal law.

From the perspective of Beccaria's theory, nodal governance appears to be *an intermediate state* between the state of nature and the monopoly on the use of force by the sovereign. Individuals not only have a choice between the state of nature and the criminal law: they also can choose the instruments of nodal governance. There are gradual differences between the state of nature, the intermediate state of nodal governance and the criminal law of the state. From Beccaria's theoretical perspective the question must be: how much freedom does a person have to transfer to the state in order to provide the necessary security and how much freedom does a person have to withhold to protect his own security? The answer to this question can be based on a Beccarian balancing of freedom and security to reach a maximum security with a minimum loss of freedom.

In his book *Anarchy, State, and Utopia* Robert Nozick argued that individuals in a state of nature do not immediately have to transfer all their freedom to the state through a social contract (Nozick 1974). They can use their freedom in the state of nature to start protection agencies on the basis of private contracts. Nozick aimed to illustrate that the state could rise out of a free market of private protection agencies in the form of a dominant protection agency or a federation of protection agencies. With this reasoning, it could also be argued that the free market would not necessarily result in one dominant agency, but in a range of protective possibilities in which the state exists alongside other forms of protection companies. They can offer private instruments to protect security, from alarm installations to surveillance services and security personnel. The Beccarian social contract could regulate certain instruments of security, like the criminal law and its institutions, on which the state has a monopoly. The social contract could also provide for the freedom to protect security through private arrangements. To a certain extent the parties to the social contract could reserve a part of their freedom for private security arrangements. The amount of freedom transferred or reserved could be based on a rational calculation of the optimum effects of the transference.

In this context the question can be raised what the status of freedom is in the intermediate state of nodal governance. Johnston and Shearing claim that no set of nodes can be given conceptual priority in a network-based approach to governance. They argue that the exact nature of governance is a matter of empirical enquiry (Johnston and Shearing 2003: 147). This point of view has been the object of critical debate in criminological literature. According to some authors, the state still has a central place in the governance of security, although the state does not provide for all instruments of security. The central place of the state has taken the form of 'anchored pluralism' in which the state is the final authority on all instruments of security provided by state institutions, private companies and citizens (Loader and Walker 2006, Loader and Walker 2007: 170-194).

Johnston and Shearing presuppose the possibility of the use of contract and property as instruments of security. The protection of 'mass private properties' and 'gated communities' is partly based on the rights of the owners of these properties and their freedom of contract. In a modern state, however, the right to property is not a natural right, but it is defined and regulated by the state and its laws.[6] Property rights are protected by the state in order to allow private owners to exercise these rights. The possibility to exercise these rights presupposes the existence of the state and the laws of the state which regulate private property.[7]

These laws also contain limitations on property rights, for instance the limitation that the owner of private property does not have the right to punish individuals who violate his property rights in the way the criminal law system can punish perpetrators. The owner of private property has the right to exclude individuals from the use of his property and to arrest violators and hand them over to the state in order to punish the perpetrators. These rights and limitations are defined by the laws of the state. When an owner transgresses these laws, he

6 The same problem occurs in Nozick 1974. He presupposes property rights and contract rights without the existence of a state. Given the complexity of these rights, it is problematic to suppose that they can be defined as natural rights without laws defining them. The complications of defining property rights may be a reason of its own to enter a social contract and to transfer ruling powers to the state.

7 This point was already argued by Rousseau in his social contract theory (Rousseau 1997: Book I, Chapter 8 and 9).

or she can become the subject of state force through private or public proceedings.

Freedom of contract is also a right defined by the laws of the state.[8] Contracts are regulated by laws and these laws also mark the boundaries of the freedom of contract. According to private law, it is not possible to regulate the use of force by private contract. The use of force falls under the monopoly of the state as it is defined by private and public law. It is allowed to contract with private companies on surveillances, but it is not allowed to contract with these companies on the arrest, trial and imprisonment of individuals in order to protect private property.[9]

From the perspective of the Beccarian theory, the state monopoly on the criminal law could be amended with additional instruments to protect the security of individuals and private companies. These instruments, like the freedom of contract and property rights, are also defined and limited by the law of the state, first of all by the monopoly of the state on the use of force, which excludes certain forms of coercion on the basis of private property or private contracts. The private law of the state regulates the legal powers of property owners and the freedom of contract on the security market.

Nodal governance can be analyzed as an *amendment* to the Beccarian theory of the social contract. The intermediate state of nodal governance can be placed between the Beccarian state which provides for security through the criminal law and the state of nature in which everybody has to provide for their own security in a war of all against all. Most instruments of nodal governance, like private contracts and property rights, presume the existence of the state, its monopoly on the use of force, and the laws of the state which regulate and limit private contracts and property rights.

The Beccarian theory on the social contract is *incomplete* because Beccaria thought that the criminal law is the only instrument to protect security. His theory of rational choice, however, suggests that individuals have more instruments from which to choose than just the criminal law. They can use their freedom to protect their security and they can make provisions in the social contract to reserve a certain amount of freedom to maximize the protection of security. The free market of private security is limited and protected by the state

---

8 Crawford calls contractual governance 'regulated self-regulation' (Crawford 2003: 488). He points out the risks of exclusion and inequality of contractual governance (501). An important gain can be the fact that contractual governance is voluntary, in contrast to the punitive coercion of the state. The voluntary character of contractual governance can make room for restorative justice (502).

9 Johnston and Shearing call 'the authority of contract' an alternative to 'state-granted coercive powers' (Johnston and Shearing 2003: 17). They add that 'the state can be called upon to use force in support of contracts and their property claims', but they also state that 'the governance of security is authorized through a variety of different, albeit related, auspices'. The legal powers of private person to make contractual rules on the governance of security, however, presuppose the existence of the state which regulates the right to property and the freedom of contract. See on these and related problems of nodal governance Loader and Walker 2007: 188-190 and 192-194.

monopoly on the use of force. On this point the free market of security differs from the state of nature where such a monopoly does not exist.

From the point of view of Beccaria's theory, the question can be asked whether private security arrangements are effective in comparison with the security offered by the criminal law and whether these arrangements comply with the principles of equality, legality and proportionality. The order of the risk program in nodal governance is not as clearly stated as the criminal law, the instruments in the form of exclusive measures can be disproportionate in relation to the unwanted behaviour, and the effects of private arrangements can lead to inequality in the protection of security. Individuals and companies who can afford it, can effectively protect their security in gated communities or business improvement districts, while individuals who lack the financial means have to live in 'no go areas' which resemble the Hobbesian state of nature. A consequence of nodal governance could be the growth of unsafe areas which may work to everybody's disadvantage.[10]

A possible solution to this problem could be state intervention in unsafe areas to protect citizens who cannot pay for their security or state subsidy of private arrangements for those who cannot pay them. Taxing the rich to finance security for to poor could also be a solution (Johnston and Shearing 2003: 111).

The best solutions according to Beccarian reasoning depend on the six or seven levels of rationality and on the possibilities of the criminal law and the private arrangements to offer effective protection. The solutions finally depend on a rational balancing of freedom and security and this balancing could lead to the conclusion that individuals should be able to use their freedom to protect their security instead of transferring their freedom to the state and the criminal law. But this reasoning also presupposes the existence of the state as the highest authority to define and limit property rights and contract rights. A rational theory of the social contract should not only describe the monopoly of the state on the use of force, but also the private freedoms of citizens and companies to protect their own security, based on provisions in the social contract and the laws of the sovereign state.

6. Conclusion

Both the theory on nodal governance as formulated by Johnston and Shearing, and the theory of Beccaria on the criminal law fall short of explaining private arrangements to protect security. Johnston and Shearing fail to see that private contracts and property rights are legal concepts which presuppose the existence of the state and its laws on property and contract. Johnston and Shearing have to clarify their use of concepts like 'the authority of contract' and 'mass private

[10] Johnston and Shearing call the private areas of security 'new feudal domains' with 'private corridors' running over the unsafe areas, for instance in the form of bridges or underground pathways between the safe areas (Johnston and Shearing 2003: 110).

property' in relation to private law and the state monopoly on the use of force.[11] Beccaria did not take into account the possibility that individuals can use their freedom to protect their security under the rule of private law. Beccaria's theory on the rationality of individuals can be used to argue that individuals must have the possibility to look for a balance between private freedom to protect security and public protection by the criminal law of the state.

The Beccarian theory on the social contract can be amended with provisions on the private arrangements of individuals to protect security. These provisions can be constructed on the basis of the Beccarian principles of equality, legality and proportionality, and also on the basis of the six or seven levels of Beccarian rationality. Johnston and Shearing also seem to reason from the rational interests of individuals in the protection of security. These interests could be specified in a theory on the rational choices between the different instruments and on the implementation of the Beccarian principles.[12]

It cannot be excluded, however, that Beccaria's dream can no longer be a source of inspiration. In that case, alternative theoretical frameworks have to be developed to explain and justify nodal governance and the diminishing of state governance: individuals are not rational in accordance with Enlightenment ideals, the state cannot meet the Enlightenment expectations of effectivity and normativity, and the free market of security has replaced the state monopoly on the governance of security. It could be disputed that this replacement is really an ideal situation. This intermediate state could also be a consequence of a failing society in which rich people retire in their 'gated communities', while those who cannot pay for their security, have to live in the 'no go area's' with a strong resemblance to the Hobbesian state of nature. As long as this situation is considered to be a state of avoidable failure, the Beccarian dream is still alive.

11 Shearing seems to acknowledge this point when he accepts concepts like 'rule at a distance' en 'state-anchored pluralism' (Shearing 2006: 24). But he denies the possibility of a conceptual priority of the state on the basis of 'conceptual claims'. He argues that priority in nodal governance is an empirical matter (27, see also Johnston and Shearing 2003: 147). Shearing, however, does not make clear what the status of concepts like contract and property is. It seems to be impossible to define these concepts only empirically, without any reference to their legal meaning which conceptually presupposes the existence of a state and a legal system.

12 Beccaria's theory of rational choice could be amended with ideas from modern rational choice theory and (neo)liberalism. The seventh level of rationality, which is absent in his theory, suggests that rational decisions on the distribution of security in society should take into account the equal moral worth of persons. Rawlsian rationality could be taken as a model of the way decisions on this seventh level should be taken. See Rawls 1999: 123 e.f. on the rationality of persons in his theory.

References

Beccaria, C. (1995). *Of Crimes and Punishments*. Cambridge: Cambridge University Press.

Crawford, A. (2003). Contractual Governance of Deviant Behavior. *Journal of Law and Society*, *30(4)*, 479-505.

Crawford, A. (2006). Networked Governance and the Post-Regulatory State? *Theoretical Criminology*, *10(4)*, 449-497.

Garland, D. (2001). *The Culture of Control*. Oxford: Oxford University Press.

Hobbes, T. (1996). *Leviathan*. Cambridge: Cambridge University Press.

Hudson, B. (2003). *Justice in the Risk Society: Challenging and Re-Affirming Justice in late Modernity*. London: Sage.

Johnston, L., & Shearing, C. (2003). *Governing Security. Explorations in Policing and Justice*. London/New York: Routledge.

Lacey, N. (2008). *The Prisoner's Dilemma*. Cambridge: Cambridge University Press.

Loader, I., & Walker, N. (2006). Necessary Virtues: the Legitimate Place of the State in the Production of Security. In J. Wood, & B. Dupont (Eds.), *Democracy, Society and the Governance of Security*. Cambridge: Cambridge University Press.

Loader, I., & Walker, N. (2007). *Civilizing Security*. Cambridge: Cambridge University Press.

Nozick, R. (1974). *Anarchy, State, and Utopia*. Oxford: Basic Blackwell.

Plato (1994) *Gorgias*, Oxford: Oxford University Press.

Rawls, J. (1999). *A Theory of Justice*. Oxford: Oxford University Press (revised edition).

Reiman, J. (2007). The Moral Ambivalence of Crime in an Unjust Society. *Criminal Justice Ethics*, *26(3)*, 3-15.

Rousseau, J.J. (1997). *The Social Contract*. Cambridge: Cambridge University Press.

Shearing, C. (2006). Reflections on the Refusal to Acknowledge Private Governments. In J. Wood, & B. Dupont (Eds.), *Democracy, Society and the Governance of Security*. Cambridge: Cambridge University Press.

Wood, J., & Dupont, B. (Eds.) (2006). *Democracy, Society and the Governance of Security*. Cambridge: Cambridge University Press.

Wood, J., & Shearing, C. (2007). *Imagining Security*. Cullompton: Willan Publishing.

Young, D.B. (1983). Cesare Beccaria: Utilitarian or Retributivist? *Journal of Criminal Justice, 11(4)*, 317-326.

Young, J. (1999). *The Exclusive Society*. London: Sage.

4. Legitimacy of Dutch Criminal Law in Increasingly Horizontal and Multi-Dimensional Relationships

Christine Cleiren

1. Introduction[1]

Contemporary Dutch society is characterised by far reaching upheavals and changes; on the one hand there is a move towards Europeanization and internationalization; on the other hand there are turbulent changes within the national boundaries. Widely used terms such as the compensation claim culture, modern citizenship, individualization, privatization, negotiation tactics, self-regulation and populism express in words the latter developments. These developments are of course not limited to the Netherlands and partly not even to Europe. They concern changes in the whole western world that have a huge influence on the role of the state. The state finds itself for example – thanks to these developments – in a split between withdrawal and action in areas such as economy, education, welfare and security. The monopoly of the government to organize and govern society cannot be taken for granted like it used to be. Since the Enlightenment society has been characterized by a vertical structure. Since then the state has taken the responsibility to protect the rights and freedom of its citizens. Society is changing more and more into a horizontal and multi-dimensional structure, and the state seems to be more of a player than a leader or keeper of the game. This development is reflected among others in the dismantling of the welfare state over the past few years in the Netherlands and the transfer or abandonment of originally public tasks to the free market. These developments go hand in hand with a change in the role of the law and in particular the role of the criminal law. Both society and the law are becoming more and more horizontal in structure and instead of a pyramid model for ordering and a pyramid model for law, a network society has come into existence and there is talk of a 'multilevel legal order'.[2] These new forms of governance seem to be the same as what has become more and more known as nodal governance (Johnston & Shearing 2003, Wood & Dupont 2006, Wood & Shearing 2007). Nodal governance is a form of governance where the state

---

1 Parts of an earlier published text by the author (Cleiren 2010) have been reworked in this contribution. Parts of an earlier published text by the author (Cleiren 2010) have been reworked in this contribution.

2 Cf. Ost & Van de Kerckhove, 2002. Also in other French scientific literature, e.g. by Michel Foucault en Mireille Delmas-Marty, there is a strong similarity with this interpretation.

monopoly on the governance of security has been replaced by forms of network governance. The state, private companies and citizens work together in networks of governance in which they use a range of instruments and strategies to organize and govern society. The term nodal governance is used in particular to describe and analyze the governing instruments for providing security and combating and controlling crime. In the Netherlands certain developments in the provision of security have already been described with the term nodal governance.[3]

Various academics from very different disciplines all seem to interpret the development to a more horizontal and multi-dimensional society and the loss of the state monopoly on certain social areas as a reaction to the failure of the government.[4] The changes towards a governance model with a nodal orientation could then be seen as the result of a conscious choice. Others see the failure of the state as a monopolist as one aspect of the social developments. The developments leading to another governance model come forth from an interaction between different social shifts, where no single architect can be indicated. Even without making a choice from either one of these positions we can determine without any reservation that the size, intensity and the close interaction of the social developments outlined are such that they have to be taken for a fact.
This observation does not mean that the changes cannot or must not have far reaching consequences for the criminal law and criminal procedure. A short explanation is appropriate at this stage.

The explanation for the above mentioned social development is relevant with an eye to the role of the law and the legal regulation of the way that all the players behave in the areas of horizontal and multi-dimensional relationships (the state, companies, citizens etc). Should it be the case that the state has lost its grip on the control of security and combating and controlling crime then the fundamental question arises what impact this has on the legitimacy of state actions, the legitimacy of the law as an instrument of control and on the regulation of actions performed by non-state players in the areas of horizontal and multi-dimensional relationships (public-private organizations, companies, citizens etc.). There is a valid enough reason to assume that the conditions for our rule of law cannot be anchored in the same way as before. Our Dutch perception of the constitutional democratic state (*democratische rechtsstaat*) is – due to its strong connection with the Enlightenment – firmly based on the classical monopoly of the state on the governance of security and the

3 See *Justitiële Verkenningen* (2009) and *Politie in ontwikkeling, Visie op de politiefunctie* (2005). The term nodal governance is by the way not used in exactly the same way in the latter collection as it is in the more theoretically orientated literature.

4 See also Klaas Rozemond in *Beccaria's Dream, On Criminal Law and Nodal Governance*, Introduction, in this volume.

determination of crimes and punishment.[5] If the monopoly of the state with regard to the criminal law is subject to changes brought about by these developments then inevitably the fundamental characteristics of the criminal law are affected. The state has had, following in the footsteps of the Enlightenment, the monopoly over the criminal law during the past centuries. Beccaria's theory completely complemented this, he advocated a rationally constructed criminal law that would prevent citizens from harmful conduct and would create the greatest happiness shared among the greater number (Beccaria 1995).[6] That monopoly also implies, according to the enlightenment thinkers, explicit obligations in securing both safety and justice. Can this double role be fulfilled or adequately fulfilled in the new situation and in what way? Equally the question arises how other guarantees that are inherent in our concept of the *rechtsstaat* can be guaranteed. Also the democratic monitoring of providing security and the governance and control of crime will no longer be able to cover the same range as before.

The state cannot automatically use the law in the new situation as it did in the past in order to stipulate goals and means and the continuation cannot be realized without the input of non-public players. If one calculates to the limits such a new social situation then it will be clear that our once trusted separation of powers offers insufficient grip for the preservation of checks and balances, now that it cannot include all the relevant players in the newly formed social environment.

Criminal law and criminal procedure are highly suitable to use for investigating the development to more horizontal and multi-dimensional relationships and the accompanying changes to the position of the state and to map the implications for the constitutional democratic state. Developments in society have a large influence on the tasks and goals of the criminal law and on the criminal law discourse, because of the fact that the tasks and goals of the criminal law are 'situated' in the heart of society.

The developments in Dutch criminal law and criminal procedure during the last two to three decades will be examined in this paper. First of all the developments in the criminal law that connect with the trend to more horizontal and multi-dimensional relationships in the social landscape will be investigated and described. From this information we can see if the state is losing its monopoly position on the criminal law and criminal procedure and what other players can also be found in that playing field. Along with this it can be made clear if and how the realization of relevant criminal law goals are coordinated,

---

5 Referring to Witteveen (2004: 75): 'There can be marked differences between political systems that either focus on legality (like Germany) or on the rule of law (as in the United Kingdom) or on constitutionalism (like the united States). The Dutch use the word *rechtsstaat* to refer to the whole family of concepts and accordingly, there are overtones of legality, rule of law and constitutionalism to be discerned in it.' See also Grote 1999.

6 See also Klaas Rozemond in *Beccaria's Dream, On Criminal Law and Nodal Governance*, Introduction, in this volume.

regulated and controlled in the changed situation and if the governance mechanisms present are the same and how this form of governance could be characterized. This descriptive objective complements the contribution of Van Calster and Schuilenburg in this collection. The overview of the present state of affairs will offer starting points in assessing the normative question of how the legitimacy of criminal procedure can be guaranteed according to the demands of the democratic *rechtsstaat* within a more horizontal and multi-dimensional criminal procedure. Along with this an attempt will be made to answer the question how in the changed – and still changing – situation the principles of the constitutional democratic state and the checks and balances by the three powers of the state (Trias Politica) are filled-in, actualized and anchored and how this can be assessed. This question connects with the scope of the normative questions that Rozemond answers in his paper 'Beccaria's dream'. Then we will take a look to the future. How can the legitimacy of the transformations of the criminal procedure be guaranteed in the future?
The question of the effectiveness of the changed way of governing and controlling will not be handled in this paper.

2. The Traditional Characteristics of Dutch Criminal Law

Dutch criminal law is part of public law according to normal perceptions. Current criminal law still relies on the idea that the detection and prosecution of offences carry such a heavy social weight that they belong to the exclusive care and task of the state. Criminal law has consequently a particular function in the relationship state-suspect/criminal and more general in the relationship state-citizen. In the Netherlands the public character of the criminal law comes particularly to expression in the principle of legality and in the prosecution monopoly of the Public Prosecution Service. Other aspects where the public character of the criminal law are emphasized are the goal of truth-finding rather than consensus, which connects to the absence of an adversarial process and the active role of the judge who makes judgements on the facts, the law and the person. Besides this the character of the criminal law is confirmed once again by the fact that the victim or the interested party have no possibilities for prosecuting themselves.

From the impression of this short sketch we could say that the criminal law legal position is a top-down relationship and a unique 'one-dimensional' vertical legal relationship. The relationship is not symmetrical because it is a case of a powerful state against a more vulnerable citizen (suspect). The relationship is not easily exchanged for another relationship because the system of prosecution implies that the players in a legal relationship are appointed by law and the players are placed in a fixed sequence to each other (police, Public Prosecution Service, examining magistrate, judge).

But, even if there is a certain amount of imbalance in the criminal law legal relationship, where one of the people concerned – the suspected citizen – is considered to be the weakest (and mostly is the weakest), the relationship is a legitimate legal relationship. The foundation of that relationship underpins the democratic decision-making process and the relationship is controlled by principles of the *rechtsstaat*. The democratic basis is permanently accentuated by the existence of the prosecution and the criminal law principle of legality. Moreover both the Code of Criminal Procedure and the principles of the constitutional democratic state, including the principle of legality guarantee as it were that the vulnerability and dependence of the suspected citizen are mitigated or 'compensated' to a certain degree. The criminal legal relationship seems to be more flexible than the system appears to be at first sight. The balance of power according to the presently accepted opinions within the three powers of state (Trias Politica) is readily recognizable in the way in which the legislature, the Public Prosecution Service and the judge do not only follow each other in a fixed sequence of reaction but keep themselves in proportion to each other in a continuous interaction of 'requesting information', checking and challenging.

3. A Changing Society

Various social developments from previous decades have had consequences that touch the domain of the criminal law and the legal relationships present within the criminal law. It is worthwhile to discuss them for a moment. I will limit myself to a brief outline.

First of all there is a shift in state ideology from the welfare state to a withdrawal of the state, a development that has influence on the law and more in particular on the role of the criminal law within society. In whatever way people judge the merits of the welfare state and its other – possibly less positive – effects, it has had its day. The ideas of the welfare state have had to give way to ideas where the citizen is thrown back on himself and left to his own devices. There is little left of the legislation created in that time for protecting the interests of many citizens. The withdrawal of the state results in a situation wherein the citizen and then the 'weak' citizen in particular can expect less protection from the state. The citizen has to carry his own social risks and – to protect himself – insure himself against possible risks. He is not pampered by the state with coaching and care but has to surrender himself to the laws of supply and demand on the free market. In this way the citizen becomes more 'susceptible' to criminal law interventions and more vulnerable when it comes to his resistance against them. On the other hand citizens get greater responsibility in society because of the withdrawal of the state. These developments are visible in the criminal law policy of the Dutch government since 1985. The state is trying to make the citizens also responsible for the treatment of crime and also to call on them in this matter.[7] You can also think of one of the past Dutch cabinet's (Balkenende III) drive to shift from public tasks to private care by means of self-regulation. The responsibilities are as it were rearranged. Social institutions and organizations, but also branches of industry, are forced to self-regulate and apply quality control by means of subsidy conditions and licensing regulations. The state is withdrawing, but not before it has put on 'handcuffs'.

The ideology of privatization and market forces is closely interwoven with this development. In the Netherlands we have witnessed, for example, the privatization of the Dutch railways and the gas and electricity companies. The trend to privatize is not only stimulated from above or imposed by the explicit decision of the government in order to relieve itself from some its tasks and leave them to the free market, but this trend also has its own dynamics from inside the market. We find this sort of development since the 80s in the rising phenomenon of neighbourhood watch groups and various forms of private security. Think of the use of security cameras in shopping centres, detection doors in department stores, property surveillance and private security at large events like football games and pop concerts. Similar developments can be seen in the private detective environment, like in the bank sector and in insurance companies.

Other important social developments are the rise of the security paradigm, thinking of our society in terms of a risk society and the rise of risk control, all further developed by Crawford in this collection (Garland 2001, Beck 1992, Boutellier 2002, Pieterman 2008). These developments permeate the whole of society and have far reaching consequences for ideas about crime and the criminal law. Safety of the citizen, both the protection of the citizen against crime as well as the protection of the suspected citizen, entails rights taken very seriously by the state. Prevention and precaution have become leading principles. Therefore the criminal law is also acquiring a more and more preventative character.[8] It is in this context easy to understand that the criminal law in such a developing society, where the balance is continuously made-up between the interest of freedom and the safety of the citizen and the interests of protecting fundamental rights, is not functioning as an ultimate remedy anymore, but is more often considered the most obvious instrument. This trend seems paradoxical now that we are also talking of a withdrawal of the state. The state actually acts very strongly on this point, but does so in a very differentiated and in a far less transparent manner. There is a divide and rule politics one could say.

---

[7] This tendency is described by the term 'responsibilisering', sometimes with 'responsabilisering'. See for this tendency in America and the U.K. Garland (2001): 124-127.

[8] This is clearly visible in the laws concerning the fight against terrorism.

4. 'Erosion' of the Traditional Characteristics of Dutch Criminal Law

The criminal law is not having an easy time with all these social developments. The core of this 'unease' can be traced back to the fact that the Dutch criminal law system is not based on relationships that are characterized by horizontality and/or reciprocity, but primarily on a vertical legal relationship: the state and the suspect. The restriction to a singly – and on top of that vertical – legal relationship does not balance up very well with the demands of the changing society. How, for example, should angry victims be handled?
Besides this it has been evident that maintaining values and norms in the wide area of security and public order and that of financial integrity for example cannot be satisfactorily and adequately realized within the fairly one dimensional criminal law relationship. How, for example, should private detection be handled and/or developing forms of self-regulation and supervision?

In such a social and legal climate we can hardly escape from a certain realignment of the vertical dimensions in our criminal law and of the primary commitment shared by the criminal law enforcement 'parties' involved. Criminal procedure has to refocus itself in a definite way in this environment of new relationships. The rationality of our traditional criminal law is under great pressure. This pressure has diverse cultural, social, theoretical and practical backgrounds that not only coincide, but also strongly influence each other. It is of course obvious that these problems are not restricted to the Netherlands, not to European countries and also not to the criminal law in the sense of a formally recognized criminal justice system. It could be argued though that Dutch criminal law is traditionally more vertical in character than the legal set-up in countries surrounding the Netherlands. For this reason it is possibly less easy in the Netherlands to attune to the horizontal developments outlined above.

Although the criminal law as a result of its characteristic vertical and one-dimensional relationship between state and citizen is not – or in any event not easily – suitably equipped to cope with the outlined pressure to more horizontal and multi-dimensional social relationships, it also has not remained 'passive'. We can see that the pressure has been met by 'creative' means in criminal legislation as well as in the criminal law enforcement and the administration of justice. As a result the indicated vertical relationships in the criminal law develop more horizontal dimensions and the unique one-dimensional vertical legal relationship state-citizen gives room to more differentiated multi-dimensional connections. At the same time is must be said that changes to more horizontal and multi-dimensional relationships are not without problems and trouble for the criminal law. The changes imply that the criminal law players must play their role in a partly changed horizontal and multi-dimensional landscape, while their instruments are for the most part, and (as yet) remain, based on a traditional vertical and one-dimensional relationship. This discrepancy leads to inevitable frictions. Further on we will highlight some adaptations made to a more horizontal, more multi-dimensional relationship in the criminal law (par. 5 and 7). Each of these descriptions will be followed by a discussion of the frictions that arise as a result of the adaptations (par. 6 and 8).

5. From Vertical to Horizontal Relationships in the Criminal Law

Criminal law in the Netherlands belongs to the exclusive care and task of the government. The Public Prosecution Service interprets the interests of society in the case of an infringement of the legal order and acts for the victim because of the infringement of his rights or interests. The relationship of the Public Prosecution Service to the suspect has priority and during the lawsuit the suspect and his alleged behaviour forms the drive behind the proceedings and are the object of the investigation. The legal relationships in criminal proceedings are consequently strongly vertical in orientation and this – in a certain sense closed and vertical – structure does not easily offer access to more horizontal legal relationships, like those between the suspect and victim and between public prosecutor and witness. But, as already said, there is some development visible, a development towards more horizontal relationships between the Public Prosecution Service and the suspect, but also between the Public Prosecution Service and the witness or victim and witness/suspect. The position of the victim will now be further developed.

The Changing Position of the Victim

Traditionally the victim has a very weak position in Dutch criminal procedure. There is the possibility to report a crime, to make a charge in case of an offence prosecutable only in case of complaint, a right to complain in case of no proceedings and to give evidence. None of these roles, specifically focused on the rights of the victim, have been put into the law. The victim is not recognized as an autonomous party. It is rather that being a victim is only a quality with an eye to and as a means of bringing the lawsuit against the suspect to a good conclusion. Within the criminal law he has no possibility for an autonomous civil action, but does have – and one can add 'only' to this – the possibility for joining the procedure as a disadvantaged party that is conducted by the Public Prosecution Service.

In the meantime some changes have appeared and Dutch legal practice is being further 'stimulated' by the ECHR, which has given, in its own way, a not be neglected position to the victim. The legislature has meanwhile agreed to give a stronger position to the victim, taking into account the existing character of the criminal proceedings. In the Code of Criminal Procedure the victim has acquired an independent section.[9] The importance of the regulation lies in the

[9] Wet tot wijziging van het *Wetboek van Strafvordering, het Wetboek van Strafrecht en de Wet schadefonds geweldsmisdrijven ter versterking van de positie van het slachtoffer in het strafproces*, Staatsblad 2010, 1 (Kamerstukken 30 143) (= Law for changing the Code

creation of an independent section where rights are granted to the victim, allowing the victim to be considered as a participant in the proceedings for the first time. The capacity has however considerable restrictions as well, most of the rights granted to the victim cannot be enforced. Although there are several adaptations to more horizontal relationships realized there is no direct horizontal relationship created between the victim and suspect. Settlements, mediation and restoration of rights have – in contrast to Belgium for example – hardly got a foot in the door of the Dutch criminal procedure and are thus not established there (Cleiren 2001, Cleiren 2003).[10]

6. Frictions Surrounding the Shifts to More Horizontal Relationships in the Criminal Law

The changes in the criminal law to more horizontal relationships do not easily fit into the traditional vertical criminal law relationships. It is a tight squeeze to fit-in the tasks of the criminal law players: legislature, Public Prosecution Service and judge.

Frictions around the Changing Ideas on Victims

The social need for a better position for the victim has also been taken-up by the legislature. The need for recognition of victimization, the recognition of the need to look the offender in the eye and to communicate the anger he has caused in front of the judge and recognition of the need for retribution have been translated into the granting of a right to speak to the victim. Soon this need will be translated into the status of participant in the proceedings. But then the vertical character of our criminal proceedings will still dominate over the relationship between victim and suspect. Here are a few examples. The victim can sometimes get damages thanks to the judgment of the court, but would be happier perhaps with a simple human gesture from the offender. The victim may speak at the trial, but there is no question of hearing both sides of the argument. There is neither an 'independent' relationship, nor a legal relationship, created between the offender and the victim. As far as horizontalization is concerned it seems that only the goodwill of the Public Prosecution Service or the mediating role of the judge can facilitate this.

In short, while there is an obvious breakthrough in the vertical relationships there are also frictions visible as a result of the growth of horizontal

of Criminal Procedure, the Criminal Code, and the Act of the Criminal Injuries Compensation Fund Act to improve the position of the victim in criminal law proceedings, Bulletin of Acts 2010, 1 (Parliamentary Documents 30 143). It is anticipated that the law will be operative from 1 January 2011.

10 See for this also the contribution by John Blad, *Restorative Justice as Criminal Justice without Threats* and by Philip Stenning *Whose conflict is it anyway? A Critique of Restorative Justice* in this volume.

manifestations that have developed in the meantime. Those frictions can be reduced to a large degree to our top-down, vertical and one dimensional criminal proceedings environment. The frictions identified point to the fact that it is not easy to realize the responsibilities in those horizontal relationships, if that has to take place using the traditional instruments – aimed at one dimensional relationships. If the Public Prosecution Service tries to mediate in the relationship between the suspect and the victim the question will quickly arise how voluntary are the parties participating in such a fabricated relationship. Besides it is especially the criminal judge who, because of his active role in our proceedings, will find these frictions on his path and as a result will sometimes be split in two himself.

7. From One-Dimensional to Multi-Dimensional Relationships in the Criminal Law

It has already been stated above that one could describe the criminal law legal relationship, from the characteristics of the Dutch criminal justice system, as a top-down relationship and as a 'one-dimensional' vertical legal relationship. The players are stipulated by law within this unsymmetrical and inflexible relationship and placed in a sequence of reactions to one another (police, Public Prosecution Service, magistrate, judge). Their powers have been carefully defined and are carefully coordinated with each other. One could say that there is one column. But in the meantime there are also strong shifts visible in these traditional characteristics of the criminal law: to a diversity of players and to a more differentiated method of work.

Extending the Social Field
There is a visible broadening of the social terrain in which the importance of compliance with behavioural rules is recognized. It is so that the attention to enforcement of the standards and regulations in public places has already extended itself to causing small irritations when they are not enforced. People are addressed for their behaviour such as urinating in public, not cleaning up dog faeces, or putting glass outside the Bottle Bank by law enforcement officials or citizens. Cooperation between citizens is sought in this way and citizens are encouraged to correct other citizens. The broadening of the social terrain in this sense also works through to the fulfilling of tasks by the players in the criminal procedure. For years the criminal law was advocated for these types of offences as an *ultimum remedium*, now the players from the criminal legal proceedings are 'pulled along' in the maintenance and compliance of these types of behavioural rules. We can see here a certain degree of entanglement between the enforcement of the criminal law and maintaining public order. We can for example see a similar broadening and entanglement of activities in the work of council ombudsmen, integrity commissions, and other complaint and disciplinary commissions with the players in the criminal justice system.

Particularly in times of social disorder, unrest, uncertainty and insecurity the criminal law is often considered and seized upon as the way to cure all evils. In the current juncture we see a strong tendency to interpret and point to the task of enforcing the criminal law as far as its goals are concerned almost completely in terms of security. All this has consequences for the way in which the enforcement of the criminal law task is interpreted, as well as for the character of the tasks that others (legislature and law enforcement) put on the shoulders of the actors in the criminal procedure. In this way for example forms of prevention and precaution become part of the task, responsibility and care of the criminal law procedure. In this way a certain amount of entanglement is created between the tasks of enforcing the criminal law tasks and those of child welfare, health care, education, psychiatry, public order, house building policies, etc. For instance, in the plan for Safe Houses that are and will be set-up in the Netherlands, we do not only recognize this entanglement, but also an attempt to realize common goals in the field of security and public order with the help of this entanglement.

A similar type of development is visible in the suppression of terrorism. There we have also an entanglement of enforcing criminal law tasks with tasks of various other state organizations such as intelligence and security services. Each of these organizations has its own roles, powers and goals, but there is both an overlap in activities and an overlap in powers.[11] In connection with this paper it is important to note that with the help of a joint venture not regulated by law (the CT-infobox) a contribution is being made to combating terrorism by bringing together and comparing information about people and networks who are in one way or another connected with terrorism and related radicalism. The intention is to make a quick, multidiscipline analysis and appraisal of the available information by means of consulting, comparing and analyzing the data that the participating services have contributed. Depending on the results of this appraisal it becomes clear which measures – intelligence, criminal law, intelligence law etc. is possible or desirable for any one of the participants. The 'collected and shared' information then becomes available for the relevant participant.[12]

The legislature is also busy with cautious attempts of trying to develop the criminal law in the direction of a more precaution and prevention orientated instrument. This can be seen for example in the recently introduced terrorism law and in a completely different field by creating compulsive admission and treatment for addicted criminals who constantly repeat committing crimes. But even after a criminal law intervention and the execution of a sentence the citizen also wants to be protected from 'dangerous' fellow-citizens, against recidivism, against a confrontation with ex-convicts and against fear.[13] We can take as an

[11] See for this the WIV 2002, in particular art. 20.

[12] See for more on the joint venture Kamerstukken (= Parliamentary Documents) II 2004/05, 29 754 and 27 925, nr. 21.

[13] I will not go into the background of the origins of the 'will' of the citizen here.

example the hanging up of posters in shopping centres with the photos of shoplifters and the requirement to be informed about the return of a paedophile to a residential area after his release from detention.

Extending to Europe and Other International Fields
The increasing internationalizing and Europeanization of the criminal law leads to the situation where the tasks and activities in the framework of our national criminal procedure are no longer restricted to our national enforcement bodies.
International cooperation with, for example, the Joint Investigation Teams, Europol, OLAF and also in the near future by means of the European acquisition of evidence order, result in the situation that the social field, the internal applicable legal standards and the internal functional players are no longer restricted to within our national boundaries and the officials operating within them. The valid treaties as well as the principle of reciprocity and the principle of trust result in a situation that we can see, also in this front, a growth in the entanglement in the enforcement of the national criminal law with non-national enforcement instruments, officials, research results etc.

The Growth of 'Private Law Enforcement'
During the past few decades there has been a growth in the privatization of security, public order and the fight against crime, partly from the market developed by the private sector itself, but also partly as an answer to the need to safeguard private interests that cannot (or not anymore) depend on being enforced by public bodies.
For this reason the need for security arose in the 70s – also because of the many burglaries – in districts, streets and private houses, in areas with a certain amount of 'well-being', while this form of public security did not have any priority within government policy. The first neighbourhood watches was formed. During the following years the involvement of private citizens and commercial companies with public security and the prevention and fighting of crime also grew. Also in the domain of private detectives and commercial detective agencies we can see that of what were originally criminal law activities many have been taken over by the private sector and there is also evidence of a similar entanglement there. Moreover there are signs of serious detective work by citizens and other private players, partly set-up out of own interest and partly with a public flavour. More recently we also see experts, like scientific researchers and ex-detectives, in the Netherlands who investigate under their own authority and responsibility and/or criticize the truth of judicial findings in real criminal cases.[14]

In short, the role of the criminal law is changing. The role of the criminal law as an instrument is losing importance on the one hand to other sectors, like child welfare, health care, private detectives and international information distributors

[14] Futher elaboration in Cleiren (2008).

but on the other hand the criminal law is also getting more involved and entwined. Moreover there is also evidence of the expansion of the criminal law as an instrument to a preventative and a precautionary role and to activity after the execution phase, as well as to areas outside the national boundaries. On this point also there is evidence of an entwinement between the work of the criminal law procedure players and the players from other government organizations. The ways in which matters are governed and managed seem to connect with the nodal governance model.

8. Frictions around the Shifts to Multi-Dimensional Relationships in the Criminal Law

Shifts to more multi-dimensional relationships, just like the shifts to more horizontal relationships, do not fit easily into and onto the characteristics of our traditional criminal law. Again there is a tight squeeze with the interpretation of the tasks of the criminal law players; legislature, Public Prosecution Service and judge. Who is controlling, who is standardizing?

Expanding the Field

In the previous part the expansion of criminal law activities was determined by an entwining of criminal law performance with security activities in such areas as child welfare, health care and public safety. One of the aspects connected to this that can lead to objections is that the need for security goes further than where the – in principle – mainly repressive character of the criminal law lends itself to or can lend itself. The criminal law faces its own limits when it comes to precautions, prevention, monitoring the compliance to conditions, aftercare, prevention of self-determination etc., due to its primarily repressive character and the restriction to punish behaviour and not intentions.[15] Worries can also arise in connection with the regulation of the exercise of power which can become diffused through the entanglement. Non-criminal law players, such as child welfare workers can have control over other information – and even worse – over information on the personal and private life of somebody. That information can be very important for criminal law interventions by police and the Public Prosecution Service. It goes without saying that criminal proceedings authorities as a result of the principle of legality and the imposed restrictions cannot get access to all of the information themselves.

It is obvious then that the police and the Public Prosecution Service at times when extremely relevant information is available from non-criminal law players want to acquire the information and where necessary to couple it with their own information in the interest of security and prosecution. For example it inevitably

[15] We have to note here that the substantive criminal law is much more occupied in the field of risks, plans and preparations that the legislature of 1886 could have imagined or found acceptable.

happens through the work practises in Safe Houses that sometimes the players in that domain allow criminal law authorities access to information.
In what cases and under what conditions can information that has come from the other players be shared, used and coupled to the need for tracking down offenders? Also the background information in the dossier cannot remain outside consideration when it concerns the decision to prosecute.

Similar friction can be seen where it concerns for example to the partly inevitable overlap and entwining that has been seen between criminal law players and the work of the intelligence and security services. The legislature has realized this, so it seems from the commentary on the law for increasing the possibilities for detection and prosecution of terrorist offences, and yet didn't have any objections.[16] It also applies here that prosecuting authorities as a result of the *rechtsstaat* and the restrictions on them that they cannot get access to all the information themselves. It speaks for itself that the police and the Public Prosecution Service, in the interests of security, try to get relevant information that is available to non-criminal law players. Certainly now that the joint venture (CT-infobox) does not have a legal basis the question arises here also if and if so in which cases and under what conditions can information from the other players be shared, used and coupled for detection purposes. We stumble on friction with this question. The judge, from his legal position, will have to be very alert to the origin of the material used for evidence, in particular the admissibility of the Public Prosecution Service in its legal proceedings. At the same time he will hardly have any possibilities for checking the route that preceded the prosecution by the Public Prosecution Service because that route chiefly took place outside the criminal justice system.

Entwining of Private and Public/Private Environments

Private enforcement of the law is not primarily aimed at the same goals as criminal law enforcement in the sense of maintaining public law – and legislation and public standards. Even though the goals and powers of these organizations are totally different to those of the players from the criminal law enforcement field, the activities of the players within the criminal column are entwined as a result of the overlap in work area. Information from private players proves moreover to be absolutely necessary sometimes in order to trace certain forms of criminality, and certainly in order to be able to tackle it afterwards. We can think for example about the information supplied by energy companies in the detection of marijuana growers. The results of private security – videotapes for example – can be very important for public enforcement of the

16 *Wet van 20 november 2006 tot wijziging van het Wetboek van Strafvordering, het Wetboek van Strafrecht en enige andere wetten ter verruiming van de mogelijkheden tot opsporing en vervolging van Terroristische misdrijven* (Stb. 580, inwerkingtreding 1 febr. 2007) (= Law of 20 November 2006 to amend the Code of Criminal Procedure, the Code of Criminal Law and several other laws to extend the possibilities for tracking down and prosecuting terrorist crimes (Bulletin of Acts and Decrees 580, valid from 1 Feb. 2007).

law, for example as a basis for raising suspicion, but also as evidence material in a public law settlement. Moreover it is also clear that the security risks that new information systems, internet banking, and internet shopping bring with them cannot even be tackled with the regular criminal law instruments. The government is often dependent on individuals, providers and international cooperation for this.
The predicament we are faced with is not so much whether information and evidence material can be collected, but to stipulate the limits of coupling, sharing and using that material. Here once again the question arises if the judge has sufficient instruments at hand to carry-out his assignment properly in view of the legal responsibilities.[17] Here also the route that preceded the prosecution by the Public Prosecution Service also took place partly outside the criminal justice system.

Briefly, even though at the present social juncture the one dimensional monopoly position of the criminal law state has been broken there are also frictions visible as a result of the growth in multi-dimensional manifestations. Those frictions can be reduced to a large degree to the fact that for the criminal law the guarantee of control on the testing of the legal action and the results on the basis of legality and unwritten principles are 'frustrated'. The criminal law players – and the criminal law judge in particular – keep their own responsibilities in the framework of the criminal law procedure. The criminal law players have a certain amount of space to operate within, but that is limited. The frictions identified point to the fact that it is not easy to realize the responsibilities in the multi-dimensional relationships if that has to happen with the traditional – aimed at one dimensional relationship – instruments. It is once again the criminal law judge who particularly, because of his active role in our legal proceedings, will find these frictions on his path and because of that sometimes find himself in a split.

9. The Role of the State on the Nexus of the Criminal Law and Other Societal Domains

Governing complex social relationships and developments is almost impossible, as outlined above. The linear logic where complicated relationships are governed does not satisfy complex relationships anymore – as Van Calster and Schuilenburg have argued in their contribution to this collection. That restriction applies even more now that the state itself is part of it – partly intentional, partly unintentional.[18] The state certainly has not sat behind the drawing table as an

[17] In extreme cases the judge has the possibility to apply the sanction of *détournement de pouvoir* or abuse of administrative competence.

[18] We see this restriction also discussed in the comprehensive literature about the 'makeable' society but also in terms of a society that shows all the characteristics of a complex, adaptive system. See Kauffman (1993, 1995).

architect to sketch the new status quo and to work out a future sketch based on this. There also doesn't seem to have been any attempt made to carry-out any form of control over these developments on the criminal law procedure that takes place within and outside its frontiers. We can conclude though that the state hasn't stood still. There have been various reactions to the different developments that together give form to the shifting relationships and sliding panels. The government has delegated to various bodies by means of legislation and policy, mandating and delegating, decentralizing and external liberation of supervisory tasks a network of tasks, powers and responsibilities and are partly realized in the form of self-regulation, compliance, subsidy preconditions and licensing schemes. In this way the government gives away a lot of her own responsibilities, and on the other hand complements her tasks with elements of verifiability, transparency, quality control and forms of legal protection. All this illustrates the split between action and withdrawal. I will give some examples, first of all in the framework of horizontalization. As far as the position of the victim is concerned the state has partly placed the responsibilities with the organization Victim Help Holland. This organization offers for example help with the composition of a written victim declaration. We can point to the laws and legislation whereby the government binds private bodies to quality norms for enforcing the law as far as the differentiation and multi-dimensional developments go. In this way activities by private organizations have to follow standards provided for in the law of protection of personal data and the state makes quality assurance guarantees with respect to the performance of security and guarding services by way of licensing schemes.

The government has deployed the help of laws and legislation to control the quality of the players and 'new' forms of legal protection and to safeguard our *rechtsstaat*. The 'reactions' by the state to withdrawal on the one hand, and taking action on the other hand with the help of the law are not illogical in view of the changing landscape. The law is not only part of the developments outlined, but also has an indisputable potential to offer a contribution as an instrument to the set-up and control of a changed social landscape. The 'reactions' are in themselves not in conflict with the law or legal rights. On the contrary, it is within the framework of the state's responsibility not only wishful thinking to maintain the legal order, but also necessary and legitimate to change the 'strategies' in accordance with the changed and changing social reality.

10. Management and Regulation in a Changed Criminal Law Landscape

On the basis of the above we can conclude that at the present social juncture we can no longer automatically describe the criminal law goals, principles and system primaryly in terms of a vertical relationship between the state and citizen (suspect/offender), or from the perspective of a one-dimensional criminal justice system where the state always has the monopoly. The criminal law work environment has been greatly extended on the one hand, but on the other hand the environment as well as the instruments and the players in the field must be shared with other systems and players. The playing field looks like a patchwork quilt; the players are a motley crew with very different backgrounds. There is evidence of a melting and entwining of national and international environments, of private and public interests and of private and public action. That playfield is not only broad, divers and complex, but above all in continuous development.

Moreover the state seems in its own way to have contributed to the creation of forms of governance and control over that broad, divers and complex playfield. Characteristic of most of the 'state reactions' is that they do not lie within, but outside the traditional criminal justice system. That means that the legal responses of the state to the more horizontal and multi-dimensional social relationships have been formed to a large extent outside the criminal justice system and are aimed at players other than the traditional criminal law players. Because of this the criminal law has lost its unique, sovereign or dominant position in the domain of both substantive and procedural law, as well as in the daily practice of law enforcement and prosecution, compared to the position it had in the past.

The basis for the roles and powers upon which the criminal law players must carry-out their work in the criminal justice system are completely determined, formulated and regulated by the criminal law, and are thus dominated by vertical and one-dimensional relationships. Legality and unwritten principles of due process regulate and standardize the behaviour of the players. That means that they have to carry-out their task in a changed, horizontal and multi-dimensional landscape while their instruments are principally based on a vertical and one-dimensional relationship. The frictions discussed earlier form an illustration of the tension that comes from this. If we look at the nature of these frictions, then we see that the tension arises because the players cannot or cannot completely safeguard or realize or even get around the traditional criminal law procedure.

In the case of the horizontalization of criminal procedure for the position of the victim the friction lies in the fact that within the criminal law no 'independent' relationship, or legal relationship, is created between the offender and the victim. The only evidence of horizontalization that exists between them comes by the grace of the mediating role of the criminal law players, because within the traditional criminal law procedure there is no judicial instrument available to give form to the relationship between the victim and the offender. The possibilities for this are then inevitably very limited.

In the case of the development towards more multi-dimensional criminal law relationships the friction comes to expression especially in the task of the judge who has to control and test the actions in the preliminary investigation and the results of these, while his instruments are not sufficient because they have been tailored for one-dimensional relationships. Because of the entwinement between the work as well as the evidence of non-criminal law players with that of the criminal law players the traditional criminal law instruments that the judge has available are not completely appropriate and sufficient in order to test the reliability of the evidence and the appropriateness of its acquisition. The judge is in any case, much more than normal, dependent for this on the way in which the Public Prosecution Service is in state, and is prepared, to offer openness and transparency as to the origin of the evidence.

11. Regulation of Responsibilities in the Changed (and Changing) Environment

If we look at the changed environment and its consequences for the constitutional state's requirements then we can observe that the constitutional guarantees that lie in our traditional criminal law within the criminal law procedure cannot or cannot sufficiently be realized in the new more horizontal and one-dimensional relationships.

At the same time we can observe that in most of the cases in question other – not traditional criminal law – instruments and (legal) guarantees are created. In this way for example the private investigation and security branches are subject to a compulsory privacy code for transparency and supply of information requirements by the state.[19] The work of the joint venture in the fight against terrorism is also subject to a form of legally regulated legitimacy control.[20] It would be going too far to say that the current state of affairs does not comply with the demands of constitutionality. The interpretation of this can for example consist of transparency, openness, supervision regulations, possibility of sanctions or withdrawing licences etc.

Responsibility for the Criminal Law Players

This state of affairs does demand serious consideration. Viewed from the requirements of the constitutionality of our traditional criminal law one could argue that these frictions form an illustration of a balancing act at the limits of the conditions for constitutionality. There is still professional responsibility for the representative of the criminal law and the criminal law procedure. Despite the fact that the role of the originally fairly monopolized role of the state as far as the criminal law goes is seriously diminished, the responsibility for maintaining the criminal law legal order in the Dutch democratic constitutional system still lies primarily with the state. Maintaining legal order cannot be optional for her. The role of the police, Public Prosecution Service and the criminal law judge cannot be missed in this. They have their own responsibility within the domain of criminal law and this is laid down in the law. They work

19 The law on privacy was published in the Staatscourant (= the Official Governmental Publication) on 13 January 2004.

20 Wet op de inlichtingen- en veiligheidsdiensten 2000 (= Law on intelligence and security services 2000).

according to a limited assignment, with a considerable ornate organization and a large arsenal of powers. The other players in the field – the non-criminal law players – mostly have a smaller assignment, less powers and less strong and limited goals than the Public Prosecution Service. The criminal law judge remains essentially at the end of the chain; punishing and checking standards as well as testing the reliability and adequateness of the evidence collected.

The question is whether the bodies responsible for enforcing the criminal law and legal procedure have enough instruments of their own to fulfil and carry-out their tasks as required in view of the constitutional democratic state in this new landscape. The instruments are tailored to a unique 'one-dimensional' and vertical legal relationship. As already said it is not easy to exchange this legal relationship for another relationship because the system of prosecution implies that the players' legal relationship is determined by law and the players are placed in a sequence of action with respect to each other. At the same time we can state that our Dutch criminal law culture shows great elasticity in tackling these challenges. The preceding description of the already existing developments towards more horizontal and multi-dimensional relationships in the criminal law forms an illustration of this. The three powers of state have proven to be flexible. The legislature, the Public Prosecution Service and the judge in the present criminal procedure do not only follow each other in a sequence, but relate to each other in a continuous exchange of 'making enquiries', controlling and challenging.

It will have to be seen if the elasticity of our current Dutch criminal law culture is flexible enough to also absorb the continuous changing environment of society. In order to realize this there is a minimum requirement of the three powers of state to have insight in the outlined developments to more horizontal and multi-dimensional relationships in the criminal law and that they are aware of the frictions that this can bring. The problem at this moment is that this consciousness and insight does not seem all too great, a state of affairs that coincides directly with the diffuse and non-transparent environment that has arisen and now lies ahead.

12. Closing Considerations: Governing Security under the Rule of Law (*Rechtsstaat*) in the Future

Remaining Questions

By means of examples from the criminal law it has become clear that the results of the social shifts are clearly visible in what we can indicate as a tendency to more horizontal and multi-dimensional relationships in the criminal law. The new environment has been mapped and set in a constitutional perspective. The question remains wether and if so then how within this more horizontal and multi-dimensional criminal procedure – and in the awareness of the related tensions – the legitimacy of the criminal procedure in the future can be garanteed.

Dynamics and Stability

The complexity of the present society asks for creative and innovative solutions. The democratic *rechtsstaat* is luckily a dynamic concept that is always open and must always remain open for new forms of realization and actualization. That means that the democratic *rechtsstaat* is mostly flexible enough to react to social developments and to adjust the rules of the game. In the previous paragraph it was already concluded that there is indeed great flexibility. But, at the same time it became clear that not all the frictions identified can be solved within the traditional criminal justice system.

The question arises for the future if there are other possibilities to compensate the limits of the traditional criminal law system and with that to withstand the (potential) tensions with our own constitutional conditions. Thereby it will have to be admitted that not all frictions can be removed, that you cannot control and regulate everything. The importance of the legal order and the importance of positive law for guaranteeing a decent society also imply that the law does not have to go to the limits with all the social developments. It is true that the law and the legal order have a dynamic function in the democratic *rechtsstaat*, but also to a certain degree an autonomous, channelling and stabilizing function as well. The law will – taking into consideration the assessment of interests that are served by horizontal and multi-dimensional relationships – also have to set its limits.

The Future on the Long Term

For the future on the long term we can point to the inevitable inherent limits to the flexibility of the legal proceedings culture. The state has a monopoly position in our criminal law system that goes back to Beccaria's dream. That position is ultimately based on the idea of protecting citizens from other citizens (taking the law into one's own hand) and against the state itself through the division of power between the three powers of state. If that protection is in danger of being shoved aside – like what seems to be the case with all the frictions – and cannot be compensated in all cases by active deployment of the three powers of state then there is a serious problem. But it would be going too far to come to such a conclusion on the basis of what has been said above. Beccaria's dream has not completely disappeared in the mist thanks to the inherent dynamics and flexibility of the law. This doesn't take away from the fact that there is reason enough to continue keeping a finger on the pulse.

The Near Future

For the near future we will have to try and exploit the dynamics that are part of the democratic *rechtsstaat* to a maximum in order to withstand the frictions outlined above. Where certain guarantees of constitutionality come under pressure in the new relationships we will have to look for new or other guarantees or forms.

It inevitably results from the above that the vertical one-dimensional criminal law system offers insufficient instruments in itself to withstand the changes and by adding new laws the limits to the system will not be solved. For the near future we must not expect any or little satisfaction in solutions along that line. That is why it would be good for us to carefully consider 'compensating' remedies to cope with the frictions outlined above. In the following – with the awareness of the complexity of the situation – a few points of departure for further research are offered for further consideration. Essentially they both point to possibilities that a responsive or reflexive law offers (Nonet & Selznick 1978).

The first research topic could be found in the active role of the criminal judge. We could find a second research topic in the idea that the legitimacy of criminal procedure is not limited to 'suitable' legislation, but can also be served and promoted through effectiveness in the criminal law procedure, through transparency and through verifiability. The effectiveness will not be considered, but transparency and verifiability will be briefly handled.

A The active criminal law judge

In the Dutch continental legal proceedings tradition the criminal judge is given an active role. In this way the role is traditionally distinguished from that of the civil law judge and the role of the judge in other, non-continental criminal law systems. While the suspect in a common law system mostly gets his protection for example from his more or less equivalent position in the lawsuit and the possibilities that that offers him, our Dutch suspect will have to get his protection through the rights granted to him by law, from the negative legal evidence system[21] (negatief wettelijk bewijsstelsel) and through the active, committed and leading role of the judge. In the meantime the systems are growing over and back towards each other. That applies to the continental criminal law and civil law as well as to the continental and non-continental criminal law systems. But there is a lot to be said for encouraging the criminal judge to firmly pick-up the old active role in that environment where the constitutional guarantees seem to come under threat.

He can try not to get around but to actively approach the frictions discussed above that get put on his plate. In this way he can weigh-up and actively try to guarantee in actual cases not only the endangered interests of the suspect but also those of society – and where applicable also those of the non-criminal law players and that of the victim. The judge can for example – fairly analogous to

21 This refers to the fact that though a judge cannot convict a defendant on the basis of evidence that is not recorded as such in the Code of Criminal Procedure (only legal evidence is valid), while the judge is not obliged to convict after having amassed enough legal evidence (in that sense the system is negative, it only stipulates when a defendant cannot be convicted).

the active manner where he tests the activities in the preliminary investigation for legitimacy since the 80s – actively question the Public Prosecution Service about the origin of evidence that was gathered in ways other than by criminal law actors in order to test the reliability and the adequacy in acquiring it.

B Transparency and verifiability

An important problem, as has already been said, is that the environment as it now lies is very diffuse and not transparent. Because of this the first positive contribution can be expected by more transparency and verifiability. Openness and transparency form the best conditions to give criminal law players the opportunity to control and fulfil with tests their legal protection role for society, suspect and victim.

Although reservation is often considered best if it concerns the transparency of the relationships discussed here, there is no reason for this taking into consideration the frictions observed above. We have observed in the argument above that the outlined shifts in the judicial field were legitimate in view of the social developments. Nevertheless a step towards openness and transparency will not be easy. The situation is different for non-criminal law players. It was noted in the preceding part that for many of the players some form of regulation exists from or within their own domain (self-regulation, codes of conduct, compliance, good governance etc.) and sometimes even explicit control on compliance. If all goes well the non-criminal law players do not have anything to hide. But in view of their private status and the workings of the market in which they operate this is probably a bit too naive. Nevertheless transparency and openness can keep them alert – and probably also must – to the fact that they, despite their position, cannot and may not act as if their field of action was a sanctuary. They also must realize that they have to be visible and controlled under a constitutional democratic state.

References

Beccaria, C. (1995). *Of Crimes and Punishments*. Cambridge: Cambridge University Press.

Beck, U. (1992). *The Risk Society, Towards a New Modernity*. London: Sage.

Boutellier, H. (2002). *De veiligheidsutopie, hedendaags onbehagen en verlangen rond misdaad en straf*. Den Haag: Boom Juridische uitgevers.

Cleiren, C.P.M. (2001). *Geding buiten geding, Een confrontatie van het geding voor de strafrechter met criminal law ADR-vormen en mediation*. Gouda: Quint.

Cleiren, C.P.M. (2003). Het opstandige slachtoffer. Genoegdoening aan slachtoffers in het Strafrecht. *Handelingen Nederlandse Juristen Vereniging, 133(1)*, 33-104.

Cleiren, C.P.M (2008). Het monopolie op de criminal law waarheidsvinding. Overwegingen over belang en risico's van private 'deskundigen'-inbreng. In J.H. Crijns, P.P.J. van der Meij, & J.M. ten Voorde (Eds.), *De waarde van waarheid*. Den Haag: Boom Juridische uitgevers.

Cleiren, C.P.M. (2010). *Evolueren naar meer horizontale en multi-dimensionale verhoudingen in het strafrecht*. Mechelen: E. Story-Scientia/Kluwer.

Garland, D. (2001). *The Culture of Control, Crime and Social Order in Contemporary Society* (pp. 124-127). Oxford: Oxford University Press.

Grote, R. (1999). Rule of Law, Rechtsstaat and 'Etat de Droit'. In C. Starck (Ed.), *Constitutionalism, Universalism and Democracy – a Comparative Analysis* (pp. 269-306). Baden-Baden: Nomos.

Johnston, L., & Shearing, C. (2003). *Governing Security. Explorations in Policing and Justice*. London/New York: Routledge.

Justitiële Verkenningen (2009). *Nodal Governance en Veiligheidszorg* en *Politie in ontwikkeling*, nr. 1.

Kauffman, S.A. (1993). *The Origins of Order, Self-Organization and Selection in Evolution*. New York/Oxford: Oxford University Press.

Kauffman, S.A. (1995). *At Home in the Universe: The Search for the Laws of Self-Organization and Complexity*. New York/Oxford: Oxford University Press.

Nonet, P., & Selznick, P. (1978). *Law and Society in Transition: Toward Responsive Law*. New York: Octagon Books.

Ost, F., & Kerckhove, M., van de (2002). *De la Pyramide au réseau, Pour une théorie dialectique du droit*. Brussels: Publications des Facultés Universitaires Saint-Louis, Boulevard du Jardin.

Pieterman, R. (2008). *De voorzorgcultuur. Streven naar veiligheid in een wereld vol risico en onzekerheid*. Den Haag: Boom Juridische uitgevers.

Politie in ontwikkeling (2005). *Politie in ontwikkeling. Visie op de politiefunctie*. Den Haag: NPI.

Witteveen, W. (2004). Inhabiting Legality, How the Dutch Keep Reconstructing their 'Rechtsstaat'. In S. Taekema (Ed.), *Understanding Dutch Law*. Den Haag: Boom Juridische uitgevers.

Wood, J., & Dupont, B. (2006). *Democracy, Society and the Governance of Security*. Cambridge: Cambridge University Press.

Wood, J., & Shearing, C. (2007). *Imagining Security*. Cullompton: Willan Publishing.

5. The Judicial Branch: A Partner in the Business of Governing Security?

Ard Schoep

1. Understanding the Judicial Role in the Governance of Security

The concept of governance of security, as Johnston and Shearing perceive it, offers a framework for analyzing security programmes and strategies. Critical to this concept is the notion that it is to be distinguished from the 'conventional' terminology of policing. Not just because of the fact that policing itself has become a hybrid model, but also because of the fact that security programmes nowadays almost presuppose various partnerships, e.g. with 'local businesses, voluntary agencies, statutory agencies and members of the local community' (Johnston and Shearing 2003: 11), which justifies the use of the concept of governance. The governance of security must therefore be considered to be a framework built on the ideas of partnership and shared responsibilities.

Using the concept of governance as they do, Johnston and Shearing themselves raise the question whether this approach is too broad. Reducing a complex of governing functions and strategies, including courts and judges, to a 'simple, generic type' might result in a denial of their specificities (Johnston and Shearing 2003: 18). Indeed, they recognize that, *for a better understanding of the specific functioning of these strategies*, their respective mentalities, procedures, structures, rules and practices must be kept in mind. In actually *describing the big picture* of the governance of security, however, they seem to leave the question unanswered whether the 'mentalities, procedures, structures, rules and practices' of the respective institutions must be considered relevant factors. Because of the judiciary's principal commitment to the Rule of Law and the democratic society it is associated with, an analysis of the role of the judiciary in governing security might give some insight in the relevance of the Rule of Law to the concept of nodal governance and the governance of security. This paper explores in essence that very question: the relationship between the governance of security, nodal governance and the judiciary from the perspective of the Rule of Law.

The question then is whether the judiciary is part of the nodal network. And, if so, in what way is the nodal governance of security influenced by the judicial role in it? Or is it the other way round: in what way does its nodal role influence the administration of justice in criminal law?

There are various and valid indications that the judiciary as an institution is not and will not be a key player in the field of the governance of security as described by Johnston and Shearing. Expectations in that direction must be questioned when put into the perspective of the judicial tasks and functions within the context of the Rule of Law. Let me address this matter by referring to the concepts of government and governance. In the following, I understand the concept of government primarily as a description of the legal order of a state (Raz 1979). In this respect, the use of the concept of the Rule of Law corresponds to constitutionalism. The concept of judicial governance is often used within this context, as it refers to models of judicial constitutional and organizational design (Piana 2010). The concept of governance in the sense used within the governance of security relates in my view to the body of regulations and practices of management and control of a certain societal phenomenon, e.g. security (Johnston and Shearing 2003). This definition clearly includes non-governmental agencies carrying responsibility for the management and control of certain societal phenomena. In some ways, this may correspond to what Raz called the political conception of government. Furthermore, from a governmental point of view, the concept of governance primarily relates to the more executive and policymaking practices. We cannot therefore take for granted a judicial role in the *governance* of security – it seems we can only evaluate the judicial role in the governance of security insofar as its governmental (or constitutional) role is concerned. Because both the concepts of government and governance are closely related to the views one has on the content and scope of the legal order of the state, in particular on the way the Rule of Law determines this (legal) order and the functioning of the state organs, I will pay more attention to these concepts when elaborating on the concept of the Rule of Law and its relevance for the functioning of the judiciary in the Netherlands.

It follows that, while much of the literature on the governance of security deals with the position of the police, local authorities, private companies and, to a lesser extent, the legislator and the law itself, not much attention is given to the position of the judiciary. But, broadly accepting the notion, also for the Netherlands, that security matters are no longer an exclusive concern of the state and that the criminal justice system must be seen as a system in which partnerships and shared responsibilities exist, several questions arise.

Therefore, it is the purpose of this paper to identify if, and to what extent, the judiciary in the Netherlands is, from a governmental point of view, considered to be a player in the partnerships that shape the 'governance of security'. Governmental strategies with regard to courts and judges can influence the relationships between the agencies within the criminal justice system as a whole and, in particular, the relationship between the judiciary on the one side and other stakeholders on the other. To what types of judicial functioning do these strategies refer to and how does this relate to the concept of the Rule of Law? Secondly, when there are indications that the judiciary must at least partly be considered a partner in the governance of security, some normative implications need to be discussed. These implications do not only involve the shape and content of the partnerships, but also bring forward views on the responsibility and task of the judiciary, bearing in mind the apparent interrelated functioning within the context of the criminal justice system.

The above results in the following structure of this paper. First, some general remarks on the position of the judiciary within the context of the Rule of Law and the criminal justice system must be made. Types and functions of judicial partnership practices need to be elaborated. By way of concluding, some normative consequences of judicial functions becoming increasingly interwoven with other functions in the criminal justice system are explored.

2. Some General Remarks on the Position of the Judiciary within the Context of the Rule of Law and Criminal Law (Enforcement)

2.1 The Rule of Law and the Judiciary

It is common knowledge that views on the content and scope of the Rule of Law vary greatly and range between (more) formal and (more) substantive conceptions (Craig 1997, Tamanaha 2004). In this respect, the Rule of Law is to be understood as a normative requirement regarding the validity of the law. Whereas the more formal interpretations of the Rule of Law stress the sources of the law and the principle of legality and are in particular silent when it comes to determining whether laws that meet these standards are good or bad laws, substantive conceptions of the Rule of Law, building on the formal requirements, stress this normative quality by referring to moral principles included in the Rule of Law: law must also be *good* law. The formal conceptions of the Rule of Law require among other things that the law be prospective, general, clear, public and relatively stable (Raz 1979). These requirements correspond closely to the principle of legality, as promoted for example by Beccaria. Substantive conceptions include requirements like the protection of individual rights (rights conception, Dworkin 1978) and are expanded to include positive obligations to improve the life of people (social welfare conception, see for an overview Tamanaha 2004). In its report to the Dutch government, the Scientific Council for Government Policy (WRR 2002) distinguished four basic positions regarding the Rule of Law: the Rule of Law as a value-oriented system (Fuller), as a formal constitution of a legal order (Rawls), as a requirement for a free market economy (Hayek) and the Rule of Law as an ideology (Unger).

In discussing the Rule of Law and its implications for the judiciary it is imperative to keep in mind the various conceptions of the Rule of law as well as their respective translation into state and legal orders. Some requirements relate to the (legal) order of the state and to the state organs and their mutual relationships, some to the functioning of the respective branches of government. With regard to the judiciary, that means in particular that the discussion on the adherence to formal or substantive conceptions of the Rule of Law is about its adjudicative function: to what extent does the judiciary have an autonomous role in the development of the law and the principles and policies underlying this development?

Differences between common law and continental European jurisdictions are relevant to understanding what exactly is meant by 'the Rule of Law'. For example, developments in continental European jurisdictions show a diversity in conceptions of the Rule of Law, relating to two ideal-type families: the *Neo-Latin* and the *Rechtsstaat*-oriented conception (Guarneri and Pederzoli 2002). The French or Neo-Latin type of judicial governance originates from the (Montesquian) strict adherence to the law made by the will of the people and results in a relatively minor role for the judiciary. The German type of judicial governance is usually referred to within the context of the *Rechtsstaat*, with traditionally a stronger judiciary. Furthermore, doctrine has made clear that the German concept of the *Rechtsstaat* does not completely correspond to the Rule of Law (WRR 2002, Palombella 2010).

In the following I will primarily focus on the way the Rule of law is to be understood in the Dutch system of government. In that respect, I will speak of the *rechtsstaat*. The Scientific Council for Government Policy came to the conclusion that the principles lying at the heart of the Dutch *rechtsstaat* are: a government bound by law, a separation of powers, and a guarantee of judicial independence (WRR 2002). It is this working definition that I will adhere to in the following.

The constitutional and institutional structure Beccaria is referring to in his treaties on crimes and punishment derives mainly from the work of Montesquieu. The framework built by Montesquieu was developed against the background of the preservation of liberty of the citizen and the protection of the citizen against the arbitrary use of state power. In order to achieve these objectives, it was necessary to separate the legislative, executive and judicial branches of power: between the government, the law and the citizen, the judiciary was the guardian against the arbitrary use of state power (Montesquieu 2006).

The promotion of the Rule of Law, and in particular the principle of legality, by Beccaria (building upon the ideas of Montesquieu) led to a specific type of judiciary. Beccaria recognised the absolute primacy of the legislator in laying down the law. In the interpretation of the law the judge's role is limited: the judge's task is merely to 'construct a perfect syllogism about every criminal case: the major premise should be the general law; the minor, the conformity or otherwise of the action with the law; and the conclusion, freedom or punishment. Whenever a judge is forced, or takes it upon himself, to construct even as few as two syllogisms, then the door is open to uncertainty' (Beccaria 2003: 14).

Both the separation of powers and the principle of legality, Foqué and 't Hart claim, serve the effectiveness of the criminal justice system and the protection of the individual who is subject to state powers (Foqué & 't Hart 1990). In this respect, however, Dupont shows that in the writings of 18th century penal theorists the principle of legality did not only stem from the desired protection of citizens against the arbitrary use of state power. Legality was also perceived to shape a modern strategy of crime control – a criminal justice system managed by rationally determined goals and foreseeable and calculable effects. Upholding the principle of legality also had important positive effects on the organisation of the criminal justice system. Managing a criminal justice system based upon the principle of legality necessarily implied a *system* of criminal justice and therefore an institutional, organisational framework (Dupont 1979). Legality therefore has had, besides a protective connotation, also a utilitarian and organisational dimension. Beccaria himself recognised the utilitarian goals behind his theoretical framework (Beccaria 2003; 103-105).

The consequences of the Beccarian theory for the criminal justice system were considered by other 18th century penal law scholars, as Dupont convincingly shows. Both systemic effectiveness and individual protection against the use of arbitrary state power were pursued emphasized. One striking feature Foqué and 't Hart put forward is the emphasis on transparency and accountability of the functioning of state powers. Beccaria's and Montesquieu's views on the primacy of the lawmaker, on the interpretation of the law and on the determination and execution of sentences are ultimately traceable to a critical analysis of the arbitrary use of state power. Transparency and accountability of the institutions of the criminal justice system are a prerequisite for safeguarding an optimum in personal freedom. As Foqué and 't Hart point out: Montesquieu's and Beccaria's concept of the separation of powers is meant to prevent the unlimited use of state power. Binding both the state and the citizen to the rules of the law makes those powers visible, transparent, which contributes to the legitimate use of state powers. Additional concepts for accountability emerge once the conception of the Rule of Law changes, as can be seen in the following description of the balance-of-power doctrine and the institutional changes the Dutch judiciary has gone through.

2.2 A Balance of Power – Partners in the Business of Law

This is not the place to exhaustively discuss how the judicial function has developed since the 18th century. It is widely known that the separation-of-powers doctrine in the Netherlands has shifted towards a balance-of-powers doctrine. The legislative, executive and judicial branches of the state all have their own and separate tasks and responsibilities. Nevertheless, doctrine and practice point to a system of checks and balances that places the state functions in an interdependent relationship with each other (Witteveen 1991). That leads for example to the conclusion that, within certain limits, the judiciary is a recognised partner in the business of the law (Rijpkema 2001; WRR 2002). Much has already been written on this subject, with many examples of a (more or less) legitimate judicial contribution to the development of the law. One example is the development of the criminal law on euthanasia in the Netherlands

(Buruma 2007). Another is the contribution of the judiciary to the system of checks and balances in the enforcement of public and private law in the Netherlands by declaring rules of administrative policy (at both state and local level) under certain conditions to be rules of law, the application of which is subject to judicial review.

It must be noted, however, that the legitimacy of judicial lawmaking in civil-law oriented countries like the Netherlands is more problematic than in common-law countries. Within this context, the legitimacy of the use of judicial power is not primarily tied to the constraints Beccaria has put on the judge's discretion. But not only a more activist attitude of the judiciary has raised legitimacy questions. Values like transparency and accountability, deriving from the principle of legality, needed modification in the light of the changing societal and political demands made upon the judiciary in the Netherlands. In that respect, some remarks on institutional changes in the Dutch judicial system are in order here.

2.3 Institutional Changes in the Dutch Judiciary – Additional Parameters for Accountability

At the beginning of the 1990s, the judiciary was facing severe problems in the field of human resource management, in the implementation of new technologies and with respect to accountability. The quality of the administration of justice in general was seriously questioned. Cases were pending too long, people could not get proper access to the courts and, as described, in certain areas of law, the courts' decisions had the appearance of arbitrariness. In the structure it had at that, time the judicial organisation could not resolve these problems on its own. Hence proposals were made to restructure the judicial organisation. This development is not exclusively Dutch and can be seen in many other jurisdictions (Voermans 2007).

In outline, the underlying idea of restructuring the judiciary was to give it responsibility for its own functioning and thereby strengthen its independence. Until then, the Minister of Justice was responsible for managing the judiciary, which was physically performed by way of the Department of Justice. Today, the physical management and control of the judicial organisation are separated from the Department of Justice and from the Minister. The Council for the Judiciary was founded to execute the managerial powers over the judiciary.

But the Council for the Judiciary was not only given powers in respect of managerial matters. The Council was also designed to improve *the quality in the administration of justice and to promote uniformity in the application of the law*. In this respect the foundation of a Council for the Judiciary was a real breakthrough in the organization of the judiciary. Never before there was an administrative judicial body equipped with powers that (within certain limits) went to the heart of the judicial work, adjudication.

To live up to expectations and to accept responsibilities, it was almost inevitable that the exercise of these powers would lead to some kind of policymaking by the judiciary. Besides pursuing traditional values of judicial functioning like independence and impartiality, the judicial organisation pursued additional values and goals. Effectiveness and efficiency in the organisation and procedures before the court and a better communication with those directly and indirectly involved became part of the long-term *strategy* of the judiciary.

In addition to the classical Rule-of-Law doctrine, in which notions of legality, separation of powers and the protection of fundamental rights of the citizen take prime place, the judiciary was influenced by what is known in the literature as the new public management theories. This coincides with a new way of giving meaning to the concept of accountability (Bovens 2006; Ng 2007). Mak refers to these theories as a truly new paradigm (Mak 2007; 33-36). Quality is the central argument in the new public management paradigm. In a certain sense the concept of quality is all about standards and goals and their relative importance. But as Ng points out, quality is also an issue of morality in the sense that it aims to realise 'the full potential that one is capable of with the resources one has' (Ng 2007; 29). Because of the need for a more efficient judiciary, legitimacy and accountability of the judiciary became also an issue of quality control. Quality indicators with respect to the management and organisation of the judiciary thus became part of realising accountability. Ng reflects on the consequences for the judicial functioning and claims that they do not necessarily pose a danger to judicial independence, because in the end it is the judiciary itself that determines the quality indicators, in cooperation with the communities it serves (Ng 2007; 31). There is a lot to be said about this claim, for instance that Ng seems very positive about the context in which these quality indicators are determined.

We have to agree with Ng that the use of quality indicators is a matter of choice and morality. There can be no doubt about the institutional necessity of restructuring the judicial organisation. But with it came what several authors call a different paradigm – the new public management paradigm in which values like transparency and accountability gained new meaning. From that moment on the administration of justice did not only explicitly involve the realisation of the classical Rule-of-Law doctrine, but also accountability for the effective delivery of justice.

The above makes clear that the judiciary has its own institutional responsibility in the criminal justice system. As for any organisation in the public administration, transparency and accountability in its institutional functioning are, in addition to the legal infrastructure that defines the legitimacy of judicial decisions, a necessary feature of a modern, legitimate judicial practice. By linking the legitimacy of the judiciary in its organisational sense to societal and political demands, the judiciary becomes by definition a partner in the administration of justice – it demands an orientation towards these demands and a balancing between them and other 'quality indicators'. It might be questioned however to what extent this additional focus of the judicial organization is in fact a new paradigm or, in line with Dupont's analyses, a mere development of one of its defining characteristics – that it is part of a modern strategy of crime control.

The prevalence and acceptance in continental jurisdictions of a purpose-bound orientation of the judiciary is highly debated and raises serious objections. The realization of certain societal or ideological goals in the context of adjudication or conflict resolution infringes directly upon the more formal conceptions of the Rule of Law. In that case following rules becomes purpose-bound policymaking – a subject that has been discussed extensively in legal theory (for an overview of the various positions, see for example Van Gerven 1973). But it must be stressed that all this concerns adjudication – the conflict resolution function of the judiciary. The institutional changes as mentioned above do not *directly* involve judicial adjudication in the Netherlands. On the contrary, one might say, because this is explicitly excluded by Dutch legislation. But it is not the adjudicative function that has become purpose bound, it is the *organization* of the judiciary that has been subject to a changing set of demands and goals.

Narrow and broad conceptions of the Rule of Law seem to converge: The necessity to meet the accountability rationale stems from the limiting and protective function of the Rule of Law. The determining factors for accountability, however, have been connected with societal en socio-economic rationalities. In that respect, a more substantive conception of the Rule of Law seems to appear. This converging picture of the rationales behind the Rule of Law finds a partner in the constitutional arrangements behind the balance-of-powers doctrine. Not only with respect to the adjudicative function, but also at the level of its organizational and/or bureaucratic functioning within the criminal justice system practices of balance, of interdependences and associations must be expected to exist. The appearance of judicial governance in the context of a balance-of-power doctrine therefore needs to be analysed not only from the perspective of judicial independence and impartiality, but also from its organizational entanglement in the criminal justice system. These practices are expected to reveal a mode of functioning that must be considered relevant to the manifestation of accountability as a requirement deriving from the Rule of Law (Piana 2010).

3. Two Relational Concepts in Judicial Partnerships: Dependences and Associations

In the following I would like to address relational concepts and judicial practices that might influence the behaviour of the judiciary in its functioning, even in the role in which the judiciary is assumed to be autonomous. The evolving role of the judiciary in the Dutch criminal justice system comes together with a nuanced view on the way judicial independence and impartiality are safeguarded and achieved. The effect which the founding of the Council for the Judiciary primarily had was an open centralisation of powers over the management over the judiciary. On the one hand, it strengthened the judicial independence, although its relationship with the government, in particular the Minister of Justice, is still under debate. On the other hand, granting the judicial organisation explicit powers in matters of criminal justice policy had an impact on the relationship between the judiciary and the others stakeholders in the criminal justice system. The relational practices described below function within this context.

For a better understanding of the relational practices of the judiciary in the governance of security, I would like to focus on two levels of relational partnerships. Within this context, I speak of judicial *dependences* and *associations* that exist in the context of criminal law and criminal law enforcement. *Judicial dependences* concern and describe the way in which the judiciary, being an independent agency at a more constitutional level, is a dependent agency where its organisational or institutional functioning within the context of criminal law enforcement is concerned. Within these types of relationships, the judiciary is in essence a passive player, at the receiving end and not involved in or left with authority in the decision-making where the judicial function is concerned. This type of partnership is, generally speaking, connected with the classical (liberal) conception of the Rule of Law: dependences are a logical product of a judicial power that is separate from the legislative and executive branches. *Judicial associations* relate to the more complex and, from a normative point of view, more problematic arrangements in the criminal justice system where the judiciary is in fact, explicitly or implicitly, visibly or invisibly, an active partner in the criminal justice system with at least some authority where the judicial function or domain is concerned. While judicial practices in the more Neo-Latin (French) type of governance tend to remain within the boundaries of a strict application of the law and a non-activist judiciary, the balance-of-power doctrine seems to enhance the probability of more activist practices to occur. They relate to Soeharno's emphasis on the concept of reciprocity (Soeharno 2006). The concept of *judicial associations* inevitably implies a certain tension. On the one hand, these practices might be considered a logical step in the development of judicial governance within the context of the balance-of-power doctrine and contribute from that perspective to the legitimacy of the judiciary. On the other hand, the weak side of judicial governance by *associations* concerns the potential threat to its independent and impartial functioning.

A 'relational sub-concept' could be added to this latter scheme, although it does not (primarily) relate to partnerships with other stakeholders in the criminal justice system. There is a category of associations, which I call mutual consultative structures, from within the judicial organisation itself therefore, which is concerned with matters of criminal policy that are typical and explicit judicial matters or are left to the judiciary.

Theoretically, the above-mentioned partnerships can and must be distinguished. In practice, however, they will tend to overlap. Also, these types of partnership function as ideal-types in the argument, primarily aimed at focussing the discussion. They are primarily descriptive concepts, useful for understanding developments concerning the position of the judiciary in governing security. That having been said, the shape of these partnerships necessarily derives from the normative paradigms of the separation or balance of powers.

4. Partner in the Business of Law (Enforcement) – Exploring Judicial Partnerships in the Criminal Justice System in the Netherlands

With respect to the relational concept of dependence, two kinds of dependence can be distinguished: input and output dependence. The first deals with the fact that according to Dutch Criminal Procedure the judiciary is completely dependent on the Public Prosecution Service for the cases brought to court.[1] The Public Prosecution Service itself, a monopolist in that respect, has since years developed a highly sophisticated and politically tuned (motivated, driven, expedient?) policy in respect of the settlement of criminal cases, both regarding the decision to prosecute and as regards the sentencing recommendation to the court. It follows that the judicial domain is determined not only by statutory arrangements on the formal and substantive jurisdiction of the courts, but also, and within the limits of these arrangements, by the policy developed by the Public Prosecution Service. What judges do in criminal cases must therefore be seen in relation to the criminal justice policy developed by the Public Prosecution Service. Changes in the penal climate in the Netherlands can therefore never exclusively be explained by referring to judicial practices (Downes and Van Swaaningen 2007). The output dependence mainly deals with the systemic arrangement that the execution of imposed sentences is not the judiciary's responsibility, but also a task primarily delegated to the Public Prosecution Service. It does however relate to the legitimacy of the judiciary, in particular considering the movement on Truth in Sentencing in the United States and/or the early-release debate (Shepherd 2002; Padfield, Van Zyl Smit and Dunkel 2010).

Judicial associations relate, as I stated, to the more complex arrangements in the criminal justice system where the judiciary is in fact an active partner in the criminal justice system with at least some authority in respect of the judicial function or domain. Their manifestation must be considered a direct result of the balance-of-power doctrine combined with the systemic and interdependent character of the criminal justice system. To actually describe these types of

1 There is one exception to this: The procedure laid down in section 12 of Dutch Code of Criminal Procedure. That section provides a statutory power to the courts to undo decisions by the Public Prosecution Service to not prosecute and, instead, order the Public Prosecution Service to prosecute in the underlying case.

practice, and to actually analyse their merits, it seems necessary to draw a picture of the background of at least some of the practices of judicial partnerships.

We have seen that, from a constitutional point of view, the judiciary is more or less absent in the governance of security, because the governance of security must in particular be seen as an executive issue. Expanding our view to a more institutional level, focussing on actual practices that occur within the judiciary, a more complex situation reveals itself. There are practices that point to the presumption that the judiciary should, in a sense, be regarded as a partner in the business of law enforcement. What kind of associations, what kind of practices are they?

A first distinction must be made concerning the scope of the partnerships. First and foremost, partnerships exist in the sense that within the judiciary itself a great number of consultative structures operate. These are the mutually consultative structures. Although these structures are not the primary focus as far as the concept of nodal governance is concerned, they do point to some extent to connections with and dependences on what might be called other stakeholders in the criminal justice system. These are the nodal consultative structures. In the latter kind of partnerships, where other stakeholders like the Public Prosecution Service or the probation service are involved, practices might point to the normative implications we are looking for.

Secondly, where partnerships occur, it is important to realise which aspects of judicial functioning these practices aim at. As we have seen, the organization of the judiciary makes a distinction between the administration of justice, in which (financial) planning and control are placed within a certain hierarchical structure, and matters of adjudication. In respect of the latter, judges are statutory guaranteed to be autonomous. Organizational structures from within the judiciary can only support initiatives to promote the quality and uniformity in the application of the law. It is obvious, under the current legislation, that where consultative structures (whether they are mutual or nodal) lead to policies influencing judicial decision-making, the normative implications are the most pressing.

4.1 Managing the Criminal Justice System

Practices of judicial partnership occur on several levels of the criminal justice system. I expect that this does not come as a surprise to practitioners. The partnerships differ however in nature and in scope. To give an idea some examples of 'partnership' practices will be outlined in the following.

Managing Input: Covenants between Public Prosecution Service and Judiciary. The court must annually assess how many cases are likely to come into the judicial domain for settlement. On the basis of these and other factors, the number of the judicial, administrative and other supporting staff is determined.

This assessment is made in close cooperation with the Public Prosecution Service, as research on existing consultative structures within the judicial organisation shows (Boone et al. 2006). Matters like these are regularly discussed between representatives of the Public Prosecution Service, other stakeholders and the courts. These consultations have multiple and various purposes. Their main function is to streamline the workflow. One striking example is the coordination taking place behind the scenes when so-called mega-cases are brought to court. Other purposes are to inform each other on existing problems and possible solutions. In times of cutbacks in the criminal justice system, representatives of the courts ask the Public Prosecution Service for example why there is a setback in the number of cases brought to court. Many courts also have informal meetings with (local) bar associations.

Managing Input: Minors in the Criminal Justice System

One particular consultation structure struck my attention: it was the so-called juvenile district platform, established in the Almelo district in the Netherlands. Members of this platform are representatives of the court, the Public Prosecution Service, the probation service and the Child Care and Protection Board. This is clearly not merely a consultation structure for the purpose of streamlining the workflow of juvenile cases in the criminal justice system. Its purpose goes beyond that and it is for that reason that I will discuss it here, on the basis of a forthcoming article (co)authored by Jeroen ten Voorde, within the context of nodal governance. It is not my intention to discuss this platform exhaustively. The only point I want to make clear at this stage is that it shows the interrelated and interdependent functioning of the court in the settlement of juvenile cases.

The Almelo juvenile district platform unites the executive agencies that carry responsibility for dealing with minors in the criminal justice system. It involves the Public Prosecution Service, detention-centres, the probation service, the Child Care and Protection Board, the National Institute for Forensic Psychiatry and Psychology, as well as members of the court and occasionally local governments (Dronkers & Ten Voorde, forthcoming). One of the goals this platform has set itself is to deal with young adults between 18-21. Because of their age, they are systematically *processed* through the regular criminal justice system. Criminal law however makes it possible that sentences available only for juveniles until the age of 18 can under specific circumstances be imposed upon young adults between the age of 18-21. Individualisation of intervention strategies for young adults was considered necessary. And although it is the Public Prosecution Service that determines whether a case is brought before a juvenile court, in the early stages of the prosecution the cooperation of (examining) judges is a prerequisite. One example may clarify this: about three days after his arrest, a young adult suspect is brought before the examining judge, who is a specialised juvenile court judge. Thereafter, when a suspect is put into pre-trial detention, suspension of the detention can be requested. At that time, reports must be available to the judge to determine whether or not this is the proper path to follow. In this process there is out-of-court judicial involvement in the policymaking concerning what to do with whom. This is clearly an example of the associations in which tensions between an effective settlement of criminal (juvenile) cases and quality in decision-making on the one hand and judicial independence on the other hand come to the forefront. Another example are the proceedings regarding fast-track settlements in criminal cases.

Managing Input: Fast-Track Proceedings

Another example, showing the interdependences in the criminal justice system and highlighting some interesting features of the nodal role of the judiciary, stems from the general consultative structures as outlined above. It concerns the fast-track proceedings in criminal procedure (Mevis 2010). Two types of proceedings can be distinguished: ordinary fast-track proceedings in which cases are dealt with within fourteen days after arrest, and super fast-track proceedings that are dealt with within three days.

In recent years, (super) fast-track proceedings have in particular proved an attractive policy instrument for event-related circumstances. New Year's Eve, football games, demonstrations and suchlike are typical events where fast-track proceedings are provided for. In addition, fast-track proceedings serve as a tail of the governance of crime and public order in urban problem areas.[2]

Serving as the tail of the governance of crime and public order, the judiciary is faced with the problem of being a reliable partner. In matters like these, where great organizational efforts are made to meet the demands of a speedy and effective administration of justice, quality parameters like due process are easily endangered. Proper cooperation between Public Prosecution Service and judiciary is used to agree on the use of fast-track proceedings, on the use of the media and on the effectiveness of these procedures and on sentencing factors. This type of cooperation might obscure the traditional point of view taken by the judiciary that a well-considered decision is preferably taken in a detached atmosphere and after a period of reflection. In practice this type of proceedings places judges in an awkward position. For instance, expectations of the Public Prosecution Service and the public regarding a quick and fierce intervention are high and put a load of pressure on the courts to meet these expectations.

4.2 Managing the Quality of Judicial Decision-Making

Mutual Consultative Structures

Uniformity in the application of the law is a central goal not only of the administration of justice itself, but also of the judicial organization. As stated above, structures within the judiciary can support initiatives and practices that relate to this goal. In matters of law and the uniformity of its application, the Supreme Court has the final say. There are matters of adjudication, however, in which the Supreme Court has only a marginal power because they are considered to be matters of fact rather than matters of law. The realization of

2 Kamerstukken II 2008/09, 31 700 VI, nr. 83 (Menukaart snelrecht).

uniformity in the application of the law in these matters is left to the so-called factual instances within the judiciary – the district and appellate courts. In general, these matters concern topics in which the legislator has left judges with wide discretion in decision-making. Mutual consultative structures have been developed to deal with issues like uniformity in decision-making on for example fixing the compensation in dismissal cases, on fixing alimony and on the sentencing decision (Schoep and Teuben 2006). As the Dutch judiciary lacks a constitutional and institutional basis for such structures, these policies are essentially developed in an informal setting.

Consultative Structures on Improving Consistency in Sentencing

One of the issues explicitly assigned to the judiciary was the sentencing problem – at the time primarily defined in terms of inconsistencies (Council of Europe 1992). The role of the judiciary in the development towards more consistency in sentencing is a good example of how the judicial branch has changed over the years. Consistency in sentencing (policy) was by then primarily seen as a responsibility of the Public Prosecutor. Beside the fact that it made the Public Prosecution Service develop guidelines for the prosecution decision and the sentencing request, the judiciary was not very active on an institutional level to promote consistency in their sentencing decision. This does not mean that they were not paying any attention to this problem. Both the need for more information on sentencing decisions throughout the country and the application of lists of tariffs for sentencing can be traced as far back as the 1950s. It is well known that certain courts (district courts as well as courts of appeal) made use of internal lists for sentencing and of small local databases for sentencing. These lists and the way they were applied were not very structured. Revision was hardly organised, it was not known how these lists influenced the court in the sentencing decision and there was no information on how other courts organised their sentencing decisions and whether they were in line with each other. Research showed however that there was great interest in achieving more uniformity in sentencing through some kind of lists and receiving better information on the sentencing decisions of other courts (Fiselier and Lensing 1995). Over the years, the judicial attitude towards the problem of sentencing began to change. It became clear that the measures taken to promote equality and consistency in sentencing did not succeed. The National Conference of Presidents of the Criminal Chambers of the Courts of Appeal (NCPCCA) took this up and stated that they, the judiciary, should make efforts to promote consistency in sentencing. In 1998 this resulted in the formulation and issuing of so-called orientation points for sentencing. These were mainly based on existing lists and they therefore reflected to some extent the aforementioned lists of tariffs and the current sentencing practices of the courts. Orientation points now exist for multiple offences in the area of for example drugs, violence, drunk-driving and theft.

The legal status of these orientation points is debated. The Supreme Court does not regard the application of these orientation points as a matter of law, which leaves many of the legitimacy questions in the development and application of the orientation points unresolved. Regardless of their legal status, however, they do play a role in sentencing decision-making. But that is not our concern here. One aspect that does seem to be of interest is the substantive part of the orientation points and the way they are being developed. In other jurisdictions, sentencing orientations, starting points or guidelines have primarily been developed by specific agencies, bodies that were specifically designed and equipped with authority to cover matters of sentencing policy (Freiberg and Gelb 2008). As the Dutch judiciary lacks constitutional and institutional powers for such bodies, these orientation points are essentially being developed in an informal setting. This raises serious questions and concerns as regards transparency and accountability. One cannot consider it necessary that the judicial organisation must support initiatives like the development of sentencing orientations in order to promote consistency in sentencing without allowing the same organisation the institutional structures that would address questions of legitimacy and accountability.

One aspect of sentencing policy raises particular concern. Since the development of a separate judicial policy on sentencing, questions have arisen on the balance between this policy and the policy developed by the Public Prosecution Service. This is still an unresolved issue and in some way it has been comfortably tucked away. The emergence of the use of public opinion on sentencing and sentencing policy by the Public Prosecution Service, however, spotlights this sensitive issue again. The Public Prosecution Service using public opinion polls on sentencing and sentencing policy puts the judiciary in an awkward position between democratic arguments on the one hand and perhaps Rule of Law based arguments on the other hand. What legitimate claim does the judiciary in the perception of the people have to put aside this sentencing policy?

5. The Legitimacy of the Judiciary under the Governance of Security

Many practices, of which only a few have been described above, give rise to the assumption that the judiciary is in many ways not only a partner in the business of the law, but also a partner in the business of law enforcement. It is a peculiar partnership though, interwoven as it is with criminal policymaking, and it raises some fundamental questions.

Boutellier for example asks himself the question how that relates to what he refers to as the ‘paradox of criminal law’ (Boutellier 2002): If criminal law and criminal policymaking have become more instrumental and more linked with societal interests and developments, where does that leave the judiciary with its traditional normative paradigm of *ultimum remedium*?

Let me first say that there is no clear answer to that question. One thing I would like to point out though is that Boutellier's assumption that the *ultimum remedium* paradigm is one of the defining paradigms must be reconsidered. Even from a Beccarian rationality, the *ultimum remedium* paradigm must be nuanced as a defining principle of the organization of the criminal justice system. As regards its punishment mentality, the traditional Beccarian principles of proportionality and restraint, into which the *ultimum remedium* paradigm has been incorporated, another discussion comes to the fore. Being input-dependent as it is, the growing importance of administrative and out-of-court settlements paradoxically confirms the traditional normative paradigm of *ultimum remedium* of the judicial function. For the Netherlands this only seems the case by the grace of its declining domain. Security programmes tend to avoid, rather than involve judicial governance. Where the judicial domain is in play, matters of constitutional domain and institutional focus are relevant parameters.

5.1 Constitutional Domain and Institutional Focus

Within the constitutional domain, influenced by the balance of powers, the judiciary claims its own role and function by addressing and achieving an institutional focus. The institutional focus we perceive has been twofold. It has been on what is known as the new public management paradigm. In the last decade one of the main focuses of the judiciary was to realise maximum quality out of the available resources. But the focus was also on topics related to the quality of decision-making, and on building a bridge between quality in decision-making and quality of the organisation. Examples of these practices have been highlighted above. Besides the well-known, but difficult to measure parameters of efficiency and effectiveness, the attempts to improve the comprehensibility of judgements, to realise the principle of equality and to improve the expertise and professionalism of judges did not necessarily lead to a lesser workload or a better workflow. So the institutional focus has been twofold and in recent years a shift in focus towards the latter has become clear, which can ultimately be traced to the normative paradigm of the Rule of Law. These institutional focuses, however, are primarily concerned with the exterior of the judicial functioning. It shapes the conditions under which a judgement is perceived to be legitimate. That is not surprising, but it leaves a blank spot where attitudes and mentalities are concerned. In that respect, there is uncertainty in some practices of judicial policy. This is the blind spot that needs further research. By way of conclusion I can best make that clear with some remarks on discretionary judging and managerialism in the criminal justice system.

5.2 Nodal Governance and Managerialism

Normative consequences of the nodal functions of the judiciary occur when put in the light of the concept of *managerialism*, a concept that Bottoms used for describing and analysing international developments within sentencing systems (Bottoms 1995). He claims that in the last thirty years international developments have taken place that seem to have changed the positions of the agencies involved in the sentencing system. This is related to the growing importance of what Bottoms called 'managerialism', a concept which views the criminal justice system *as a system*, as a chain of functions and responsibilities that necessarily exposes the interdependences of the police, Public Prosecution Service, judiciary and legislator (see also Feeley and Simon 1992). According to Bottoms, the emphasis on the systemic character of criminal justice seemed to develop into four main features:

> '1. An emphasis on inter-agency co-operation in order to fulfil the overall goals of the system;
> 2. An emphasis on creating, if possible, an overall strategic plan for the whole of criminal policy (...) with each separate criminal justice agency having its own mission statement, integrally related to the goals of the remainder of the system;
> 3. The creation of key performance indicators (...), in order to measure aspects of efficiency and effectiveness (...);
> 4. Active monitoring of aggregate information about the system and its functioning (...), with special (though not exclusive) attention being given to information concerning the "key performance indicators".'

Some of the features described by Bottoms seem to correspond very well to the developments described above. According to Bottoms, the concept of *managerialism* has implications for the law, for the way in which the individuals are viewed in the context of the criminal justice system and, so he argues, for the courts. Where the position of the judiciary is concerned, his argument might meet with objections saying that these developments relate to executive agencies and cannot be 'nearly so true of the courts'. While admitting that some of these objections are justified, he argues nonetheless that the language of (systemic) managerialism tends to embrace the courts within it. In addition, he claims that it is a mistake to believe that the courts can remain totally immune from its effects, even if it does not directly influence or constrain the courts or the judges' discretionary powers. Thirdly, Bottoms points to the fact that, with respect to the sentencing decision, it can directly be impinged by legislator, sentencing commission or whatever agency that functions on this matter within the rules and procedures of the specific jurisdiction.

Apart from its systemic aspect, managerialism has, according to Bottoms, two other dimensions, namely a consumerist and an actuarial dimension. Leaving the latter aside, as it would require a paper in itself, the consumerist aspect of managerialism may be interesting to look into. The consumerist aspect derives, according to Bottoms, from the systemic aspect. This systemic dimension can lead to an increasing pressure from the legislative and executive branches for an 'efficient service delivery'. Bottoms argues that one (side)effect of this approach is a growing orientation of responsible agencies towards the views of those to whom the services are delivered, 'to test whether the services are delivered satisfactorily' (Bottoms 1995: 31). This argument completes in my view the realisation in practice of what above has partly been described by Ng as quality as a neutral concept. The question of choice and morality lies in the orientation. Would a judiciary of the kind existing in the Netherlands in the end be strong enough to avoid this consumerist perspective?

6. Conclusion

The argument of Johnston and Shearing concerning democratic security arrangements, necessarily (but not everywhere) involves the judiciary as part of the system. As we have seen in the above, there are many judicial practices in the Netherlands that make it possible to put the traditional (Beccarian) judiciary into perspective and put emphasis on the 'partnership role' of the judiciary. While there is nothing new in this statement, the constitutional argument, derived from the separation of powers and shifted to the balance of powers, leaves the judiciary in theory some flexibility in developing its desired functioning. The independence of the judiciary still stands, but its organisation and its functioning in society and within the criminal justice system are necessarily intertwined both with societal goals and demands as well as with the public prosecutor's office and the latter's criminal policy. That leaves us with a quest for new ways of giving meaning to the demands of control and accountability, as Ng and Mak (amongst others) clearly put forward. A more activist role of the judiciary, in the shape of the growing importance of the associations as described above, must be seen as a direct result of the development of the judiciary in the Netherlands within the context of the balance-of-power doctrine.

Implications of the partnership role of the judiciary in the criminal justice system on the normative fundamentals underlying the *organization* of the judiciary became visible once they were confronted with theoretical models of institutional focus. The distinction between a Rule-of-law based institutional focus and a new public-management based institutional focus appeared to be useful for describing and understanding some of the judicial practices. On the other hand, the analysis of concrete consequences of these shifts in paradigm need further sociological research. Bottoms' *managerialism* has put, in addition, an emphasis on some substantive implications of an increasing involvement of the judiciary in the organizational environment of criminal justice policy. Dutch judicial policies, dependences and associations as described above do not show a clear inclination towards either side – in a way it must be considered reassuring that the Council for the Judiciary has put great emphasis on the substantive quality of judicial decision-making and made great efforts to support initiatives to increase this quality. But there are practices that must be maintained and they are a matter of concern. The inevitable relevance of criminal justice policy for judicial functioning meets with fundamental objections when judicial policies are expected to converge or correspond to overall criminal justice policies. The Rule of Law and also the Dutch *rechtsstaat* require that the judiciary is left at least partly free to independently define the parameters for its accountability. Not isolated, but independently and with due regard to its controlling function. That would, in my view, be a parameter for partnership practices of criminal justice policy, with or from the judiciary.

References

Beccaria, C. (2003). *On Crimes and Punishments and Other Writings* (Cambridge Texts in the History of Political Thought). Cambridge: Cambridge University Press.

Boone, M. e.a. (2006). *Het functioneren van de rechterlijke organisatie in beeld. Onderzoek naar de stand van zaken binnen de rechterlijke organisatie na de invoering van de Wet OBG en de Wet Raad voor de rechtspraak.* Den Haag: WODC.

Bottoms, A. (1995). The Philosophy and Politics of Punishment and Sentencing. In C.M.V. Clarkson, & R. Morgan (Eds.), *The Politics of Sentencing Reform* (pp. 17-49). Oxford: Clarendon Press.

Boutellier, H. (2002). *De veiligheidsutopie.* Den Haag: Boom Juridische uitgevers.

Bovens, M. (2006). Analysing and Assessing Public Accountability. A Conceptual Framework. *European Governance Papers* (EUROGOV) No. C-06-01, <http://www.connex-network.org/eurogov/pdf/egp-connex-C-06-01.pdf>.

Buruma, Y. (2007). Dutch Tolerance: On Drugs, Prostitution, and Euthanasia. In M. Tonry, & C. Bijleveld (Eds.), *Criminal Justice in the Netherlands. Crime and Justice. A Review of Research* (pp. 99-106). Chicago: The Chicago University Press (35).

Council of Europe (1992). *Recommendation* (92) 17, *Concerning Consistency in Sentencing.*

Craig, P. (1997). Formal and Substantive Conceptions of the Rule of Law. *Public Law* 467.

Downes, D., & Van Swaaningen, R. (2007). The Road to Dystopia? Changes in the Penal Climate of the Netherlands. In M. Tonry, & C. Bijleveld (Eds.), *Criminal Justice in the Netherlands. Crime and Justice. A Review of Research* (pp. 31-72). Chicago: The Chicago University Press (35).

Dronkers, C., & Ten Voorde, J. (forthcoming). *OM-gaan met gestoorde ontwikkeling bij jongvolwassenen. De regiefunctie van het Openbaar ministerie bij strafzaken van jongvolwassenen.*

Dupont, L. (1979). *Beginselen van een behoorlijke strafrechtsbedeling.* Antwerpen: Kluwer.

Dworkin, R. (1978). Political Judges and the Rule of Law, 64 *Proceedings of the British Academy, 259*, 262.

Feeley, M.M., & Simon, J. (1992). The New Penology: Notes on the Emerging Strategy of Corrections and its Implications. *Criminology*, 449-474.

Fiselier, J.P.S., & Lensing, J.A.W. (1995). Afstemming van de straftoemeting. *Trema*, 105-117.

Foqué, R., & 't Hart, A.C. (1990). *Instrumentaliteit en rechtsbescherming. Grondslagen van een strafrechtelijke waardendiscussie.* Arnhem: Gouda Quint.

Freiberg, A., & Gelb, K. (Eds.) (2008). *Penal populism, sentencing councils and sentencing policy*. Devon: Willan Publishing.

Gerven, W. van (1973). *Het beleid van de rechter*. Antwerpen/Zwolle: Standaard Wetenschappelijke Uitgeverij/W.E.J. Tjeenk Willink.

Guarnieri, C., & Pederzoli, P. (2002). *The Power of Judge : a Comparative Study of Courts and Democracy*. Oxford: Oxford University Press.

Johnston, L., & Shearing, C. (2003). *Governing Security. Explorations in Policing and Justice*. Londen/New York: Routledge.

Mak, E. (2007). *De rechtspraak in balans. Een onderzoek naar de rol van klassiek-rechtsstatelijke beginselen en 'new public management'-beginselen in het kader van de rechterlijke organisatie in Nederland, Frankrijk en Duitsland*. Nijmegen: Wolf Legal Publishers.

Mevis, P. (2010). Niet bij snelheid alleen: Hoe snelrecht een toegevoegde waarde kan krijgen. In *OM Congres 2010. Snelrecht: Hoe sneller, hoe beter?* Den Haag: Openbaar Ministerie.

Montesquieu, C-L. de S. (2006). *Over de geest van de wetten*. Amsterdam: Boom uitgevers.

Morlino, L., & Palombella, G. (Eds.) (2010). *Rule of Law and Democracy. Inquiries into Internal and External Issues*. Leiden: Brill.

Ng, G.Y. (2007). *Quality of Judicial Organisation and Checks and Balances*. Antwerp: Intersentia.

Padfield, N., Van Zyl Smit, D., & Dunkel, F. (Eds.) (2010). *Release from Prison: European Policy and Practice*. Devon: Willan Publishing.

Piana, D. (2010). Beyond Judicial Independence: Rule of Law and Judicial Accountabilities in Assessing Democratic Quality. In L. Morlino, & G. Palombella (Eds.), *Rule of Law and Democracy. Inquiries into Internal and External Issues*. Leiden: Brill.

Raz, J. (1979). *The Authority of Law. Essays on Law and Morality*. Oxford: Clarendon Press.

Rijpkema, P. (2001). *Rechtersrecht*. Den Haag: Boom Juridische uitgevers.

Schoep, G.K., & Teuben, K. (2006). Rechterlijke samenwerking. In E.R. Muller, & C.P.M. Cleiren (red.), *Rechterlijke Macht* (pp. 403-432). Deventer: Kluwer.

Shepherd, J.A. (2002). Police, Prosecutors, Criminals, and Determinate Sentencing: The Truth about Truth in Sentencing. *Journal of Law and Economics* (XLV), 509-543.

Soeharno, J. (2006). From Guardian of the Rechtstaat to Ruler in the Rule of Law: An Inquiry into the Increased Role of the Judiciary. In A. van Hoek et al (Eds.), *Multilevel Governance in Enforcement and Adjudication*, pp. 157 - 177). Antwerpen: Intersentia.

Tamanaha, B.Z. (2004). *On the Rule of Law. History, Politics, Theory*. New York: Cambridge University Press.

Voermans, W. (2007). Judicial Transparency Furthering Public Accountability for New Judiciaries. *Utrecht Law Review 3 (1)*, 148-159.

Witteveen, W.J. (1991). *Evenwicht van machten.* Zwolle: W.E.J. Tjeenk Willink.

WRR (2002). *De toekomst van de nationale rechtsstaat (Rapporten aan de regering - 63*). Den Haag: Sdu Uitgevers.

6. Torture as a Lesser Evil? Governing Security in Times of Terrorist Emergencies

> 'It is well that, when the act accuses him, the result should excuse him; and when the result is good, (..), it will always absolve him from blame. For he is to be reprehended who commits violence for the purpose of destroying, and not he who employs it for beneficent purposes.'
>
> Niccolo Machiavelli

> '(...) hard cases make bad law, and (...) artificial cases make bad ethics.'
>
> Henry Shue

Jean-Marc Piret

1. Torture and the Law

The normative legal issue about torture is (at first sight) quite plain and simple: In the Western world torture has been absolutely and unconditionally prohibited. In 1980 the U.S. 2nd Circuit Court held that 'the torturer has become, like the pirate and the slave trader before him, *hostis humani generis*, an enemy of all mankind.'[1] The international Criminal Tribunal for the Former Yugoslavia reinforced this characterization in the proceedings against a Croatian torturer, underscoring that the prohibition is a peremptory norm of international law (*ius cogens*) imposing obligations upon states *erga omnes*.[2] States have the obligation to enforce the prohibition of torture toward all and no state can shirk out of its obligations, regardless whether it has signed international treaties on the subject or not. Torture is also prohibited in all the major human rights conventions.[3] Under international law it is also prohibited to expel or extradite

---

1 *Filártiga v. Peña-Irala*, 630 F.2d 876. It is ironic that John Yoo, the lawyer who precisely contributed substantially to the justification of torture in the war against terrorism while he was a Deputy Assistant Attorney General under the Bush administration, implicitly referred to the formula 'hostis humani generis', and argued that the practices it is referring to, should also enclose terrorism.

2 *Prosecutor v. Furundžija*, International Criminal Tribunal for the Former Yugoslavia, 10-12-1998.

3 The UN Convention against Torture and Other Cruel, Inhuman or Degrading Treatment or Punishment defines torture as 'any act by which severe pain or suffering, whether physical or mental, is intentionally inflicted on a person for such purposes as obtaining from him or a third person information or a confession, punishing him for an act he or a third person has committed or is suspected of having committed, or intimidating or coercing him or a third person, or for any reason based on discrimination of any kind, when such pain or suffering is inflicted by or at the instigation of or with the consent or acquiescence of a public official or other person acting in an official capacity.'

persons to states where they would be in danger of being tortured (prohibition of 'refoulement'). And finally of the utmost importance is the fact that the universal right not to be tortured is absolute; no derogations are possible from the prohibition of torture. Article 2(2) of the U.N. Torture Convention provides that 'No exceptional circumstances whatsoever, whether a state of war or a threat of war, internal political instability or any other public emergency, may be invoked as a justification of torture.'[4] The term 'whatsoever' is particularly powerful, because it rules out any possibility of an exception. So wherever torture is practiced, it is extra-legal and based on might, not on right. But precisely this absolute and categorical character of the ban on torture has been challenged by lawyers and philosophers, particularly since the 'war on terror' started.

2. Exceptions and Emergencies

In his famous treaty on *Crimes and Punishments* the Italian enlightenment philosopher Cesare Beccaria explains why the death penalty and cruel punishments including torture are unacceptable. Beccaria gives two types of arguments: utilitarian and social contract arguments. The latter argument is based on principle: the associates in the social contract only give up the smallest possible portion of their natural freedom, but still big enough for the addition of all these individual portions of freedom to constitute a state power that has the capacity to enforce the laws and to protect and guarantee the residual freedom of the citizens. As the transfer of freedom is limited, people did not hand over their most fundamental right to life. He infers from there that capital punishment cannot ever be based on the law. Most of the comments on Beccaria's text then proceed by pointing out that the author further argues that capital punishment is neither necessary nor effective or useful. But they often omit to comment on the intriguing text fragment immediately following his statement that capital punishment can not be based on right. There he acknowledges the existence of the extra-legal reality and exceptional necessity of capital punishment: when a person, even if deprived of liberty, still has connections and power such as to endanger the security of the nation or when his mere existence can produce a dangerous revolution in the established form of government. 'The death of a citizen thus becomes necessary when a nation is recovering or losing its Liberty or, in time of anarchy, when disorders themselves take the place of laws' (Beccaria 1995: ch. 16). To execute the death penalty in such a situation would not be based on the law (which is impossible) but it would be the consequence of a state of war between the state and one or more individuals. So even for Beccaria, exceptional situations where necessity can be invoked as a state of nature plea, do exist. But one has to reckon them as what they are: exceptions to

[4] The same applies to the European Convention on Human Rights: article 15 (2) holds that no derogation is possible from the prohibition of torture formulated in article 3 ('No one shall be subjected to torture or to inhuman or degrading treatment or punishment').

one of the most fundamental norms of penal law. Such exceptions by definition can not be integrated into the normative body of the law, but they do exist. If it were not for the principled social contract argument, there would still be another loophole in Beccaria's argumentation against the death penalty and torture. It is located in the utilitarian aspect of his theory, which is not based on principle: he is opposed to capital punishment and torture because they are ineffective, they don't work as instruments of deterrence. If it would be possible to demonstrate on empirical grounds that this assumption is wrong and that torture can be effective under certain circumstances as a means to realize a greater good, then it may become acceptable as a lesser evil to consequentialists.

Because in the Beccarian contractualist paradigm the exception of torture cannot be integrated in the normative framework of the state under the rule of law, it can only be introduced as a practice when it is situated at the outskirts of civil society, in an intermediate space between the state of nature and state regulated praxis (see also Rozemond's characterization of 'nodal governance' in this book). The Beccarian social contract operates between the citizens of a state. It has often been said in political philosophy that the relations between states are analogous to the relations between individuals in the state of nature. However since its inception in the seventeenth century, modern international law has been a huge enterprise of civilizing inter-state relations by creating a normative framework of international obligations through treaties and multilateral covenants. In the last paragraph of this article, I will argue that the practice of torture as it developed in the 'war against terrorism' in Afghanistan and Iraq (and elsewhere) could become a reality only because the U.S. government defined its relation to the suspects of terrorism captured on the battlefield as a relation to outlaw enemies who could neither be considered as strangers who nevertheless had rights under the domestic penal and constitutional law (as they are neither participants in nor beneficiaries of the social contract), nor as soldiers who had rights under international humanitarian law. As a precondition to the normalisation of torture, a type of 'nodal' security governance (Johnston and Shearing: 2003) had to be deployed in which state agencies and non-state actors worked together in normalizing a torture culture that operated in an interstitial space between state-regulated praxis and war considered as a state of nature. But before I can elaborate on that, I will first explain in the next paragraphs how politicians, lawyers, philosophers, ethicists and courts have been dealing with the problem and the reality of torture.

After 9/11 some politicians, philosophers and lawyers have claimed that the traditional standards and principles governing security policy and (penal) law no longer apply because we have entered an emergency situation that justifies a state of exception. Sanford Levinson, a prominent American law Professor wrote in a comment on the torture scandal in Iraq that not the political philosopher Leo Strauss, who had been repeatedly designated as such, but the legal philosopher Carl Schmitt was the intellectual guide of the Bush policy.[5] Schmitt who was one of the leading constitutional lawyers in the republic of Weimar, and the sharpest analyst of the constitutional crisis of that regime (Piret 1996: 5-26), had written that there exists no constitutional norm that is applicable to the state of emergency. When the state confronts its own internal disintegration and possible destruction the only hope to avert this catastrophe lies in a sovereign power that has the capacity to define and enforce the new rules that apply in the state of exception and that is effective in redefining what is 'normal' for the time being. And that is precisely what the Bush administration did.

According to the U.S. Government the war against terrorism could only be won with exceptional means. The USA Patriot Act[6] allowed warrantless Government wiretapping and warrantless secret searches of homes and premises of those belonging to a vague class of persons some of which might have been potentially dangerous. Numerous people were detained without charge and without having access to a lawyer. Shortly after the attacks Congress passed the Authorisation to Use Military Force (AUMF) which authorized the President 'to use all necessary and appropriate force against those nations, organizations, or persons he determines planned, authorized, committed, or aided the terrorist attacks that occurred on September 11, 2001 (...)'.[7] Subsequently the Bush administration announced that aliens suspected of terrorism arrested on American soil as well as fighters captured on the battlefield in Afghanistan and deported to Guantanamo Bay would be treated as 'unlawful enemy combatants' who would neither be tried before civil courts nor be granted the rights and protections of prisoners of war under the Geneva Conventions.[8] The Office of Legal Council (OLC) argued that the President's power as commander in chief meant that he had complete discretion in conducting the military operations against hostile forces. A March 2003 memorandum for the defence department on the subject of extraterritorial interrogation of alien unlawful combatants provided that 'in order to respect the President's inherent constitutional authority

5 Interestingly, Levinson (2004b: 7-8) points at some parallel between Schmitt and Alexander Hamilton's statements in the *Federalist* n° 41.

6 The controversial Patriot Act was reauthorized by Congress in early 2006, but on condition that there would be more oversight of its application by Congress. The intention of this agreement, as usual, was nearly annihilated by Bush's signing statement of 9th March 2006: 'The executive branch shall construe the provisions (...) that call for furnishing information to entities outside the executive branch, (...), in a manner consistent with the President's constitutional authority to supervise the unitary executive branch and to withhold information the disclosure of which could impair foreign relations, national security, the deliberative processes of the Executive, or the performance of the Executive's constitutional duties.' Signing Statement available at: <http://www.whitehouse.gov:80/news/releases/2006/03/20060309-8.html>.

7 Cf. Authorization for Use of Military Force, September 18, 2001, Public Law 107-40 [S. J. RES. 23]; 107th CONGRESS.

8 On the subject of privileged and unprivileged combatants and the laws of war see Piret (2008: 59-111, especially 73-87).

to direct a military campaign against al Qaeda and its allies; general criminal laws must be construed as not applying to interrogations undertaken pursuant to his Commander-in-Chief authority'. The federal anti-torture legislation had to be 'construed as inapplicable' to interrogations undertaken pursuant to his authority. Following this interpretation international law prohibiting torture had to be considered as 'unconstitutional'.[9] According to the infamous 'Bybee memo' of 1 August 2002 written in response to a CIA request for legal guidance, arguments pertaining to necessity and self-defence could provide justifications that would eliminate any criminal liability. According to the OLC lawyers, this reading was justifiable as article 2(2) of the Torture Convention prohibiting any derogation had not been incorporated into the federal anti-torture statute. Moreover, as the federal anti-torture law did not define the term 'severe' pain, the OLC lawyers were also capable of redefining torture as being 'equivalent in intensity to the pain accompanying serious physical injury, such as organ failure, impairment of bodily function, or even death'.[10]

There are also very strong indications that the government relied on a massive scale on 'extraordinary rendition' of detainees to countries where torture is practiced, and that constitutes not only a breach of an explicit provision (the right to 'non refoulement') in the U.N. Convention Against Torture to which the U.S. is a party, but it can also be interpreted as the intentional policy to 'torture by proxy'.[11]

3. Can Interrogational Torture Be Justified in 'Ticking Bomb' Situations?

Even liberals are ready to accept emergency suspension of rights on the conditions that it is only used as a last resort, that it is precisely targeted and applied to the smallest possible number of people, that it will be subject soon after its introduction to a process of adversarial justification, and that it is limited in time (Ignatieff 2004). But liberals diverge as to the question of how far these exceptional measures may go. Can they include actions that are incompatible with the respect of human dignity such as torture? And how could this possibly be justified in the light of the categorical ban on torture described above? Since 9/11 extensive attempts have been undertaken in order to justify the use of torture in 'ticking bomb' (TB) situations. Roughly the TB scenarios all have a

9 March 14, 2003 Memorandum for William J. Haynes II, General Counsel of the Department of Defence, available at http://www.torturingdemocracy.org/documents/20030314.pdf# page=13.

10 Cf. Bybee Memo, full text at http://fl1.findlaw.com/news.findlaw.com/nytimes/docs/doj/bybee80102mem.pdf.

11 Art. 3(1) provides 'No State Party shall expel, return ("refouler") or extradite a person to another State where there are substantial grounds for believing that he would be in danger of being subjected to torture.' For the phenomenon of extraordinary rendition considered as 'torture by proxy' see CHR&GJ (2005) and Garcia (2009).

comparable structure to this: the police has caught a member of a terrorist group who has planted a bomb in a crowded area that will go off in the near future, but he refuses to talk. The investigation team has very good reasons to assume that the detainee knows the location of the explosive device. If the bomb explodes many people will die. If the authorities know where it is planted, the massacre can be prevented by evacuating the area and defusing the explosive device. May we torture the location of the bomb out of the detainee in order to save many innocent people from death and mutilation? Some of the proponents of interrogational torture in TB situations, have underlined that this kind of torture has nothing in common with cruelty or sadism or the will to humiliate the detainee, but that it can be understood as a moral duty owed to the potential victims who will die or be mutilated if the interrogators don't succeed in their aim of averting the threat. In this perspective, so they argue, the torture of one or two prisoners can be considered as a lesser evil in order to forestall a greater one (Luban 2005: 1439). It is a case of self-defence of a community against its mortal enemies.

The proponents of the use of torture in TB situations argue on a consequentialist and mostly act-utilitarian basis: if the harm that is prevented from happening by torture is greater than the harm that will be caused by it then non-lethal interrogative torture is justified. Jeremy Bentham was the first to elaborate this line of argumentation. For Bentham to torture one guilty person who has the information that can save the lives of many innocent people is justifiable as it satisfies the cost-benefit test (Twining and Twining 1973: 305-356). In the same line of reasoning Richard Posner, a well known American Court of Appeal judge and Professor at the university of Chicago Law School, thinks that the acceptability of interrogational torture should be subjected to a cost-benefit analysis where the alleged inefficacy of torture, the costs in terms of possible corruption of our institutions and the risk of 'normalization' of torture as a practice even in less dramatic cases than that of the TB scenario are al taken into account. Posner writes that 'there is such a thing as a lesser wrong committed to avoid a greater one'. That is why he sees no reason for a categorical ban that always ought to be enforced, whatever the circumstances: 'if the stakes are high enough torture is permissible. No one who doubts that should be in a position of responsibility' (Posner 2004: 295). Nevertheless Posner thinks that it is better not to legalize torture, but to leave the decision to executive discretion. By legalizing torture, officials will be tempted to explore the outer bounds of the rules and the practice would be likely to become regular. That is why he thinks it is better to uphold the customary legal prohibitions with the understanding that they will not be enforced in extreme circumstances (ibid.: 296).

The most controversial proposition in favour of accepting torture as a means of preventing a catastrophe to happen, was formulated by Alan Dershowitz (2003), a well known American defence attorney, and Harvard law Professor. The starting point of Dershowitz was the conclusion that torture is a widespread phenomenon, even under nations that have signed treaties prohibiting all of it.

Tolerating that torture is being practiced 'below the radar' by low level law enforcement officials without accountability is hypocritical and worse according to Dershowitz than bringing the phenomenon to the surface by requiring a judicial warrant as a precondition for initiating a process of interrogational torture under any circumstances. To understand how he came to this idea one has to reckon that Dershowitz was very impressed by the discussion about the issue during a stay in Israel. Long before September 11, 2001, in the late 1980s there was a controversy in Israel about the coercive interrogation techniques that the security services, the GSS, were using with terrorist suspects. Dershowitz (2004: 258) asserts that there is little doubt that many lives of potential victims were saved by using these methods but that Israel paid an extraordinary high price for saving these lives in terms of violation of basic human rights.

At that time in Israel the TB scenario, although occurring very rarely, served as an intellectual justification for a pervasive system of torture that was also played down as 'coercive interrogation'. Dershowitz asked his audience at the Hebrew University why, given the fact that non-lethal torture was widely considered as justifiable in TB situations, it should not be limited exclusively to that exceptional situation by introducing a system of prior judicial approval, a 'torture warrant'. Dershowitz assumes that by introducing more visibility and accountability, the burden of proof needed in order to justify the use of coercive interrogation would be made heavier and that this would reduce the use of torture to the smallest degree possible.[12] In 1987 the Landau Commission inquired about the torture practices of the GSS, after some detainees had died in custody. The Commission adopted the view of the GSS that the use of coercive interrogation techniques often was a requisite for the effective interrogation of terrorists and argued in favour of legalization of the methods used by the security service. The justificatory argumentation of the Landau Commission was based on choosing the 'lesser evil' in a TB situation. Interestingly though the Commission did not insist on the fact that the threat of the terrorist outrage had to be *imminent* as is mostly the case when TB scenario's are used for the purpose of justifying interrogational torture. 'The deciding factor is not the element of time, but the comparison between the gravity of two evils (...) To put it bluntly, the alternative is: are we to accept the offence of assault entailed in slapping a suspect's face, or threatening him, in order to induce him to talk and reveal a cache of explosive materials meant for use in carrying out an act of mass terror against a civilian population, and thereby prevent the greater evil which is about to occur? The answer is self-evident'.[13] Although the Israeli government did not follow the Landau Commission's recommendation to formally legalize the coercive interrogation techniques used by the GSS, they were more or less informally considered as normal practice by the Israeli government.

[12] He already published on the subject at that time. See Dershowitz (1989), Moore (1989: 280-344), Kadish (1989: 345-56).

[13] Quoted in Evans and Morgan (1998: 45).

After the attacks on the World Trade Centre and the reports about coercive interrogation techniques used by the CIA and the military, Dershowitz wanted to reopen the debate in the U.S. If torture is a fact, which it obviously is, then it would be better that judges take the responsibility and dirty their hands in order to restrict the use of torture to exceptional cases when the lives of many are at stake. In those extreme situations judges should be the ones to give the permission by issuing a warrant because accountability and democratic visibility require that any use of torture be subjected to judicial control. Ultimately that would also imply that the specific techniques of non-lethal torture for which the warrant was requested, would have to be duly specified. Dershowitz's plea for the introduction of torture warrants in exceptional cases argues in favour of an *ex ante* lawful justification of 'necessity', a paradoxical attempt to legally regulate the state of exception, although he construed his argument as a *conditional normative position*. Only *if* we assume that the executive authorities would in fact use torture in extremely dangerous TB situations, then it would be better to bring the practice to the surface and let the judiciary take the responsibility to give the permission and to control, circumscribe and confine its use.

4. The Dangers of the TB Scenario as an Intellectual Framework

Several critical arguments have been raised against the justification of interrogational torture on the basis of the TB scenario.[14] The case is extraordinarily rare to occur, especially when the conditions of the scenario are tightly framed: the catastrophe must be *imminent* and the detaining authority must be almost *certain* that the detainee knows where the bomb is hidden. In reality the authorities are seldom sure about the guilt of the suspect and mostly they don't know what he knows or doesn't know.[15] The risk of torturing innocents is high. One also doesn't know whether torture will be effective because the victim could resist, or he could lie. However Dershowitz (2003: 137) gives the example of the Philippine police who in 1995 tortured a Pakistani Al Qaeda terrorist almost to death (they tortured him for weeks), until he disclosed the information about a plot to assassinate the Pope and to crash eleven airplanes with thousands of passengers into the ocean. If they hadn't tortured him, thousands of innocent travellers might have died. David Luban

[14] Cf. Luban o.c. (2005); Bufacchi and Arrigo (2006: 339-357).

[15] Steinhoff (2006: 343) thinks that this is a weak argument, because if not knowing for certain whether you have the right person or whether he has the knowledge that the authorities need in order to avert a catastrophe, would be sufficient reason not to harm that person, we would not only have to abstain from self-defence (because we do not know 'for certain' whether the robber pointing a gun at us is actually determined to shoot) but also from punishment, because 'you *never* know for certain!' whether you have convicted the right person. Moreover that doesn't exclude that there are cases when the police or the security services are pretty sure about what they know.

(2005: 1442) criticizes Dershowitz's example and argues: 'You cannot use the argument that preventing the al Qaeda attack justified the decision to torture, because at the moment the decision was made no one knew about the al Qaeda attack.' So the problem is this: if the authorities have captured someone who may, or may not know about a catastrophic plot, is it acceptable to torture him? How certain must we be? And for how long torture him ? (ibid.) The information obtained by interrogational torture is also deemed unreliable according to the critics, because the tortured person will tell his torturers everything that could put an end to his ordeal.

There are other pragmatic arguments against the use of interrogational torture. It would become problematic for a state in which torture would be legalized to demand from its enemies in the war on terrorism to treat its captured soldiers (for example in Afghanistan) according to the rules of international humanitarian law. Given the improbability of the occurrence of a genuine TB case, the real goal of inter-rogational torture is likely to be a 'general phishing' operation in order to collect any valuable information that might be useful to dismantle the terrorist organisation. We already saw in the example of the Landau Commission that there is a tendency to widen the scope of situations in which interrogational torture would be deemed acceptable. Even in cases where the danger is not imminent and the interrogation could only lead to the discovery of a cache of explosives, the answer as to the legitimacy of torture was considered as 'self-evident'. Following that logic one might argue that 'al Qaeda is itself the ticking time bomb, so that unwinding the organisation meets the formal conditions of the TB hypothetical' (ibid.: 1443). The next station on the slippery slope would than be to torture in any case that would help us to get more information that would be of use in the war on terrorism. And if suspects resist even under torture, then why not torture their sons, their daughters and wives? If the stakes are high enough and if only the numbers on the cost-benefit balance count, as act-consequentialists would have it, then there are no more limits.

But rule-consequentialists should be sensitive to the long term 'costs' of corrupting the institutions of democratic states in a way that is beyond repair, and also to the risk of slippage that starts with the acceptance of torture in extraordinary rare cases and ends with it's normalization. The classic example of this process of slippage is the case of the French in Algeria (Bellamy 2006: 142-145, Branche 2007). Torture there was initially justified as a measure for the exceptional cases when imminent terrorist attacks on the civil population had to be averted, but it rapidly grew like a cancer and became a widespread practice (Vidal-Naquet 1998, 2001). François Mitterand who at first was minister for the interior and later responsible for the justice department, was convinced that the Algerian insurrection could only be countered by a harsh repression ('the only negotiation is war' said Mitterand). He had granted wide ranging powers to the military in order to repress the insurrection in Algiers. General Massu who was then military governor of Algiers had approved of the brutal interrogation techniques (beating, water boarding and electroshocks) that were already widespread at his arrival in Algeria early 1957. Massu pretended to never have seen prisoners tortured or to have practiced torture himself, his activities were 'above' those details, as he said in an interview.[16] However in a book published 1971 in reaction to the condemnatory tone of the Italian film 'the battle of Algiers', he defended the torture which he refused to call that way, preferring the term 'la question par force' as a necessary means of counter-terrorism. According to Massu the real barbaric methods were used by the FLN insurrection movement and not by the French paratroopers. Later he had the courage to admit that the use of torture had been an unnecessary error in Algeria. Massu's insinuation that the coercion practiced by the French was rather moderate in comparison to what the terrorists did to the French colonists, the *pieds noirs*, was not confirmed by general Aussaresses who was personally involved in the so called 'details', not only as a commander but also as torturer. Aussaresses admitted to have killed 24 prisoners. What he regretted the most was that some of the victims which were tortured died in the process before they had given valuable information. He participated in disguising several murders and summary executions as suicides. When 'explaining' his actions he said that 'once a country demands its army to fight an enemy who is using terror, it becomes impossible to avoid using extreme measures'.[17] In 2002 Aussaresses was convicted, not for what he had done,[18] but for making an apologia of it in a book.[19] In 2004 the conviction was confirmed by the Cour de Cassation, which decided that freedom of expression did not justify glossing over war crimes. Nevertheless the Cour de Cassation confirmed that Aussaresses could not be prosecuted for the facts themselves. In 2005 he was stripped of his rank, the right to wear his army uniform and his Légion d'honneur by Presidential decree.[20]

---

16 Interview available at http://www.ina.fr/economie-et-societe/justice-et-faits-divers/video/I00018231/massu-sur-la-bataille-d-alger-en-janvier-fevrier-1957.fr.html; see also another interview at http://www.ina.fr/histoire-et-conflits/guerre-d-algerie/video/CAB00060096/plateau-invite-general-paul-aussaresses.fr.html.

17 http://www.military.com/NewContent/0,13190,SOF_0704_Torture,00.html.

18 Because the French military had been granted a collective amnesty by decree in 1962, which was confirmed by the *loi d'amestie* of July 1968.

19 Aussaresses (2001).

20 In 2009 though the old general won one of his last battles. The European Court of Human Rights convicted France for not having respected the general and his editor's right to freedom of expression (art. 10). The Court held 'that the Court of Appeal's finding that the author's aim had been to persuade readers of the legitimacy and inevitability of the torture and summary executions carried out during the war in Algeria was not decisive for assessment of the facts at issue in relation to Article 10. It regarded the book in question above all as a witness account (...) The publication of a witness account of this kind unquestionably formed part of a debate on a matter of public concern which was of singular importance for the collective memory. The account, (...) supported one of the conflicting theories in the debate, defended by the author, to the effect that such practices had not only existed but had had the blessing of the French authorities. In the Court's view, the fact that the author had not taken a critical stance with regard to these horrifying practices and that, instead of expressing regret, he had claimed to have been acting in

That the danger of a slippery slope is not a cheap rhetorical argument used by absolute prohibitionists of torture, but a very realistic danger is confirmed by the Algerian case. Paul Teitgen who was appointed as secretary general of the Algiers police department in 1956 and who had refused to approve the torture of even one TB terrorist at the beginning of his activity, had to resign in protest less than a year later because he could no longer bear the massive use of torture and the high numbers of disappearances (more than 3000) of persons whose arrests had been sanctioned by him (Bellamy 2006: 144).[21] The justification of torture begins with the exceptional TB case and then it moves on to cases that fall short of that scenario: torture suspects who might know of an arms cache or how the terrorists are organised etc (Bellamy 2006: 145). According to Raphaëlle Branche (2007: 558) the general absence of sanctions and criminal convictions of torturers allows the conclusion that 'torture – albeit prohibited – was in fact permitted in Algeria.'

5. Is Torture Morally Worse Than Killing?

What is it that makes torture morally so peculiar that we prohibit its practice in a way that is even more categorical than the prohibition of killing? After all, the police may kill criminals under certain conditions, and according to the rules of *ius in bello* soldiers engaged in combat have a license to kill their enemies. The Enlightenment philosopher and publicist Voltaire gives us a first explanation why we (should) abhor torture more than killing. In his Treaty on Tolerance, written on the occasion of '*the murder of Jean Calas, committed in Toulouse with the sword of justice*', Voltaire draws our attention to the difference between killing in war and the torture of an innocent (Jean Callas was tortured to death on the wheel the 9th of March, 1762):

> 'We soon forget the crowd of victims who have fallen in the course of innumerable battles, not only because this is a destiny inevitable in war, but because those who thus fell might also have given death to their enemies, and did not lose their lives without defending themselves. Where the danger and the advantage are equal, our wonder ceases, and even pity itself is in some measure lessened; but where the father

accordance with the mission entrusted to him, formed an integral part of that witness account. (…). The Court reiterated that freedom of expression within the meaning of Article 10 was applicable not only to "information" or "ideas" regarded as inoffensive or as a matter of indifference, but also to those that offended, shocked or disturbed. Accordingly, penalizing a publisher for having assisted in the dissemination of a witness account written by a third party concerning events which formed part of a country's history would seriously hamper contribution to the discussion of matters of public interest and should not be envisaged without particularly good reason.' Cf. Mathias Vermeulen at <http://legalift.wordpress.com/2009/01/16/orban-and-others-vs-france-article-10-covers-dissemination-of-witness-accounts-of-torturer>.

[21] The impressive letter of resignation from Paul Teitgen is available at http://www.histoire-en-questions.fr/guerre%20algerie/terreur-tortures-lettre.html.

> of an innocent family is delivered up to the hands of error, passion, or fanaticism; (...) where the arbiters of his destiny (...) may murder with impunity by decree, then every one is ready to cry out (…)'

Voltaire points to our abhorrence of assaulting the defenceless. In his classic article about torture he wrote some thirty years ago, Henry Shue (1978: 124-143) demonstrated that even if death can be considered as a greater harm than torture (for a limited period), this by no means implies that there could not be a justification for the greater harm that is not available for the lesser harm. Like Voltaire, Shue thinks that the principle that prohibits assaults upon the defenceless is fundamental in this respect. The victim of torture has no possibility whatsoever to defend himself in a fair fight. He is entirely at the mercy of his torturer and that is why torture is more reprehensible than killing while respecting the laws of war. Torture is an absolute negation of someone's autonomy.

David Sussman (2005: 4,8) has added another reason why torture is morally more horrendous than killing or other forms of cruelty. Interrogational torture 'forces the victim into the position of colluding against himself as simultaneously powerless and yet actively complicit in his own violation', it manipulates its victims through their own responses in a context where they are extremely vulnerable, dependent and disoriented. If the victim does not respond to the questions of his interrogator, his silence may well be considered as a continuation of his attack. In this way the victim is led to think that he is responsible for his own torment, 'some part of him serves as the eager agent of his tormentor' (ibid.: 24). The helpless victim is forced to be complicit in her own violation, creating a perversion of any basic moral relations that an individual bears both to others and to herself (ibid.: 30). Not everybody is convinced by Sussmann's arguments though. The feature that makes torture so despicable is by no means unique to torture according to Uwe Steinhoff. If in an armed robbery, the robber points a gun at a victim and threatens to kill him if he does not give his money, the robber also turns the agency of the victim against himself. The robber makes his victim's fear express *his*, the robber's, will, making the victim complicit in his own violation when he hands over the money for fear of death (Steinhoff 2006: 340). Steinhoff is not convinced either by Luban's argument that torture is more despicable than killing because it 'strips away from its victim all the qualities of human dignity that liberalism prizes'; and that for that reason it is a 'microcosm raised to the highest level of intensity, of the tyrannical political relationship that liberalism hates the most' (Luban 2005: 1430). But prisons are also 'microcosms of tyranny' and yet most liberals do not find them unacceptable. Even if the level of tyranny is much higher in torture than in imprisonment, it is far from clear that one hour of non-lethal torture is more tyrannical than 15 years of prison (Steinhoff 2006: 344). To Steinhoff liberalism is not so much about 'dignity', which he considers to be an elusive concept, but about the liberty of the innocent. They are the ones who have to be protected against aggressors. That is why he does not consider it irrational or immoral in a genuine TB situation to weigh the risk of torturing an innocent against the risk that innocent people die in an explosion. Demanding to enforce the absolute prohibition on torture as it is embodied in the law, no matter the circumstances cannot be morally justified in a compelling way: '*Fiat justitia et pereat mundus* is an irrational and immoral maxim' (ibid.: 346).

6. Torture and the Israeli Supreme Court

The arguments in favour of upholding an absolute ban on torture summed up until now, cannot occult two facts. The first is that exceptional situations do exist where the amount of information that the authorities have, makes them sure that a catastrophe could be prevented if the detainee would be talking. The second is that torture, regardless of how unfortunate we may find that reality, is sometimes effective (even if it is not most of the time). The widespread use and normalization of torture by the French army in Algeria enabled the French in some cases to prevent terrorist attacks and to destroy a fraction of the terrorist infrastructure in Algiers. Even if the French strategy in Algeria proved to be counter-productive in the long run because it fuelled the insurrectional energies in the population, and it constituted a blot on the reputation of the army that has not been wiped out until today, it cannot be denied that there were particular cases when lives of many innocent people have been saved by the means of torturing FLN terrorists. Analogously the Israeli Supreme Court, who prohibited a number of coercive interrogation procedures that had been used on a regular basis by the security services, admitted that sometimes this practice had 'led to the thwarting of murderous attacks'.[22]

So let us have a closer look at the Israeli experience. We already saw that in the years after the report of the Landau Commission had been published, torture became a more or less 'normal' practice in the GSS interrogation of Palestinian terrorist suspects. Between 1995 and 1997 several complaints had been formulated, accusing the GSS of torture such as sleep deprivation, shaking, beating, excessively tight handcuffs and the prolonged use of the 'Shabach' position which causes serious muscle pain in the arms, in the neck and headaches. The government did not contest the use of the majority of these methods, but denied that they presented an inherent danger to the lives of the suspects or that they would cause irreversible damage. They also argued that doctors were present during the interrogation. The government also emphasized that these methods did not intend to inflict pain or damage, but that they were functional in rendering the interrogation more effective. Moreover the government argued that these methods did not violate international law as they did not constitute torture, nor cruel, inhuman or degrading treatment.[23] The

22 Levinson (2004a: 34); for concrete examples see Israel Supreme Court (2005: 30). Meanwhile vol. II and III of 'Fighting Terrorism within the Law' have also been published on the internet.

23 Public Committee Against Torture in Israel v. State of Israel, H.C. 5100/94 (1999). Ibid.: 31-35.

government argued further that these methods were legal under the 'necessity defence' provided for in Israeli penal law, as they were only used as a last resort in order to save the lives of innocent victims of terrorism (the TB scenario).[24] The Government held that it was it's moral duty to fight terrorism in an effective way and to employ the necessary means to realize that purpose.

The Supreme Court however ruled that these methods did not fall into the sphere of a fair interrogation; that they are not reasonable and that they infringe upon the suspect's dignity, his bodily integrity and his basic rights in an excessive manner. According to the Court these methods could not be considered to be included in the general power to conduct interrogations.[25] The Supreme Court did not deny that the 'necessity defence' could in exceptional cases be available *post factum* to investigators indicted of a criminal offence. What the Court denied was that the authorities could infer from that possibility an *ex ante* legal authorization to allow the interrogator to use physical coercion. The Court emphasized that the necessity defence does not constitute a source of authority, which would allow GSS investigators to use physical means during the course of interrogations. When the necessity defence is successful, it has the effect of allowing one who acts under the circumstances of 'necessity' to escape criminal liability. But that does not in itself authorize the act and the concomitant infringement of human rights.[26] The Court also held that the rule of law requires that an infringement of human rights be prescribed by statute.

The Supreme Court concluded that it was aware that this decision could possibly hamper the ability to deal properly with terrorist emergencies. But according to the Court, a democracy must sometimes fight with one hand behind its back. The unique situation of Israel is that this search by the Supreme Court for balance between human rights protection and security often has to be achieved in real time as the judicial adjudication may take place during combat or while the interrogation of suspects is going on.[27] Judicial review of the counter-terrorism measures may render counter-terrorism harder in the short term, but it also strengthens democracy and the rule of law in the long term.

---

[24] Cf. Art. 34 (1) of the Israeli criminal code: '*A person will not bear criminal liability for committing any act immediately necessary for the purpose of saving the life, liberty, body or property, of either himself or his fellow person, from substantial danger of serious harm, imminent from the particular state of things [circumstances], at the requisite timing, and absent alternative means for avoiding the harm.*'

[25] Public Committee Against Torture in Israel v. State of Israel, H.C. 5100/94 (1999) Ibid.: 45-46.

[26] See also Kremnitzer (1989: 244-247).

[27] The events being reviewed are often still taking place, making it necessary for the Court to order the immediate stoppage of an unlawful type of interrogation, or the immediate halt of a deportation action or the interruption of the demolition of buildings of Palestinian people. In doing so the Court does not replace the commander's executive discretion with its own operational judgement but it reviews the actions in the war against terrorism as to their legality and legitimacy. Cf. Israel Supreme Court (2005).

'There is no security without law. The rule of law is a component of national security'.[28]

Concerning the torture case it can be concluded that the Israeli Supreme Court on the one hand does rule out torture as a legal and acceptable practice, but on the other hand it does not exclude the *post factum* possibility of a necessity defence if in exceptional situations torture would have been effectively used in order to save the lives of innocent people.[29] The Court also does not rule out the possibility for the legislative branch to enable and specify the use of 'physical means' of interrogation by legislative act, which seems to be in contradiction with the Court's conclusion that Israel is bound by its international obligations to accept the absolute character of the prohibition of torture, ruling out any form of derogation or balancing against other interests. This contradiction could be overcome by legalizing only 'moderate physical means' that can be 'construed' as to their legal significance in such a way that they are not torture and do not amount to cruel, inhuman or degrading treatment.[30] But even if the latter would be the case (that the 'moderate physical means' would not amount to torture but nevertheless constitute 'degrading treatment') an 'exceptional circumstances' derogation could be available according to some lawyers because art. 2 (2) of the U.N. Torture convention prohibiting any derogation exclusively mentions 'torture' (Parry 2004: 149).

7. Emergency Exceptions and the Problem of 'Dirty Hands': Justification or Excuse?

In his classical article on the problem of dirty hands Michael Walzer (2004: 67) reminds us of the difference between justification and excuse: an excuse is typically an admission of fault; a justification is typically a denial of fault and an assertion of innocence. As Walzer rightly points out, Machiavelli's famous dictum that in some cases 'the act accuses, but the results excuse', is politically consequentialist but not morally. Indeed why should an act 'accuse' if it were not intrinsically bad? But an intrinsically bad act can possibly be excused afterwards from a political and legal point of view, when the public experiences

[28] Ibid. p. 20.

[29] In 2002 the Israeli parliament enacted the *General Security Service Law* providing for a restriction of liability in its art. 18: 'A Service employee (...) shall not bear criminal or civil responsibility for any act or omission performed in good faith and reasonably by him within the scope and in performance of his function (...)'. As to the actual 'rules, service directives and service procedures' the law itself only says that they 'need not be published (...)'. In my opinion this constitutes an attempt to legalize the exception and hence to lighten the burden of proof in comparison to the 'necessity defence' already present in Israeli penal law, 'good faith' and 'reasonableness' being requirements which are easier to fulfil than 'necessity'.

[30] See for example Amos Guiora's (2008) attempt (drawing on the Israeli experience) to construe a 'hybrid paradigm' legitimizing methods of 'lawful coercive interrogation' (for the U.S.) that do not amount to 'torture'.

the results of that act *post factum* as overwhelmingly good. The political realist who gets his hands dirty knows that political action involves a great risk, for bad things must be done well if he wants to have a chance to be excused afterwards. 'There is no reward for doing bad things badly, though they are done with the best of intentions' (ibid.: 70). Politicians, law enforcement agents and soldiers sometimes cannot avoid acting immorally in order to do what they subjectively consider to be good. The genuine TB scenario, however rare it may be, is such a situation.

And even Henry Shue (1978: 57), who explains why torture is morally worse than killing 'can see no way to deny the permissibility of torture in a case just like this'. However, for Shue this does not imply that the legal prohibitions against torture should be removed for 'there is a saying in jurisprudence that hard cases make bad law, and there might well be one in philosophy that artificial cases make bad ethics. If the example is made sufficiently extraordinary, the conclusion that the torture is permissible is secure. But one cannot easily draw conclusions for ordinary cases from extraordinary ones, and as the situation described becomes more likely, the conclusion that the torture is permissible becomes more debatable' (ibid.). In a world of uncertainty the burden of proof that it is *necessary* for someone to act illegally, should rest on the shoulders of that person who is going to overstep the law and commit a crime. Considering the metastatic tendency of torture, such an act ought to remain illegal 'so that anyone who sincerely believes such an act to be the least available evil is placed in the position of needing to justify his act morally in order to defend himself legally' (ibid.). By upholding the criminal liability and refusing to specify the conditions under which the 'necessity defence' or even a plea in mitigation would be successful, society introduces moral and legal uncertainty that raises a dam in order to prevent a torrent of state brutality to overflow the land. As Alex Bellamy (2006: 147) convincingly argues 'moral and legal uncertainty guards against slippage and normalization while not prejudging the outcome of individual cases. Instead in each case the mitigating circumstances need to be balanced against the broader necessity of preventing torture. It is important that the torturer and those who authorize torture do not know in advance how their action will be morally and legally assessed. Such uncertainty forces them to accept dirty hands; to realize that their own society and the wider world may regard them as immoral and criminal for what they are about to do'.

We saw that this position was first articulated in general terms by Henry Shue and Michael Walzer; it is also very similar to the position of the Israeli Supreme Court and of several authors who, in the aftermath of 9/11, reflected on the problem of torture in exceptional cases.[31] Whether the actor who violates the

[31] Gross (2004: 1481-1555) has defended this position as a case of 'pragmatic absolutism and official disobedience'. He argues that an absolute ban is the appropriate legal position but that certain extreme circumstances must not be brushed aside as morally or legally irrelevant. In such exceptional circumstances public officials can take the responsibility to act extra legally on their own peril and accept the possible consequences of their breach of

absolute ban would be punished, remains to be decided afterwards by society. The mere possibility of an (uncertain) *ex post* excuse has not the same corrupting effect on our institutions as an *ex ante* justification such as Dershowitz's torture warrants. It can not serve as a precedent because it will be an opportunistic *ad hoc* decision depending on the results. If the positive results massively outweigh the gravity of the violation of the law in the perception of the public, no court will be willing to punish the actor severely, although courts may be ready to punish them leniently in order to symbolically confirm the legal norm.

8. The Daschner Case: 'Rescue-Torture'?

The unfortunate fact that (the threat with) torture sometimes works, can be exemplified by a German case that has nothing to do with terrorism, but that nevertheless bears some very significant similarities with the TB scenario. In September 2002 the then 27 years old law student Marcus Gäfgen kidnapped Jacob von Metzler, the 11 year old son of a rich banker from Frankfurt am Main. He lured the boy into his apartment and killed him by suffocation. Then he demanded one million Euros of ransom from the parents in a written note. He wrote also that the boy was kidnapped and that the parents would see their son again if the kidnappers managed to leave the country with the money. Then he hid the body on a private property. From the moment that he picked up the ransom, he was under police surveillance. The same day in the afternoon he was arrested at Frankfurt airport. The police found half of the ransom money and a note concerning the planning of the crime in the suspect's flat. From then on the investigators think that the boy is in mortal danger and that the time to save him is running out. But Gäfgen refuses to tell where the child is; he only tells the police that he is somewhere in a hut near a lake. Wolfgang Daschner, deputy chief of the Frankfurt police gave the order to threaten the suspect with considerable physical pain and, if necessary, to subject him to such pain in order to make him disclose the boy's whereabouts. The officer who interrogated Gäfgen told him that a person specially trained to torture without leaving traces was on his way by helicopter. The officer also hit the suspect several times on the chest and shook him so that, on one occasion, his head hit the wall. Some ten minutes later, without the torture threat being executed, Gäfgen told the police where the boy was kept. This led to the discovery of the child's corpse.

---

the law. The risk for the public official is considerable because of the uncertainty of *post factum* ratification of his acts by the public and the judiciary. An absolute ban minimizes the risk of normalizing the practice of torture (the slippery slope); it has an educational function because it emits an unambiguous moral message, creates moral inhibitions and raises the spectre of public exposure and criminal indictment (ibid.: 1501-1507). The rule establishing an absolute ban implies a strong presumption in favour of obedience 'that is rebuttable in exceptional cases where the wrong of disobedience is outweighed by the greater wrong that would follow from obeying the rules' (ibid.: 1521).

In July 2003 Gäfgen was convicted to life imprisonment for kidnapping and murder. He then started a series of appeals (because he considered that his conviction was based on evidence obtained through coercion) up to the European Court of Human Rights (ECHR). Meanwhile the police officers Daschner and his subordinate were prosecuted for coercing a suspect. In December 2004 the Frankfurt regional Court convicted the two police officers very mildly to suspended fines. The Court rejected the 'necessity defence' because the threat to torture the suspect, even if it had not been executed, had violated human dignity as codified in Art. 1 of the German Constitution and the prohibition on torture as expressed in art. 104 (1) of the Constitution and art. 3 of the European Convention on Human Rights. The Frankfurt regional Court held that the protection of human dignity and the prohibition of torture are absolute, allowing no exceptions or any balancing of interests, irrespective of the conduct of the person concerned and the nature of the offence of which he is suspected and irrespective of the fact that the life of a person is at stake (ECHR 2010: 12, 28). In determining the sentences, the regional Court considered that important mitigating factors had to be taken into account. The officers thought that the boy was alive and they had to take decisions under considerable pressure in order to (so they assumed) save his life. After the events they had both been removed from their function.

The Court in fact convicted the two without really punishing them. After his conviction Daschner was appointed as chief of the Police headquarters for Technology, Logistics and Administration. In June 2010 the Grand Chamber of the ECHR found (in the Gäfgen case) that 'such punishment, which is manifestly disproportionate to a breach of one of the core rights of the Convention, does not have the necessary deterrent effect in order to prevent further violations of the prohibition of ill-treatment in future difficult situations' (ibid.: 35). As a consequence there has not been sufficient redress and the applicant (Gäfgen) may continue to consider himself a victim of a breach of Art. 3 of the Convention. Six judges (of the 17) filed a partly dissenting opinion in which they criticized the decision because in their opinion the quantum of the penalties given to the police officers should no longer be relevant after they were declared guilty and were sanctioned. Determining the appropriate sentence should remain under the exclusive jurisdiction of the national criminal courts (ibid.: 65). I think this critique is appropriate because it is one thing to firmly uphold the prohibition of torture irrespective of the reasons for which the authorities whish to extract a statement of a suspect, but it is yet another thing when the European Court, as if it were a supra-national jurisdictional sovereign, highhandedly interferes with the courts on the national level regarding the quantum of the punishment in a particular case. One can only insist on judicial restraint in this respect. The regional Court has punished the police officers very leniently, because there were massive mitigating factors, as not only the Court, but also society at large felt.[32]

Following the Daschner-case there has been a lively discussion in Germany whether the state's duty to protect human dignity as provided in the Constitution should not require torturing a suspect if the life of an innocent person is at stake. The term 'Rettungsfolter' was coined for that purpose. The proponents pointed out that, after all the police is allowed to shoot hostage takers if necessary to save the lives of hostages, so why not allow the use of a certain amount of 'physical means' for their interrogation? The proponents argue that those who rule out that possibility prefer to respect the dignity of the hostage-taker to saving the life of the hostage. The absolute prohibitionists argue that in such a case the life of the hostage may have to be sacrificed to what is 'right'.[33] The core of the debate followed reasonings analogous to those in the American discussion.

9. Torture and Nodal Governance

The big majority of the torture cases that have been reported in the 'war against terrorism', did not fit the genuine TB scenario. As Luban (2005: 1445) explains, this scenario has a build-in error when it is used to justify normal legal practices: it assumes a single *ad hoc* decision about whether to torture in a desperate emergency. But 'the real world is a world of policies, guidelines, and directives. It is a world of *practices*, not of ad hoc emergency measures'. In the real world of counter terrorism policy and enforcement, the interrogator and the decision-maker are not the same person. When the interrogators, as was the case in Afghanistan and Iraq, get mixed messages about whether the Convention against Torture or the Geneva Conventions apply; when they hear rumours about secret locations and special CIA teams doing much harsher things in interrogation than they do; when there is no strict supervision and the chain of command and responsibility is blurred by unclear and equivocal orders ('give him the treatment', 'make sure he has a bad night', 'loosen this guy up for us' etc.), than the tyranny that is inherent in the interrogator's job, has nothing to hold it within limits. The risk of slippage from deception to abuse, to torture lite,[34] to beatings, water boarding and sexual humiliation is then very much increased (ibid.: 1449).

[32] The fact that the Frankfurt Court had excluded the extorted confession and the real evidence that was found as an effect of it from use at Gäfgen's trial (he was convicted on other grounds), in my opinion sufficiently served to condemn and prevent the future use of investigation methods in breach of Art. 3.

[33] See for example Lienemann (2005).

[34] The concept of torture 'lite' has been coined for the use of 'moderate physical and psychological pressure' in interrogation (stress positions, loud music, sleep deprivation). Those who think that this type of coercion should be allowed in emergency situations don't call it 'torture lite' because any type of torture is prohibited. The problem of the exact definition of torture will be of great importance in the years to come because interrogation of suspects (of serious crimes) by the police or by the military is an activity

As we already saw in the testimony of the French general Massu, this process is also reinforced by pushing the operational 'details' and the 'guilty knowledge' down the chain of command (ibid.: 1450). The torture culture running out of control can be described as the consequence of a bad type of 'nodal governance' (Johnston & Shearing 2003), a type of security governance that leads to a concentration of unaccountable power. A multitude of actors and nodes of governance participated in this process of de-responsabilisation and re-normalisation: from the President to the OLC lawyers and Congress who sanctioned their proposals, from the Pentagon officials to the military personnel and private contractors on the ground, from policy makers to the security agents on the working floor. The fact that the U.S. is fighting the war against terrorism extraterritorially had the consequence that the regime under which terrorist suspects labelled as 'unlawful enemy combatants' were detained, was neither the domestic regime of penal law (which ought to comply with the principles of legality and proportionality) nor the regime of international humanitarian law, as the U.S. denied the detainees the status of prisoners of war. The war became a war against outlaws which, analogous to the sate of nature, knows no clear and enforceable rules. The use of force and coercion which in a domestic regime, falls under the authority of the executive and can be checked by the judiciary as to its legality and legitimacy, shifted to the muddled responsibility of military commanders on the field, intelligence officers and private security contractors. At Abu Ghraib for example, the torturers (one of the *local nodes* heterogeneously composed of soldiers, military police, intelligence personnel and private contractors) felt themselves empowered to act in a 'creative' way as they were taking part in a forward looking common enterprise of risk reduction, a security program in which state and non-state actors worked together in redefining what was acceptable and shirking responsibilities in such a way that what happened had been 'nobody's' plan.[35]

---

which can not be stripped of its inherently coercive dimension. When a distinction is made between the prohibition of torture on the one hand and cruel, inhuman or degrading treatment (which is also prohibited, but for which a derogation may be available) on the other, then there will always be attempts to argue that some types of 'moderate' coercion (but what is moderate?) are not torture. Moreover, the U.S. have made reservations concerning the prohibition of 'cruel inhuman and degrading treatment'. While art. 2 of the Torture Convention prohibits the infliction of mental harm, the U.S. have restricted this to the infliction of 'prolonged mental harm' and whereas art. 16 prohibits cruel, inhuman and degrading treatment, the U.S. have limited this to treatment that would 'shock the conscience', which creates considerable space for interpretation and possibly also for interrogation techniques that will not yet 'shock the conscience' (whose conscience?) but are nevertheless highly coercive. Cf. Schlink (2007: 85-89).

[35] The unaccountability was reinforced because of the increased use of private contractors to whom military and security duties are outsourced. Military officials do not have the legal authority to supervise private contractors who are accountable only to their corporate employer. Military personnel may be prosecuted under the Uniform Code of Military Justice for their misbehaviour, but with private contractors it is a different and difficult issue, especially when the facts occurred abroad. Cf. Bina (2005: 1237-1263), Rosemann (2005: 77-100).

The torturers could consider themselves as the responsible executioners of a community policy, even if their superiors never gave them explicit and written orders to 'torture' detainees.[36]

[36] Here again there is a significant parallel with the Algerian case. When Aussaresses, who then was an officer under the command of general Massu, told his superior in the evening that by the next morning a specific prisoner would be dead, Massu only growled. General Massu never gave the explicit order to torture FLN suspects to death. Nevertheless Aussaresses was firmly convinced that he had the assent of his superior for what he was about to do. And they both were convinced that the French politicians who were responsible for what was happening in Algeria knew and approved what they were doing (Aussaresses 2001).

References

Case Law:

ECHR, Grand Chamber, *Gäfgen v. Germany (Application no. 22978/05)*, 1 June 2010, p. 12, 28.

Books and Journal Articles:

Aussaresses, P. (2001). *Services Speciaux, Algerie 1955-57*. Paris: Perrin.

Beccaria, C. (1995). *Of Crimes and Punishments*. Cambridge: Cambridge University Press.

Bellamy, A.J. (2006). No Pain, No Gain? Torture and Ethics in the War on Terror. *International Affairs, 82*, 121-148.

Bina, M.W. (2005). Private Military Contractor Liability and Accountability after Abu Ghraib. *John Marshall Law Review, 38,* 1237-1263.

Branche, R. (2007). Torture of Terrorists? Use of Torture in a 'War against Terrorism': Justifications, Methods and Effects: The Case of France in Algeria, 1954–1962. *International Review of the Red Cross, 89(867).* Available at http://www.icrc.org/Web/eng/siteeng0.nsf/htmlall/review-867-p543/$File/irrc-867-Branche.pdf.

Bufacchi, V. & Arrigo, J.M. (2006). Torture, Terrorism and the State: A Refutation of the Ticking-Bomb Argument. *Journal of Applied Philosophy, 23 (3)*, 355-373.

CHR&GJ (Center for Human Rights and Global Justice), (2005). *Report Torture by Proxy: International Law Applicable to 'Extraordianary Renditions'*. New York: NYU 2005. Available via <http://chrgj.org/docs/APPG-NYU%20Briefing%20Paper.pdf>.

Dershowitz, A.M. (1989). Is it Necessary to Apply 'Physical Pressure' to Terrorists — And to Lie About It?. *Israel Law Review, 23*, 192-200.

Dershowitz, A.M. (2003). *Why Terrorism Works. Understanding the Threat, Responding to the Challenge*. New Haven: Yale University Press.

Dershowitz, A.M. (2004). Tortured Reasoning. In S. Levinson (Ed.), *Torture. A Collection* (pp. 257-281). Oxford: Oxford University Press.

Evans, M. & Morgan, R. (1998). *Preventing Torture: A Study of the European Convention for the Prevention of Torture and Inhuman or Degrading Treatment or Punishment*. Oxford: Oxford University Press.

Garcia, M.J. (2009). *Renditions: Constraints Imposed by Laws on Torture*. Washington: CRS (Congressional Research Service) Report for Congress. Available at <http://www.fas.org/sgp/crs/natsec/ RL32890. pdf>.

Gross, O. (2004). Are Torture Warrants Warranted? Pragmatic Absolutism and Official Disobedience. *Minnesota Law Review, 88* , 1481-1555.

Guiora, A. (2008). *Constitutional Limits on Coercive Interrogation*. Oxford: Oxford University Press.

Ignatieff, M. (2004). *The Lesser Evil. Political Ethics in an Age of Terror*. Princeton/Oxford: Princeton University Press.

Israel Supreme Court (2005). *Judgments of the Israel Supreme Court: Fighting Terrorism within the Law*, with an introduction by Aharon Barak, President of the Israel Supreme Court. Available at <http://www.mfa.gov.il/NR/rdonlyres/599F2190-F81C-4389-B978-7A6D4598AD8F/0/terrorirm_law.pdf>.

Johnston, L. & Shearing, C. (2003). *Governing Security. Explorations in Policing and Justice*. London: Routledge.

Kadish, S.H. (1989). Torture, the State and the Individual. *Israel Law Review, Spring/Summer*, 345-356.

Kremnitzer, M. (1989). The Landau Commission Report—Was the Security Service Subordinated to the Law or the Law to the Needs of the Security Service? *Israel Law Review, 23*, 216-279.

Levinson, S. (Ed.) (2004a). *Torture. A Collection*. Oxford: Oxford University Press.

Levinson, S. (2004b). Torture in Iraq and the Rule of Law in America. *Deadalus, Summer*, 7-8.

Lienemann, W. (2005). Gnade an den Grenzen des Rechts. Die Debatte zur Aufweichung des Folterverbots aus ethischer Sicht. *Neue Züricher Zeitung*, 23.04.2005.

Luban, D. (2005). Liberalism, Torture and the Ticking Bomb. *Virginia Law Review, 91*, 1425-1461.

Massu, J. (1971). *La vraie bataille d'Algers*. Evreux: Plon.

Moore, M.S. (1989). Torture and the Balance of Evils. *Israel Law Review, Spring/Summer*, 280-344.

Parry, J.T. (2004). Escalation and Necessity. Defining Torture at Home and Abroad. In S. Levinson (Ed.), *Torture. A Collection* (pp. 145-165). Oxford: Oxford University Press.

Piret, J.-M. (1996). Legaliteit en Legitimiteit bij Carl Schmitt en Hans Kelsen. *Nederlands Tijdschrift voor Rechtsfilosofie en Rechtstheorie*, 5-26.

Piret, J.-M. (2008). The 'War against Terrorism', International Law and the Growth of Unchecked Executive Power in the U.S.. *Revue Interdisciplinaire d'Etudes Juridiques, 60*, 59-111.

Posner, R.A. (2004). Torture, Terrorism, and Interrogation. In S. Levinson (Ed.), *Torture. A Collection* (pp. 291-298). Oxford: Oxford University Press.

Rosemann, N. (2005). The Privatization of Human Rights Violations – Business' Impunity or Corporate Responsibility? The Case of Human Rights Abuses and Torture in Iraq. *Non-State Actors and International Law, 5*, 77 - 100.

Schlink, B. (2007). The Problem with Torture Lite. *Cardozo Law Review, 29 (1)*, 85-89.

Shue, H. (1978). Torture. *Philosophy and Public Affairs, 7 (2)*, 124-143.
Steinhoff, U. (2006). Torture - The Case for Dirty Harry and against Alan Dershowitz. *Journal of Applied Philosophy, 23* (3), 337-353.
Sussmann, D. (2005). What's Wrong with Torture? *Philosophy and Public Affairs, 33 (1)*, 1-33.
Twining, W.L., & Twining, P.E. (1973). Bentham on Torture. *Northern Ireland Law Quarterly, 24 (3)*, 305–356.
Vidal-Naquet, P. (1998). *La torture dans la République: essai d'histoire et de politique contemporaine, 1954-1962*. Paris: de Minuit.
Vidal-Naquet, P. (2001). *Les crimes de l'armée française en Algérie 1954-1962*. Paris: La Découverte.
Walzer, M. (2004). Political Action. The Problem of Dirty Hands. In S. Levinson (Ed.), *Torture. A Collection* (pp. 61-76). Oxford: Oxford University Press.

Part II: Changing Perspectives in the Governance of Security

7. Whose Conflict Is It Anyway? A Critique of Restorative Justice

Philip Stenning[1]

> 'We must be careful not to attach any notion of something real to this word 'justice', such as a physical force or an actual entity. It is simply a way whereby humans conceive of things, a way which influences beyond measure the happiness of all.'
>
> Cesare Beccaria, 'On Crimes and Punishments' (1764/1995: Ch. 2, p. 11)

1. Introduction

'Restorative justice' is, of course, 'a way whereby humans conceive of things' which is different, in important respects, from the way things are conceived of in our modern criminal justice system. But it shares many of the objectives of the criminal justice system – delivery of 'justice' for offenders and victims, acknowledgement of wrongdoing by the offender, prevention (or at least reduction) of future wrongdoing, 'rehabilitation' of the offender, the fostering of a more peaceful and safer community, etc. – although it prioritises these objectives differently from the criminal justice system and seeks to achieve them through very different processes. Restorative justice, in other words, is an alternative approach to 'governing security under the rule of law' which emphasises restoration and restitution over punishment and stigma

Restorative justice is certainly not a new concept, although it is only relatively recently (in the last twenty years or so) that it has come to be commonly known by that name. In fact, if you look back to Anglo-Saxon (pre-Norman Conquest) England, you find dispute resolution practices in small rural communities which bear a close resemblance to modern restorative justice practices (Jeudwine 1917: Ch. V; Maitland, 1885/1974; Radcliffe and Cross 1954; Duff *et al.* 2007: Ch.2). This, I believe, is no coincidence, and should come as no surprise; modern restorative justice seeks to displace the state as the central actor in dispute (or conflict) resolution, and instead place the parties (offender and victim) and the 'community' in which they live at the heart of the process. Back in Anglo-Saxon times, there was no central state or sovereign as we know it today, and people lived virtually all of their lives in small, closed, intimate rural communities.

---

1 I'm most grateful to Professors Adam Crawford and Ronnie Lippens, for their very helpful comments and suggestions on an earlier draft of this article. The remaining flaws, of course, are entirely my responsibility.

2. Sources of Inspiration for Modern Restorative Justice Practices

Modern restorative justice, however, is not conceived so much as a return to earlier, simpler ways of life and dispute resolution, as an alternative approach – alternative to formal legal procedures – to modern problems. It has two main sources of inspiration. The first is dissatisfaction with the formal legal system, and in particular the criminal justice process, and a desire to find a better, more effective process for dealing with conflicts (Zehr 1990). And the second are some still relatively recent Aboriginal governance practices, particularly in New Zealand, where modern restorative justice practices were first experimented with as an alternative to European formal state youth justice processes – specifically, approaches to governance practised on Māori *marae* (Pratt 1996; Tauri 1998).[2]

A *marae* is a community meeting place in a typically small rural Māori community (although as a result of migration to cities there are now urban *marae*). It is the centre of community life, and serves political, social, religious, administrative and judicial purposes. Decisions of all kinds (including the resolution of disputes) are taken collectively, and involve any member of the community who wishes (or is expected) to attend, under the supervision of elders and under the supposed gaze of ancestors, in community meetings on the *marae*. These practices reflect Māori cultural norms which, like those of many other Aboriginal peoples around the world, stress collective kin-based living rather than individualism based in nuclear families, and rule by collective consensus rather than by executive fiat. When Europeans first colonised New Zealand in the 19th Century, they initially recognised the value of not attempting to disrupt or replace these Māori forms of community self-governance. As we all know, however, that tolerance did not last very long (Hill 2004: Ch.1; Stenning 2008: 90-95).

Adapting such practices to the very different political, social and cultural realities of modern 21st century urban environments, as an adjunct or alternative to formal legal processes, however, has posed significant challenges, and it is these (as well as restorative justice's real potentialities) that I want to explore in this paper. In doing so, I stress that I am not expressing opposition to attempts to implement restorative justice principles and practices in present-day societies, or arguing that they do not offer real potential for better decision-making and conflict resolution in some circumstances. Rather, my critique is animated by what I (and some others) perceive to be the tendency of some of restorative justice's more ardent proponents to significantly 'oversell' the plausible applications and potential benefits of such practices in our 21st Century world, and to gloss over their very real limitations. It is all too often presented, along with motherhood and sliced bread, as a self-evident, unalloyed good.

---

2 Several commentators have questioned whether modern restorative justice practices in New Zealand and Australia can legitimately be claimed to be based on *traditional* Aboriginal justice practices, as opposed to Aboriginal practices that were adapted to reflect European values after colonisation (Bull 2001: Ch. 2; Daly 2002).

3. Key Features and Principles of 'Restorative Justice'

Before proceeding to my critique, however, I need to briefly set out what are generally agreed to be the key features of 'restorative justice' that distinguish it from modern formal institutions and processes of conflict resolution. In doing so, I draw particularly on the writings of three of modern restorative justice's principal theorists: Nils Christie, John Braithwaite and Howard Zehr. Modern restorative justice theory finds its roots in the writings of criminal justice abolitionists such as Thomas Mathieson (1974) and Louk Hulsman (1991), and advocates of 'peacemaking' such as Harold Pepinsky (1991). But it was Christie, Braithwaite and Zehr who most successfully translated these frustrations with formal criminal justice into positive proposals for alternative institutions and processes for dispute resolution.

It was the Norwegian criminologist Nils Christie who first articulated the idea of 'conflicts as property' in a lecture he delivered at Sheffield University in England in 1976 (Christie 1977). His argument was basically that conflicts should be regarded as the 'property' of the specific parties to them, and of the 'communities' of which those parties are members. The state, and in particular the legal profession, he argued, had expropriated this property in imposing formal legal institutions and processes on conflict resolution. In doing so, conflicts were transformed from being conflicts between individuals in communities into conflicts between individuals and the state, representing 'society'. Conflicts and the responsibility for their effective resolution, he proposed, should be returned to their rightful owners, and the role of the state should be strictly confined to facilitating such self-governance. Christie's argument has been further developed more recently in his thought-provoking 2004 book, *A Suitable Amount of Crime* (Christie 2004).

Meanwhile, in New Zealand the authorities were growing increasingly frustrated at the seeming ineffectiveness of formal youth justice institutions and processes in responding to increasing levels of crime, especially among Māori youth (who, as has been the case with many indigenous groups in other countries, had become statistically seriously 'over-represented' in the criminal justice system). To put it simply, this frustration reflected what the British criminologist, Leslie Wilkins, had observed about formal criminal justice in the early 1970s, when he noted that: 'Crime is the only problem in the world that we consider 'solved' when we've found somebody to blame for it.'[3] It was in this context that *marae*-based Māori conflict resolution practices were turned to as providing a possible alternative to the formal youth justice system's response to these problems. The adapted format that was developed came to be known as a 'family group conference' (later renamed in some other jurisdictions as a 'community accountability conference'), which has since then remained the

[3] In an unpublished public lecture at the University of Toronto, 1970.

principal, but by no means exclusive, format for 'restorative justice' (Stenning 2008: 272-281).

This format attracted attention in neighbouring Australia, and became the subject of John Braithwaite's seminal book, *Crime, Shame and Re-integration* (Braithwaite, 1989), in which he sought to theorise restorative justice and place it within the context of the development of criminological and justice theory more generally. At about the same time, Howard Zehr, in North America, was developing his own Quaker-based critique of formal criminal justice, and alternative proposals for 'restorative justice' principles, institutions and practices, in his influential book, *Changing Lenses* (Zehr 1990). The rest, as they say, is history.

So the basic principles on which restorative justice practices are based can be briefly summarised as follows:

- Conflicts (or disputes) 'belong' to the particular parties involved in them and to the 'communities' to which they belong, and the primary responsibility for addressing and resolving such conflicts rests with these parties and communities, not with the state, or 'society' more generally.
- The role of the state should be limited to facilitating such local community resolution of conflicts (e.g. through funding, provision of facilitators and venues, etc., and other support).
- Resolution of conflicts should be achieved through relatively informal, facilitated dialogue between the parties and representatives of their community, and should be consensus-based. Such dialogue should be conducted in non-technical everyday language which can be easily understood and participated in by those involved.
- Resolutions should be remedial rather than punitive, emphasising a desire to 'restore' good relations in the future, rather than punish offenders for past behaviour. They should aim to 're-integrate' offenders as valued and respected members of their communities, rather than degrade, stigmatise and exclude them from community life. In short, resolutions should be focused primarily on the future rather than on the past.
- Resolutions should pay as much attention to addressing the circumstances and needs of victims as those of offenders. Victims should be fully involved both in voicing their experiences as a result of the offending behaviour (so that offenders can appreciate and take responsibility for the consequences of their behaviour) and in reaching satisfactory resolutions together with offenders and their communities.
- Responsibility for ensuring and monitoring the successful implementation of resolutions should be shared by those who have participated in the process, and not just left to facilitators or other officials.

4. A Critique

4.1 Issues Arising from RJ Principles

My critique has two branches. First I consider some difficulties which are inherent in the principles themselves as an alternative to the principles which underlie our formal criminal justice institutions and processes. Then I address some problems which arise in attempting to apply these principles to the realities of modern 21st Century life. As will be apparent, these two branches of critique intertwine at various points.

The first and most fundamental difficulty that arises from the principles themselves concerns the idea that conflicts are usefully regarded as the 'property' of specific offenders, victims and the 'communities' to which they belong. It is true, of course, that most crime and conflicts are very local in character and involve offenders and victims who are known to each other. Nevertheless for a significant amount of crime and conflict this is simply not the case. Not only does a considerable amount of behaviour that we consider unacceptable and respond to as crime not involve any easily specifiable victim beyond 'society in general', but even in the case of crimes that do involve identifiable victims, the victims and offenders often do not both belong to any one identifiable 'community', and may in fact live in completely different and distant communities. Furthermore, even if the specific offender(s) and victim(s) in a particular case do belong to the same local community, the offending may have been influenced by forces or conditions, and/or have repercussions, beyond that community (e.g. it might be related to wider networks of organised crime or international terrorism), as result of which others in the wider society beyond that community may have a legitimate interest in how the offending is dealt with. So while this fundamental restorative justice principle may be applicable to many if not most crimes and conflicts, its application to a lot of others is much more problematic.

A second difficulty which arises from the principles themselves concerns the 'responsibilisation' of the parties and 'community'. This principle assumes that the parties and the community have both the will and the capacity to take responsibility for dispute resolution, and for overseeing the successful implementation of resolutions. This in turn presumes a minimally functional 'community'. The difficulty with this is that there is reason to believe that quite a bit of crime and conflict arises precisely out of the *dysfunctionalities* of communities in the first place (see e.g. Sampson 2004). To assume, then, that these communities will be sufficiently functional to successfully undertake responsibility for addressing and resolving these problems may be simply unrealistic in many cases. Related to this, of course, is the concern that effective restorative justice will only be accessible to 'better-off' communities, which have sufficient 'social capital' and 'collective efficacy' to enact it (Sampson 2004). I will return to this point later.

Related to this is the issue of power. Restorative justice principles, and their advocates, tend to be less than candid about this issue. For these principles to be workable in practice, power differentials which allow some parties to dominate others (and which may be a primary source of crime and conflict in the first place), must somehow be neutralised (Braithwaite 2003: 9). Otherwise, restorative justice processes risk simply reproducing and reinforcing the inequalities and injustices to which these power differentials give rise. Some feminists in particular have raised concerns of this kind in opposing attempts to address sexual assaults through restorative justice processes in the context of what they consider to be unreconstructed patriarchal societies (Stubbs 1995). Yet beyond imposing on facilitators (perhaps in many cases quite unrealistically) the responsibility for persuading participants to renounce their power in participating in conflict resolution processes, the principles themselves, and those who advocate them, seem to have little to offer by way of addressing this problem. And this is a problem, of course, that is merely compounded by the fact that in practice restorative justice processes cannot occur unless all those who ought to be involved in them agree to do so. Consequently, restorative justice processes are unlikely to be viable in cases involving long-entrenched and obdurate differential power relations among the parties and/or within the 'community' concerned. As Dickson-Gilmore & LaPrairie (2005) have noted, this has proven a major obstacle to the effective implementation of restorative justice in some remote Aboriginal communities in Canada (for which, for other reasons, one might have thought that they would be particularly well suited). Attempting to introduce restorative justice in such communities as an alternative to formal criminal justice can actually make matters much worse than much better, since their members often have no choice but to live with the consequences, which sometimes may involve recriminations and further retaliatory offending.[4] Sometimes communities welcome formal criminal justice interventions precisely because they are unable to resolve conflicts effectively without them. It simply cannot be assumed that restorative justice processes will offer more acceptable 'justice' than can be expected from the formal criminal justice process in every case, regardless of the social, political and cultural context. In this respect, Willem de Haan's (1990:167) caution needs to be heeded:

> 'Emphasis on participatory processes of definition or the contextuality of conflicts may be welcome, but it can also lead to problematic outcomes, particularly in situations "where the participants do not have equal power, where no prior relationship existed, or where suspicion, fear, and prejudice flourish" (Harris 1987, p. 34). For these reasons, legal form is still required to ensure fairness.'

---

4 Note Crawford's (2002: 107) important reminder that: 'History teaches us that extra-legal forms of social control, upon which restorative justice relies for much of its normative persuasion, can appear both in desirable and undesirable guises with malign as well as benign consequences'.

4.2 Practical Concerns

The second branch of my critique concerns practical problems of implementation. At the heart of these is the common practical difficulty of realising and instantiating 'community' for the purposes of restorative justice. The problem here is that the kinds of communities which are envisaged by restorative justice principles are becoming increasingly difficult to find in 'advanced' 21st Century societies. No-one, I think, has better articulated this problem than the sociologist Zygmunt Bauman in his path-breaking writing on what he calls 'liquid modernity'. His ideas on this are most eloquently developed, I think, in his book *Liquid Love - On the Frailty of Human Bonds* (Bauman 2003). In this remarkable book, which to me reads more like a post-Orwellian nightmare than a bright vision for the future, Bauman paints a picture of social relations in which the moral economy – which he argues provides the foundation for philanthropy and *communitas* – is replaced by an increasingly globalised consumer economy; the citizen is replaced by the consumer; 'communities of sameness', as we think of them today, are replaced by the Price Club, loyalty cards, and 'communities of occasion'; and long-term personal relationships and bonds are replaced by shorter-term, opportunistic 'connections of convenience', the most important feature of which is their impermanence and the associated ease of *disconnection* as changing circumstances and new opportunities dictate. Like everything else in such a society, public goods – the stock in trade of governments – including security and justice, begin to resemble exchangeable commodities, and government itself is conducted like a business in a competitive market. In short – and of course I am not doing justice to Bauman's sophisticated analysis here – he seems to be arguing that in the new 'liquid modernity' towards which we are heading, the kinds of 'communities' on which most proposals for 'community justice' and 'restorative justice' alternatives to the criminal justice system are premised, will cease to exist.

Now I've no doubt that the picture Bauman paints is an exaggerated one which does not reflect the reality in all societies, or everywhere in any society. But it is not simply a nightmarish fantasy, and I think we can all recognise features of our own societies and communities in his account. And even if it is only half true, his account of 'liquid modernity' poses a huge challenge for the effective and widespread implementation of restorative justice as an alternative to formal legal processes for conflict and dispute resolution in the 21st Century. Perhaps – and this is pure speculation on my part – the development of 'virtual communities' may be able to compensate to some extent for the decline of the kinds of terrestrial communities which have been so central to conceptions of restorative justice so far (Putnam 2000; *The Economist* 2007; Christakis and Fowler 2010). But I do not feel optimistic about this.

Even if we assume that Bauman is quite wrong, however, some challenges for instantiating communities for the purposes of restorative justice remain. For even if the offender and the victim of crime (or the parties to conflict) are actually members of the same community, how is that community to be adequately represented in restorative justice practices? This, as you will probably know, has proven as much of a challenge for the implementation of so-called 'community policing' as for restorative justice (Brogden and Nijhar 2005: Ch. 3). The solutions which have been tried have, unfortunately, proven less than satisfactory. John Braithwaite (1999) has referred to the kind of 'community' which is typically represented in a family group conference as a 'community of care' rather than the wider 'community' which restorative justice principles seem to envisage – that is, it is a community of those most intimately associated, through family, work, school or other social connections, with the individual parties to the conflict which, he argues, is the community most directly affected by the offending behaviour. While this might be an acceptable definition of 'the community concerned' in some cases, as I have agued above, it certainly would not be in others, in which the wider community, even quite narrowly defined as the local neighbourhood, let alone the wider society, most certainly has a legitimate interest in how a conflict or offence is dealt with. And in this respect, the fact that most restorative justice processes are held in private gives rise to a major concern, not only in terms of adequate public accountability with respect to their outcomes,[5] but also in terms of any notion of fair and equal justice for offenders *and* victims (Hudson 2003). While restorative justice principles justifiably promote individualised justice (in the sense of resolutions tailored to the particular circumstances of each conflict), they do not, I think, include sufficient safeguards against what in Britain have come to be referred to as 'post code' outcomes. Nor, arguably, do they adequately guard against excessively punitive or discriminatory resolutions imposed by reactionary or racist community members.

Even assuming that Braithwaite's 'community of care' is an acceptable one to be entrusted with responsibility for resolving conflicts and 'doing justice' in individual cases, however, difficulties remain in assembling such credible 'communities' in cases involving adult offenders and victims. In this respect it is probably not a coincidence that restorative justice has in most jurisdictions (although with some exceptions) been largely confined to addressing problems involving young offenders (who often do actually still live with their families), and has proven much more difficult to implement effectively for adult offenders who will often no longer have such easily identifiable or mobilisable community roots (see e.g. Triggs 2005).

Next in this catalogue of challenges is the issue of participation. Advocates of restorative justice commonly place great emphasis on its benefits for victims, and support this claim with research findings which show a high degree of satisfaction among victims who participate in restorative justice processes, contrasting this with much lower victim satisfaction with formal criminal justice processes (Strang, 2002). While I do not, of course, dispute these findings, they must be properly considered in the context of rates of victim participation which, in many jurisdictions, have proven to be disappointingly low. In 2004,

[5] For a contrary view, see Roche (2003).

for instance, New Zealand researchers Gabrielle Maxwell *et al.* (2004: 84) reported that victims or their representatives attended less than 50% of the youth family group conferences that they studied in which a victim had been identified. Bauman's conception of the realities of 'liquid modernity' may well offer some understanding of why persuading victims and other potential participants to participate in family group conferences poses such a challenge these days. The attempts in some jurisdictions to substitute surrogate victims for actual victims in some family group conferences do not, I think, satisfactorily resolve this problem, and are in any event tenuously compatible with restorative justice principles.

As for offenders, one might reasonably suspect that they will be most likely to agree to restorative justice processes if they estimate that they will result in a better outcome for them than if they submit to the criminal justice process (Hudson 2003). This in turn is more likely to be the case if they are recidivist and/or more serious offenders (and therefore more likely to receive harsher punishment on conviction in the courts). Yet in many jurisdictions access to restorative justice processes is still restricted to first-time and less serious offenders. So unless and until these processes are made available to chronic and serious offenders, they are unlikely to constitute a significant alternative to criminal justice processes, or have a significant impact on levels of crime,[6] since most first offenders do not re-offend even when processed through the formal criminal justice system. The evidence of the impact of restorative justice processes in reducing re-offending is not impressive (Morris and Maxwell 2003: 264-267; Sherman & Strang, 2007: Ch. 10), and recent criminological research suggests that factors other than the criminal justice process are more important in accounting for desistance from crime (Kazemian and Maruna 2009).

We need also to consider the challenges of persuading other 'community members' to participate, voluntarily and without compensation, in restorative justice processes. This, of course, relates to my earlier discussion of the capacities of communities and the willingness of their members to volunteer their time for community work such as restorative justice. Bauman's concept of 'liquid modernity' suggests that both may be diminishing, although Sampson (2004) argues that such trends are unequally reflected in different communities, depending on their social cohesion and collective efficacy. Experience with attempts to involve community members in 'community policing' and crime prevention, however, are not especially encouraging in this respect, suggesting as they do that typically the only community members who find the time for such participation are the retired and the unemployed, who of course will not typically be representative of the community as a whole (Schneider 2007), and that sustained participation even of these people is difficult to achieve (Skogan 2004). Indeed there is recent evidence that volunteering in general is declining

[6] In their review of the evidence about restorative justice, Sherman and Strang (2007: 68) note: 'The key finding is that *RJ may work better* [in reducing repeat offending] *with more serious crimes than with less serious crimes*, contrary to conventional wisdom' (italics in original).

somewhat, at least in England and Wales (Travis 2010; Ipsos Mori 2010: Ch. 4). So while I am sympathetic to Willem de Haan's (1990: 167) call for 'forms of social regulation which are not located in or defined by the state but operate (semi)autonomously as alternative, progressive, and emancipatory forms of dispute settlement and conflict resolution' to displace the dominant state criminal justice system, I think we need to be realistic about the potential of restorative justice to achieve such forms to any significant degree in our increasingly atomised societies.

Next, I want to compare and contrast the functions that restorative justice can be expected to perform with those that the criminal justice process is intended to perform. I have argued elsewhere (Stenning 2004) that the criminal justice system is designed to perform four key functions: a *forensic* function (investigating crimes and adjudicating criminal charges); a *prophylactic* function (anticipating and preventing crime); a *corrective* function (responding to crime by punishing and rehabilitating offenders and providing redress for victims); and a *symbolic* function (communicating society's values and standards of acceptable behaviour, and its intolerance of unacceptable behaviour). Of course, how successful the criminal justice system is in performing each of these functions is certainly not self-evident, and would be a subject for another paper. But what I want to raise here is the extent to which we can look to restorative justice to perform these functions as well or better than the criminal justice system.

Restorative justice is often presented by its proponents as an alternative to the entire criminal justice process. But I don't think this claim is justified. The *forensic* function is only partially performed through restorative justice processes. Although 'the facts' of a case, from both the offender's and the victim's point of view, are certainly an important subject of discussion in most restorative justice processes, this discussion is predicated on the fact that the offender has already admitted to the offence in general terms as a condition of participation in the process. In this sense, restorative justice process are not so much an alternative to the forensic functions of the criminal justice system, as an alternative to criminal justice sentencing hearings which, of course, involve less formal proceedings than the adjudicative phase of a trial, and in which victims are increasingly being given an opportunity to participate and be heard (Hoyle and Zedner 2007: 473-481; Stenning 2008: Ch. 9).

Restorative justice processes may well perform the *corrective* and *prophylactic* functions as well or better than the criminal justice process, although the evidence on this is by no means conclusive. But the private nature of restorative justice process severely limits their capacity to perform the *symbolic* communicative function that criminal justice is designed to perform. So these are, I think, limitations on the extent to which restorative justice processes can rightly be regarded as a full alternative to the criminal justice process.

Finally, there is the matter of cost. As is the case with the economics of criminal justice, by no means enough good research has been done on the economics of restorative justice to allow us to state with any confidence that it is a more economic form of justice than criminal justice, even if this may turn out to be the case. To the extent that resort to restorative justice rather than criminal justice results in less resort to incarceration, we could certainly expect that this would be an economic benefit as well as a correctional one. But given the kinds of cases to which restorative justice processes are typically limited, this seems quite unlikely. So the question of cost remains an open one so far as I can see.

5. Conclusion

This has been a critique of restorative justice, so I make no apology for having focused particularly on the challenges it faces and its limitations as an alternative to the formal criminal process, rather than its potential (Johnstone and Van Ness 2006). Nothing that I have said, however, is intended to deny that restorative justice has the potential to offer real benefits in terms of decision-making, conflict resolution and restoration of peace and harmony in communities (including possibly national and international communities). But I hope I may have convinced you of the need not to exaggerate this potential, and to recognise that restorative justice is unlikely ever to be a complete, satisfactory and acceptable substitute for formal legal processes that have been developed and refined over centuries of experience, as some of its more ardent advocates sometimes seem to suggest.

References

Bauman, Z. (2003). *Liquid Love: On the Frailty of Human Bonds*. Cambridge: Polity Press.

Beccaria, C., & Bellamy R. (Eds.) (1764/1995). *On Crimes and Punishments and Other Writings*. Cambridge: Cambridge University Press - English translation edited by R. Bellamy, translated by R. Davies, with V. Cox.

Braithwaite, J. (1989). *Crime, Shame and Re-Integration*. Cambridge: Cambridge University Press.

Braithwaite, J. (1999). A Future Where Punishment Is Marginalized; Realistic or Utopian? *U.C.L.A. Law Review*, *46 (6)*, 1727-1750.

Braithwaite, J. (2003). Principles of Restorative Justice. In A. von Hirsch, J. Roberts, A. Bottoms, K. Roach, & M. Schiff (Eds.), *Restorative Justice & Criminal Justice: Competing or Reconcilable Paradigms* (pp. 1-20). Oxford/Portland, OR.: Hart Publishing.

Brogden, M., & Nijhar, P. (2005). *Community Policing: National and International Models and Approaches*. Cullompton, UK: Willan Publishing.

Bull, S. (2001). *The Land of Murder, Cannibalism and All Kinds of Atrocious Crimes? An Overview of 'Maori Crime' from Pre-Colonial Times to the Present Day*. Ph.D. thesis, Victoria University of Wellington, New Zealand.

Chrisatakis, N., & Fowler, J. (2010). *Connected: The Amazing Power of Social Networks and How They Shape Our Lives*. London: Harper Collins Publishers.

Christie, N. (1997). Conflicts as Property. *British Journal of Criminology*, *17(1)*, 1-15.

Christie, N. (2004). *A Suitable Amount of Crime*. London/New York: Routledge.

Crawford, A. (2002). The State, Community and Restorative Justice: Heresy, Nostalgia and Butterfly Collecting. In L. Walgrave (Ed.), *Restorative Justice and the Law* (pp. 101-129). Cullompton, UK: Willan Publishing.

Daly, K. (2002). Restorative Justice: the Real Story. *Punishment and Society*, *4*, 55-79.

Dickson-Gilmore, J., & LaPrairie, C. (2005). *Will The Circle Be Unbroken? Restorative Justice, Aboriginal Communities, and the Challenges of Conflict and Change*. Toronto: University of Toronto Press.

Duff, A., Farmer, L., Marshall, S., & Tadros, V. (2007). *The Trial on Trial: Towards a Normative Theory of the Criminal Trial*. Oxford/Portland, OR.: Hart Publishing.

Freedland, J. (2007). The Internet Will Revolutionise the Very Meaning of Politics. *The Guardian*, 30th May 2007, p. 27.

Haan, W. de (1990). *The Politics of Redress: Crime, Punishment and Penal Abolition*. London: Unwin Hyman.

Harris, K. (1987). Moving into the New Millennium: Toward a Feminist Vision of Justice. *The Prison Journal, 67*, 27-38.

Hill, R. (2004). *State Authority, Indigenous Autonomy: Crown-Maori Relations in New Zealand/Aotearoa 1900-1950.*Wellington, NZ: Victoria University Press.

Hoyle, C., & Zedner, L. (2007). Victims, Victimization and Criminal Justice. In M. Maguire, R. Morgan, & R. Reiner (Eds.), *The Oxford Handbook of Criminology*, 4th ed. (pp. 461-495). Oxford: Oxford University Press.

Hudson, B. (2003). Victims and Offenders. In A. von Hirsch, J. Roberts, A. Bottoms, K. Roach, & M. Schiff (Eds.), *Restorative Justice & Criminal Justice: Competing or Reconcilable Paradigms* (pp. 177-194). Oxford/Portland, OR.: Hart Publishing.

Hulsman, L. (1991). The Abolitionist Case: Alternative Crime Policies. *Israel Law Review, 25(3-4)*, 681-709.

Ipsos Mori (2010). *Our Nation's Civic Health - Main Report* A Report for the Department for Communities and Local Government. London: H.M.S.O. also accessible at <http://www.communities.gov.uk/documents/communities/pdf/1519846.pdf>.

Jeudwine, J. (1917). *Tort, Crime, and Police in Mediaeval Britain: A Review of Some Early Law and Custom.* London: Williams and Norgate.

Johnstone, G., & Van Ness, D. (Eds.) (2006). *Handbook of Restorative Justice.* Cullompton, U.K.: Willan Publishing.

Kazemian, L., & Maruna, S. (2009). Desistance from Crime. In M. Krohn, A. Lizotte, & G. Penly Hall (Eds.), *Handbook on Crime and Deviance* (pp. 277-295). New York: Springer Publishing Co.

Maitland, F. (1885/1974). *Justice and Police.* Reprint. New York: AMS Press.

Mathieson, T. (1974). *The Politics of Abolition.* London: Martin Robertson.

Maxwell, G., Kingi, V., Robertson, J., Morris, A., & Lash, B. (2004). *Achieving Effective Outcomes in Youth Justice: Final Report.* Wellington, NZ: Ministry of Social Development.

Morris, A., & Maxwell, G. (2003). Restorative Justice in New Zealand. In A. von Hirsch, J. Roberts, A. Bottoms, K. Roach, & M. Schiff (Eds.), *Restorative Justice & Criminal Justice: Competing or Reconcilable Paradigms* (pp. 257-271). Oxford/Portland, OR.: Hart Publishing.

Pepinsky, H. (1991). Peacemaking in Criminology and Criminal Justice. In H. Pepinsky, & R. Quinney (Eds.), *Criminology as Peacemaking* (pp. 299-327). Bloomington, IND.: Bloomington Indiana University Press.

Pratt, J. (1996). Colonization, Power and Silence: A History of Indigenous Justice in New Zealand. In B. Galaway, & J. Hudson (Eds.), *Restorative Justice: International Perspectives* (pp. 137-155). Monsey, NY: Criminal Justice Press/Amsterdam: Kugler Publications.

Putnam, R. (2000). *Bowling Alone: The Collapse and Revival of American Community.* New York: Simon & Shuster.

Radcliffe, G., & Cross, G. (1954). *The English Legal System* (3rd ed). London: Butterworth & Co. Ltd.

Roche, D. (2003). *Accountability in Restorative Justice.* Oxford: Oxford University Press.

Sampson, R. (2004). Neighbourhood and Community: Collective Efficacy and Community Safety. *New Economy, 11(2)*, 106-113.

Schneider, S. (2007). *Refocusing Crime Prevention: Collective Action and the Quest for Community.* Toronto: University of Toronto Press.

Sherman, L., & Strang, H. (2007). *Restorative Justice: The Evidence.* London: The Smith Institute.

Skogan, W. (2004). Representing the Community in Community Policing. In W. Skogan (Ed.), *Community Policing (Can it Work?)* (pp. 57-75). Belmont, CA.: Wadsworth/Thompson Publishing.

Stenning, P. (2004). *The Death of the Community? Prospects for Justice in the 21st Century.* Unpublished Inaugural Professorial Lecture, Victoria University of Wellington, New Zealand, 1st June, 2004.

Stenning, P. (2008). *The Modern Prosecution Process in New Zealand.* Wellington, NZ: Victoria University Press.

Strang, H. (2002). *Repair or Revenge: Victims and Restorative Justice.* Oxford: Clarendon Press.

Stubbs, J. (1995). 'Communitarian' Conferencing and Violence Against Women: A Cautionary Note. In M. Valverde, L. MacLeod, & K. Johnson (Eds.), *Wife Assault and the Canadian Criminal Justice System* (pp. 260-289). Toronto: Centre of Criminology, University of Toronto.

Tauri, J. (1998). Family Group Conferencing: A Case Study of the Indigenisation of New Zealand's Justice System. *Current Issues in Criminal Justice, 10(2)*, 168-182.

Travis, A. (2010). Not the Big Society: Volunteering Declines in England. *The Guardian*, 30th April, 2010, p. 18.

Triggs, S. (2005). *New Zealand Court-Referred Restorative Justice Pilot: Evaluation.* Wellington, NZ.: Ministry of Justice.

The Economist (2007). Social Graph-iti: There's Less to Facebook and Other Social Networks than Meets the Eye. *The Economist*, Vol. 385, No. 8551, 89-90.

Zehr, H. (1990). *Changing Lenses.* Scottdale, PA.: Herald Press.

8. Restorative Justice as Criminal Justice without Threats. An Interpretative Approach to Restorative Justice Potentials for Public Safety

John Blad

An American soldier, who had just been granted guardianship over a little girl of 4 years old, used the technique of so-called water-boarding to force his step-daughter to say the alphabet. Apparently she refused to say it while she could: he must have threatened the girl that something nasty would happen if she kept on refusing. She was a 'bad girl' and was supposed to be frightened into saying what she was required to say. This news-item appeared on a website on February 8, 2010.

To my mind the soldier did something awful and must have been out of his mind. Or was he? Did he not just replicate and imitate a crude model, used and defended by American security forces recently, of squeezing the 'truth' out of those suspected of terrorism? It was a cultural model available to him, there was an example that gave him the notion that this might be a way of achieving his aim. The results, of course, were terrible for the poor girl, and will be bad for the guardian as well. Now he will find out...only now. He will be made clear he showed personal lack of morals, empathy and social skills.

To threaten with pain however, in order to make people behave in a certain desirable way, is a commonly accepted type of social behavior, which is fundamental to the traditional criminal justice systems in our world.[1] I must be more precise: the substantive criminal law tells you how not to behave, it proscribes certain actions and you are presumed to be deterred from these types of conduct by the punishment that the law states you will or might get.

Is it a coincidence that, after more than two decades of intensified use of the punitive model and intensified punitive political discourse, we can witness a growing tendency in our population to use threats to get what they desire? Threatening politicians or authors that you disagree with through the internet, threatening aid-givers to give aid swifter or in a special way, threatening

1 Of course there may be threats which are unjustifiable and others that are not. But even if the threats of the penal law could be justified, f.i. by saying they serve the interests of self-protection of society (Quinn 1995), I want to discuss whether they could really serve this interest and, whether this interest could not be better served by other means than holding out a threat.

teachers to change school-reports, threatening civil servants if they are or seem unkind, and threatening police who then produce their ticket-book immediately. Is not a general cultural model of intimidation[2] spreading and should the state become ever more intimidating to trump the intimidations of its citizens? I believe this is the case, despite and even through most of the forms of 'responsibilisation', 'horizon-talisation' and 'nodal governance' that are described, analysed and discussed in recent academic literature. One could wonder (with Hoogenboom 2009:65) whether nodal governance is not just a new and fashionable way of talking about 'old' phenomena , which at the surface seem to imply different modes of social control, but which at a deeper level imply predominantly a further elaboration and deeper penetration of the traditional punitive model of influencing conduct.

Our criminal justice systems, while seeking new forms of co-operation with societal partners such as corporations and local councils, are at the same time seeking ever increasing levels of deterrence and blurring the boundaries between crime and 'social nuisance', making the latter amenable to criminal justice interventions. Although these interventions are often called 'preventive' and 'pro-active', they obviously increase the scope of the punitive model: a breach of instructions or conditions of suspended prison-sentences leads inevitably to imprisonment. The latest development in the Netherlands is the new authority of the public prosecutor to impose instructions with regard to the conduct of the suspect, who is likely to cause nuisance to others: the breach of *such an instruction* will be a crime, penalized with a maximum of one year imprisonment. Step by step the scope of provisions in the substantive criminal law increases, bit by bit the procedural criminal law loses its normative grip upon criminal justice agencies (Claessen 2010: 87-105), a 'quasi-penal-law' in the hands of non-governmental organizations develops (Schuilenburg 2009: 14) and the free citizen we once projected as a political ideal is primarily treated as a risk, to be controlled by making all citizens functionaries of the security-state (Blad 2005).

Packer (1968) was right in stipulating that we should *only* criminalize conduct when we are deeply convinced that the conduct is of such a damaging nature that imprisonment would be justified in order to protect society against serious harm. But the limits of the criminal sanction seem to be a long forgotten theme.

---

[2] I am aware that intimidations could be distinguished from justified threats by their lack of justification. But an excessive use of punishment in general and in particular cases and excessive – even obsessive – stress on punishment in public discourse tends to bring about a cultural state of intimidation in which people begin to believe that they and/or their fellow-citizens are fundamentally incapable of doing the right thing without the threats under which they are placed. I surmise that the self-efficacy of society and the capacities for self-regulation and informal social control are undermined by this actual development.

The punitive model should however be restricted again to the utmost, to the margin in which it may have to remain, to the *last resort* it should be. And my contention is that restorative justice offers theoretical and practical ways to achieve that: but only if criminal justice interventions are liberated from the obligation to punish, in so far as this obligation *only* derives from our initial consequence-driven threat.[3] In this contribution I will first deal with what should be obvious: the defectiveness and costs of the punitive model in criminal law, which is one of the main reasons why classical utilitarian thinkers insisted on parsimony. Then I shall continue by discussing restorative justice as an urgently needed strategy of depenalisation. Restorative justice can be defined as 'a theory of justice that emphasizes repairing the harm caused or revealed by criminal behavior.' The definition continues with a most important reference to a procedural aspect: 'It is best accomplished through cooperative processes that include all stakeholders' (www.criminaljustice.org). Approached in this way restorative justice can easily be recognized as a phenomenon fitting in the categories of nodal governance (Burris, Drahos and Shearing 2005) and such, but importantly different in its capacities to avoid the imposition of punishment.

1. The Catascopic Steering Model of Criminal Justice

The deterrence model that has been proposed by Beccaria and Bentham is a top-down (a catascopic) model with seemingly only two entities: the sovereign state and the (legal) subject and the latter was supposed to be directly informed and influenced in his or her choices by the actions and communications at the state level (Hulsman 1986). The state is mainly seen as a legal entity and structure, keeping self-centred, hedonistic, free-floating and rationally calculating citizens (Vervaele 1990: 87 a.f.) in control. In Beccaria's view, the actor is even supposed to have contributed to a social contract and is thus expected to be fully aware of what types of conduct would constitute a breach and therefore be punishable (hence the juridical myth 'that everybody knows the law'). This means that the citizen who breaks the law is fundamentally assumed to have done that consciously and willingly, choosing against the social contract and its adherents. Of course, the social contract is nothing but an axiomatic – fictitious – legitimation of the criminal law, which in fact brings about a system of steering citizens from a long distance by the centre of the state, through legal definitions and legal threats, combined in the legality principle. As a consequence, in the legally allowed reaction to legally defined criminal conduct only the legal aspects of the interaction (action and reaction) count and the subjective and intersubjective (social), psychological and moral meanings of the

[3] This way of stating things implies that retribution theory is not discussed here and that retribution remains a possibly acceptable legitimation of punishment. But the difference is that, in principle, we than speak of the need to punish a criminal action that we did not expect to prevent (and possibly even expected). With some interpretative changes retribution can be a foundation also for restorative justice (Walgrave 2008).

conduct in question are either suppressed or seen as of marginal importance. Because the basic mechanism of influencing behavior is inherently an ethically negative one (intentionally inflicting pain) the criminal procedure has become shaped as the due process that should facilitate and monitor the decision to exercise the right to punish: again here only two actors count (legal subject and the state) and only the legal aspects of the charge and the procedures followed are relevant. And since the only relevant conflict is that between the state and the suspect, fundamentally the victim remains the victim who is only passively to win or lose with the defeat or the victory of either primary adversary. This may (and can) not be a fundamental objection from the viewpoint of punitive reasoning, it is from the perspective of many victims and of restorative justice.

It is evident that if we decide – after due consideration – that this or that type of conduct deserves to be punished, we would also demand that this punishment can only be imposed after due process has taken place. But both in cultural and performative sense the costs of such a penalization are high.

The cultural implications are that, first, we have decided to *threaten* our fellow-citizens which is an ethically negative action in general (projecting a rather insulting image of man[4] and giving up on the attempt to convince) and second, because the prospect of a punishment of some sort has been held out, we have become obliged to actually inflict the pain when the conditions which allow that have been fulfilled. The actual imposition of that punishment becomes an essential element of the experience that justice is done. That is simply a matter of the criminal justice authorities keeping their word and maintaining a sort of credibility of the threat for those who are aware of it. In the process, we run the risk of dissociating ourselves from the fellow-citizen we punish, especially when we share popular assumptions about crime being conduct of persons ('others') with a criminal identity. But what we may need to do, to be effective in changing conduct, may precisely be the opposite: associating with the culprit.

Performatively, should we have trusted that our threat would *prevent* crime from happening, the realized offence suggests that we clearly have failed to do so, and by imposing the punishment we promised we would impose, we all know that this will probably exacerbate the problems of the offender and his social network, especially when we impose prison-sentences which have the strong tendency to (inter)subjectively confirm criminal identities and prolong criminal lifestyles. But, unfortunately, we must do what we promised. And we should and often do realize that this will undermine our initial endeavor to stimulate 'good conduct'. Even if we decide not to impose a prison-sentence, because we feel that the offender is able to learn, shows signs of conventional morality and could

[4] Once described by the Dutch psychiatrist Trimbos (1963) as projecting a 'primitive mentality in all those, on who the fear of punishment should have an effect'. This projection in its consequences implies the necessity to cultivate this fear and to promote such a primitive mentality.

effectively be helped, we are in a position in which our offerings will all *have to have* the content and meaning of some sort of infliction of pain: even in our 'alternative sanctions' something of a *hard treatment* has to be built in, so as not to be seen as an undeserved reward.

2. Reasonable Doubts

Apart from the fact that the deterrence model presupposes a special unworldly kind of psychology in human beings – in the words of the Dutch legal scholar Pompe (1928: 4) 'bourgeois with great inclination to calculate and with few passions' – there are sociological reasons why it works so badly that we can conclude that it does not work at all. To remain in the interactional and interpretative approach we are using here we can refer to an interesting article by Thomas Mathiesen (1994), who discussed general prevention as a form of communication and analysed how and why this communication is weak and even failing. This fact, in his view, explains why the results of research into the reality of general prevention are so inconclusive and contradictory.

As already indicated above the theory of deterrence presupposes a simple and direct communication between senders and receivers of messages (conveying approval or disapproval) in a simple, unequivocal and relatively surveyable situation like a nuclear family or a classroom. These situations do exist in societies of course, but society itself does not have that character and does not conform to that situational condition.

If we consider the criminal justice system as a system of authoritative signification, it is embedded in the wider politics of signification that the state entertains, which is 'exercised in a long string of institutional contexts' implying that even the one-way communication (the sending of the message) may go wrong and fail. As Mathiesen (1994: 224) demonstrates, legislative changes in the sanction levels and developments in the sentencing practices of courts thought to have general preventive effects are simply too subtle and too much part and parcel of the everyday routine of criminal policy to be picked up and received by the addressees with a meaning corresponding to that of the senders.

The penal law, announcing punishment as a carrier of meaning may not reach certain members of the audience (supposedly watching carefully that and how their fellow is punished), and if it reaches them, the message will be interpreted against the background of their own symbolic understanding of the world. Communication is not a one-way process: the meaning of punishment or any other message has to be *recreated* by those who receive it and can only be recreated in the way the sender has meant it if there really is a *common* symbolic understanding (Mathiesen 1994: 222).

Moreover, as we all know, the chance of detection of and apprehension for a breach of the law is of much greater importance for effectively influencing behavior than the normative message itself. With modern technology we can sometimes enhance the chances of getting caught.

The starkest example of general deterrence I know from experience is the Rotterdam Maastunnel (a tunnel under the Maas river) that was a racing track for many years but which is now intensively camera-controlled: a driver exceeding the maximum speed of exactly 50 km per hour is guaranteed to be flashed and receive a fine. In this context it appears to be enough for *some* drivers to adjust their speed in order to avoid a fine, to create a situation in which *all* drivers constantly 'abide by the law'. It is not allowed to change lanes and if you did you would end up in a row of cars driving the same speed below 50 km an hour. The tunnel-traffic is now perhaps the only traffic in Rotterdam with almost 100% compliance. Perhaps other parts of camera-supervised roads and streets also show high levels of compliance, but the important point to note is that the normative message (the speed-limit) is enforced with technical means that seem to guarantee almost a 100% chance of detection and punishment, for those parts that are under camera-surveillance. In my living region routine users of the road system know exactly where the camera's are and step on the gas – for whatever reasons – as long and as soon as they are out of reach of these detection instruments. In general they will drive safely – even if only for their own sake – but not necessarily following each and every rule. These observations tell us that even when people are fully aware of normative expectations they are dealing with these norms differentially and flexibly according to the context and, one must add, according to the priorities of their day: if one is perhaps already too late for an important appointment one may decide to break the law and pay the fine. And taking this risk, the driver may discover that in fact the camera was inactive (which they often are).

If even in this domain of – one may say superficial kind of – conduct that is easy to survey the behavioral influence is so momentary, temporary and uncertain, why and how could we hope for a decisive influence (by the penal threat alone) on more deeply rooted and emotionally invested conduct, that is subjectively expressive of great ambitions, deep frustrations, jealousy, anger, hate, love, wanting to belong etc.?

Contrary to conventional deterrence research, that was situated at the macro-level and abstracted from subjective interpretations, *perceptual* deterrence research – which looks at the interpretative micro-cosmos of the individual – has shown the decisive importance of what a person expects to achieve (Kleemans 2001; Moerland 1991): these subjectively expected results are *biographically* determined and can simply not be known objectively and beforehand (as the classical criminal law theory of deterrence presumes).

As Mathiesen (1994: 231) argues, a large part of an average population has committed – sometimes serious – criminal acts, and we might also concur to Maruna's observation that the 'true criminal' whose life consists of committing crime and only crime everyday does in reality not exist (Maruna 2001: 44).

Both the 'law-abiding citizen' and the 'true criminal' are social stereotypes without much empirical support and in many ways crime is a normal, everyday thing. However, says Mathiesen: 'we also know that those who remain criminally active, and who recidivate frequently and who end up with long-term sentences in our prisons, show an accumulation of indices of social and personal problems – alcohol use, poor education, family disruption etc. (...) when facing people with such a complex and problematic background, a background which, as a life context, increases the probability of criminal behavior, the preventive effect of punishment is also neutralized. Put briefly and in bold relief: general prevention functions in relation to those who do not 'need' it. In relation to those who 'need' it, it does not function' (Mathiesen 1994: 231).

In terms of communication-sociology: 'With a background in complex problems related to alcohol, family life, work situation and educational situation, which together constitute the relevant sign structure or context of interpretation, the signal [*of possible punishment, jrb*] is not interpreted as a (threat of a) deterrent sanction or an educational message. Rather, it is for example interpreted as more oppression, more moralizing and more rejection' (Mathiesen 1994: 231).[5]

3. The Production of Criminal Identities: Not Just Collateral Damage

Would it not be more realistic to say that we write legal prohibitions because we expect the proscribed conduct to happen rather than to expect that we prevent it by proscribing it?

Would sentencing authorities not be more free and able to respond to the real qualities and dimensions of the criminal conduct and its victimizing consequences if they were liberated from the myth of general deterrence? Is this illusion of general deterrence not one of the most important factors in our international trends towards ever higher sentencing levels? Another cause is the desire to incapacitate through longer periods of detention.

But apart from the fact that general deterrence is not a very realistically conceived model of influencing conduct of citizens, there are high costs

[5] It is especially the last named experience: rejection, that needs our further attention in the sense that restorative justice attempts to censure the harmful conduct without communicating a moral rejection of the person of the perpetrator. To the contrary, a structural and cultural attempt is made to not let the act define the actor. See most notably J. Braithwaite's works including Crime, Shame and Reintegration (1989).

involved. One of the main, and generally acknowledged, problems of criminal justice are the high rates of recidivism. According to the latest fact sheet (2009-5) relating figures of 2006 recidivism has decreased in the Netherlands for the first time since 1997. Of the convicted adult perpetrators in general 28,2% was prosecuted again within two years after conviction; importantly however, of those who were put in prison 54,1% relapsed within a period of two years. Juveniles who were detained in Juvenile (offender) Institutions showed a prevalence of recidivism of 58,2% after having been 60% for a long number of years.

Disregarding this fact implies disregarding the costs of future victimizations, that might be avoided by sanctioning in ways that avoid stigmatization and structural des-integration (or negative integration) of offenders.

That stigma and negative social integration hang together has been made clear by the sociology of deviance. It was argued, that many young perpetrators become shunted on the track of a criminal career in the process of reacting on their first offence(s). The secondary deviances resulting from the reaction on primary deviance are explained as the outcome of a successful labeling of the culprit as a true criminal. Successful labeling implies, on the one hand the firm establishment of a person's criminal identity in the social world, on the other hand an adjustment of the self-image of the perpetrator and of his perspective on the social world in which he will be 'a criminal'. The secondary deviant is a person whose life and identity are organized around the facts of deviance (Lemert 1972: 63). In the famous Dutch school of thought about criminal law called the 'Utrecht School' this idea was already brought forward as early as 1954 by its leading scholar Pompe, who defined the criminal person as someone who has not only committed a crime *but also* develops afterwards such a close relation to that crime that his whole personality is changed and built around that misdeed (Pompe, 1954:168 my translation): 'A perpetrated crime is a burden for the perpetrator.' And, in Pompe's view, 'He could liberate himself from that burden' if he and us – if we all – consider punishment as the road to redemption. Unfortunately, as Pompe also notices, the criminal procedure and the punishment do not liberate and redeem the offender, but most often they 'nail the offender to his crime', strengthening the psychological and defining bond between actor and act.

As a consequence of the successful labeling of a person as criminal, legal opportunities to achieve legitimate aims in life (f.i. an official job) are blocked by distrusting members of 'law-abiding' society, making it easier for the stigmatized person to pursue a criminal, rather than a non-criminal career.

Although sociology of deviance and its theories of how the criminal is a product of an elaborated social process was rather popular for a short time in the 1970s its influence seems to have waned from the beginning of the 1980s, only to return with the development of restorative justice and the growing interest in sanctions that 'really work'. In epistemological terms sociology of deviance is an expression of a relatively new (phenomenological) image of man which is more realistic and more adequate for dealing with our problem than the two ontological images of man that seem to have been dominant respectively in the classic school (the indeterministic image of the basically immoral and selfish homo economicus) and the modern school (the deterministic view of man as a puppet animated by unconscious cause-effect relations) (Ter Heide 1965).

It is the phenomenological image of man being open to the world (Glastra van Loon 1957 and 1980; Ter Heide 1965; Van Haersolte 1970), in constant interaction with other social actors, developing his identity through social interactions in concrete social settings with specific social meanings attached to them. The essentialist objectivity of the social world has been replaced by a view on social reality as an intersubjective reality, produced and maintained by processes of externalization, objectivation and internalization of meaning (Berger and Luckmann 1966). The world that presents itself as objectively there, is in fact constantly reproduced by us, by our thoughts and actions.

4. How Restorative Justice Could Help...

The process of attributing and accepting a criminal identity is concluded and ritually confirmed by the demonstrative punishment of the culprit. He is considered to have consciously and deliberately done a wrong that he is not allowed to repair and for which he will suffer, *because we promised that.* He is robbed of his other 'selfs' and acquires the dominant social status of the criminal. Even if he does restore the damages of the victim it has little relevance for his supposed debts toward society. He is caught in a career that he will find fully prepared for him, he will find *he is expected to relapse*: that is what makes the true criminal. But as Maruna (2001: 166) claims: 'Essentially, societies that do not believe that offenders can change, will get offenders who do not believe that they can change.'

If the criminal is a *social production*, produced by the existence of a 'virtual criminal identity' which is attributed to concrete individuals in the process of criminal conviction (becoming convinced of their criminal identity), it would be a transformation of justice when criminal connotations are not anymore in play, or their meanings fundamentally changed, or their scope of application drastically limited. Since many of our convicted offenders relapse, and many often, theoretically safety and security would be served greatly by such a transformation. And it could all be arranged under the rule of law, as many legislatures have already demonstrated even though the application of restorative justice seems to remain too marginal. It seems to me that the main reasons for this marginal and often frail existence and discontinuity of restorative practices – even where they have independently been evaluated positively – relate to penal populism and the widespread belief in general (and specific) deterrence.

If we can accept that penalization for the reason of deterrence appears to be dysfunctional, there will no longer be a perceived necessity to make true the threat of punishment and we can begin to reorganize our criminal justice systems much more fundamentally (Blad 2010). On the one hand we can look for sanctioning arrangements that avoid or even counteract the social production of criminal identities and on the other hand we can see whether we can do victims more and a better service by offering them a more fundamental role.

Whether it is correct or not to claim, as Van Dijk (2006) does, that the origins of the penal law lie in the concept of 'penos' – which does not mean pain or punishment but compensation – nothing would stand in the way of making reparation, restitution and compensation much more central in our justice interventions if we did away with the myth of general deterrence. And we still would perform all the functions that Mathiesen (1994: 221) aptly ascribes to punishment: retribution, moral education and habit formation. The latter two functions we might call 'positive general prevention': it is indeed in all respects positive to have types of interventions that communicate effectively the type of relations and interactions that we would like to see entertained by our citizens: horizontal, equal relations ruled by reciprocity. And when this equality and reciprocity is breached and damaged by the 'high-handedness' of an offense, the offender should have the primary obligation to set things right and to make amends. Doing this in a morally acceptable way, as both Duff (2001) and Walgrave (2008) have argued (but in a different way with different implications), can be understood as retribution.

In all definitions of restorative justice making the offender accountable for his offence and urging him to make amends and repair the damage done (to the extent possible) feature and victim-offender-mediation and conferencing are the two primary and mostly used procedural interventions of criminal justice. Conferencing should be prioritized whenever feasible, because of the much richer input you get when the deliberations involve many (significant) others both in terms of communicating the normative message that what the offender has done is unacceptable *and* in terms of proposing and finding ways to address both the various harmful consequences and the criminogenic needs. As is the case in a number of countries, these procedures should and often will lead to realistic restorative plans, intersubjectively acceptable to the participants, to be independently scrutinized by justice officials with regard to their fairness[6] and

6 The concept of fairness is deliberately preferred here above the concept of proportionality, because restorative agreements are fundamentally a figure of private law that is introduced into the criminal procedure. In this sense it is comparable to the civil claim that

conformity with the law. The restorative obligations that the offender accepts will have to be complied with and function as the core sanction, if necessary with some supplementary sanction *imposed* later by judicial authorities.

In such arrangements the victim and his rights, needs and interests regain a fundamental importance, both in procedure and in sanctioning the offender. Both are procedurally and culturally *empowered* to address the consequences of what happened and to experience a certain level of control over their futures. This is essential in view of the victim's feelings of having been overpowered by the offender and the offenders feelings oscillating between denial and taking responsibility but not knowing how (Mooren 2001; Bastiaensen 2000). The offender is offered a way to deny any suggestion that he might be a criminal and to focus – perhaps for the first time – on someone else – his victim –, take on the role and perspective of 'the other' and discover the deeper moral and social implications of his high-handedness. Crucially, in the approach of restorative justice the opposite of 'deviant-smithing' is happening: 'normal-smithing' as Maruna called it in reference to Lofland: 'Communicate to him the message that, despite what Actor thinks of himself, despite what normal and deviant others think of him, there lurks within him – underneath, after all, essentially – a core of being that is normal' (Maruna 2001: 140). Only within such an approach conditions can be created in which the offender could allow others into his deepest thoughts, his internal dialogue, the personal source of his life script (Jonckheere 2009).

By taking on restorative duties the offender can not only show that he wants to dissociate himself from his misdoing, by complying with his obligations he himself learns he can do something good, which would allow him to believe a bit more in his 'normal self'. As Maruna shows redemption is about 'learning through doing, and becoming transformed as a result.' Making wooden cupboards in a prison is given as an example: 'You can't teach people self-esteem. These pine shelves and cabinets (made by ex-offenders in a reintegration-program's woodwork training) are the vehicles for self-esteem' (op.cit.: 155). Another example may be doing meaningful work for the victim and the community.

Having been censured for their offence, the offenders can be praised for their making amends and for the positive turn that they seem to be making. New Zealand youth justices are doing precisely that in court sessions after the completion of a set of restorative obligation, checked in court as a final moment in the procedure. This functions as the kind of 'reintegration ceremony' that Maruna considers of importance to strengthen the process of going straight: it must be certified in some way for the process to gain momentum. 'Some

---

a victim can introduce into the criminal procedure, according to Dutch criminal procedural law. Also this claim should be scrutinized with private law criteria.

recognized members of the conventional community must publicly announce and certify that the offender has changed and that he/she is now to be considered essentially non-criminal' (Maruna 2001: 159).

For the sample in the LDS the redemption took more or less place through *unsuccessful degradation* ceremonies: 'Groups of friends, intimates, and conventional others publicly testified on the desisting person's behalf, leading an agent of social control to formally acknowledge the ex-offenders change in behavior.' The interaction was unprecedented and unanticipated, merited and formal (op.cit.: 159). 'All three narrators knew that they were "trying". They were making some progress toward staying straight. Yet, none of them had any confidence that this effort would aid them in any way in the eyes of society. Recall that desisting ex-offenders still generally view the world as unfair and assume that the deck is always stacked against them. Suddenly and unexpectedly, though, there is justice. They have done well, and someone actually "believes in them"'(op.cit.: 161).

The psychological impact of these rituals may be even more important than the social: 'They realize, for what they claim is "the first time" in their lives, that they have some control over their own destinies.' This is a newfound control and one that carries on to other aspects of their lives. They now experience 'They have the ability to act positively and be rewarded for it' (op.cit.: 161).

What I have discussed so far in this paragraph is that restorative justice has the potential to sanction in ways that do not communicate and affix a criminal identity to offenders and in this way a lot of the criminogenic damage that is done by the traditional punitive system can be avoided. Also the victims can be served better and experience more justice when restorative programs are run well. A final point that I want to bring forward about the qualities of restorative procedures is that they offer ways to work more realistically and more effectively on the causes of the offending behavior. That is to say, in the process of being held accountable the offender is not only confronted with his responsibility for the harm and damages done, but often also questioned about how his conduct came about and what seems to be problematic in his life in so far as it contributed to his wrong behavioral choices. I am not saying that this always happens, but I would propose that some attention to the backgrounds of offending behavior should be given and – when appropriate and possible – activities should be included in restorative plans to address serious causative problem-areas ('criminogenic needs') such as forms of addiction, unaddressed earlier failures (such as having dropped out of school, not having been able to find a job etc.) and structural problems in the family-context. This type of activities often are included in restorative plans and make sense both in helping the offender to address unresolved problems that seem to stand in the way of a positive integration into conventional society and in *preventing further victimizations*: something participating victims often express as something they would like to see coming out of the restorative meeting. Support and monitoring tasks can be assigned in the same restorative plan and when professional aid and consultations are needed also these can be planned and function more adequately and truly 'demand-driven'. The offender should also in this respect be stimulated to take a leading responsibility, not 'to be rehabilitated' but to *rehabilitate himself*, to recover from the explicit or implicit damages done to his own life-perspectives and to give a new direction to his personal biography.

In that last respect there is a link again with Maruna's book, that pleads for building in forms of narrative therapy, that encourages 'rebiographing' to develop more liberating life-stories: 'Therapy must teach people write the scripts or their future instead of reading it as an unchangeable blueprint of life plans' (Maruna 2001: 140). This is important because 'despite the individualistic bias and tone of explanations for desistance, the change process, like the process of juvenile involvement in crime, is a social and interactional one' (Maruna 2001: 154).

As they stand today, the results of investigations about the effectiveness of restorative justice procedures for preventing crime are rather promising. Nowhere restorative justice does worse than traditional criminal justice and many programs have consistently shown better results (Morris & Maxwell 2001; Walgrave 2006; Sherman & Strang 2007).

Strikingly, the three programs identified by Sherman and Strang (2007: 74 a.f) as counterproductive were schemes, in which some element of subjectively experienced disrespect or distrust seems to have been prevalent, inducing forms of *defiance* that can also be noticed in traditional criminal justice. It fits the symbolic-interactionist analysis developed in this article that fundamentally respecting the offender as a person would enhance the effect of our endeavor to make him accountable.

Sanction Cocktails and Depenalisation

In terms of sanctioning the development of restorative justice and its integration into the criminal justice system – as exemplified f.i. in the New Zealand youth justice system – many of the obligations that are established in the restorative agreements are equivalents to 'traditional' non-custodial sanctions (community sanctions, financial compensation orders etc.), but importantly they are not *imposed* by the courts but *proposed by the parties involved and based on their interests*, and the courts may and do sometimes supplement these obligations with other sanction elements, *considered necessary in the general interest*, all of which are presumably of a non-custodial nature. So what arises is a praxis of establishing 'sanction cocktails' with a primary focus on restoration and reparation in a differently organized procedure, with different participants and, crucially, avoiding the use of imprisonment with its totalizing effects on disintegration and criminal status. So what we are witnessing is a very new strategy of *depenalisation* (Council of Europe, 1980), which is important because of the necessity of avoiding the social production of criminal identities and future victimizations by ex-prisoners (and of course other social and economic costs). Depending on the scope of offences that will be allocated to this 'new' restorative justice department within the criminal justice system what could be achieved is an important level of *decarceration* – in New Zealand the population detainees in juvenile institutions has decreased with approximately 75% – making possible a shift of public expenditure to activities which are more fundamentally preventive of crime because they can enhance the general quality of life, such as family care and – support and better schools.[7]

5. Brief Summary and Conclusion

The criminal law addresses a certain construct of the subject, in which the subject is reduced to a legal entity who is aware of his being a legal subject (bearer of subjective rights and subjected to law). The anthropological assumptions of the classical criminal law are however outdated and wrong. For, as we all know, subjective reality is much more complex and multi-dimensional and awareness of the law and its implications is generally absent or marginal. Even if some awareness of the legal context is there, there is no way of knowing what this awareness implies. It may have been neutralized or turned into a challenge. Practically, the most important claim I want to make here is that it is of great importance that – in general – people break the law as a consequence of what they perceive – from within their (for others beforehand unknowable) biographical situation – as the best ways to achieve what they are trying to achieve. They will generally have made a variety of mistakes (either in choosing their aims or in their methods) if they have broken the law and they may have caused serious damages and harm in their activities, for which they should be held accountable. Their best choice was our worst and they should learn to behave better. But if the deeper rationale for our criminal justice system lies in the desire to protect society ('ourselves') against crime, we should think again about our strategies to achieve that protection. What we should not want to do is actually produce the criminals that we have to protect ourselves from. So in holding people accountable for their breaking the law, we should not provide them with the motives to see and accept themselves as the 'criminals' that general culture portrays as the perpetrators of crime.

The popularized ideas about the possibly positive behavioral effects of deterrence, that penal populists capitalize on, amount to an important blockade

---

7 In a recent article (Blad 2010) I developed a proposal to reorganize the substantive criminal law into four categories of offences. Those which are restorable only and not punishable, those which are in principle restorable but also punishable as must be, those which are in principle punishable but might also be restorable if the parties so wish, and those which are only punishable.

against making real progress in our criminal justice interventions. What I have tried to demonstrate is the *interactional strait-jacket* in which deterrence places everyone in the system having to deal with offences and offenders.

Hulsman – building upon sociology of deviance and labeling theory – was right in claiming that we need an anascopic approach to understanding criminal conduct to develop new ideas about how to respond to it more adequately. In restorative procedures we are able to organize attention for and nearness to the real biographies – their 'times' and 'spaces' - of offenders and victims, through their own language and their own conceptions of what is really important. These biographies can become reconnected to the legal order by acknowledging these expressed needs and interests in a tailored legal response. The procedures and aims of restorative justice *could* facilitate much more realistic and responsive sanctioning than those of conventional criminal justice, which in effect predominantly seem to facilitate criminal careers by producing symbolic and real impediments to (positive) reintegration. Impediments, as Maruna has demonstrated, that are often too hard to overcome.

References

Bastiaensen, R. (2000). Aanzet tot reflectie omtrent grondwoorden van de herstelgerichte praxis: 'verbondenheid' en 'verantwoordelijkheid'. In T. Peters (Ed.), *Herstelgerichte detentie. Van Actie-onderzoek naar Beleidsvoering* (bijlage 2). Leuven: Katholieke Universiteit van Leuven.

Beccaria, C. (1764). *Dei Delitti e delle Pene*. As translated by J.M. Machielse (1971) Over Misdaden en Straffen (tweede druk). Antwerpen: Kluwer Rechtswetenschappen/Zwolle: Tjeenk Willink.

Bentham, J. (1802). *The Theory of Legislation*. As introduced and presented by Upendra Baxi (1975). Bombay: N.M. Tripathi /New York: Dobbs Ferry.

Berger, P., & Luckmann, T. (1966). *The Social Construction of Reality*. Middlesex: Penguin Books.

Blad, J. (2005). Deprivatisering van veiligheidszorg en de nieuwe dominantie van het publiekrecht. De burger als functionaris van de veiligheidsstaat. In L.C. Winkel, J.J.M. Jansen, H.O. Kerkmeester, R.J.P. Kottenhagen, & V. Mul (red.), *Privatisering van veiligheid* (pp. 21-38). Den Haag: Boom Juridische uitgevers.

Blad, J. (2010). More Conciliation, Less Punishment: Demanding a Public Choice. *(e-)Journal for Law and Conflict Resolution, Vol. 2 (5)* 80-90.

Braithwaite, J. (1989). *Crime, Shame and Reintegration*. Cambridge: Cambridge University Press.

Burris, S., Drahos, P., & Shearing, C. (2005). Nodal Governance. *Australian Journal of Legal Philosophy*, *30*, 30-58.

Claessen, J. (2010). *Misdaad en straf. Een herbezinning op het strafrecht vanuit een mystiek perspectief*. Nijmegen: Wolf Legal Publishers.

Council of Europe (1980). *Report on Decriminalisation*. Straatsburg.

Dijk, J.J.M. van (2006). *The Mark of Abel; Reflections on the Social Labeling of Victims of Crime*. Inaugural lecture Tilburg: Intervict.

Duff, R.A. (2001). *Punishment, Communication and Community*. Oxford: Oxford University Press.

Glastra van Loon, J.F. (1957). *Norm en Handeling*. Groningen: Wolters Noordhof.

Glastra van Loon, J.F. (1980). Recht en menselijke natuur. In J.F. Glastra van Loon (Ed.), *De eenheid van het handelen* (35-56). Amsterdam: Boom uitgevers.

Haersolte, R.A.V. Baron van (1970). Een nieuw rechtstheoretisch klimaat. In *Handelingen van de Vereniging voor Wijsbegeerte, LIV, part one (3-25)*. Zwolle: Tjeenk Willink.

Heide, J. ter (1965). *Vrijheid. Over de zin van de straf.* Den Haag: Bakker/Daamen.

Hulsman, L. (1986). Critical Criminology and the Concept of Crime. *Contemporary Crisis, 10*, 63-80.

Jonckheere, A.M. (2009). Justitiepastoraat en 'herstel': een poging tot positiebepaling. *Tijdschrift voor Herstelrecht, (9) 4*, 26-40.

Kleemans, E. (2001). Rationale keuzebenaderingen. In E. Lissenberg, S. van Ruller, & R. van Swaaningen (red.), *Tegen de regels IV. Een inleiding in de criminologie* (pp. 153-170). Nijmegen: Ars Aequi Libri.

Lemert, E.M. (1972). *Human Deviance, Social Problems and Social Control* (second edition). Englewood Cliffs, N.J.: Prentice Hall.

Maruna, S. (2001). *Making Good: How Ex-Convicts Reform and Rebuild their Lives*. e-book. Wolters Kluwer.

Mathiesen, T. (1994). General Prevention as Communication. In R.A. Duff, & D. Garland (Eds.), *A Reader on Punishment* (pp.218-237). Oxford: Oxford University Press.

Moerland, H. (1991). *Winkeldiefstal, een te riskante zaak?* Arnhem: Gouda Quint.

Mooren, H. (2001). Recht maken wat krom is. Herstelbemiddeling in het perspectief van zingeving. *Tijdschrift voor Herstelrecht, (1) 2*, 26-37.

Morris, A., & Maxwell G. (2001). Restorative Justice for Juveniles. Oxford-Portland Oregon: Hart Publishing.

Packer, H.L. (1968). *The Limits of the Criminal Sanction*. Stanford: Stanford University Press.

Pompe, W.P.J. (1928). *De persoon des daders in het strafrecht*. Inaugural lecture Utrecht University. Zwolle: Tjeenk Willink.

Pompe, W.P.J. (1954). De misdadige mens. *Tijdschrift voor Strafrecht*, 153-171.

Quinn, W. (1995). The Right to Threaten and the Right to Punish. In A.J. Simmons, M. Cohen, J. Cohen, & C.R. Betz (Eds.), *Punishment* (pp. 47-93). Princeton, New Jersey: Princeton University Press.

Schuilenburg, M. (2009). De securisering van de samenleving. Over de relatie tussen veiligheidszorg, bestuur en quasistrafrecht. *Krisis*, *3*, 6-22.

Sherman, L.W., & Strang, H. (2007). *Restorative Justice: the Evidence*. Report for The Smith Institute, London.

Trimbos, C.J.B. (1963). Straf en rechtspraak. In: *Misdaad zonder straf* (pp. 9-31). Utrecht/Antwerpen: Spectrum.

Vervaele, J. (1990). *Rechtsstaat en recht tot straffen*. Antwerpen: Kluwer/Arnhem: Gouda Quint.

Walgrave, L. (2006). Herstelrecht: internationaal evaluatieonderzoek. *Tijdschrift voor Herstelrecht, (6) 2*, 9-21.

Walgrave, L. (2008). Restorative Justice, Self Interest and Responsible Citizenship. Devon: Willan Publishing.

WODC (2009). *Recidivemonitor* Factsheet 2009-5. Den Haag.

9. Doing Restorative Justice to Beccaria's Dream. Roads to Reconciliation and Realization of Prevention, Retribution, Restorative Justice and the Rule of Law

Hendrik Kaptein

1. Introduction

As noted before, the title of Beccaria's famous book on crimes and punishments is about as often quoted as its contents go unread, apart from standard reference to its brief conclusion (ch. 47, p. 113, all quotations here from the Bellamy edition, 1995, italics original):

> '*In order that punishment shall not be an act of violence perpetrated by one or many upon a private citizen, it is essential that it should be public, speedy, necessary, the minimum possible in the given circumstances, proportionate to the crime, and determined by the law.*'

Lots of lip-service notwithstanding even this fundamental injunction is well-known to go more or less unheeded in the actual administration of criminal justice, even in so-called civilized jurisdictions. In academia Beccaria's work did not fare that well either. More or less scholarly discussion is generally limited to reformist lip service and standard criticism of Beccaria's presumably utilitarian emphasis upon general prevention and its supposed incompatibility with human equality and retributive justice. Again, such discussion seems to be unconnected to Beccaria's main text at times indeed.[1]

More interesting for now are important parts of Beccaria's conception of criminal law and punishment that seem to have escaped both practical and academic attention. Thus an attempt will be made here to reinterpret and improve upon Beccaria's ideas of penal servitude, with an eye on reinterpretation of retribution as reparation and attendant reform of the administration of criminal justice. Indeed Beccaria advocates life-long penal servitude as the main and most effective kind of punishment for serious offences (ch. 28).

Elsewhere (notably so in chs. 22 and 34) Beccaria considers the usefulness of penal servitude not just in terms of deterrence, but also in terms of redress of harm done to society or even to individual creditors. Indeed – and sometimes forgotten – '*retribuere*' means: 'to pay back', 'to compensate', 'to restitute', 'to redress' and so on. Thus Beccaria's often assumed anti-retributivism may not be

1 See also Bellamy ed., 1995, pp. ix v., not much seems to have changed here since then.

such a simple matter as it seems. His emphasis on social engineering may be compatible with fruitful reinterpretation of retribution, not as infliction of pain in the first place but as offenders' restoration of harm done in as far as feasible.

Discussion of this will here proceed as follows. Next there is a brief outline of Beccarian main lines in as far as relevant for the issue of retribution as reparation, stressing his thoughts on the importance of proportionality and subsidiarity in the administration of criminal justice and punishment, as nowadays expressed in terms of 'nodal governance' or otherwise. Then there is discussion of Beccaria's ideas on penal servitude as retributive reparation. On things go with further development of Beccarian ideas on retribution into civilized criminal law, offering reparation not just for society but also for specific victims of crime. Penal servitude is shown to be superior to the pain of punishment anyway. In the end it is argued that there is no conflict between prevention and retribution suitably reinterpreted as undoing consequences of crime in principle. The need for subsidiarity and reform of criminal law and punishment remains pressing, both on behalf of legal security for crime victims and in order to do away with the pain of punishment as infliction of pain.

2. Beccaria Reconsidered

Beccaria's theory of criminal law and punishment is generally depicted as science and utility oriented, social contract based and egalitarian, forward looking, focusing on general prevention, and generally optimistic.[2] Broadly correct as this is, a couple of issues need to be briefly discussed in order to pave the way for introduction of retribution to be further developed on the basis of Beccaria's theory of crimes and punishments.

Beccaria's mechanistic psychology is a case in point. Though rather common in his times and even found in Kant's moral and political theories, such psychology still is important for an understanding of his conceptions of criminal law and punishment. Desires, wants, motives and intentions are depicted as forces acting in different directions. Human conduct is regarded as the result of summation and cancellation of forces brought about by such psychic factors. Thus desires, wants, motives and intentions may be directly compared to, or may even be regarded to come down to natural causes, the effects of which may be exactly calculated in principle. Thus Beccaria wrote (in ch. 6, p. 19):

> 'It is impossible to foresee all the mischiefs which arise from the universal struggle of the human emotions. They multiply at a compound rate with the growth of population and with the criss-crossing of private interests, which cannot be geometrically directed towards the public utility. In political arithmetic, we must substitute the calculus of probabilities for mathematical exactitude.'

[2] See Kaptein (1997) offering a more or less adequate outline for Dutch readers.

This interesting paradox is not so simply solved by any legislator and public administrator, not even in limited application of this kind of calculus to criminal justice (ch. 6, pp. 19 v.)

> 'That force which attracts us, like gravity, to our own good can be controlled only by equal and opposite obstacles. The effects of this force are the whole confused gamut of human actions; if these interfere with and obstruct each other, then the punishments, which we may call *political obstacles*, eliminate their evil effects, without destroying the moving cause, which is the very sensibility inalienable from man's nature. And the legislator behaves like the skilled architect, whose task it is to counteract the destructive forces of gravity and to exploit those forces that contribute to the strengthening of the building.'

This approximation of the idea or even optimistically scientific ideal of *l'homme machine* is a presupposition of Beccaria's ideas on exact calculation of amounts of punishments to be meted out against different crimes. The expectation of punishment is just one more force influencing courses of action and thus such force, or different forces related to different kinds of more or less serious crime, should generally outweigh forces driving to misconduct as clearly defined by criminal law.

This also relates to Beccaria's utility oriented approach of criminal law. If happiness is the result of harmonious satisfaction of wants and desires, the administration of criminal justice and public administration in general for that matter ought to create conditions under which all members of society are optimally encouraged to abstain from crime, at a price not so high as to outdo the gains realized by rational administration of criminal justice and public administration in general.

Thus regarded the administration of criminal justice is part of a public administration directed to the construction of a better human future. Governing human motivation and conduct in order to create a less criminal and generally happier society is predominant, then. Indeed Beccaria's normative orientation is mechanistically utilitarian, as beautifully expressed in ch. 23, p. 55 (see on this also Bellamy 1995):

> 'This is the way to avoid muddling the relations and the invariable nature of things, which, being unlimited in time and perpetually operative, breaks down and overturns any limited regulations which deviate from it. It is not only the arts of taste and pleasure that have faithful imitation of nature as their inevitable principle. Politics itself, when it is true and lasting, is governed by this general rule, since it is nothing but the art of guiding and concerting the immutable sentiments of men.'[3]

Well-known objections against public well-being as the ultimate end relate to the supposed incompatibility of utilitarianism with equality or even justice. Though Beccaria's writings do not really deal with this issue (apart from a rather

3 'Politics' here means 'public administration'.

isolated reference to persons v. things, in ch. 20, see later on here), there may still be an indirect answer. His justification of the state and its coercive powers – no doubt influenced by Rousseau – is based on the idea of a social contract, the terms of which are expressed by laws limiting parties' liberties to the minimum possible extent compatible with freedom for everybody. Parties involved in such a social contract, or in fact all citizens, may not be expected to contract in such a fashion that their own interests may be sacrificed in the name of some or other common good like any highest sum or average of human happiness. Whether this bare minimum of distributive justice solves the problem of utilitarianism v. equality and justice remains to be seen. Adding to this are persistent problems in concepts and conceptions of social contract, Rousseauan or otherwise (see on this Rawls, 1999).

What are 'the happiest forms of punishment', at least according to Beccaria? Contrary to common scholarly opinion Beccaria was not so 'modern' as to advocate detention as the main mode of punishment for serious offences. In fact locking up people is to be used mainly for pre-trial detention and then only if no other adequate means are available. In fact his criticism of detention awaiting trial (in chs. 19 and 29) has lost nothing of its pressing importance, given widespread and persisting misuse both in The Netherlands and abroad.

In a few brief passages Beccaria advocates public shaming (ch. 23), corporal punishment (ch. 20), banishment (ch. 24), imprisonment (ch. 33, mentioned in passing as fairly heavy punishment) and penal servitude (mainly for serious crime, from theft up to murder, see chs. 22 and ch. 28) as the main forms of punishment.

Permanent penal servitude is advocated as superior to the death penalty,[4] at least in terms of prevention, as is vividly described in ch. 28 (p. 68):

> 'Therefore, permanent penal servitude in place of the death penalty would be enough to deter even the most resolute soul: indeed, I would say that it is more likely so. Very many people look on death with a calm and steadfast gaze (...). However, neither fanaticism nor vanity survives in manacles and chains, under the rod and the yoke or in an iron cage; and the ills of the desperate man are not over, but are just beginning.'

In fact Beccaria tries to explain that his preferred forms of punishment are not just optimal from the point of view of prevention, but also more equal than alternative forms of punishment.[5] Thus fines favour the rich – then and now – while corporal punishment hits rich and poor alike. One more advantage of penal servitude is criminals' contribution to society through their own labour. Such penal servitude is less costly than mere imprisonment as well (ch. 22), one more lesson to be learnt yet.

---

4 The death penalty is also opposed by Beccaria on the basis of its supposed incompatibility with the social contract, see again ch. 28.

5 Remember equality of citizens as parties in the social contract, as outlined above.

Indeed Beccaria did not offer anything like a systematic treatment of different kinds of punishments. Schafer (1970) and Foucault (1975) offer more detailed description of 18th century penal servitude and its pains. May such practices have been what Beccaria envisaged as the prime form of punishment for not so petty crime? Discussion of any non-punitive orders is well-nigh absent as well. This may relate not just to the virtual non-existence of psychopathology, let alone forensic psychiatry in Beccaria's days, but also to his scepticism concerning the relevance of *mens rea* for degrees of punishment (see ch. 7).

Still Beccaria was ahead of his – and our – times in advocating confrontational measures against crime. Thus he wrote (in the context of tax fraud, generally deserving 'fairly heavy punishment', ch. 33, p. 88):

> 'For instance, the prison regime of a tobacco smuggler ought not to be the same as that of a hired assassin or a thief, and, to be the most fitting sort of punishment, his work ought to be limited to toil and exertion in the excise service which he wished to defraud.'

Some more use of this insight may be made, not just by making drink and drive offenders (probably a non-issue in Beccaria's times, at least in the administration of criminal justice) clean up first aid units, so that they may gain some impression of possible consequences of their misconduct.

Preventing crime however is not just an issue of adequate punishment, the administration of criminal justice being part of public administration in general. In fact Beccaria stresses the importance of proportionality and subsidiarity as criteria for criminal law and punishment. Some crimes may be better prevented by measures ranging from 'street-lighting at public expense' and 'sober and moral sermons delivered in the silence and sacred peace of churches' (ch. 11, p. 29) to the public and open registration of all contracts (!, ch. 34, p. 90). Some of this sound advice may still be apposite in our times as well.

Indeed this is one more important aspect of Beccaria's theory of criminal law and punishment not always duly taken into account. Thus Johnston & Shearing (2003: ch. 3 and elsewhere) depict Beccaria's conception of crime and punishment as well-nigh exclusively focused on state intervention legitimized by criminal law. Concepts of nodal governance are presented as at least equally important answers to crime, both in preventive and in restorative respects (see among others Shearing 2001). Though Beccaria probably was not yet acquainted with the concept of nodal governance, basic ideas behind it are not at all at odds with his theory of crime and punishment, then.

Again, this is far from a complete overview of Beccaria's theory of criminal law and punishment. So many interesting issues and insights are left out of account here, in order to pave the way for retributive reinterpretation of Beccarian concepts and conceptions of punishment.

3. Rewards of Retributive Reinterpretation (Repairing Beccaria)

Beccaria is generally regarded as anti-retributivist, though his writings may not be very explicit on this issue. In fact his book does not even contain any mention of the concept of retribution, let alone of *lex talionis*. Still the following remarks imply fundamental criticism against the core idea of retribution by infliction of pain as justified by crime itself, as different from justification of punishment in terms of its possibly beneficial consequences (ch. 16, p. 40):

> '(...) the purging of infamy presupposes that pain, which is a sensation, can purge infamy, which is a mere moral relation.'

This is famously echoed by Modderman:[6]

> 'It is evident from the simple considerations set out that the purpose of punishment is not that of tormenting or afflicting any sentient creature, nor of undoing a crime already committed. How can a political body, which as the calm modifier of individual passions should not itself be swayed by passion, harbour this useless cruelty which is the instrument of rage, of fanaticism or of weak tyrants? Can the wailings of a wretch, perhaps, undo what has been done and turn back the clock?'

Anyway, nothing like *fiat justitia pereat mundus*, Kantian or otherwise, is to be found with Beccaria. Thus he stated (again in ch. 16, p. 40):

> 'A misdeed already committed, and for which there can be no redress, need be punished by a political society only when it influences other people by holding out the lure of impunity.'

Beccaria's ideas on penal servitude may appear crude and cruel (as discussed before) but then they may also serve to show that retribution in a different sense is at least implicit in his conception of punishment for a number of serious offences. Thus he writes (ch. 22, p. 53, see also chs. 28 and 34):

> 'Thefts without violence should be punished with fines. Whoever seeks to enrich himself at the expense of others ought to be deprived of his own wealth. But, since this is generally the crime of poverty and desperation, the crime of that unhappy section of men to whom the perhaps "terrible" and "unnecessary" right to property has allowed nothing but a bare existence, (...) the most fitting punishment shall be the only sort of slavery which can be called just, namely the temporary enslavement

6 In 1864, p. 39, at least for Dutch readers: trying to compensate for crime by punishment is like trying to make cloth out of iron. Beccaria also stressed the impossibility of undoing crime (ch. 12, p. 31).

> of the labour and person of the criminal to society, so that he may redress his unjust despotism against the social contract by a period of complete personal subjection.'[7]

Thus Beccaria used the idea of the social contract to 'civilize' crime and punishment in terms of breach of contract and enforced full compensation as remedy for this. Indeed in most cases of crime mere civil law remedies of performance after all or payment of damages will not do. Not just theft, but also murder, manslaughter, grievous bodily assault and serious property crimes other than theft are so many more breaches of social contract, then. Amounts of redress may be more difficult to establish, as loss of life and limbs may be less easily valued than loss as a consequence of theft.

This is no retribution in the sense of *ius talionis* or any other principle relating pain of punishment to seriousness of crime, independent of possible beneficial consequences of punishment. But the idea of penal servitude does relate to retribution in a more original sense, as restitution.[8] Or: offenders are to make good for what they did wrong.

Relationships of such retributivism to social contract conceptions and to contract in general may be clear enough. But even apart from issues of contractual justice in general the idea of a social contract may not be sufficiently plausible to justify punishment as redress. Thus it may be more interesting to inquire into utilitarian considerations as possible backings for punishment as redress and retribution as reparation.

At first sight, retribution not just as infliction of pain but as assigning offenders with any special burden because they are offenders is incompatible with principles of utilitarianism, however differently worked out in detail. The pain experienced by offenders being punished is of no greater or lesser worth in itself than any other pain, experienced by victims of crime or by any sentient beings. So if it would be more generally useful not to make offenders redress their wrongs by their own labour, then there would be no justification for penal servitude. Thus the administration of criminal justice may be more costly than 'solutions' of consequences of crime by civil law remedies to be initiated by victims. Even leaving (some) serious offenders alone and/or paying damages to crime victims by public means may be the best things to do in terms of the public good.

Beccaria's ideas on redress by penal servitude seem as interesting as lacking any real foundation in his general utilitarianism, then. However, human nature and its presumably immutably fixed mechanisms of desires and avoidances may come to the rescue here. Mill, one of Beccaria's posthumous philosophical brothers in arms, expressed fundamentals of this as follows (in 1861, p. 63):

---

7 Again, Rousseau's influence shines through here. Or: Marx is presaged in criticism of property rights, among other things as presuppositions of crimes of theft in more than one respect.

8 '*Retribuere*' indeed means 'to pay back', 'to compensate', 'to restitute', 'to redress' and so on.

> 'We have seen that the two essential ingredients in the sentiment of justice are the desire to punish a person who has done harm and the knowledge or belief that there is some definite individual or individuals to whom harm has been done.
>
> Now it appears to me that the desire to punish a person who has done harm to some individual is a spontaneous outgrowth from two sentiments, both in the highest degree natural and which either are or resemble instincts: the impulse of self-defense and the feeling of sympathy.
>
> It is natural to resent and to repel or retaliate any harm done or attempted against ourselves or against those with whom we sympathize. The origin of this sentiment it is not necessary here to discuss.'

So any calculation of social utility, mathematically rigorous or not, has to take such sentiments of justice into account. Indeed such sentiments are of no higher or lower value than any other sentiments, desires or motives in themselves. Remember that there can be no ranking in terms of moral qualities, or any other qualities apart from contribution to the common good for that matter. But given such sentiments – not found irrational by Mill, in as far as human and social life would be conceivable without them at all – singling out offenders as agents of redress becomes rational from a general utility point of view.

First, offenders must be punished some or other way, or sentiments of justice may not be satisfied. Diminishing sums or averages of utility by pains of punishment may be outweighed by gains in utility through satisfaction of sentiments of justice. For utilitarians such sentiments cannot be of any moral value per se. Still such sentiments may strongly influence utilitarian consideration and its results.

Second, making offenders pay for what they did better contributes to social utility than just making them suffer. Undoing harm for wrong done is better (or better: more useful) than leaving harm as it is, just as mere suffering is rather less useful than penal servitude. The burdens of penal servitude may serve to satisfy sentiments of resentment and justice felt by victims of crime and the general public. Also, and duly stressed by Beccaria, penal servitude may be rather more preventively effective than other forms of punishment (see before).

Beccaria may have wrongly left the distinction between personal and external preferences out of account here. Personal preferences relate to goods and opportunities people want for their own enjoyment, external preferences relate to assignment of goods and opportunities to others. Dworkin (1978: 234 v.) made this distinction in his trenchant criticism of utilitarianism and its inability to categorically distinguish between these two kinds of preferences. Beccaria's application of utilitarianism to the administration of criminal justice however may well gain by paying attention to sentiments of justice leading to external preferences. Oddly enough Beccaria does discuss gratitude, one more external preference, as an important condition for social cohesion (ch. 26), but indeed leaves its ressentimental counterparts out of account.

Please note that this attempt to reconcile prevention and retribution is rather different from other attempts in terms of retribution as infliction of pain in the first place. Thus Rawls (1955), Hart (1959) and Benn (1967) among others developed justifications of punishment in terms of general utility and retribution *in casu*. Interpretation of Beccaria in such terms was attempted by Young (1983) and Bellamy (1995) again among others. Such reconciliatory interpretation may founder both Beccaria's at least implicitly strong objections against and indeed the general implausibility of retribution as infliction of pain for that matter (see on this Kaptein, 2004).

4. Beyond Beccaria: Retribution as Civilized Restorative Justice Serving Legal Security

Still, Beccaria's plea for punishment as redress may not be very firmly backed by act or even rule utilitarianism after all. Act utilitarianism requiring calculation of all interests at stake in all specific cases may well lead to very different reactions to crime, ranging from doing nothing to letting victims and the general public do with real or supposed perpetrators whatever suits vengeful sentiments.[9] Even rule utilitarianism, requiring design and enforcement of rules in the service of general utility, may not inexorably lead to meaningful penal servitude as the main kind of punishment for serious crime. In the end, it is all a matter of complex calculation of so many ressentimental and other forces, with uncertain outcomes at best.[10]

Also, resentment has rather negative connotations. Immoderate resentment and its concomitant external preferences against real or supposed offenders may lead to inappropriately harsh punishment, according to utilitarian calculation or otherwise. This makes one think of Beccaria's own brief but vivid description of penal servitude and its cruelties (as cited before).

But then there is a rather different and more meaningful relationship between what me be called rational resentment and answers to crime in terms of retribution as reparation. Results of this will appear to be not just compatible with Beccaria's ideas on penal servitude and redress, though their realisation will appear to be rather less cruel in the first place. Retribution as reparation may even be regarded as a logical next step in the development of Beccaria's reformative ideas.

Main lines of this may be developed as follows. In his justifiably famous 1962 essay, Strawson argued against 'hard' determinism denying freedom of will as presupposition of responsibility, on the basis of personal and moral resentment as rational presuppositions of personality, community and society. Human beings cannot take themselves seriously when they equate wrongful harm done to them with any harm possibly happening to them. Such lack of any personal resentment or a totally fatalistic attitude is incompatible with distinct

---

9 See Benn (1967) for a summary of this and related issues.

10 See Brandt (1959) for the definitive treatment of act v. rule utilitarianism.

personality. In the same way, total solitude would be the consequence if nobody felt and uttered moral resentment as a necessary consequence of wrongful harm done to others. Strawson even argued that human life and society are inconceivable without personal and moral resentment.

Interesting here in the first place are consequences of Strawson's (highly plausible) anti-determinism in terms of unavoidably rational resentment, not worked out by himself. Or: what would be optimal handling of wrongdoing and consequent rational resentment in general, in a wider sense than just relating to state reactions to crime? A simple example may serve to show some main lines.

Somebody receives an invitation for dinner at a friend's home. She appears as agreed upon, but nobody opens the door. Later on, the victim expresses some kind of resentment to the offender, who was not there when he ought to have been there. In the absence of convincing excuses, the offender is expected to apologize and to try to make up for the wrongful harm he inflicted upon the invited person. Thus he may promise to prepare a still more elaborate dinner, as soon as possible. If to the contrary his reaction to the invited person's resentment were to display indifference, then the victim would feel like not being respected. Then the indifferent offender acts as if he does not take his own conduct seriously, thereby not taking himself seriously either. On the other hand, if the victim does not display any kind of resentment at all, then the offender may think of her as somebody not imposing any limits to the conduct of others towards her. Then she will not be taken seriously either.

In the absence of exonerating excuses for wrongdoing, expression of resentment ought to lead to recognition of victims by offenders, apology, reparation and reconciliation, as essential elements of human relationships. Without apology and reparation, however variable their forms and expressions may be, there can be no reconciliation and relationships based upon respect and self-respect. This is of basic importance not only for victims, but for offenders as well. Offenders will not be respected by victims and others as long as they do not take responsibility for their conduct and its consequences.

Personal resentment of victims is indeed complemented by moral resentment of others and society as a whole against offenders. Solidarity presupposes such moral resentment about harm done to others, as a kind of compassion essential for community. Moral resentment is to supplement personal resentment in bringing offenders to repair their wrongdoing. Moral resentment may even be regarded as a form of love, as solidarity in reciprocal self-realization.

Thus both rational resentment and eventual reparation and reconciliation between offenders, victims and others in society are essential for reciprocal respect and self-respect, probably the most important immaterial values in life (as explained by Rawls, in 1999).

Individual responsibility, liability and retribution as reparation are ingredients of essential solidarity and sense of community. Community is constituted by individuality in the sense of 'being there for the other' by assuming full responsibility and acting on its consequences. This is one of the

'cements of society'. Part of this was already preached by Butler (in 1726, published in 1729,
p. 115, so Beccaria might have taken notice), though he probably did not think of reparation as superior to punishment as infliction of pain yet:

> 'The indignation raised by cruelty and injustice, and the desire of having it punished, which persons unconcerned would feel, is by no means malice. No; it is resentment against vice and wickedness: it is one of the common bonds, by which society is held together; a fellow feeling which each individual has in behalf of the whole species, as well as of himself.'[11]

These essential relationships between crime, responsibility, reparation, respect, self-respect and community hold good not only for more or less intimate human relationships as in the example above, but also for anonymous human relationships making up society as a whole. Hence its importance for criminal law and punishment. Civilized criminal law answers to crime are to conform to the basic scheme of rational resentment and recognition of wrongful harm, leading to compensation and reparation for victims. Moral resentment comes to the fore, then. The state, representing and realizing the public interest, acts on behalf of personal resentment of victims and of moral resentment of other citizens, in order to force offenders to compensate for harm done to victims and to society in general. Serious crime is to be compensated for by penal servitude, the rewards of which are due to victims and to the state.

Civilized criminal law is not just solidarity with victims, but also with offenders. Penal servitude is more than backward-looking retribution by offenders' suffering. It is first and foremost about reconstitution of community. Penal servitude is offenders' symbolical and material return to socially acceptable relationships with victims and citizens in general. Penal servitude is community service, restoring the 'cement' of society as noted before.

Indeed and rather different from Beccaria's crude and cruel forms of penal servitude however briefly described, reparation by offenders is to be determined by its productivity in the first place. Offenders' pain as a consequence of extra exertion is no more than a not always unwelcome by-product. Detention may not always be necessary. The state may intervene, paying crime victims beforehand. Confrontation with possible consequences of specific crimes may be part of penal servitude, and so on. In terms of total costs and profits, net results are to be positive, certainly so in comparison to the huge human and financial costs of any punitive detention regime, however suitably reformed.

Compensation for crime victims as essential for really civilized criminal law isnot predominant in Beccaria's own work, apart from oblique reference to redress to be offered by offenders (see before). The ideal would be complete restoration of victims to their original states, as if nothing wrong was done to

[11] Compare these common bonds or 'cement' to Beccaria's building as a metaphor for society, and to gratitude as a condition for social cohesion, as cited before.

them at all. Thus crime may be undone after all, turning back the clock in principle – considered by Beccaria to be an impossibility in principle (see before).

This turning back the clock in a positive sense may be further explained as follows (see Kaptein, 2010, for details). First and foremost: how is legally relevant wrongful harm to be determined? Generally, this is done by comparing two futures, one actual and another potential, in principle. Or: wrongful harm is the difference between somebody's or some body's total future without any conduct (in a wide sense) having caused the harm, and the future including consequences of harmful conduct involved.

Such a counterfactually conditional concept of harm is not really necessary in simple cases of harm, as caused by breaking glasses and like things. Consequences of bodily and (associated) mental and emotional harm however may well need to be determined by comparison of different life expectancies. Even this elementary concept of harm suffices to show that any categorical distinction between past and future is rather implausible, at least in legal respects. Related to this is the basic and uncontested function of compensation for wrongful harm: guaranteeing a future for the harmed person or body concerned as if no harm was ever inflicted at all. Such 'undoing' of a harmful past is analogous to forbearing harm in the future. Thus regarded past and future are symmetric, from a legal point of view.

In many cases of wrongful harm, paying money may do by way of restitution and/or compensation. In other cases, undoing mental and emotional harm may presuppose identification of wrongdoers, to be made to pay for what they did wrong themselves. Such 'undoing of guilt' may still be essential for undoing serious harm.

Thus realization of retribution as reparation changes the future and the past for the better, however at odds with common sense which has it that the past is what it is and the future is what it may become. Practical realization of this in the administration of criminal law is another matter. The more serious the wrongful harm, the less can it be really undone of course.

Still Beccaria's ideas on penal servitude may be fruitfully further developed in these directions (see Kaptein, 2004). Reform and reintegration of criminal law and tort law are high on the agenda, then. Interestingly enough this is already to be found in Beccaria's work as well.[12] Still, and also stressed by Beccaria, strict codification of sanctions is to remain essential for retribution as reparation by penal servitude.

Justification of what may be called civilized criminal law and punishment directed to victims' and state compensation by offenders themselves in terms of respect and self-respect as ultimate human values is rather different from Beccaria's utilitarianism, however qualified. Such respect and self-respect may still be implicit in Beccaria's none too strictly utilitarian outlook, at least

[12] See for example ch. 22, on redress of consequences of theft, ch. 34, on debtors obligation to pay back, and so on.

compared to Bentham's radicalism. Hart expressed this as follows (in 1966, p. 51):

> 'I think that very often where Bentham and Beccaria differ in detail this is traceable to Beccaria's conviction that what may be done in the name of utility should be limited by consideration of what befits the dignity of a man.'

Such dignity may be implicit in the social contract as discussed before, as every citizen is presumed to have an equal say in such a contract. Beccaria also presages Kant's conception of man as an end in himself in the following rather isolated passage (ch. 20, p. 50, italics are Beccaria's):

> 'There is no freedom when the laws permit a man in some cases to cease to be a person and to become a *thing*: then you will see the efforts of the powerful devoted to discovering from amongst the mass of civil relations those in which the law most favours his interests.'

Whether this will do to counteract Beccaria's general utilitarianism is another matter. But even purely utilitarian considerations may offer further backing for civilized criminal law (as already suggested here). Also, special and general preventive effects of punishment as civilized penal servitude may not be worse than consequences of other regimes, including detention and its well-known adverse effects on offenders.

5. Beccaria's Dream (To Be Continued)

So Beccaria has not been so well-read indeed, at least concerning important retributive elements in his work, to be interpreted in terms of reparation by offenders. This again relates to his emphasis on the importance of the psychology of human sentiments and feelings as constituting both the foundations and the operating conditions of rational criminal law. Indeed reason is not to be contrasted with emotion here and elsewhere. There can be no rational criminal law or any other human practice for that matter without taking human sentiments, feelings and emotions into account (ch. 2, p. 10):

> 'If we consult the human heart, we find in it the fundamental principles of the sovereign's true right to punish crimes, for it is vain to hope that any lasting advantage will accrue from public morality if it be not founded on ineradicable human sentiments.'

Which is of course not to say that emotion, sentiments and feeling are rational per se. However, Beccaria may have wrongly left out of account both the sense and the force in personal and moral resentment in their positive senses, as presuppositions of respect and self-respect as cements of society. His grand project is not finished yet in this sense too, both in theory and in practice.

Still any administration of criminal justice, however suitably reformed, has to take another kind of sentiment into account as well. Punitive attitudes in the general population will not abate in any near future, as Beccaria already foresaw (ch. 34, p. 89):

> 'Men's most superficial feelings lead them to prefer cruel laws. Nevertheless, when they are subjected to them themselves, it is in each man's interest that they be moderate, because the fear of being injured is greater than the desire to injure.'

Negative resentment may not always stay within reasonable bounds. 'The fear of being injured' may not put much weight in the scales. Most citizens and officials have no real experience of punishment and its drastically underestimated consequences, deservedly so or not. Reform of the administration of criminal justice however wrongly perceived as too mild will not stand much change to be realized on any scale. But civilized criminal law as outlined above may not meet with much popular resistance. Offenders still seem to be suffering, albeit as a not unwelcome by-product of penal servitude serving retribution as reparation in the first place. Thus restorative justice may be realized against odds of punitive public opinion.

Beccaria was undoubtedly right in his moves toward retribution as reparation, however implicit. He may have been less right in his optimism on crime prevention by means of punishment. His mechanistic psychology is a case in point. Directly comparing human motives with natural causes and explaining human conduct in terms of products of such forces is all too simplistic. Thus calculating measures of punishment in terms of counteractive forces is too simplistic as well, if punishment is to be generally preventive against crime at all.

More specifically Beccaria presumed that enlightened citizens know about the laws and their possible adverse consequences for ill-behaving individuals, such citizens having contracted to such laws themselves in principle. Even this presupposition may be proven wrong. Thus it is maintained that one reason for doubt on preventive effect of criminal law and punishment is public ignorance of criminal law and law in general.[13] This may not be the only problem with prevention.[14]

Let it be kept in mind that issues of preventive effect are empirical issues in principle. Whether actual or potential measures against crime may be effective and if so to what extent depends on highly complex causal and motivational regularities, to be applicable to still more complex realities and their interrelations. Statistics are notoriously unreliable here, both in themselves and

---

13 See for example Robinson and Darley (2004) at odds with Beccaria's dream on the advantages of the printing press, as beautifully expounded in ch. 5.

14 See among many others Garland (2001), Johnston and Shearing (2003) and Levitt and Dubner (2005) on unexpected explanations of crime reduction in terms unrelated to any administration of criminal justice.

in causal and/or motivational conclusions to be drawn from them, inductively or otherwise. Standard tests of causal connection like falsification are impracticable anyway, even apart from possibly undesirable consequences of temporarily doing away with the administration of criminal justice. So any general conclusion on any preventive effect of whatever measures is tentative at best. All this is evident enough but still sometimes kept out of account in more or less a priori thought about prevention of crime and its modalities. (Beccaria was aware of this: see his remarks on the complexity of human driving forces as cited before).

Still there may be good reasons to assume that sanctions aimed at reparation in the first place will not do worse in terms of special and general prevention, compared to punishment as infliction of pain by detention (see on this again Kaptein 2004).

Also, subsidiarity as criterion for administration of criminal justice is and remains of foremost importance, as stressed by Beccaria himself as well. So many other kinds of public administration may sensibly reduce crime, however difficult it may be to relate causes to effects here too.

Less Beccarian but certainly not at odds with main lines of his argument is the need for informal restorative justice, offering redress without recourse to formal administration of criminal justice. Thus victim-offender mediation and other ways to adequately handle consequences of crime are important parts of any retribution as reparation scheme. Such mediation may even serve purposes of special and general prevention. Again this is in line with Beccaria's emphasis on the importance of proportionality and subsidiarity as criteria for public administration of criminal justice and punishment.

Again, repairing consequences of crime is not categorically different from forbearing such consequences. Remember retribution as reparation in its ideal sense as undoing crime, turning back the clock. At least in this ideal sense, meaningful concepts of retribution and prevention have more in common than is commonly taken for granted. In line with this, legal security is not just realized by prevention of crime, but also by restoring crime victims to their original positions in as far as possible.

So Beccaria's grand project, suitably reformed in terms of retribution as reparation, is still the main agenda for reform of criminal law and punishment. As in his own times, no really revolutionary measures are needed to realize this. Main features of the administration of criminal justice in so-called civilized jurisdictions may remain as they are, at least on paper.

What does need long due and radical reform however is the double punishment of punishment as infliction of pain and the – again double – bereavement of crime victims, victimized a second time by being left alone, to be replaced by retribution as reparation for victims and society in as far as possible. Or, one more time: end the pain of punishment as mere infliction of pain.

Though civilized criminal law may still be sufficiently punitive in order to gain public acceptance at least in this respect, changes for any reform within foreseeable futures may still be dim. This was not really different in Beccaria's own times, as he noted in ch. 34 (p. 91):

> 'But easy, simple and great laws, which await nothing but a sign from the lawgiver to spread prosperity and vigour throughout the nation, laws which would earn him immortal hymns of gratitude down the generations, are those which are least considered and least wanted. A nervous and nitpicking spirit, the fearful prudence of the present moment and an unadventurous dourness toward novelty take over the feelings of those who regulate the multifarious activities of little men.'

Beccaria may have been too pessimistic. His book has exerted major influence to the good, by any standards of historical explanation in terms of causal and/or motivational laws. Anyway – as again already explained by himself (in ch. 11, p. 30):

> '(...) but if, in upholding the rights of men and the invincible truth, I were to contribute to relieving some blighted victim of tyranny or, equally lethal, ignorance, from the spasms and anxieties of death, the blessing and tears of joy of even a single innocent man would console me for the scorn of the multitude.'

This does not just relate to even a single victim of wrongful capital punishment. It relates to the sense of trying not just to add to already interminably endless scholarship on criminal justice but also trying to reform however piecemeal real administration of criminal justice as well. And lest it be thought this is the end of the story, let one last consoling thought of Beccaria be cited, on the administration of criminal justice (from ch. 14, p. 36):

> 'We shall not point out other refinements and provisions which these kinds of institutions call for. If it were necessary to say everything, I should have said nothing ...'

References

Beccaria, C.B. (1764, [1766]). *Dei delitti e delle pene*. Livorno, also in R. Bellamy (Ed.) (1995), *On Crimes and Punishments and Other Writings*. Cambridge: Cambridge University Press.

Bellamy, R. (1995). *On Crimes and Punishments and Other Writings*. Cambridge: Cambridge University Press.

Benn, S.I. (1967). Punishment. In P. Edwards (Ed.), *The Encyclopedia of Philosophy*. New York: Free Press & Macmillan.

Brandt, R.B. (1959). *Ethical Theory*. Englewood Cliffs: Prentice Hall.

Butler, J. (1729). Sermon upon Resentment. Also in J. Butler (1827), *Sermons, To Which Are Added, A Charge To The Clergy Of Durham And Correspondence With Dr Clarke*. Cambridge: Hilliard & Brown/ Boston: Hilliard, Gray, Little & Wilkins.

Dworkin, R.M. ([1977], 1978). *Taking Rights Seriously*. Cambridge: Harvard University Press.

Foucault, M. (1975). *Surveiller et punir: Naissance de la prison*. Paris: Gallimard. Also in M. Foucault (1977). *Discipline and Punish: The Birth of the Prison*. London: Penguin Books.

Garland, D. (2001). *The Culture of Control: Crime and Social Order in Contemporary Society*. Oxford: Oxford University Press.

Hart, H.L.A. (1959). Prolegomenon to the Principles of Punishment. *Proceedings of the Aristotelian Society*. Also in J. Gardner (Ed.) (2008), *Punishment and Responsibility: Essays in the Philosophy of Law*. Oxford: Oxford University Press.

Hart, H.L.A. (1966). Bentham and Beccaria. *Atti del Convegno Internazionale su Cesare Beccaria promaosso dall'Accademia delle Scienze di Torino nel secondo centenario dell'opera 'Dei delitti e delle pene', Memorie dell'Accademia delle Scienze, Classe di scienze morali*, IV, 9, Turin. Also in H.L.A. Hart (1982). *Essays on Bentham: Studies in Jurisprudence and Political Theory*. Oxford: Clarendon Press.

Johnston, L., & Shearing, C. (2003). *Governing Security: Explorations in Policing and Justice*. London/New York: Routledge.

Kaptein, H.J.R. (1997). Rechtsfilosofie van de 18de eeuw. In C.W. Maris, & F.C.L.M. Jacobs (Eds.), *Recht, orde en vrijheid: Een historische inleiding in de rechtsfilosofie*. Groningen: Wolters Noordhoff.

Kaptein, H.J.R. (2004). Against the Pain of Punishment: On Penal Servitude and Procedural Justice for All. In H.J.R. Kaptein, & M. Malsch (Eds.), *Crime, Victims and Justice: Essays on Principles and Practice*. Burlington: Ashgate Publishing.

Kaptein, H.J.R. (2010). Virtues of Truth in Forbearing Wrongs: Client Confidentiality Qualified by Legal Symmetry of Past and Future Harm. In A. Amaya, & H.L. Ho (Eds.), *Virtue in the Law*. Oxford: Hart Publishing Co, forthcoming.

Levitt, S.D., & Dubner, S.J. (2005). *Freakonomics: A Rogue Economist Explores the Hidden Side of Everything*. New York: HarperCollins Publishers.

Mill, J.S. (1861). Utilitarianism. *Frazer's Magazine*. Also in O. Priest (Ed.) (1957), *Utilitarianism*. Indianapolis/New York: The Bobbs-Merrill Company, Inc.

Modderman, A.E.J. (1864). *Straf - Geen Kwaad*. Amsterdam: Frederik Muller.

Rawls, J. (1955). Two Concepts of Rules. *Philosophical Review, 64/1*, 3-32. Also in S. Freeman (Ed.) (1999), *Collected Papers*. Cambridge, Mass. /London: Harvard University Press.

Rawls, J. ([1971], 1999). *A Theory of Justice*. Cambridge, Mass.: The Belknap Press of Harvard University Press.

Robinson, P.H., Darley, J.M. (2004). Does Criminal Law Deter? A Behavioural Science Investigation. *Oxford Journal of Legal Studies, 24/2,* 173-205.

Schafer, S. ([1960], 1970). *Compensation and Restitution to Victims of Crime*. New Jersey: Patterson Smith.

Shearing, S. (2001). Punishment and the Changing Face of the Governance. *Punishment and Society, 3,* 203-220.

Strawson, P.F. (1962). Freedom and Resentment. *Proceedings of the British Academy*. Also in P.F. Strawson, (1973) *Freedom and Resentment, and Other Essays*. London: Methuen.

Young, D.B. (1983). Cesare Beccaria: Utilitarian or Retributivist? *Journal of Criminal Justice*, *11*, 317-326.

10. A Transaction Approach to Fighting International Corruption

Abiola O. Makinwa

1. Introduction

A rapidly expanding world market is a catalyst for the formulation of supranational rules to ensure the order, certainty and stability essential for continued growth. Unfortunately, along with a global market comes increased insecurity from transnational crimes such as international corruption. Safeguarding security is a challenge where there is no clear nexus of governance and sovereignty is dispersed. The state as the primary provider of security is limited in the terrain beyond the state. Furthermore, international corruption occurs in agreements reached in private commerce on a scale that impacts global political, social, economic development. This blurs the traditional roles assigned to the public and private sectors. Shearing recognises this blurring of roles and strongly criticises the continued focus on the state as the primary provider of security in the face of the de facto reality of private government that has resulted from an explosion of 'mass private property' (Shearing 2006). This is particularly true in respect of international corruption where the diminished power of the state and the pre-eminence of private corporations in corrupt exchanges motivate the need to map out the nodes of governance (Johnston and Shearing 2003) in a world where the goalposts have moved.

Shearing aptly summarizes a fundamental question of these times. He asks how a theoretical jump can be made to 'positions that recognize a diversity of governing auspices; that is, to positions that recognise the role of the state while at the same time recognising, and bringing clearly and explicitly into the equation, the role of non-state auspices as well as non-state providers of governance' (Shearing 2006). This paper attempts to make such a jump with regard to international corruption by proposing a *transaction approach* to fighting international corruption. This approach seeks to restore interactions damaged by corrupt activity so as to create an environment where the risk of engaging in acts of international corruption outweighs the gains of non-compliance.

The *transaction approach* proposed in this paper embraces a multi-level perspective of the interactions affected by a corrupt exchange in a single narrative. Anticipating and addressing the issues that arise across levels of interaction and in particular the contract that results from the successful violation of the anti-corruption rules provides more coherency and effectiveness in devising anti-corruption strategy. The corollary is also true. Pursuing a single-level approach in the face of interconnected levels can create paradoxes and fault lines of incoherence. Furthermore, a multi-level approach enlarges the conceptual scope of redress for damage caused by corrupt activity thus increasing accountability and risk for corporations engaging in corrupt behaviour.

Section A of this paper lays the foundation for a *transaction approach* by examining the current sanctioning of international corruption and suggests that the single-level approach of criminalisation results in a schism between the public law consensus to criminalize international corruption and the private law contract that results from the successful violation of the anti-corruption laws. This creates a paradox that encourages inefficient implementation and encourages risk taking. Section B moves beyond the single level approach of criminalisation and identifies various levels of transacting affected by the corrupt exchange. Effective anti-corruption strategy must anticipate the issues that arise across the *mandate*, *violation* and *consequence* levels to the extent that they create and influence the environment in which international corruption occurs.

Section C of the paper focuses on the contracts that result from the corrupt exchange. The interactions across the various levels of transacting are impacted by the contract tainted by international corruption. The status of this contract is critical to shaping the environment in which international corruption occurs. Such contracts should arguably constitute a category whose enforceability is connected to their public interest dimensions. The more insecure the contract tainted by corruption the greater the risk for parties contemplating corrupt activity.

Section D examines the potential of the contract tainted by corruption as a regulatory tool in the fight against international corruption while Section E summarises the advantages of a *transaction approach*. The paper ends by concluding that a *transaction approach* connects the various levels of interaction that shape the environment in which international corruption occurs. This creates an opportunity to change this environment in a manner that increases the risk of engaging in corrupt activity and, by so doing, positively impact the fight against international corruption.

2. Section A: The Paradox of Consensus and the Contract Left Standing

International corruption is typically of the sort referred to as *grand corruption*. It occurs at the highest levels of governance and 'distorts the central functions of government' (UN: 2004). International corruption is defined as having three primary elements (1) an international element, (2) a commercial element and (3) as involving government officials (OECD: 1997). This means that while the criminalisation of international corruption is an important and necessary first step it presents a structural conflict of interest problem. Implementation using the criminal process is dependent on government officials who are a key actor in international corruption. Implementation is also strongly influenced by political as well as economic interests.[113] The dependence on the apparatus of the state in initiating, investigating and sanctioning international corruption is a grave impediment to prosecution. The degree of success is dependant not so much on the fact of criminalisation but on the political will to prosecute.[114]

Perhaps not surprisingly, despite an array of international and domestic regulations, international corruption remains a pressing issue (Transparency International 2009).[115] It would seem that the establishment of common rules is not enough. The quest for effective schemes of 'restraint' still continues (Beccaria 1764a). A second phase in the fight against international corruption is therefore emerging in the necessary translation of rules prohibiting such corruption into the operative elements of legal interactions and legal systems.

The positive effect of the international regulatory framework has been the emergence of a global standard or consensus condemning international corruption (Makinwa 2007). This consensus is symptomatic of an international society held together not by territory or sovereignty but by the dynamics of mutually dependent relationships in a series of collaborative agreements (Velasquez 1992).[116] The consensus against international corruption has shaped the objectives of the international anti-corruption discourse in its acceptance of three basic propositions.

The first proposition is that international corruption is detrimental to the common good (Abed 2002; Rose.Ackerman 1999; Dreher 2005). This has resulted in international business practices, once regarded as legal becoming criminalized as a violation of the norms that coexist for the good of international society. Ilias argues that corruption should in fact be viewed as a crime against

[113] The attempts of the Blair government to stop the investigations into bribery allegations involving BAE, a British defence, security and aerospace company are a rather apt example of this. See Corner House Research & Campaign against Arms Trade, R (on the application of) v Director of the Serious Fraud Office; Corner House Research & Ors, R (On the Application of) v The Serious Fraud Office.

[114] The United States stands in the forefront of prosecuting anti-corruption cases. This is to be contrasted with the very meagre levels of enforcement demonstrated by the rest of the World. For statistics on US Anti-corruption enforcement efforts under the Foreign Corrupt Practices Act. See Shearman and Sterling LLP (2008).

[115] The international framework is a patchwork of rules namely the Inter-American Convention against Corruption (1996), the OECD Convention on Combating Bribery of Foreign Public Officials in International Business Transactions (1997), the Council of Europe's Criminal Law Convention on Corruption (1999), the Council of Europe's Civil Law Convention on Corruption (1999), the Convention on the Fight Against Corruption involving Officials of the European Communities or Officials of Member States of the European Union (1997), the UN Convention against Transnational Organised Crime (2000), the African Union Convention on Preventing and Combating Corruption, (2003) and the UN Convention against Corruption (2003).

[116] Velasquesz points out the importance of a core common morality as necessary for international economic interaction. Without this, economic interactions would be 'nasty and brutish if not short'.

humanity (Ilias 2006). The establishment of a base line of legality is the first requirement of the rule of law. It removes international corruption from the realm of purely private commercial agreements. At this point, the private activities international traders move into the domain of public safety. Criminalisation is thus the litmus against which the norm eschewing international corruption is identified.

The second proposition posited by the consensus is that that there is a need for common rules to tackle international corruption. The need for a collaborative response is necessary in an integrated world market characterized by high volumes of trade occurring outside the domestic jurisdictions of states (Teubner 1997a).[117] International corruption occurs within the purview of international trade, an activity fostered and promoted by the State but carried out mainly by private persons (Teubner 1997b).[118] The business practices in this supranational space emanate not so much from national institutions but from the actors and merchants in an essentially self regulatory environment (Teubner 1997c).[119]

A third proposition embraced in the consensus on criminalisation is that systems of 'effective restraint' should accompany the de-legitimisation of corrupt practices. Minor and Morrison write that the predominant response to criminal behaviour today '(...) reflects an adversarial conception of justice and is characterized by retribution and utilitarianism. The aims of traditional sanctions (...) are to achieve vengeance, just deserts, deterrence, incapacitation, and/or rehabilitation by punishing offenders and placing them in treatment programs Minor' (Morrison 1996). The assumption in classical criminal punishment theory is that effective punishment of the offender will deter the commission of further acts of international corruption that harm society.

These propositions are at the heart of the global consensus criminalising international corruption and undeniably hold true. However, the stability of this consensus is challenged by the *paradox* of the contract that results from the successful violation of the rules prohibiting international corruption. The persistence of international corruption as a transnational crime confirms the fact that contracts tainted by international corruption continue to flourish. Where the rules prohibiting international corruption are successfully violated the proof of such success is the contract that comes into being as a consequence of the bribe that has exchanged hands.

---

117 Teubner remarks that '[t]oday's globalization is not a gradual emergence of a world society under the leadership of interstate politics, but a highly contradictory and fragmented process in which politics has lost its leading role'.

118 Teubner points out that the 'lex mercatoria, the transnational law of economic transactions, is the most successful example of global law without a state'.

119 Teubner emphasizes that 'the new living law of the world is nourished not from stores of tradition but from the ongoing self-reproduction of highly technical, highly specialized, often formally organized and rather narrowly defined, global networks of an economic, cultural, academic or technological nature.

Anti-corruption rules have criminalized international corruption but the status of transactions resulting from the successful violation of the prohibition is not so clear. This is not uncommon and MacQueen speaks about the 'silence of regulatory legislation' that accompanies criminal prohibitions (MacQueen 2004). The 'silence' on the part of regulation raises the question of the effect of criminalisation on resulting private transactions.

The contract tainted by international corruption undermines the proportionality of response that should discourage further acts of international corruption. Beccaria has remarked that 'punishments and the means adopted for inflicting them, should, consistent with proportionality, be so selected as to make the most efficacious and lasting impression on the minds of men (...)' (Beccaria 1764b). A system that does not address with equal severity the consequence of the successful commission of international corruption but rather focuses principally on its perpetrators leaves opens windows of opportunity that encourage risk-taking.

Two major windows of opportunity emerge as a result of what can be referred to as the 'contract left standing' and act as a counter force to the effects of criminalisation. The first window is the potential trade off of the gains to be made from the contract that results from a corrupt exchange. The second window is the potential to protect the contract tainted by corruption with private law principles of freedom of contract as well as resorting to international arbitration. The windows of the 'trade-off' and 'resort to international arbitration' undermine current approaches to tackling international corruption and support an environment where the risk of engaging in corrupt behaviour may not offer significant advantages over non compliance.

I The Trade Off

The choice between the violation of the prohibition against corruption and the contract that may result from a successful violation presents a net gain or net loss proposition. This encourages speculative behaviour that is premised on several factors; firstly, the risk of discovery; secondly, even where discovered, the risk of successful prosecution; and thirdly, whether the potential profit to be made from the resulting contract outweighs the risk posed by punishment.

The fundamental ethic of a corporation is the need to make a profit. Companies will favour a course of action that best boosts company earnings and satisfy shareholders. An environment that is essentially 'silent' on the contract tainted by corruption motivates choices that may not be present to the same degree in an environment that extends the punitive effects of criminalisation to resulting contracts or transactions. Where the *satisfaction* of shareholders can be quantified in terms other than company profits the choices of corporations will reflect this changed environment. Factors such as increased awareness about a corporation's corrupt activity, damage caused to peoples or the environment, penalties, fines, disgorgement of profits, reputational implications, and suits by shareholders themselves are few examples of actions that are encouraged by an environment that seeks to restore the interactions damaged by corrupt activity.

The risk to the corporation that results from such actions can positively influence compliance.

The conditioning effect of the environment also applies to the demand side of the bribery equation. The fact that contracts resulting from the corrupt exchange are not the focus of the criminal sanctioning process strengthens the hand that demands the bribe. An environment that renders such consequential actions insecure weakens the strong position of the party demanding a bribe.

II Resorting to International Arbitration

A second window of opportunity created by the contract tainted by corruption is the opportunity to protect the contracts by utilising private systems of dispute settlement. For several decades the internationalisation of world trade has resulted in strategies to minimize the risks associated with the lack of uniformity in national laws and practices. International arbitration is regarded as a risk efficient and neutral method to resolve disputes regarding contracts with an international character and is premised on the fact that within the private sphere persons are given the freedom to regulate their private transactions. The arbitration process is controlled by the parties to the dispute in a secret and confidential process (Redfern and Hunter 2004).

The principle of party autonomy gives parties to arbitration the freedom to decide on the place of arbitration, the rules that will govern the dispute, the procedure to be followed and most importantly the arbitrators that will decide the dispute. This process is safeguarded by an international framework of rules that ensures the worldwide enforcement of arbitration awards[120] and limited court intervention.[121]

The fact that the bulk of international commercial contracts contain an arbitration clause means that contracts tainted by international corruption are more likely to fall under the jurisdiction of a private international arbitration panel than a national court of law (Makinwa 2009). In short, the secrecy and confidentiality of the international arbitration process can act as a layer of protection for contracts tainted by international corruption.

III Effect of 'Windows of Opportunity'

The reality of the contract left standing creates an incentive for actors in the corrupt exchange to influence the discourse in a manner that protects the contract. This leads to a sort of double speak. On the one hand there is the worldwide acknowledgement of the detrimental consequences of international

---

[120] See in particular the United Nations Economic and Social Council 1958 New York Convention on the Recognition and Enforcement of Foreign Arbitral Awards and the United Nations Commission on International Trade Law 1985 UNCITRAL Model Law on International Commercial Arbitration.

[121] For example, Art. 5 of the Model Arbitration Law adopted in many countries worldwide provides that 'in matters governed by this Law, no court shall intervene except where so provided in this Law'.

corruption and collective desire to see it eliminated, and, on the other hand, the exasperation of companies faced with real losses where the contract left standing goes to a more 'amenable' competitor. The official dialogue may become no more than mere talk while the business of corruption continues in the 'real' world. Blundo describes this in terms of the 'real' functioning and the 'official' functioning of a state beset by corruption (Blundo and Sardan 2006).

Thus, while the existence of the anti-corruption rules may lend itself to best practices, the reality of the 'street' sustains a strong incentive to do what it takes to survive the competitiveness of international business. A tipping point of futility may be reached where the gains of the anti-corruption rules are eclipsed by the inadequacy of the system. This dynamic may lead to cracks in the consensus and the unified front against corruption. The contract left standing is at the heart of this dichotomy and profoundly influences the environment that shapes the occurrence of international corruption.

Criminalisation creates a false separation between transactions that occur in the corrupt exchange and those that occur after the commission of the offence. Yet, all these transactions are in fact connected and shape the environment in which international corruption occurs. This suggests the need for an approach to sanctioning international corruption that accommodates transactions occurring at all levels of interaction.

3. Section B: Corruption in Transactions

Three features stand out in the environment that influences international corruption. Firstly, the regulatory framework; secondly, the contract that comes into being as a result of the successful violation of the anti-corruption and thirdly, the damage suffered by persons affected directly or indirectly by the effects of the contract.

The direct line of consequence between the legal rules prohibiting international corruption, damage to victims and the resulting tainted contract is one that is somewhat blurred by the division between the public and private law. While some aspects are caught within the ambit of traditional criminal law regulation, several aspects of this interaction lie beyond the reach of criminalisation in the sphere of private law. An artificial public/private boundary does not accord with the realities of the corruption environment. Adopting a *transaction approach* can provide a holistic view of the processes of the corruption exchange.

Corruption occurs in interactions. It stands to reason that attempts to curtail corruption should address this process of interaction. Changing the focus of the fight against corruption from the individual to the transactions that arise between persons involved in a corrupt exchange enables the complex mechanisms that underlie the process of international corruption to be viewed as a cohesive whole. Typical international business interactions that may involve corruption include corporate fraud, private to private corruption, private to public corruption, market collusion, cartels as well as corporate lobbying. (Transparency International 2009).[122] Attempts by succeeding governments,[123] the competitor who has lost a bid as a result of unethical practices,[124] shareholders,[125] principals,[126] non governmental organisations along with ordinary citizens[127] to institute claims based on acts of bribery and corruption provides a rough typology of 'victims' (Makinwa 2010). For such victims civil remedies may offer a more effective method of recovery and relief (Graham 2002). There is however an even larger group of persons that suffer the damage of international corruption. These are the indirect victims, citizens of states whose social, economic and political progress is negatively impacted by corruption. The direct and indirect victims of international corruption are much closer to damage suffered than a paternalistic state. They are also motivationally better situated to seek redress for the harm they have suffered.

I Levels of Interaction in a Corrupt Exchange

The interconnectedness of acts of corruption and their consequences suggests that to effectively address the damage caused by international corruption the various levels of interactions impacted by the corrupt exchange should be taken into account. This paper identifies three main levels of such interactions. These can be referred to as the mandate, violation and consequence levels.

---

122 Report on Corruption in the Private Sector. <http://www.transparency.org/policy_research/surveys_indices/gcb/2009>

123 See for example BBC News report '"Abacha accounts" to be frozen' Wednesday, 3 October, 2001, available at <http://news.bbc.co.uk/2/hi/africa/1576527.stm>.

124 An example is the US the case of Lamb v Philip Morris, where Kentucky tobacco farmers filed a civil suit against Philip Morris and BAT arguing that the 'donations' promised by the defendants' subsidiaries amounted to unlawful inducements designed and intended to restrain trade.

125 A good example is the case of In re Immucor. After Immucor announced that it was to be formally investigated by the SEC for violations under the Foreign Corrupt Practices Act, this prompted shareholders to file a complaint under sections 10-b and 20(a) of the Exchange Act. The shareholders claimed that Immucor had understated the potential number of FCPA violations for improper payments that it was facing, reporting the SEC investigations as an 'isolated event'. It turned out that there had been several acts of corruption committed by Immucor over a period of several years.

126 For example in the 2003 Tesco Stores Case, a Mr. Pork, a manager, in Tesco's e-commerce was found to have received a bribe of £323,749.99 from a customer that did business with Tesco, Delta Computer Systems (UK) Ltd.

127 As for example the civil action by Transparency International (France) and Mr. Gregory Ngbwa Mintsa, a Gabonese citizen, in December 2008 to call for an investigation into large amounts of real estate and other assets acquired in France by presidents Denis Sassou N'Guesso of Congo, Omar Bongo-Ondimba of Gabon and Teodoro Obiand Mbasogo of Equatorial Guinea. See Press release by Transparency International (France) http://www.transparency.org/news_room/latest_news/press_releases_nc/2009/2009_05_06_france_case.

I (1) The Mandate Level

Government officials do not exist in a vacuum but are bearers of a mandate granted to them as the representatives of individual citizens. The government official is an agent not just of the government on whose behalf the official negotiates but, more pertinently, of the people who put the government in power. Actions that harm the public interest are outside the mandate of representatives. Where an act of international corruption occurs, there is a breach of mandate. This public interest is at the heart of anti-corruption regulations and strategy.

Outside of this foundational context, international corruption is sometimes viewed as victimless crime because it is conceptualized as a private agreement occurring with the consent of transacting parties. Ruggiero makes the point that the study of corruption tends to focus on the individuals who have been involved in a corrupt exchange with the result that corruption ends up 'being assimilated to a form of victimless crime, where the actors involved are equally determined to participate in the exchange and pursue their private if illegal interest' (Ruggiero 2000). However, such a viewpoint disconnects from the mandate level of interaction. Rugerrio rightly argues that the impact of the corrupt exchange may not be perceived when attention is only centered on the specific setting in which it takes place (Ruggiero 2000). Indeed the full impact of corruption is felt beyond the specific instances in which it takes place precisely because it represents an abuse of a mandate that results in harm to the givers of that mandate.

A *transaction approach* makes a direct link between acts of international corruption and the abuse of mandate that it represents. Such a perspective views criminal law boundaries as artificial to the extent that the definition of the criminal offence excludes the actual victims. Framing the discussion in mandate terms broadens the conceptual scope of anti-corruption strategy to enable the articulation and protection of the interests of the grantees of the mandate. Seen in this way a primary function of anti-corruption rules should be the restoration of the trust breached by addressing the damage suffered to the grantees of the abused mandate. This parallels the notion of trust and the duty of loyalty in the agency relationship of the private law. The challenge this raises is how to encourage and facilitate the process of restoration of trust in the sanctioning processes for international corruption.

I (2) The Violation Level

The next level of interaction can be described as the violation level where the giving and acceptance of a bribe occurs. This is the familiar terrain of the criminal law. It is also the level at which the private law discourse about corruption primarily occurs. The public and private law articulation of corruption share a common core and the fundamental substance of the interaction in question is the same. It stands to reason that the consequences of this interaction should be consistent across the private and public law domains.

The violation level is evidenced by an agreement to enter into a transaction that creates a conflict of interest. Such a position is a breach of mandate because of the secrecy that accompanies the agreement to give a bribe. Secrecy is often referred to as a key distinguishing element of the bribery transaction. In the interactions between the parties involved in the corrupt exchange, the mandate giver is kept in the dark. This secrecy can only be directed at the mandate giver and from this perspective the *harm caused* by the act of secrecy accrues *to* the mandate giver. As such, the harm occasioned by the violation identifies the real victims at international corruption.

The term secrecy in the international corruption discourse is probably best interpreted as a lack of consent (Makinwa 2007b). In many countries, particularly those rated poorly on the Transparency International indexes, corruption is an open secret. The perception of people is that it is an increasing phenomenon and that their government officials are on the take. Clearly there is knowledge about the general fact of bribery if not the specific case. However general knowledge does not equate to consent. For a bribe to lose its character as a bribe there has to have been consent to its occurrence.

Referring to the lack of secrecy in terms of a lack of consent emphasizes the relationship between the mandate giver and the perpetrators of international corruption. A *transaction approach* sees the party whose trust is betrayed not only in the narrow terms of the classic 'principal' of a corrupted agent but more broadly in terms in the mandate givers who have entrusted a public official with specific duties. The challenge lies in formulating the theoretical framework for this notion of '*trust*' and the consequent remedies for its breach. Adopting such a formulation broadens the conceptual scope of the crime of international corruption and brings to the fore the victims of corruption.

1(3) The Consequences Level

A third level of interaction is the consequence level. The consequence level results from the breach of trust at the mandate level and the successful breach of anti-corruption rules at the violation level. The primary focus of interaction at this level is the contract that comes into existence where anti-corruption rules have been successfully violated. The contract left standing influences behaviour and affects the deterrent effect of anti-corruption strategies. To allow persons to benefit from contracts resulting from bribery transactions is a contradiction to the logic of the anti-corruption rules.

Without due consideration of the effects of the consequence level, progress in the fight against international corruption is seriously compromised. The contract left standing, as a contract between 'consenting parties' is often a private contract to which the rules and principles of private contracts should apply. However to adopt this reasoning is to ignore the manner in which the contract came into being in the first place and could set up the private law as a cloak for transactions that go against the public interest.

The traditional dichotomy between the public and private sector is under strain in the world of international corruption. Harden has remarked that the conceptual divide between 'public' and 'private' has … ceased to correspond to the way the world actually works …[and]…[L]egal structures and ways of thought need to be re-adapted accordingly,' (Harden 1992). Interactions at the consequence level are complicated by the blurring of the lines between the public and private sectors. In modern times, the state is increasingly joining the fray as a private contractor and shareholder (Backer 2008). This challenges the notion that the state as represents and protects the public interest in a public/private transaction.

Liberal notions of freedom of contract assume a freedom to create and confer legal rights and obligations in a private self regulating system. In this private sphere the interest of the individual is the primary focus and not that of the society. However, as Friedman pointed out as far back as five decades ago, 'the increasing participation of public authority in contracts creates the wider and as yet generally unexplored problem of the dual function of the state, *as a superior and as an equal*' (Friedmann 1951-52a). The position today would seem to confirm the urgency of this problem (Backer 2008). At the level of consequence the provision of security cannot always be automatically ascribed to the state.

Figure 1. Summary - Levels of Interaction.

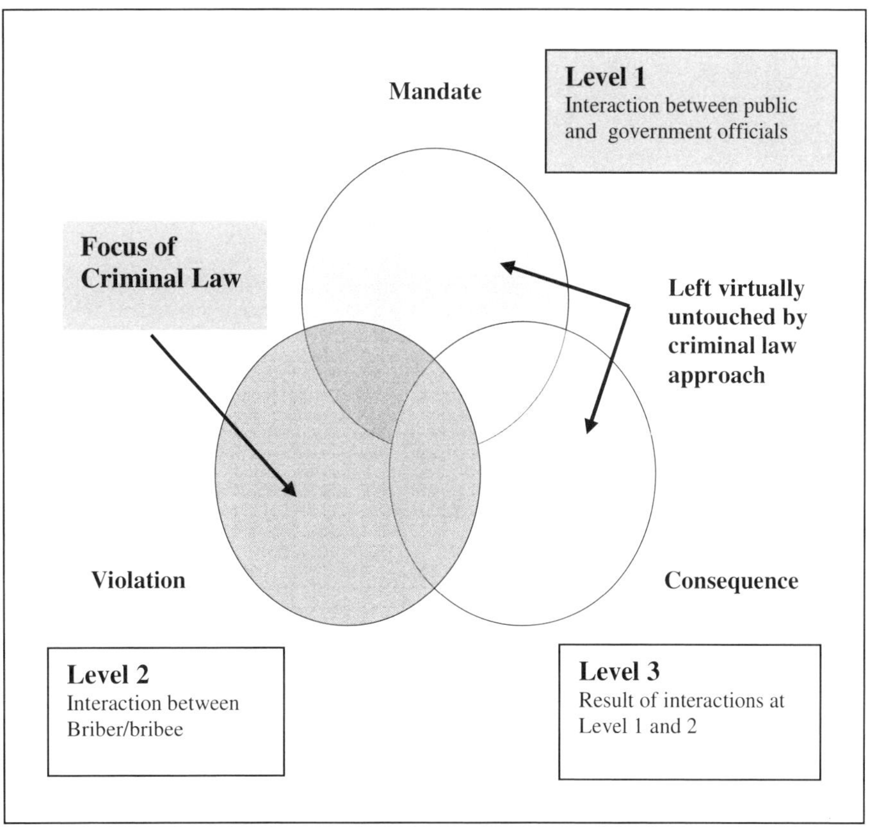

4. Section C: The Contract Tainted by International Corruption

The contract tainted by international corruption impacts all the levels of interaction. It motivates the breach of mandate; it is the substance of the violation of the anti-corruption laws and it is the consequence of their breach. As such this contract stands at the center of the environment shaped by these interactions and its status can positively or negatively impact the fight against international corruption.

The contract tainted by international corruption raises questions about the role of contracts in the ordering an international society that is defined not so much in terms of a sovereign with a monopoly on violence but by agreements based on pragmatism and mutual interest. It could be argued that, from the perspective of the fight against international corruption, principles of contract law must be viewed in the particular context of the commercial society in which they operate. In this society the private rights embraced in the law of contract are challenged by a global framework of anti-corruption laws. The mandatory nature of these rules carried to their logical conclusions impact upon the operation and validity of private agreements. In this sense, the contract resulting from corruption in a *transaction approach* raises a fundamental question. Should contracts arising in such circumstances be enforced? Does contract theory interact positively with the objectives of reducing or eliminating international corruption?

Contracts that result from the process of international corruption are by definition contracts that have a public element because of the twin facts of the involvement of government officials. They are clearly in a different category from contracts between private parties whose consequences are primarily restricted to the parties themselves. By and large principles of contract law tend towards generalisations to ensure certainty, order and stability. Such generalisations tend to view all contracts alike and do not address the particularities of the special case. Collins points out that the abstraction and generality of the private law system means that 'it lacks the mechanisms for differentiating in its regulation between different kinds of contracts' (Collins 1999b). He remarks that 'the price of the advantages obtained from the generality of private law systems is the incapacity to develop an adequately differentiated system of regulation of contracts' (Collins 1999b).

Yet, there is clearly a difference between contracts resulting from international corruption and, for example, the sale of a book in a bookstore. A *transaction approach* puts the connection between the contract tainted by corruption and the larger society into focus. It is a contract with a very public element. A distinction between public and private contracts is one that is found in some civil law systems. Friedman explains that in French and German law a distinction is made between contracts involving the state that are primarily of a financial or commercial character which are categorized as private ordinary contracts and those of a more public character that arise in connection with defense, the police or public service as administrative contracts. The main distinction he points out is 'the element of discretion in public policy, including, for example, the right to terminate a contract in certain circumstances, gives to the public authority greater latitude than in a private law transaction (Friedman 1951-52b). The question with contracts tainted by corruption is the role such public policy based latitude should play regarding the interpretation and enforcement of such contracts.

Putting contracts tainted by corruption in a special category helps to provide the foundation for a treatment of such contracts in a manner that recognizes the social underpinnings and public character of the consequences of such transactions. Such contracts are not mere private agreements but rather 'the way by which social and economic policies are expressed in legal form' (Friedman 1951-52b).

The negative influence that the tainted contract has on the environment in which international corruption occurs should engender a central role for public policy and state intervention in its regulation. Freedom of contract is, in certain instances, recognized as illusory and curtailed.[128] In these cases, the rigidity of the private law system of contracts has been mitigated by legislative intervention in the particular case (Collins 1999c). This illusion of freedom is arguably even truer in the age of the mega multinational corporation in international markets.

5. Section D: The International Contract as a Regulatory Tool

Criminalisation provides a necessary starting point in the fight against international corruption. In the absence of a normative framework there cannot be common objectives, methods or solutions. However, a criminal law system based on theories of punishment and retribution sits rather oddly on a society with no sovereign that is centered on promises and obligations entered into primarily by artificial persons.

In this scenario, a more logical basis for punishment and regulation may be one that is based on the obligations between parties. This may occur by limiting enforceable obligations to those that benefit the larger international system within which the parties operate. Interventions can be encouraged not only by the state, but more importantly, by the contracting parties themselves or by third parties affected by the actions of the contracting parties. This implies an approach to contract that accommodates the relational aspects of the parties in the purposes they seek to achieve (Macneil 2000; Zumbansen 2007).[129] The fight against international corruption may require that principles of freedom of

[128] For example in special conditions for consumer contracts that underscore the social welfare responsibilities of the modern states and the increasing power of group organisation, collective bargaining.

[129] This is in line with the relational theories of contract. Contracts cannot be divorced from the complex, interconnected relationships they evidence. There is no 'universal' law of contract.

contract be subsumed to an overreaching aim of economic and social stability in international market.

The contract tainted by international corruption can serve as a unique fulcrum in developing anti-corruption strategy. The interactions at the mandate, violation and consequence levels coalesce around the contract that results from the corrupt exchange. From a transaction perspective this contact is seen not only as a private act between parties but as a potential instrument of public social control. As the regulations criminalising international corruption show, there are limits to contractual freedom and party autonomy. Contracts tainted by international corruption constitute a category of contract whose regulation should be consistent with the overall objectives of the consensus criminalising international corruption.

6. Section E: Advantages of a Transaction Approach

The *transaction approach* seeks to rebuild interactions negatively impacted at the mandate, violation and consequence levels of international corruption. This broadens the idea of sanction in the fight against corruption. Focusing on the transaction lays the emphasis on repairing the harm caused by crime, in a restitutive process. In this sense the *transaction approach* can be viewed as a form of restorative justice where the aim is to repair the 'harm caused or revealed by criminal behaviour' (Zehr and Toews 2004).[130] It also portrays security in terms of a process that seeks to retie the cords of broken interactions in a bid to promote social harmony.

From the standpoint of international corruption where the principal offenders are international corporations and government officials, restitution can expiate the 'outrage to morality' by making corporations 'pay' for their crimes, taking the profit out of their misdeeds or rendering null and void contracts tainted by corruption. This translates the need for vengeance into a format that corresponds with a 'soulless' corporation. Restitution can also have a preventative effect. The effect of undoing the harm caused by the transaction may provide a powerful incentive to ensure that transactions are not of the sort that may suffer the risk of 'being undone'.

A *transaction approach* follows the chain of interactions associated with the corrupt exchange and not just the offender. This increases potential points of intervention, redress and accountability. It can also trigger economic and reputational consequences that can be of serious significance for commercial players. Furthermore, a *transaction approach* makes the link between the criminalisation of international corruption and private law processes that may in

[130] See <http://www.restorativejustice.org/>. There is no consensus definition of the term 'restorative justice'. However one aspect that seems to be shared by writers in this field is the viewpoint from the perspective of the victim rather than the offender or in terms of restoring the social contract of society rather than punishment of the victim.

many ways be better equipped to deal with such white collar crime (Simpson 2002).

The normative framework that gives content and definition to international corruption puts the state, government officials and international companies at the center of the corruption conundrum. This raises questions about the ability of the state via its government officials to act as an effective and independent provider of security regarding international corruption. The persistence of international corruption motivates the need for new models of intervention. By linking the interactions affected by the corrupt exchange at various levels and drawing a consistent line from mandate to consequence, a *transaction approach* provides a basis to review existing principles and theory in a coherent single narrative.

This *transaction approach* throws up three basic challenges. Firstly, the articulation of the notion of trust and the consequences for its breach that occurs at the mandate level. Secondly, the incorporation of the process of restoration of trust in the sanctioning processes for violations of anti-corruption rules and, thirdly, the regulation of the consequences of corruption in the differentiation, interpretation and enforcement of contracts tainted by international corruption. Addressing these challenges may help to move the fight against corruption in a positive direction.

7. Conclusion

In a changing international society, principles of justice must adapt to new terrain. Governing security under the rule of law may require looking at old concepts with new eyes. Looking at corruption as a series of interactions helps to emphasize the fact that the path to progress in the fight against corruption must explore nodes of governance beyond the state and capitalise on the fact that a vital node of governance is emerging from the growing role of private actors in public space.

The *transaction approach* proposed in this paper identifies the mandate, violation and consequence levels of interactions as critical stages in the corrupt exchange where interventions to provide security can be made. By seeking to restore interactions damaged by corrupt exchanges the *transaction approach* can empower victims, bypass the monopoly of the state to initiate sanctions and exploit the pragmatism of the international marketplace. In this terrain, the dynamics of contracting that underpin the entire trading system can be harnessed as a regulatory tool.

The *transaction approach* presents a model that looks to the environment of international trade as the critical element in encouraging or discouraging compliance with the anti-corruption rules. The purpose of sanction is seen not so much in terms of vengeance and retribution but rather in terms of *creating an environment* that encourages compliance. It calls for an anti corruption strategy that moves beyond the offender to the *restoration of interactions* negatively impacted by corrupt exchanges. The *transaction approach* looks beyond state centered theories of punishment and opens the door to developing a model that may be more consistent with the realities of the environment in which international corruption occurs. Finally, while this paper is specific to the challenge of international corruption, a larger script that emerges is a viewpoint that sees the provision of security as a *shared function* of the public and private law in the emerging international society.

References

Abed, G. (2002). *Governance, Corruption, and Economic Performance*. Washington: International Monetary Fund.

Beccaria, C. (1764a). *On Crimes and Punishment* (Chapter 2, The Right to Punish). Translation by D. Young. Indiana: Hackett publishing Company.

Beccaria, C. (1764b). *On* Crimes *and Punishment* (Chapter 12, The Purpose of Punishment). Translation by D. Young. Indiana: Hackett publishing Company.

Backer, L. (2008). The Private Law of Public Law: Public Authorities as Shareholders, Golden Shares, Sovereign Wealth Funds, and the Public Law Element in Private Choice of Law. *Tulane Law Review, 82(1)*, 1-62.

Blundo, G., & Sardan, O. de (2006). Everyday *Corruption and the State*, 4. London/ New York: Zed Books.

Collins, H. (1999a). *Regulating Contracts*. Oxford: OUP 47.

Collins, H. (1999b). *Regulating Contracts*. Oxford: OUP 54.

Dreher, A., & Herzfeld T., (2005). *The Economic Costs of Corruption: A Survey and New Evidence* (Monograph on file at Wageningen University and Research Center Publications (Netherlands). http://129.3.20.41/eps/pe/papers/0506/0506001.pdf

Friedmann, W. (1951-1952a). Changing Functions of Contract in Common Law. *University of Toronto Law Journal, 9,* 15 at 23.

Friedmann, W. (1951-1952b). Changing Functions of Contract in Common Law. *University of Toronto Law Journal, 9,* 15 at 40.

Graham, T. (2002). *The Implications for Intermediaries Handling the Proceeds of Corruption: The Abacha Case Study*. Presented at the 'Stop Money Laundering!'-Conference, 26th February 2002, London. http://www.antimoneylaundering.ukf.net/papers/tgraham.htm.

Harden, I. (1992). *The Contracting State*. Buckingham/Philadelphia: Open University Press.

Johnston, L., & Shearing, C. (2003). *Governing Security Explorations in Policing and Justice*. London: Routledge.

Ilias, B. (2006). Corruption as an International Crime and Crime against Humanity: An Outline of Supplementary Criminal Justice Policies. *Journal of International Criminal Justice, 4(3)*, 466.

MacQueen, H. (2004). Illegal and Immoral Contracts. In M. Hesselink, & M. Veldman (Eds.), *Towards a European Civil Code* (pp. 287-289). Ars Aequi Libri.

Macneil, I. (2000). Contracting Worlds and Essential Contract Theory. *Social & Legal Studies*, *9*, 431.

Makinwa, A. (2007). The Rules Regulating International Corruption: Achieving a Common Standard? *International Business Law Journal, 1*, 17.

Makinwa, A. (2007b). Wilson v. Hurstanger Ltd: Secret Commissions - Extent of Duty to Disclose. *International Company and Commercial Law Review, 18 (10)*, 365-368.

Makinwa, A. (2009). The Role of International Arbitration in the Fight against Corruption. In O. Meyer (Ed.), *Civil Law Consequences of Corruption* (Schriftenreihe des Zentrums für Europäische Rechtspolitik an der Universität Bremen) 53 (ZERP) Nomos Verlag, 257 – 280.

Makinwa, A. (2010). International Corruption and the Privitisation of Security. In M. Hildebrandt, M. Makinwa, & A. Oehmichen (Eds.), *Controlling Security in a Culture of Fear* (pp. 99, 112-119). The Hague: Boom Juridische uitgevers.

Minor, K., & Morrison, J. (1996). A Theoretical Study and Critique of Restorative Justice. In B. Galaway, & J. Hudson (Eds.), *Restorative Justice: International Perspectives* (p. 118). Monsey, NY, USA: Criminal Justice press/Amsterdam: Kugler Publications.

Redfern, A., & Hunter, M. (2004). *The Law and Practice of International Commercial Arbitration.*London: Sweet and Maxwell.

Rose-Ackerman, S. (1999). *Corruption and Government: Causes, Consequences and Reform*. Cambridge: Cambridge University Press.

Ruggiero, V. (2000). *Crime and Markets: Essays in Anti-Criminology*. Oxford: Oxford University Press, 106.

Shearing, C. (2006). Reflection on the Refusal to Acknowledge Private Governments. In J. Wood, & B. Dupont (Eds.), *Democracy, Society and the Governance of Security* (11-32, 26). Cambridge: Cambridge University Press.

Shearman, & Sterling, LLP. (2008). *Recent Trends and Patterns in FCPA Enforcement.* http://www.shearman.com/files/upload/FCPA_Trends.pdf.

Simpson, S. (2002). *Corporate Crime, Law, and Social Control* (p. 78). Cambridge: Cambridge University Press.

Teubner, G. (1997a). Global Bukowina: Legal Pluralism in the World Society. In G. Teubner (Ed.), *Global Law without a State* (5). Dartmouth: Aldershot.

Teubner, G. (1997b). Global Bukowina: Legal Pluralism in the World Society. In G. Teubner (Ed.), *Global Law without a State* (3). Dartmouth: Aldershot.

Teubner, G. (1997c). Global Bukowina: Legal Pluralism in the World Society. In G. Teubner (Ed.), *Global Law without a State* (7). Dartmouth: Aldershot.

Transparency International (2009). *Global Corruption Barometer Report Executive Summary* (English Version) 3 http://www.transparency.org/policy_research/surveys_indices/gcb/2009

Transparency International (2009). Report on Corruption in the Private Sector 2009 *Global Corruption Barometer Report* Chapter 1 p.1 http://www.transparency.org/policy_research/surveys_indices/gcb/2009 www.unodc.org/documents/corruption/publications_toolkit_sep04.pdf

Transparency International (2009). Report on Corruption in the Private Sector *Global Corruption Barometer Report*. pp. 13-75. http://www.transparency.org/policy_research/surveys_indices/gcb/2009

UN (2004). *Anticorruption Toolkit (2004).* Vienna: United Nations Office on Drugs and Crime, UN 3rd Edition.

Velasquez, M. (1992). International Business Morality and the Common Good. *Business Ethics Quarterly,* 2-27.

Zehr, H., & Toews, B. (Eds.) (2004). *Critical Issues in Restorative Justice* (1-47). Money, NY: Criminal Justice Press/ Devon, UK: William Publishing.

Zumbansen, P. (2007). The Law of Society: Governance through Contract. *Journal of Global Legal Studies, 14 Ind.,* 191.

Cases

Corner House Research & Campaign against Arms Trade, R (on the application of) v Director of the Serious Fraud Office & anor. EWHC 714 [CA 10 April 2008].

Corner House Research & Ors, R (On the Application of) v The Serious Fraud Office (UKHL 30 April 2008) 60.

Lamb v Philip Morris, Inc, 498 US 1086; 111 S Ct 961; 112 L Ed 2d 1048 (19 Feb 1991.

In re Immucor Inc., No. 1:05-CV-2276-WSD, 2006 WL 3000133 (N.D. Ga. Oct. 4, 2006).

Tesco Stores Ltd v Simon Pook & Ors [2003] EWHC 823 (Ch).

International Conventions

Inter-American Convention against Corruption Inter-American Convention against Corruption (1996), 35 ILM 1996 at 724.

OECD Convention on Combating Bribery of Foreign Public Officials in International Business Transactions (1997), 37 ILM 1998 at 1 Article 1.

Council of Europe's (1999) Criminal Council of Europe Criminal Law Convention on Corruption, European Treaty Series No. 173.

The Council of Europe Civil Law Convention on Corruption (1999) European Treaty Series No. 174.

Convention on the Fight Against Corruption involving Officials of the European Communities or Officials of Member States of the European Union (1997), 37 ILM 1998 at 12; Official Journal of the European Union 1997 C 195.

UN Convention against Transnational Organised Crime (2000), 40(2) ILM 2001 at 353

African Union Convention on Preventing and Combating Corruption (2003), 43(1) ILM 2004 at 5.

UN Convention against Corruption (2003), 43(1) ILM (2004) at 37.

United Nations Economic and Social Council 1958 New York Convention on the Recognition and Enforcement of Foreign Arbitral Awards. http://www.uncitral.org/uncitral/en/uncitral_texts/arbitration/NYConvention.html.

United Nations Commission on International Trade Law 1985 UNCITRAL Model Law on International Commercial Arbitration.
http://untreaty. un.org/cod/avl/ha/crefaa/crefaa.html.

Part III: Security Assemblages

11. Governing Security: Including the Molecular into the Molar

Patrick Van Calster & Marc Schuilenburg

Current governmental policy often hinges on the fallacious assumption that individuals and actions can be steered by 'outside' systems (Van Calster 2008). It is assumed that individuals act as an integral part of a system purported to have a pre-determined impact on action. While this may be a successful way of controlling and organizing particular social phenomena characterized by a low level of organization; it is seriously lacking when it comes to higher levels of organisation such as crime and criminal policy. A second problem with criminal policy is that it is often linear in character. Upon being confronted with the disappointing truth that governments (and other institutions) have little or no grip on non-linear interaction and their influence on an individual's choice, their automatic response is to expand the system of control as extensively as possible (Van Calster 2010a, 2010b). However, policy intervention very often achieves very little of that originally intended. Frequently, the outcome attained will not be particularly effective or efficient, since extensive intervention often leads to extensive unintended complications. A third problem is the emergence of undesirable side effects such as the curtailment of fundamental rights and liberties (Onsea 2002). In fact, current criminal policy often results in inefficiency and perverted outcomes. To make matters worse, these new and unintended outcomes are frequently poorly understood, resulting in precautionary intervention, i.e. interventions before problems even emerge (Pieterman 2008). As a result, it has become very difficult, if not impossible, to manage new problems with 'old school' laws, regulations and structures. Policy tends to boil down to a collection of symbolic gestures and manoeuvres aimed at creating the impression that all is under control (Beck 1986).

The aim of this article is to analyse the above phenomenon from a philosophical point of view. It is argued below that the way to do this is to recognize that the traditional approach to understand and combat the lack of security and criminality is merely a derivate of what could be called 'molar thinking'. We borrow the denomination 'molar' from thermodynamics, which studies the interactions between large collections of particles on a macroscopic level. It is precisely this macroscopic approach with its focus on order, stability and control that is the centre of the largest part of social scientific research on governing security and criminality. In this contribution, it is proposed that the research on security and criminality could benefit with the study of 'the molecular', a level of description with which the molar is inseparably connected. The level of the molecular, similarly a concept from thermodynamics, consists in interactions between separate elements that in a sense constitute the molar but are seldom studied or considered in policy strategies.

1. The Molar as Dominant Practice of Research

In his *Problems of Involvement and Detachment* Norbert Elias (1956) makes a distinction between two ways of addressing reality. The first he calls *involvement*. It reflects the way nature was (or is) experienced in a pre-scientific era. Nature here is experienced as a collection of mysterious forces to which one is exposed. People did (or do) not understand nor control these forces, and were afraid of them. They were *involved* in what they experienced and had great difficulties with simple sustenance. The second approach, Elias calls detachment. Scientific method enabled man to conquer his fears and to reflect on nature as something that can be controlled, even mastered. By approaching nature in a *detached* way, and by acting as a (supposedly) *objective* observer, man felt less emotionally involved in his experience of nature. His fears disappeared to a large extent and arguably led to a level of mastery of nature. Let us try to elaborate on this.

Social scientists, like all researchers, tend to break down reality into parts in order to focus attention on isolated and controllable matters (Van Calster 2006a). They draw boundaries around that which they research or scrutinize. Doing this they make their object of research discernible from the rest of the world. That which counts as the undisputed research program of a particular discipline is then what determines such boundaries (see also: Foucault 1988; Kuhn 1962). They divide social reality into certain categories, which are presented as largely homogeneous. Simplifying social reality in this way allows scientists to study the relations between the categories. Consequently, scientists try to formulate solutions for emerging problems. As a result, researchers study the parts in terms of what they contribute to 'the whole' (Van Calster 2010a). The logic here assumes that the system, the whole, moves towards its final state or a condition, which can be known in advance (Brittan 1978). The parts *function* to form the whole or the end condition. The whole is assumed as a 'thing' (Van Calster 2010b). Little or no attention is given to interactions between parts or to the diversity of the parts; they are assumed to be 'the same' and being 'average'.

This dominant view can only explain the origin of newness and fundamental change by pointing, *ex machina*, to the exceptional qualities or visions of particular individuals (leaders, entrepreneurs, brokers, and so on) who happen to appear within the system. Such individuals, it is then believed, initiate and control new projects and are therefore not subjected (and quite enigmatically so) to mechanisms of determination. This means scientists search for those systems that (seem to) determine human interaction. The causes of what people do are then located in a system which is supposed to determine human behaviour, e.g. economic dynamics, culture, values, mentality, and so on. They are supposed to *precede* interaction and develop in a knowable and predictable way. In this way an impression is cultivated that provided these basic systems are optimal, human action and interaction could be directed in an orderly (and controllable) fashion.

In this perspective many are convinced that it is possible to intervene in human systems in such a way that aims and goals (e.g. in policies envisaged) can be achieved in a controlled way. Unfortunately this is simply not so. Moreover, this misleading concept often leads to the desperate creation of more and stronger forms of intervention which produces effects but not the best effects in the best way (Van Calster 2006b). The profiling of risk is one such model. Profiling assesses specific characteristics of individuals that might classify them as potential offenders. The fight against security and crime, therefore, resembles a never-ending cycle in which it becomes necessary to deploy ever more and stronger strategies and measures. In many western societies we have now reached a point where everyday behaviour is criminalized (Presdee 2000) and where penal measures are born from precautionary prevention of hypothetical problems, which could cause damage in the future (Romein and Schuilenburg 2008). In addition, such strategies often have side effects: endangering fundamental rights and liberties for example (Onsea 2002). It seems that Western societies are prepared to burn down their habitat in their battle against crime and search for security. Apparently, all means are justified in the fight to conquer crime. The efficacy of the means, however, remains unclear.

2. Attention for the Unstable: Matters of the Molecular

Previously, we have argued that in the molar, the focus lies on stability and control. It is a macroscopic approach, by which the system of control gets expanded in order to deal with problems of crime and disorder. Currently, new systems of control are being introduced which try to streamline human behaviour. However, social reality is much more complex than the molar can or will research. We argue the molar cannot be properly understood without the molecular, a concept with which we try to express the unpredictable and the liquid, constantly in a state of flux, never to be absolute.

The molecular level focuses on the motion and transformation of the parts of a system or whole (Kubinga 2003: 65). Physicists and chemists speak, therefore, of interactions between molecules (proteins, lipids, metabolites and so on). Although scientists consider the molecular as the most fundamental level of interaction, they recognize that information in this area is still poor and incomplete. Knowledge as to why interacting molecules group into spontaneous order is lacking (Sijbesma 2007). The molecular resembles what scientists such as Stuart Kauffman (1993; 1995) and Gregoire Nicolis and Ilya Prigogine (1989) call *complexity*. The latter scientists remark that complexity cannot be located in one identifiable place in a system (Nicolis & Prigogine, 1989: 5). Stuart Kauffman (1993; 1995) discovered that com-plexity is the result of *interactions* between the different components of a system. It manifests itself on the level of the system itself.

Kauffman (1993; 1995) and Tom Ray (1992) point to the possibilities offered by technology to study non-linear interactions. Technology enables us to study things which we do not fundamentally understand. According to Cilliers (1998) powerful computers are able to simulate the behaviour on the molecular level without understanding the complexity of it. In Kauffman's and Ray's computer simulations, each phenomenon consists of a large number of agents, and each agent behaves according to its own interests, intentions, behavioural patterns, and so on. Because the focus lies on an agent-based approach, the object of their research is expressed as a population of agents which interact according their own local 'if… then' rules (Mainzer 1996; Lewin 1993). Research on a molecular level does not work with rules, laws or regulations that are deemed valid for the whole population, but, rather, with rules for individual entities that together form a population or system. No agent has ultimate control over the interactions and reactions of others, nor over the behavioural patters of the system, or the way in which the system develops. This approach makes no appeal to someone or something 'outside' the system, imposing their/its will.

Kauffman (1995: 63–64) demonstrates that systems which consist of a large number of randomly interacting agents will develop into connected, autocatalytic networks (see also Mainzer, 1996: 97). In other words, when entities interact with each other randomly, some entities will start to play a part in the constitution of other entities. This is catalysis. Eventually the strings of emerging catalytic interaction will fold back and form autocatalytic networks. This means that entity X will play a part in the construction of entity Y which will play a part in the construction of Z that will play a part in the construction of X. There is no design or blueprint for this network. Interactive cooperation has the intrinsic capacity to produce both transformation and coherence. Both, however, are unpredictable (Mertens 2000: 91–96). According to Kauffman, variation simply emerges in interaction between entities. The amount and strength of the connection(s) between the entities in a network make up the dynamics of the network (Taylor 2001: 188).

Notice the difference with the molar approach. Typical for the molar approach is the process of reification by which one reduces phenomena to 'things'. Rules of conduct, for example, are supposed to exist outside the system from which they structure and determine the behaviour of the system. Alliez (2009) is right in stating that the molecular level revolves around 'small complex relations', rather than 'huge dialectic structures' that direct the whole. Consequently, small changes could have huge and unpredictable effects. In terms of the social, it means that attention goes out to interactions that have no reference to a centre, standard or norm. The focus lies on *becoming*, and not on *being*.

3. Characteristics of the Molecular

At the risk of simplification, we would like to distinguish three characteristics of the molecular. These characteristics do not present new abstract principles intended to provide a new representation of reality. Rather, they coincide separately with each 'event' or each 'case'.

First, the molecular is about the *immediate*. It deals with believes and desires that represent the world 'here and now' and which transcend actions from a rational-calculating portrayal of mankind, as represented in the classical judicial works of Beccaria (1764/2009) and Hobbes (1651/1985). They assume that people prefer to choose an action (for example obeying rules or the violation of it) of which they think the benefits would be huge. The problem with this approach, is that rationalism 'expects ideas to stand for something which cannot be constituted within experience or be given in an idea without contradiction: the generality of the idea, the existence of the object, and the content of the terms 'always,' 'universal,' 'necessary,' and 'true' (Deleuze 1991: 30). As is well known, one of the other problems is the all too narrow timeframe of rationalism. After all, the effects of such a choice are spread over a long period of time. The immediate instead, deals with interactions (such as pride, frustration, pleasure, anger, shame) which exist in *real time*, that is here and now. From a molar perspective these interactions are seen as exceptional and are largely kept outside 'the order of the discourse', to quote Foucault (1988). In fact, they fall outside the structural frame of uniformity or a knowable goal (Schuilenburg 2008; 2009: 210).

Second, the molecular is characterised by a *heterogeneous* series that produce differences. Rather than representation by means of 'identity, opposition, analogy and resemblance' (Deleuze 1994: 137) a system of series is a differenciating of differences by means of the coupling of heterogeneous series (whose elements are already heterogeneous). This actualization is not a unilateral process, but rather the result of a whole series of mutually reinforcing effects e.g. non-linear relationships, series of events and affairs, or open series of interactions that lead to directions that are not previously agreed or established. As such, molecular relations are never solid. They are in a constant state of flux and permit an infinite number of connections, creating with every connection something new. This means – that against the laws of classic causality – coincidence must be seen as a cause of social change.

Third, the molecular is about *perspectivism*, i.e. accepting that all truth can only be known in the context of one's own perspective. Perspectivism, which takes root in Hume's empiricism and Kant's idealism and was further developed by Schopenhauer and Nietzsche, rejects the idea of a specific interpretation of social reality, which is 'complete' or 'total'. Perspectivism claims that all knowledge is perspectival. Concrete circumstances and behaviour will always been seen from different viewpoints. Or as Nietzsche points out in *The Will To Power*: 'In so far as the word "knowledge" has any meaning, (...) it has no meaning behind it, but countless meanings – "perspectivism" ' (1967: section number 421). Yet perspectivism has nothing to do with relativism. Perspectivism may develop sensitivity for different points of view or interpretations. It compels people to see the conditions and actual circumstances under which a certain view may appear.

In short, contrary to the molar, the molecular knows neither univocal definition nor individual boundaries. It is fundamental, ambiguous and paradoxical. Perhaps it is this intangibility that causes suspicion and mistrust with researchers on security and criminality towards the idea of researching the molecular. Researchers in sociology and economy, for instance, tend to categorize interactions in terms of 'usefulness' and 'interest' for the bigger whole (profit, sales, and so on). By so doing they focus their attention on the molar. Even criminologists who research processes of groups actually focus on the characteristics of a group, such as rivalry, structure and leadership, which underline the static and therefore spotlight the molar.

4. Including the Molecular into the Molar

It would be wrong to see the molar and molecular as two separate levels of social reality. Both levels are intertwined. In fact, they co-exist. They revolve around the interaction between stability and transformation. Change or transformation can therefore emerge out of even the smallest expression or gesture of an arbitrary actor. Such approach, which works intensely in the *beta* sciences, is underdeveloped in the field of criminology. This is possibly caused by the view that the molecular is seen as a minimal order or – even worse – as chaos and disorder.[1] Perhaps researchers assume the molecular is capable of neutralizing the molar? In that case, the force of the molecular would be more powerful than that of the molar. Clearly, these assumptions are misconceptions. It is not about chaos or revolution, not about the molecular as dogmatic and conservative. Let us therefore clarify three errors about the difference between the molar and the molecular.

The molar and molecular do not refer to collectives on the one side and small unities on the other. That would mean one has to deal with macro and the other with microphysics. In reality, both levels are not distinguishable in terms of size or scale. It would be better to speak of a difference in composition, organization and consistency between the elements on the level of the molar and the molecular. The molar and molecular are not defined by the amount of elements they bring together and therefore not by their multiple characters, but by the nature of the relationships between their elements. In the case of the molecular, it is about characteristics such as nomad, rhizomes, many-voiced, smooth, intensive and indivisible. The molar is connected with features such as

---

1 The concept of 'molecular chaos' is, for instance, used in thermodynamics for the description of behaviour of independent molecules before they collide (Prigogine and Stengers 1984).

sedentary, arborescent, unanimous, striated, extensive and divisible (Deleuze and Guattari 1987: 33, 505).

The distinction between molar and molecular is not between form and substance. Earlier we suggested that the molar is about the whole and isolated and controllable parts. That means the molar is more visible, because its actions are (on first sight) fixed and framed by univocal and compelling laws and regulations. However, it would be a mistake to reduce the molar to an abstract or judicial form (for example Hobbes' and Beccaria's *social contract*), which may be unrelated to human actions. In that case, the molar would be reassuring, while the molecular would be a matter of disruption. Each segmentation brings into play both forms and substances. Therefore, the molar is not an interaction-free structure or lacking in interactions. Characteristic for the functioning of the molar is the 'centering, unification, totalization, integration, hierarchization and finalization' (Deleuze and Guattari 1987: 41) of the molecular by inserting it into larger wholes. Foucault would speak here of 'disciplinary techniques' (allocation, classification, consolidation, normalization, etc.), to make visible the insertion of human activities in the institutions of the disciplinarian society, in its schools, prisons, factories, hospitals, army barracks.

The difference between the molar and the molecular is not absolute or a dualist opposition. In fact, both cannot independently exist from each other. Or, as Deleuze and Guattari write in *Anti-Oedipus*, 'there is not one molecular formation that is not by itself an investment of a molar formation' (1983: 340). Both levels are constantly interfering, reacting upon each other, introducing to each other either a current of suppleness or a point of rigidity. As a consequence, everything always functions at the same time ('and-and') and in parallel. Although both levels are usually separately studied (as if about two different kinds of social reality), only one process underlies both levels. The two levels are constantly running into each other and are connected in, what we would like to call, a 'zone of indiscernibility'.

5. A Zone of Indiscernibility

From a criminological perspective, it is important to recognize that the molar is only one way of looking at social reality. At the same time, paying only attention to the issue of functionality and stability leads to a drastic simplification of the same reality. Then, the molar is affirmed as the positive general, without taking into account the pool of spontaneity: the random, unpredictable and heterogeneous. It is striking that the molar level cannot encompass these matters and leaves them out of the research framework. The consequence of this is that the molar only manages to grip of a small part of the mentioned question at hand in social reality. For that reason it needs to put its own position in perspective. Moreover, it should address a more permanent and dynamic system that is difficult or impossible to formalize, i.e. that cannot be interpreted from mandatory categories or abstract principles. This raises the question of how the relation between the molecular and the molar can be understood.

As mentioned earlier, a whole or totality (police organization, public-private partnership, court and so on) consists of a collection of heterogeneous elements that relate to each other. This implies a certain consistency and coherence. Viewed from a molecular perspective, a whole is always an open set or combination because the different elements are related to specific circumstances and are constantly mediated by the relations between them (Schuilenburg 2009). In a philosophical sense, this means that an element is immanent to specific and local conditions and the relations in which it exists. In fact, essence and unity are replaced by a dynamic 'middle' that connects different elements to each other. This 'middle ground' is 'not an average' (Deleuze and Guattari 1987: 293) or principle that gives reality a new direction and unity, but a process where new relations pop up and connections are made.

In a more general sense, the middle is related to the changing conditions by which something new can appear and with everything that differs. Illustrative for the middle is the verb 'connect'. This principle can be physical, linguistic or conceptual, and ensures that elements are connected together into a larger whole. Especially important here is that at any time a connection can ensure that a separate element changes and as a consequence therefore the whole. Moreover, the connection makes it possible that new elements are taken up in a whole and old elements disappear or are plugged into a new whole in which its interactions are different. One element may dislodge and go on to function in another assemblage. It can be taken out of one assemblage and be incorporated in another context (Schuilenburg 2009: 209; see also: DeLanda 2006). In turn, this context is formed by new variables, unforeseen interactions and other outcomes. This guarantees that 'the whole' can change constantly. Or put another way, the dynamic between the elements at a molecular level allows the possibility that the interactions between different parts may result in new syntheses.

If we translate this 'principle of connecting' in terms of interactions between the different elements of the whole, this means that each interaction can ensure that a social field becomes adrift, meaning that an existing field of organization is broken up and moves into directions which are not formally established or legally regulated. Interactions are in fact always in the middle and create with each connection something new. In this respect, interactions mediate the elements in the whole permanently. It is therefore important to understand that interactions exist before they connect elements and continue to exist if elements become detached from the whole. In that sense, they are external to the elements and remain in force after certain events have occurred, specific forms or structures are created, or social acts are performed. This means that interactions cannot be traced to the elements they connect. They can change without the elements changing (Deleuze and Parnet 2002: 55). But also the properties of the elements do not explain all the interactions that give the whole a certain autonomy. In this light, the elementary social fact is not the individual or the whole, but a molecular series of interactions that produce a difference; movements that differentiate something qualitatively and quantitatively (Barry and Thrift 2007).

It will be obvious by now that we are far removed from the classical way of considering meaning or purpose, in which the human subject is at the centre of attributing meaning and purpose, a logic inspired by Descartes' magical maxim 'I think, therefore I am'. In this way of thinking, the actions of a person are the product of a free, autonomous, and immutable actor. This individual is in opposition to his immediate environment without forming part of it. From an external position he can comprehend and grasp social reality in its entirety. However, from the relation between the molar and the molecular we should assume that interactions can not be reduced to the action of the individual, that is: of the substance or subject it refers or is ascribed to. The interaction is an autonomous process; it expresses a 'becoming' or 'movement', which makes it problematical to discern cause or consequence. Moreover, the relation between cause and effect is ambiguous and difficult to determine. Order and unity are therefore not provided *a priori*. They emerge immanently 'from below', from the interactions on a molecular level, rather than constrained from above by large molar structures.

6. Processes of Interaction

It may be clear by now that, from a molecular perspective, all knowledge (including criminological knowledge) is a social activity that can evoke varied reactions from and within the professional field. Criminologists and policymakers should not, therefore, be placed outside the reality and social dynamics. When, for example, they devise new methods of conflict settlement to be imposed on that reality, they do not do this from 'outside' the system. Researchers unavoidably participate in what they research, while policymakers participate in the policies they design. Hence, they contribute considerably to what they attempt to research or reform (Heisenberg 1962: 19). It is more plausible, therefore, to define the criminal justice system as a complex social process of interactions (which includes both linguistic and non-linguistic dimensions), not only between people, but also between objects – including abstract items such as rules, regulations and territories (the court, a police station and so on) (Van Calster 2005). This is because people constantly interact, and it is precisely in and through those series of interactions that all kinds of actions, such as cooperation and conflict, emerge. Those interactions can take many different forms and may include innocent, conformist and deliberate, but also confrontational or unintentional interaction.

A focus on these series of interactions raises the question of *how* reforms actually occur, and what the impact is of the actions of people commonly considered the source of those reforms (legislators, politicians, practitioners in management positions, policymakers or scientists). These reformers, after all, design the desired changes. They devise models and plans and draft legislative texts or policy documents. This process takes form through and in the very interactions these actors have with others – actors with different interests, or conflicts; actors that harbour particular rational and emotional considerations. Hence, at the time when these models, action plans or legislative texts are actually being introduced or implemented, reformers have no certainty about their impact.

In criminal justice, for example, the impact of interactions that the many managers have *with* the lower echelons will undoubtedly be far greater than the impact of interactions *within* and *from* the lower echelons since actors in management positions tend to reach a far greater audience and, in addition, may be able to enforce their decisions and measures. But practitioners in management positions, politicians, policymakers, legislators and criminologists cannot *de facto* determine what the reactions from the professional field to their plans and intentions will be. The value and importance of the measures they take depend, therefore, on how others respond to them. Thus it is in and through series of interactions that the dynamics and developments of the process of criminal justice and its many institutions emerge. No one person will ever be able to determine the dynamics of interactions within an institution or during a collaborative undertaking because those dynamics depend on what others will do. Moreover, the manner in which *external* organizations and actors respond co-determines these dynamics of transformation. In short, the whole process can better be described as – to borrow a notion from complexity sciences – *emergent* as it will never be the exact realization of a preceding design.

7. Emergence

The question that immediately arises is how can it be that interactions of thousands of people are able to produce, for example, a particular policy or 'culture'? The answer to this question relates to the intrinsic self-organizing, *emergent* properties of interaction itself (Mainzer 1996; Taylor 2001; Kauffman 1993; 1995). Recent scientific complexity research has shown that, under certain conditions (such as diversity), interactions between large numbers of entities that react to one another's locally-oriented behaviours, customs and principles generate coherent and potentially *renewed* behavioural patterns. To put it differently: interactions possess the inherent capacity to spontaneously form a coherent pattern *in itself*.[2] Abstract systems thus have the ability to self-organize and hence produce patterns and behavioural patterns without these having been imposed. This process of interaction between people who are sufficiently different from each other can thus be described as a self-organizing process with an intrinsic capacity to form behavioural patterns. We define this as a complex

2 Relatively accessible studies about this process of self-organization include Nicolis and Prigogine (1989), Prigogine and Stengers (1984), Gell-Mann (1994) Mainzer (1996) and Taylor (2001).

process of interaction. We should add, however, that not only does the pattern of interaction organize itself on a molar level, but also on a molecular level. Since these two levels appear together and concurrently, separating them will be problematic. As the scientists Kauffman and Ray have shown, the molecular level forms the molar level, while at the same time it itself is formed by that molar level. Let us examine these complexity sciences in more depth.

In the computer simulations performed by Stuart Kauffman (1993; 1995) and Tom Ray (1992), every agent is represented as a computer program. Each computer program contains a set of rules and instructions determining its interaction with other computer programs. As the emphasis is on an agent-based approach, the research object is represented as a population of agents that interact according to their own local 'if-then' rules (Mainzer 1996; Lewin 1993). So, rules or patterns should not be formulated that apply to entire populations, but rather interaction rules for the individual entities that together make up a population or system. A complex adaptive system consequently comprises a large number of agents, with each agent behaving in accordance with its own local interaction rules. As we argued earlier, no individual agent, or group of agents, determines the behavioural pattern displayed by the system as a whole, or the manner in which this pattern evolves. This approach does not include anything imposing its will from outside the system. As mentioned earlier, there is no blueprint for the organization of the entire system. It emerges and sustains itself in a self-referential manner. The emerging pattern is self-organizing. Here, self-organization is an intrinsic property of interaction, which causes the emergence of patterns (Mertens 2000).

Once again, note how different this line of thought is from thinking in terms of the molar, stability and reification. Reification implies giving a certain content to various concepts, which is then used as a reference to give meaning to social reality (see also Van Calster and Verfaillie 2007). This causes them to become systemic or molar frameworks (feedback mechanisms), where the rules of conduct are seen as being outside the system, and which are referred to in order to correct or streamline behaviour. One consequence of this can be that 'culture' is individualized as a collective to which we can then ascribe values and motives. This way of thinking depicts the collective as an acting individual. The behaviour of members of an organization, a society or, for example, the criminal justice system is then driven by the values of that 'whole'. Hence, norms and values become abstracted from daily life. In short, reification idealizes the collective, which is represented as a personality that can justify the actions of the members. This idealization, however, diverts attention from interactions in everyday life and interactions in the *here-and-now*. And it is precisely this everyday-life dimension, which continuously affects the formation of stabilities and which he believes deserves research attention.

8. The Control of Criminality as a Process

By taking series of interactions as his point of departure for analyzing life in society, the molecular lays the foundation for 'process thinking'. Process thinking assumes a long concatenation of forms of interaction that have often completely lost their original meaning. The relationship between cause and effect in those concatenations is highly ambiguous and difficult to determine, and it is very difficult to even discern cause and consequence. Take Kauffman's autocatalytic networks, for example. The problem is aggravated by the many coincidences that look like causes, but are actually relational in nature (Cilliers 1998). This makes it difficult to accurately predict what will happen in a specific place over a specific period of time. To summarize, if we were to research the operation of the penal system (often labelled as a persistent penal culture or obstinate practice),[3] as a pattern of interaction that is not so much the implementation of a preceding design, but rather the result of an ever-emergent process of interactions, the focus of research would be on interaction *themes* that organize experiences, such as themes that are considered unpleasant and are usually avoided (Van Calster 2005).

It then becomes evident that the criminal justice system is simply a series of temporary 'successful' patterns and themes of interaction, accepted by the participants as 'good enough' to be repeated, and thus becoming organizational customs. The repetition of these patterns and themes creates stability in the collective identity (or organizational culture) and organizes cooperation. These patterns and themes are expressed through a certain organizational language; in other words, in certain ways of doing and saying things. These ways create the collective identity (the criminal justice system, for example), as well as various aspects of their individual identities. The repetition of organizational customs (culture or language) that are 'good enough' will increase efficiency as the constant repetition of these customs in a similar way will improve people's performance. These customs (a certain way of speaking, for instance) are safe themes that organize cooperation. They reflect what has emerged as a standard of conduct, and make prevailing power relations seem natural. Newcomers to 'the criminal justice system' then believe that they have to use this particular way of speaking to express involvement in or commitment to the organization. We hasten to add, however, that these patterns are not recorded anywhere and

---

[3] This, of course, does not alter the fact that there are frequently elements of rational planning and determination through and in the many processes of research and policy. Just as it does not alter the fact that intense negotiations (and thus social networks) will be entered into and result in various agreements that may or may not be observed. In other words, from the perspective of process thinking, the issue of control and the extent to which social change can be brought about by government intervention or policy seem only relative. Attempts to achieve them may produce unintended outcomes over which one has little control. For that reason, objectives, models and good intentions often 'lose their innocence' after a 'confrontation' with social reality itself.

are not fixed. Precisely because they are repeated constantly, they always have the potential for transformation and thus for change.

But if the dynamics of the police and the judicial system are emergent and do not necessarily, therefore, correspond with the predetermined designs and intentions, how do these institutions change? As the research by Kauffman (1993; 1995) shows, new patterns, and thus new meanings, arise primarily in interactions that are characterized by diversity. When there is little diversity between people and they have developed solid (and often rigid) conceptions and ways of interacting with each other, their interactions are unlikely to generate anything new. Their patterns of interaction are more likely to be repetitive. Conversely, groups with a full range of diversity will have to contend, incessantly, with dissonance and forms of 'disobedience'. Successful transformation, therefore, falls somewhere in between these two extremes, in a zone Kaufman (1993) calls 'the edge of chaos.'

As we noted earlier, there is a strong probability that behaviours arising from these complex processes of interaction become routines and customs, stabilizing themselves on a molar level. Routines and customs are identifiable by their clear and delineated meaning. That is what determines the reliability and robustness of these routines. If such routines are deemed successful, that success will strengthen them, and this may make them seem rigid to reformers. Routines are often accompanied by a certain formal use of language (usually excluding other forms of interaction), within which tasks and roles are clearly defined. As a result, they exert considerable influence on cooperation. This way, the constant repetition of customs generates stability of the collective and, for example, a penal culture. Criminal law and criminal justice, then, should be considered as stable series of interactions, rather than determining forces. These customs embody the official standards of conduct and generally make the power relationships formed in this process seem natural. Over time, actors tend to abstract, objectify or reify this repetitive behaviour, and consider it to be something that has always existed and as self-evident. In other words, they 'forget' that it has been generated in and through human interactions. People in organizations become habituated to this stability and feel threatened, or may even become aggressive, if new ways of interaction are introduced.

We believe that those applying themselves to studying the criminal justice system must *also* focus on the smallest deviations or slightest changes in series of interactions. Research by Elias and Scotson (1994) may provide an interesting source of inspiration in this respect. Elias and Scotson examined what happened when a group of workers moved into a new apartment block adjacent to an older one inhabited by other workers. Even though there were no substantial differences between the two groups, hostility soon developed. The older residents started to denigrate the newcomers. Elias and Scotson explained this in terms of cohesion among the older group of workers. The older residents had come to think of themselves as 'we', a group with common attachments, likes and dislikes, and interests that had emerged because of their cooperation. They had developed a sense of identity. The newcomers lacked this cohesive identity because they had no history of working together and that, according to Elias and Scotson, made them vulnerable. The more cohesive group, therefore, was quick to label the newcomers and to attribute to them hateful qualities such as 'dirtiness', 'unreliability' and 'criminal', even though there were no obvious differences between the two groups. One group used the fact that the others were newcomers to generate hatred and thus maintain a power difference.

9. Conclusion

The present social scientific perspectives on the governance of security are based on a linear logic and are breaking down reality into parts in order to focus attention on isolated and controllable elements. We have called this 'the molar'. One of the consequences of this approach is that it deals with problems by expanding the systems of control. The efficiency, however, is unclear. We have argued that the molar cannot be understood without knowledge of the molecular. Attention for the molecular means attention for small variations and transformations that may form the basis of new social-cultural stabilities. Elsewhere we reported on the research we did on assemblages in which police and assurance companies work together to combat transport criminality (Schuilenburg *et al.* 2009). Personal preferences, frustrations and tensions have a huge impact on the outcome of the agreements between the parties. Exchange of information also occurs through informal interaction. New ways of interaction come into existence, such as new languages ('camping contacts', 'rock & roll'). In other words, the interactions between the actors change continuously. Their cooperation is not a static theme, but rather a dynamic process that requires constant interpretation in terms of relationships, unexpected events, adaptations and coincidences. As a consequence, the partnership is constantly on the move, and therefore a complex and utterly dynamic process, which can only exist in the infinitive mobility of social reality. This poses the task of researching 'what happens' without reducing it to a collective structure or a fixed order.

References

Alliez, E. (2009). Gabriel Tarde. In G. Jones, & J. Roffe (Eds.), *Deleuze's Philosophical Lineage* (pp. 209-218). Edinburgh: Edinburgh University Press.

Barry, A., & Thrift, N. (2007). Gabriel Tarde: Imitation, Invention and Economy. *Economy and Society, 36 (4)*, 509-525.

Beccaria, C. (1764/2009). *On Crimes and Punishment.* New Brunswick: Transaction Publishers. Fifth edition.

Beck, U. (1986). *Risikogesellschaft; auf dem Weg in eine andere Moderne Frankfurt am Main, Suhrkamp (Risk Society; Towards a New Modernity*). London: Sage Publications.

Brittan, G.G. (1978). *Kant's Theory of Science.* Princeton: Princeton University Press.

Cilliers, P. (1998). *Complexity and Postmodernism. Understanding Complex Systems.* London/New York: Routledge.

DeLanda, M. (2006). *A New Philosophy of Society: Assemblage Theory and Social Complexity.* London: Continuum.

Deleuze, G. (1991). *Empiricism and Subjectivity: An Essay on Hume's Theory of Human Nature.* New York: Columbia University Press.

Deleuze, G. (1994). *Difference and Repetition.* New York: Columbia University Press.

Deleuze, G., & Guattari, F. (1983). *Anti-Oedipus: Capitalism and Schizophrenia.* Minneapolis: University of Minnesota Press.

Deleuze, G., & Guattari, F. (1987). *A Thousand Plateaus. Capitalism & Schizophrenia.* Minneapolis: University of Minnesota Press.

Deleuze, G., & Parnet, C. (2002). *Dialogues II.* New York: Columbia University Press.

Elias, N. (1956). Problems of Involvement and Detachment. *The British Journal of Sociology, 7(3)*, 226-252.

Elias, N., & Scotson, J. (1994). *The Established and the Outsiders.* London: Sage.

Foucault, M. (1988). *De orde van het vertoog.* Amsterdam/Meppel: Boom.

Garland, D. (2001). *The Culture of Control. Crime and Social Order in Contemporary Society.* Chicago: Chicago University Press.

Gell-Mann, M. (1994). *The Quark and the Jaguar: Adventures in the Simple and the Complex.* London: Abacus.

Heisenberg, W. (1962). *La Nature dans la physique contemporaine.* Paris: Gallimard.

Hobbes, T. (1651). *Leviathan.* Amsterdam: Boom. Editie 2007.

Johnston, L., & Shearing, C. (2003). *Governing Security. Explorations in Policing and Justice.* London: Routledge.

Kauffman, S.A. (1993). *Origins of Order. Self-organization and Selection in Evolution.* Oxford: Oxford University Press.

Kauffman, S.A. (1995). *At Home in the Universe*. New York: Oxford University Press.

Kubinga, H. (2003). *De molecularisering van het wereldbeeld, Deel I.* Hilversum: Verloren.

Kuhn, T.S. (1962). *The Structure of Scientific Revolutions.* Chicago: Chicago University Press.

Lewin, R. (1993). *Complexity: Life at the Edge of Chaos*. London: J.M. Dent.

Mainzer, K. (1996). *Thinking in Complexity. The Complex Dynamics of Matter, Mind, and Mankind*. Heidelberg/New York: Springer-Verlag Berlin.

Mertens, R. (2000). *De Ge-heel-de Mens. Een Nieuw Denkkader.* Leuven: Davidsfonds.

Nicolis, G., & Prigogine, I. (1989). *Exploring Complexity. An Introduction.* New York: W.H. Freeman & Company.

Nietzsche, F. (1967). *The Will To Power* (Ed. W. Kaufmann and trans. W. Kaufmann & R.I. Hollingdale). New York: Random House.

Onsea, I. (2002). *De Bestrijding van georganiseerde criminaliteit in het Belgische strafrecht: de subtiele grens tussen waarheidsvinding en grondrechten.* Proefschrift Voorgelegd tot het Behalen van de Graad van Doctor in de Rechten aan de Universitaire Instelling Antwerpen, unpublished PhD dissertation.

Pieterman, R. (2008). *De voorzorgcultuur. Streven naar veiligheid in een wereld vol risico en onzekerheid.* Den Haag: Boom Juridische uitgevers.

Presdee, M. (2000). *Cultural Criminology and the Carnival of Crime.* London, New York: Routledge.

Prigogine, I. & Stengers, I. (1984). *Order Out of Chaos. Man's New Dialogue with Nature.* New York: Bantam Books.

Ray, T.S. (1992). An Approach to the Synthesis of Life. In G.S. Langton, C. Taylor, J. Doyne Farmer, & S. Rasmussen (Eds.), *Artificial Life II* (Santa Fe Institute, Studies in het Science of Complexity, 10, pp. 371-408). Reading MA: Addison-Wesley.

Romein, E., & Schuilenburg, M. (2008). Are You on the Fast Track? The Rise of Surveillant Assemblages in a Post Industrial Age. *Architectural Theory Review, 13 (3)*, 337-348.

Schuilenburg, M. (2008). The Dislocating Perspective of Assemblages. Another Look at the Issue of Security. *Open. Cahier on Art and the Public Domain*, no. 15, 18-35.

Schuilenburg, M. (2009). Assemblages. In E. Romein, M. Schuilenburg, & S. van Tuinen (Eds.), *Deleuze Compendium* (pp. 205-223). Amsterdam: Boom.

Schuilenburg, M., Coenraads, A., & Van Calster, P. (2009). Onder de mensen; de aanpak van transportcriminaliteit door politie, verzekeraars en schade-experts. *Justitiële Verkenningen, 35 (1)*, 43-62.

Sijbesma, R. (2007). *Pakkende verbindingen. Zelf-organiserende moleculen voor functionele materialen.* Intreereden, uitgesproken op 23 februari 2007 aan de Technische Universiteit Eindhoven.

Taylor, M.C. (2001). *The Moment of Complexity. Emerging Network Culture.* Chicago: University of Chicago Press.

Terpstra, J. & Kouwenhoven, R. (2004). *Samenwerken en netwerken in de lokale veiligheidszorg.* Zeist: Uitgeverij Kerckebosch.

Van Calster, P. (2005). *Georganiseerde criminaliteit als emergent fenomeen van complexe wisselwerkingsprocessen.* PhD thesis: Brussels University Press.

Van Calster, P. (2006a). Naar een criminologie van het lichaam? Over angst, het nemen van risico's, belevingen en identiteit. *Justitiële Verkenningen, 32 (5/06)*, 45-62.

Van Calster, P. (2006b). Re-visiting Mr. Nice. On Organized Crime as Conversational Interaction. *Crime, Law and Social Change, 45 (4/5)*, 337-359.

Van Calster, P., & Verfaillie, K. (2007). Het strafrechtsysteem als narratief proces. Over de illusie van maakbaarheid en controle. In J. Christiaens, E. Enhus, A. Nuytiens, S. Snacken, & P. Van Calster (Eds.), *Liber Amicorum Christiaen Eliaerts* (pp. 319-332). Brussels: University Press Brussels.

Van Calster, P. (2008). De publieke veiligheidssector als cult. Over 'prestatie' en 'presteren' als cultwaarden in de organisatiecultuur van de publieke veiligheidssector. In A. Collier, & E. Devroe (Eds.), *Politiecultuur* (pp. 147-169). Brussel: Politeia.

Van Calster, P. (2010a). Wetenschap in Tijden van Gevaar en Bedreiging. Over slechte wetenschap en pseudoafstandelijkheid. In R. Pieterman, & M. Hildebrandt (red.), *Zorgen om Voorzorg* (pp. 179-216). Den Haag: Boom Juridische uitgevers.

Van Calster, P. (2010b). Studying Society, Safety, and Security: Notes on Observer Involvement. In R. Lippens, & P. Van Calster (Eds.), *New Directions for Criminology. Notes from Outside the Field* (pp. 17-39). Antwerpen/Apeldoorn/Portland: Maklu.

12. European Surveillance Assemblages: Preventing Crime and Terrorism through Data Monitoring

Monica den Boer & Jelle van Buuren

1. Introduction

The concept of the 'surveillance assemblage' can be applied to the governance of practices of data-exchange, both at the level of the European Union as well as that within the individual Member States. In line with the argument of Johnston and Shearing (2003) that plural security practices have emerged widely, data can be interlinked and shared at a variety of levels by a substantial number of different actors, who may function in the context of a highly differentiated governance system. At the same time, it can be argued that criminal justice governance is transforming into a remote crime control mechanism, where gradually – instead of territorial patrol and physical encounters between police and citizens – law enforcement organizations compose collages of deviant (future) conduct. The popularization of the precautionary logic – in internal as well as external security environments – has encouraged wide acceptance of surveillance and mass-data gathering for the purpose of preventing crime, terrorism or military conflict. Through preventive monitoring, social ordering and mental disciplining (Foucault 1995; Haggerty and Ericson 2000; Zedner 2006; Elden 2003: 242; Lyon 2003), law enforcement can seek to deliver and distribute safety in a more efficient manner, as the sector can seek to limit its focus on serious criminal offences and public order issues. At the same time, however, the legitimacy of this managerially driven focus may come under pressure when viewed from the perspective of equal justice distribution (Van Buuren 2009).

From a criminal justice governance perspective, a few observations can be made about the emergence of a surveillance complex in Europe: 1) at the national and European level, a range of surveillance instruments has been coined which enable the law enforcement arena to gather, store and analyze data about citizens in order to control crime and terrorism; 2) these organizational surveillance 'nodes' are aggregated, concatenated and even fused into a larger surveillance complex which is jointly operated within the European Union; 3) the interoperability of surveillance nodes in the Member States allows for a large-scale sharing of information about European citizens which in turn flexes the margins for storage, use and interpretation of high volumes of data; 4) the rise of technological means and the interface with the military world have enlarged the surveillance potential; 5) the encouragement of multi-disciplinary co-operation within these agencies has nourished the erosion of fire-walls between the different agencies, gradually loosening the hitherto applicable information regimes; and 6) the enlargement of the mandate of existing agencies such as Europol and the creation of new agencies has expanded the counter-terrorism and intelligence potential, furthering the application of the precautionary surveillance of terrorism, crime and deviance.

Our main contention is that the European Union, which is in a position to initiate, facilitate, finance and implement surveillance instruments, is in the process of developing itself into a supernode, which is tentacled by smaller but powerful nodes that interlink public and private actors throughout the Member States through surveillance systems. Instead of drawing a sharp distinction between 'surveillance nodes' (assemblages, networks) on the one hand, and a Panopticon that is centrally operated by one powerful actor, we prefer to define surveillance as a continually changing theatre of activity, spurred on by the sheer Utopian dream of making societies maximally controllable. Neither will we dwell on the distinction between mass surveillance and targeted surveillance. Our emphasis is more descriptive than theoretical, and also more focused on the evolution of several smaller and larger surveillance practices, that sometimes compete and at other times seem to neatly fold into each other. Also, we seek to accentuate that surveillance has gone adrift, like a larger technocratic instrument which can no longer be controlled by one single actor. Finally, our emphasis is on analyzing how the European Union as a security actor has been caught by the logic of prevention and seeks to expand its recently adopted role of security actor through surveillance measures.

In the course of this chapter, we seek to further unpeel the role of surveillance systems in preventive security governance, and we will transpose it to shifting patterns in security governance as well as to the European policy-making level. Moreover, we will seek to clarify how vocabularies and conceptualizations in national and international discourses on security influence – or even bedevil – each other.

2. Preventive Security Governance through Surveillance

The concept of 'surveillant assemblage' was introduced by Deleuze and Guattari (1987) and further developed by Haggerty and Ericson (2000). In the context of our analysis, it provides a conceptual tool for the analysis of data-gathering and information across Europe. 'Surveillance' is understood by us as watching over, i.e. monitoring the behaviour and movement of persons, goods and systems. Surveillance includes a range of measures, exercised by public and private authorities, and is considered to enhance objective and subjective security. As such, surveillance has become closely intertwined with security. Gill (2006: 28) writes – comparably but more extensively – that global surveillance is argued to be an intrinsic part of the general economic restructuring of capitalism, and that 'security intelligence processes' are 'essentially a sub-set of the more general surveillance that constitutes contemporary governance. Thus, since intelligence is one of the two defining components of surveillance, and, in turn governance, then security intelligence is one of the defining components of security governance.'

Our discussion does not merely focus on data-systems which are widely used in European states and at the level of the European Union itself, but also on the adjacent (and interrelated) practices of de-centralized, networked, transnational data-processing and surveillance, which may not fall within the delineated lines of accountability (Gill 2006: 45). Ericson (2007: 1) observed an 'intensification of security measures' through an incremental series of legal transformations, as well as through 'innovative surveillance technologies and networks'. Below, we seek to illustrate this development by giving some examples. Closed-circuit television (CCTV), for instance, has been introduced in several environments (European Parliament 2009: 7; Hempel and Topfer 2009: 27-34). Face recognition has been proposed, for instance by Interpol, and in some instances has been introduced at local and international levels of security governance; fingerprint controls and facial recognition are and will be introduced at border entry points, allowing for the matching of personal biometric information with travel watch lists.[1]

Except for the growing acceptance of methods of surveillance such as data matching,[2] data mining,[3] and profiling, there has been a widespread introduction of smart cards, body scans, body-cams, storage and interception of telecommunication, the use of GPS for detection purposes, and environmental designs. Radio Frequency Identification (RFID) tags and electronic chips implanted in goods and vehicles are used as instruments of surveillance, often for the purpose of security governance (Ericson 2007: 2; House of Lords 2009: 17; Rathenau Instituut 2007; Van 't Hof, 2007). Although not (yet) widely used by law enforcement authorities because the information is too fragmented, RFID chips can and are used for guiding and monitoring processes such as luggage-handling. The European Commission announced recommendations and a citizens' summary for the implementation of privacy and data protection safeguards for RFID applications. The guidance directs organizations to perform privacy impact assessments, apply risk minimization techniques, and inform individuals about RFID.[4]

---

1 Electronic Privacy Information Centre, <http://epic.org/privacy/facerecognition/>. In the meantime, automated face-recognition systems have also been introduced in local public transport environments.

2 According to the American Civil Liberties Union ACLU (2004), data-matching is a loosely coupled set of techniques to tap into a wide number of data-bases containing details on the individual's behaviour, aggregate the data and scrutinize them en masse for criminal or terrorist intentions. See also House of Lords (2009: 14).

3 Data mining involves the use of mathematically based analytical tools to detect patterns in large sets of data with the purpose of predicting certain kinds of behaviour, such as the propensity to engage in criminal activity or to purchase particular consumer goods (House of Lords 2009: 14).

4 <http://epic.org>.

National surveillance assemblages as well as international data-exchange practices gradually evolve into 'horizontal' strategies, whereby de-central i.e. local law enforcement authorities can exchange information and intelligence with their foreign counterparts in other EU Member States.[5] This can be illustrated by referring to vehicle registration, a practice which gradually gains popularity within law enforcement organizations.

Vehicle recognition is extensively discussed in the European Parliament report on CCTV (2009: 14):

> 'In the UK, one of the first major applications of ANPR was launched in 1996, as part of the city of London's defences against the IRA terrorist threat: all vehicles entering the City of London had their license plates checked against police databases. In 2003 the Home Office drew up plans to extend this for more routine crime prevention purposes, and launched a national pilot scheme which involved 300 officers operating as part of 50 intercept teams across 23 police forces (...) in the first nine months 22.8 million vehicle registration marks were read (...) of which 900,000 (4%) were of immediate interest to the police. Within the resources available, the intercept teams stopped 136,857 vehicles (PA Consulting 2004). These stops led to the arrest of 10,546 people for offences ranging from burglary to drug related offence, and 2611 persons for driving offences. In other words, *seventy-five percent of the arrests were neither for traffic nor for driving related offences* (our emphasis). The significance of ANPR is that it integrates a surveillance device, the camera, with the police national computer and all of its associated databases. Like open street CCTV it targets all under its gaze but greatly enhances its surveillance capacity as it creates a major investigative resource of a vehicle's movements and locations, regardless of the status of the driver. As Watson and Walsh, in their Australian review of ANPR argue, the British Police have exploited the system's potential for: data mining as a means of building a picture of a person's (i.e. offender's) habits and lifestyle. The risk in this approach, however, is that profiles of non-offenders can also be derived from ANPR databases using data mining techniques (2008:8). The Australian Privacy Commissioner noted the British system would soon be collecting and storing around 35 million images per day and stated that they planned to keep this data for two years. Further, the ANPR data that is collected is not only mined and matched with a number of databases, but also then stored for future use. The Australian Privacy Commissioner regards this as an expansive and invasive practice.'

In short, for law enforcement organizations that seek to co-operate across the national borders of EU Member States, a wide range of surveillance possibilities has become available for the active monitoring of individuals and commodities. Ericson and Haggerty have labeled this the 'surveillant assemblage' (see also Sheptycki, 2007). Increasingly, a vast volume of data is available to government in general and to law enforcement and security agencies in particular, to the extent that the physical movement, the decisions, and even the mental state of

5 See e.g. the application of the Council Framework Decision 2006/960/JHA of 18 December 2006 on simplifying the exchange of information and intelligence between law enforcement authorities of the Member States of the European Union in the form of guidelines (Council doc. 16870/08, Brussels, 7 January 2009).

each individual is subject to continuous observation. Over a decade ago, Marx (1998) referred to this development by arguing that:

> 'New technologies for collecting personal information which transcend the physical, liberty enhancing limitations of the old means are constantly appearing. They probe more deeply, widely and softly than traditional methods, transcending barriers (whether walls, distance, darkness, skin or time) that historically made personal information inaccessible. The boundaries which have defined and given integrity to social systems, groups and the self are increasingly permeable. The power of governmental and private organizations to compel disclosure (whether based on law or circumstance) and to aggregate, analyze and distribute personal information is growing rapidly.'

Whether or not international data-gathering practices are subject to 'horizontal' or 'vertical' governance, warning shots have been given that we may be 'sleepwalking into a surveillance society'.[6] Data which have been gathered by different public authorities can be concatenated in a powerful manner, such that new knowledge or intelligence may arise from it. The justification for these practices is the elevation of security for those individuals and society as a whole, mainly through the minimization of risk and uncertainty. The interlinkage between surveillance practices and the prevention of terrorism and crime is a relatively new one within the realm of European policing. Never before did European or intergovernmental security actors such as Europol or SitCen have the possibility to gather and analyze information proactively with a view to early intervention in illegal markets or radicalization contexts; never before was the European Union in such a powerful position to stimulate the interoperability between security-enhancing databases, or to finance research on technologically advanced surveillance systems.

Preventive security governance is an area of activity where the European Union can act potently, without upsetting the sovereign Member States that hold the monopoly of violence, and thus of coercive powers which are used in the context of reactive or repressive security governance. With its encouragement of crime and radicalization prevention programmes, the European Union reinforces national developments rather than competes with national arenas which cultivate preventive security governance through surveillance. According to Ericson, 'risk is the way organizations make sense of their environment and act upon it. External sources of harm are converted into organizational risks through technologies such as early warning systems, risk profiling, and red flag indicators. Internal sources of harm are converted into operational risks through technologies such as inspections, audits, reporting procedures, and electronic surveillance. Risk management has become engrained in the social imaginary of organizations.' (Ericson 2007: 11).

6 UK Information Commissioner Richard Thomas in 2004, quoted in House of Lords Select Committee on the Constitution report, Surveillance: Citizens and the State, 2009, HL Paper 18-I, p. 5.

More than ever before, today's risk societies are preoccupied by a need to predict. Unpredictability, uncontrollability and invisibility are gradually defined as undesirable practices and thus ruled out from late modern governance (Trommel 2009; Sackers 2010). Longing for a safety utopia (Boutellier 2002), we have landed in a so-called *non-permissive society*.[7] The tendency to prevent disasters, calamities, crises, accidents, crimes and terrorist attacks has influenced the transition from reactive to proactive intervention (Den Boer 2010).

This preventive logic (also referred to as the 'precautionary principle') is not new as it has been apparent in 'high policing' strategies (Borgers and Van Sliedregt 2009), which can be characterized as the gathering of intelligence which may lead to a proactive intervention, often without an explicit criminal procedure. Scenario's, risk assessments and intelligence models have become part and parcel of accepted working methods for police and military, allowing for the prediction of patterns of uncertainty, crimes and security gaps, and allowing for a smart and timely intervention. The preventive logic involves a transition from accusation to an orientation; a transition from individual risk citizens to their environments (social network analysis; money transfers; virtual communication); from penal to administrative intervention; and from repression to the mental disciplining of citizens.

A law enforcement image that presents itself is that of '*policing by the velvet glove*', where physical encounters with the citizens are substituted by electronic data-collection (Den Boer and Van Buuren, forthcoming). The gathering of data, the conditioning, and the restyling of citizens have become part of a larger complex of '*datawars*'. Several police forces have welcomed the introduction of (smart) camera's in public spaces (Sackers 2010: 14), allowing law enforcement authorities to keep a constant watch on mobility and flows of traffic, people, goods, finances and information. This fits in a new strategy of intelligence-led policing which is labeled 'nodal policing' and which has – in a rather technocratic fashion (Den Boer, forthcoming) – become an accepted modus operandi within several law enforcement agencies'.[8]

3. Evolving Surveillance Systems

Surveillance – particularly exercised through electronic i.e. technological means – has become an inescapable reality, primarily because governments seek to reduce risk by means of preventative control (Zureik and Salter 2005: 1), culminating in a 'risk aversive Panopticon' (Whitaker 1999: 44). In a few decades, spurred on by security crises such as 9/11, the surveillance climate has altered dramatically. Below, we seek to illustrate this development by highlighting different dimensions of surveillance: its potential, its depth (pervasiveness), its application, its finality, its interaction and its effect.

---

7 Quotation from Chief Constable Bernard Welten, 11 March 2010, Public Lecture, VU University Amsterdam.

8 Rapport 'Politie in Ontwikkeling', Raad van Hoofdcommissarissen, 2005.

Function Creep

Governments and law enforcement authorities have principally sought to justify the introduction of new surveillance measures by arguing that the scrutiny of millions of data helps in identifying would-be terrorists. But gradually, anti-terrorism surveillance measures can also be used for the monitoring and registration of minor crimes or public nuisance. Or, '(W)hat is developed as an anti-crime surveillance device can be redirected against refugees, political dissidents, or striking trade unionists. Such technologies are also moving into the hands of private, corporate security, which stands outside whatever regulation and democratic accountability may constrain state agencies' (Whitaker 1999: 85).[9] Moreover, large amounts of data can now cross national borders either formally or informally, between public as well as private users (Adviescommissie Informatiestromen Veiligheid 2007; Gill 2006: 33).

Penetration of Social and Private Life

As mentioned previously, practices like data-matching, data-mining and text-mining have become widely introduced. Whitaker (2006) for instance refers to the FBI's CARNIVOR, which is a super search engine capable of trolling through e-mail traffic and flagging communications of interest, e.g. on the basis of key word recognition. In Europe, there has been discussion about the well-known ECHELON system (Whitaker 1999: 93, 105), which, allows SIGINT (signals intelligence collection) and operates on behalf of the five signatory states (Australia, United States, Canada, United Kingdom and New Zealand). ECHELON is capable of (mass) interception and content inspection of telephone calls, fax, e-mail and other data-traffic communicated across a range of media (radio, microwave, cyber-optic, cellular or satellite).[10]

More pervasive surveillance methods include data-profiling practices, which can be based on the collection and sharing of DNA-material and fingerprints.[11] Biometric information systems are thus increasingly woven into existing practices and procedures of international police co-operation (Lewis 2005: 97). According to the House of Lords (2009: 14), data-profiling is used in the public sector 'to predict a variety of risk patterns in the population, thereby enabling public services and law enforcement resources to be appropriately focused. Although this process may enable benefits and social services to be targeted more accurately and effectively, it may arguably lead to discrimination by singling out individuals or social groups for adverse treatment on the basis of incorrect or misleading assumptions.' Profiling is done on the basis of a variety of criteria, e.g. race or ethnic group, and used in security settings.

---

9 On the issue of democratic accountability, see *Parliamentary Oversight of the Security Sector.*

10 For the European Parliament Report on intelligence in general and Echelon in particular (11 July 2001), see: http://www.au.af.mil/au/awc/awcgate/echelon/echelon_eur_parliament.pdf.

11 For a discussion, see European Parliament Working Document on problem of profiling (2008).

From Evidence to Intelligence

As has been noted above, if there is one dimension of information-gathering that has changed considerably, it is the moment at which information is collected about an individual's behaviour: the last few decades have seen a steady increase of pro-active intelligence gathering (instead of reactive information-gathering in response to a concrete suspicion concerning the role of an individual in a reported crime). Hence, there has been a move from tagging real suspicions to possible suspicions. An emergent 'precautionary logic' (Ericson 2007: 25) combined with administrative anxiety about accountability has paved the path for more pro-active data-gathering and risk management: 'While other approaches to government seem to yield more uncertainty, governing through crime sends a strong signal of certainty. When there is a persistent threat that is said to affect the quality of life, or a catastrophic failure in a risk management system for which the government is held responsible, criminalization through counter-law provides an ending to the political narrative of uncertainty in the short term, and perpetuates the myth of governability in the long term.' (Ericson 2007: 207). The evolving finality can also be demonstrated in the new application potential of the Schengen Information System (SIS), which functions in the context of the Schengen Implementing Convention (1990): it allows the submission of data which are defined as indicators of future criminal action; these data will also be used for counter-terrorism purposes by virtue of the Prüm Treaty (2005).

Multiple Users, Shared Information Spaces

The House of Lords (2009: 15) reminds us that: 'The role of technology in surveillance is pre-eminent and poses formidable regulatory problems. The Information Commissioner told us that individuals 'leave electronic footprints behind with the click of mouse, making a phone call, paying with a payment card, using 'joined up' government services or just walking down a street where CCTV is in operation. Our transactions are tracked, our interactions identified and our preferences profiled – all with potential to build up an increasingly detailed and intrusive picture of how each of us lives our life. This has increased the capability for surveillance of the citizen through data collection.' New technology allows for ambient intelligence and ubiquitous computing, enabling a total information awareness on the side of government and law enforcement authorities, exercised by means of Real Time Intelligence Rooms. A condition for this practice is the cultivation of multi-disciplinary co-operation, primarily between security agents, but increasingly also between public and private agents. It is contended that public authorities organize a co-production (or 'conscription') with private business to enable the construction of a surveillance society (ACLU 2004). Air carriers have been included in this public-private security co-operation, for instance as a consequence of the Air Carrier Sanctions in the Schengen Implementing Agreement or in the context of PNR (see below): 'Multiple airlines have admitted turning over the records of their customers' travels to the government. In each case, the information was turned over not to help the government solve a particular crime or track a particular suspect, but in order to examine each traveler's records in the hopes of identifying terrorists by detecting 'suspicious' patterns in his or her travels – in effect, turning every traveler into a suspect (...)' (ACLU 2004: 10). Private vigilantism thus becomes part of the surveillance complex, and it becomes more difficult for customers or citizens to distinguish the roles and responsibilities of the surveillance agents.

Meanwhile, technology becomes smarter and more sophisticated, for instance due to the introduction of swift and massive hard drives and content analysis (ACLU 2004: 9). A new generation smart cameras has been introduced in several (semi) public spaces, such as shopping malls and railway stations, which can register a concentration of people, irregular behaviour (such as shouting, pushing), allowing for a direct notification to security agents. Within the law enforcement field, netcentric 'warfare' as well as rapid automatic intervention by means of intelligent technology are close to being applied on a vast scale.[12]

Hybrid Interaction and 'Interoperability'

At the level of the European Union, several instruments have been adopted and good practices shared in law enforcement circles which enable the connection between public order policing and overt ('forward intelligence') as well as covert surveillance of audiences, to enable a prognosis of the behaviour of political dissidents, football hooligans, mentally deranged people etc., in order to prevent riots, or in the worst case, attacks. In the UK, this is called 'forward intelligence'. Moreover, as indicated above, there is an increasing development towards authorized access to large national and international databases for police and law enforcement authorities, which increases the possibilities for multi-disciplinary usage of data and data-fusion and which enhances the interaction between intelligence-led policing and public order policing. 'Interoperability' has become the magic wand in European and transnational security arrangements.

Internalization of the Gazing Eye

The effect of total surveillance or total information awareness is that individuals are conscious of being continuously watched by state and private authorities, to the extent that they discipline themselves mentally. This 'panopticism' has become a core element of the modernist project. In this regard, Ericson (2007: 29) noted that 'The police power is perfected when it results in self-policing among members of the population. The liberal social imaginary of the 'house of certainty' is a house of discipline as self-policing. The individual who knows that she is seen through by the surveillant assemblage, who recognizes her visibility, will internalize the gaze. That is, she will not only assume responsibility for the constraints of power, but will have that power inscribed in

12 See 'Neoconopticon', Report of the Transnational Institute, 2009 (this report can be accessed through http://tni.org/report/neoconopticon).

her to the point where she polices others as well as herself.' The Leviathan-like surveillance net is incrementally enlarged through new legislation (not always passed by parliament but de-centrally widened by municipal authorities who then 'export' their new surveillance practice to other cities) to include ever new groups of the population, who for reasons of safety, education, health, housing or social benefit are made subject of more active monitoring.

4. Surveillance in the EU

Security has become one of the essential pillars in the EU polity, particularly through the construction and promotion of an 'Area of Freedom, Security and Justice'. This policy domain, previously known as the field of justice and home affairs co-operation or the 'Third Pillar', has gradually matured since the adoption of the Maastricht Treaty in 1991, and now encompasses hundreds of legal instruments, as well as several action and financing programmes.

The development of the EU Area of Freedom, Security and Justice has been flanked by wider and more general developments. On the one hand, globalization and informatization have reinforced networked (security) governance and the commodification of public security (Van Buuren 2009), whilst on the other hand, a merging process between internal and external security has facilitated the criminalization and 'securitization' of migratory flows (Bigo 1994). Furthermore, terrorist attacks have sent accelerating shockwaves through EU decision-making machinery and has culminated in the adoption of several legal instruments which entail deep consequences for information-gathering, such as the Passenger Name Record agreement and the EU Retention Directive on Telecommunication.

Particularly noticeable is the reliance of law enforcement authorities – both at the European and the national level – on information, principally gathered and dispersed through large data-bases (Van Linde 2002). Examples of European, cross-border data-bases that are used by law enforcement authorities (including customs and border control authorities) are the VIS (visa information system),[13] SIS I and II[14] (Schengen Information System), the CIS (Customs Information

[13] Access to VIS by law enforcement authorities and Europol is based on Regulation (EG) No 767/2008 of 9 July 2008 (OJ L 218/60, 13.8.2008) and Council Decision 2008/633/JHA of 23 June 2008 (OJ L 218/129, 13.8.2008), for the purpose(s) of prevention, detection and investigation of terrorist offences and of other serious crime. This can only be done when it is deemed necessary, when there are reasonable grounds and when the request is expected to substantially contribute to solving the crime, and should be performed by means of an electronic request via central access points. Source: Lecture Kurt Hager, ERA, 23 April 2009.

[14] Legal basis of SIS II: Regulation (EC) No 1987/2006 of 20 December 2006 (OJ L 318/4, 28.12.2006) and Council Decision 2007/533/JHA of 12 June 2007 (OJ L 205/63, 7.8.2007) on the establishment, operation and use of the second generation Schengen Information System.

System), and Eurodac[15] (fingerprint system for asylum-seekers) and the EIS (Europol Information System). Meanwhile, the creation of new data-bases has been announced, such as the (interlinking of) national DNA-databases (flowing from the Prüm Treaty which was signed in 2005), the creation of a European Border Surveillance System (Eurosur)[16] and the creation of an entry-exit system that registers the entry and exit of all visitors to Europe.[17]

These large data-systems are geared around the principle of verticality, i.e. data-input organized inside the Member States and mediated by a central (law enforcement) authority. The reason for this is the stronghold of national sovereignty: the prime locus of control on law enforcement activity still resides with national authorities. A vertical, central, hierarchical system of data-gathering and exchange suggests that information practices are correctly, intelligibly and transparently subjected to national and international data protection systems.

Retention of Telecommunications Directive

A core element of the EU counter-terrorism strategy is the facilitation of electronic surveillance (Akdeniz and Walker 2003), which has been formalized by means of the EU Directive on the Retention of Telecommunications, which was adopted on 15 March 2006.[18] Data retention or data preservation generally refers to the (temporary) storage of internet traffic, electronic message exchange and mobile telephony. This allows governments traffic analysis as well as mass surveillance.

The Directive requires Member States to ensure that communications providers must retain, for a period of between 6 months and 2 years, necessary

15 Council Regulation (EC) No 2725/2000/EC of 11 December 2000 (OJ L 316, 15.12.2000). Eurodac became operational on 15 January 2003 and is used by all EU Member States, Iceland, Norway and Switzerland. The EU Council Conclusions (11004/07) under the German Presidency recommended access to Eurodac by police and law enforcement authorities for the purpose of prevention, detection and investigation of terrorist offences and serious criminal offences. It was suggested by Kurt Hager at the ERA Conference on 23 April 2009 that around 1100 criminals could be detected by this system.

16 For a report of the European Parliament's Policy Department C on Citizen's Rights and Constitutional Affairs on Eurosur, see PE 408.295 Briefing Paper 'An Analysis of the Commission Communications on Future Development of Frontex and the Creation of a European Border Surveillance System (Eurosur)', June 2008. The briefing paper opines that the evaluation of Frontex falls short of 'critically assessing the consistence of Frontex activities with the fundamental values upheld by the EU.'

17 Commission of the European Communities (2008) Communication from the Commission to the European Parliament, the Council, The European Economic and Social Committee and the Committee of the Regions. Preparing the next steps in border management in the European Union. COM (2008) 69 final, Brussels, 13 February 2008.

18 Directive 2006/24/EC of the European Parliament and of the Council of 15 March 2006 on the retention of data generated or processed in connection with the provisions of publicly available electronic communications services or of public communications networks (OJ 2006 L 105, p. 54).

data as specified in the Directive to trace and identify the source of a communication; to trace and identify the destination of a communication; to identify the date, time and duration of a communication; to identify the type of communication; to identify the communication device; to identify the location of mobile communication equipment. The data are required to be available to competent national authorities in specific cases, 'for the purpose of the investigation, detection and prosecution of serious crime, as defined by each Member State in its national law'.

In its verdict on the 10th of February 2009, the European Court of Justice ruled that the Data Retention Directive is founded on an appropriate legal basis, correctly adopted on the basis of the EC Treaty and predominantly relating to the functioning of the internal market.[19] Prior to the adoption of the Directive, EU Member States had already introduced measures to oblige service providers to retain data. These measures differed substantially however, in view of the data to be retained as well as with regard to the data retention periods. This may have been the result of the EU Framework Decision, which had been proposed in 2004 by France, Ireland, Sweden, and the United Kingdom. In its ruling, the ECJ also established that the provisions of the directive are essentially limited to the activities of service providers and do not govern access to data or use thereof by the police and judicial authorities of the Member States: 'The measures provided for by the directive do not, in themselves, involve intervention by the police or law-enforcement authorities of the Member States. Those issues, which fall in principle within the domain covered by police and judicial cooperation in criminal matters, have been excluded from the provisions of the directive.'[20] It has however been claimed that access to these data is provided to law enforcement authorities without a warrant and for crimes that are not necessarily serious in nature.[21] For the access of law enforcement authorities to e.g. mobile phone records, additional measures are mostly to be found within the realms of the individual Member States.

Guild (2010: p. 3) explains that the EU Directive on Data Retention ran 'into serious trouble in the national courts in the EU', also because since the ruling of the ECJ, the Romanian Supreme Court ruled against the national implementing legislation in October 2009, and the German Constitutional Court struck down its national implementing legislation on 2 March 2010; in both cases the intrusive nature in combination with the individual right to privacy was at the heart of the argument. Guild (2010, p. 3):

> 'The German court was particularly concerned about the purpose of the collection and the storage of the data, which was precautionary in nature, that is to say not directed at events that had already taken place but at some future possible action or

19 Judgement of the Court of Justice in Case C-301/06, Ireland v. Parliament and Council.

20 Judgement of the Court of Justice in Case C-301/06, Ireland v. Parliament and Council, par. 82.

21 <http://en.wikipedia.org/wiki/Mass_surveillance#Mobile_phone_tracking>

event. It found that retention of such data must not lead to the possibility to virtually reconstruct any activities of citizens'.

PNR agreement

Since 2003, USA authorities have demanded on-line access to the Passenger Name Records which are kept by European flight carriers on flights to the USA. By screening the data, the American and Canadian authorities[22] seek to decrease the possibility that (would-be) terrorists enter their territories from Europe. The PNR's comprise several data, such as name, date of birth and telephone numbers, as well as credit card numbers, seat numbers and meals. The USA authorities may also demand information from the Advanced Passenger Information System, including gender, passport number and nationality of the passengers (Rathenau Instituut 2007).

The screening method raises several questions however as to how the PNR's help to identify risks, what the substance of the precise procedure actually is, and whether the data are run against existing criminal data (Kuipers, 2008). There are several bilateral agreements which have shaped the basis for the exchange of PNR-data by airlines. These comprise the 2004 EU-US PNR agreement, in 2006 ruled by the European Court of Justice to be founded on the wrong legal basis (Balzacq 2008: 91); the 2005 EU-Canada agreement on API (Advanced Passenger Information) and PNR data; the 2006 EU-US interim PNR agreement (replaced by the 2007 definitive EU-US agreement on the submission of PNR-data), and the PNR agreement between the EU and Australia from June 2008 (Kuipers 2008: 17f).

Foreign authorities can use these data of individuals travelling from Europe for the purpose of data-matching, data-mining and profiling. In the meantime, it has been ventured that these data have also been used to detect criminals and to control land borders. Hence, vast numbers of data are put on stock by American,[23] Canadian and Australian authorities which demonstrates the increasingly dense information web and the way in which the EU has actively developed an external security link in its counter-terrorism policy.

Members of the European Parliament, privacy organizations, airlines and data protection authorities are increasingly concerned about the transmission of personal files without the approval of the relevant individual (Kuipers 2008: 3). One of the concerns is the potential function creep, i.e. the use of data for other

22 United States' Customs and Border Protection (US-CBP) and the Canada Border Services Agency (CBSA).

23 On 14 July 2008, the American Civil Liberties Union ACLU announced that the US authorities had tagged the names of 400.000 individuals on the terrorist suspects list, 95% of whom are foreign or not a resident of the United States. 50.000 people were tagged as potentially suspicious with regard to (terrorist attacks on) air transport, while only 16 names were known to the authorities when the 9/11 attacks took place (ANP Press, 14 July 2008).

than counter-terrorism purposes, as well as the lack of reciprocity in the obligation to transfer data on passengers.[24]

Europol

Although Europol had been established before 9/11, its competences were extended considerably thereafter, partly as the consequence of a long-term programme for the Area of Freedom, Security and Justice, partly as an *ad hoc* response to large-scale terrorist attacks (Madrid 11 March 2004, London 7 July 2005 in addition to the September 2001 attacks in the USA). After 9/11, Europol established a team of counter-terrorist specialists, later transferred to the entity SC 5 (Serious Crime), with – in principle – two Liaison Officers from each EU Member State, one from the police and one from the intelligence service. The team was requested to collaborate directly with American counterparts.

Furthermore, the Director of Europol was instructed to conclude an 'informal agreement' with the USA, which provided for the exchange of liaison officers between Europol and US law enforcement agencies: at present, the FBI, the US Secret Service, the DEA and the US Postal Inspection have Liaison Officers at Europol, while Europol has seconded two Liaison Officers to a bureau in Washington DC (Ratzel 2007: 289). In addition, on 6 December 2001 Europol and the US signed an agreement on the exchange of strategic and technical information, and negotiations were started on a supplemental agreement concerning the exchange of personal data.[25] Hence, Europol has played its part in the post 9/11 tendency to blur the distinction between police and secret service intelligence, mainly by managing to overcome hitherto existing firewalls, the one being the gulf between police and intelligence agencies (MacVean 2008: 67), the other being the transatlantic gap. The question whether this has eroded restrictions to information-gathering and intelligence-exchange should be regarded as a prime subject for research.

The most important issue in the light of this paper is however the role which the agency plays in (electronic) surveillance. Europol bases itself on information which is made available by the Member States. Hence, the agency has the capacity for electronic data-storage and data-warehousing,[26] and does so by means of its information system EIS. The analytical capacity of Europol implies systematizing and assessing the data, mainly through the European Crime Intelligence Model (ECIM), as well as in OCTA (Organized Crime Threat Assessment), TE-SAT (Trends and Situations Report on Terrorism), and

---

24 The European Parliament rejected a former SWIFT-agreement (Terrorist Finance Tracking Programme) as it was of the opinion that the agreement was not in line with European data protection standards, represented an disproportionate invasion in people's private lives, and was asymmetric in the sense that the EU does not require private financial data of American citizens to be analyzed for counter terrorism investigation purposes. In the meantime however, the European Parliament adopted a minor revised version of the agreement (8 July 2010).

25 <http://www.europol.europa.eu/legal/agreements>.

26 See Article 7 Europol Convention.

selected Analytical Work Files (AWF's).[27] Moreover, there is frequent interaction between the Europol database and other international data bases which contain information on criminals and their activities, such as the Schengen Information System, Interpol data systems and data held by Eurojust. The most salient aspect is the strong emphasis on (pro-active) intelligence gathering in combination with risk assessment strategies. Europol has a rather elaborate data protection system and is subjected to the control of the Joint Supervisory Board. In the new SWIFT-agreement which facilitates USA authorities to track terrorist financing, Europol shall even be entrusted with the task of controlling the data requests from the USA.

The European Internal Security Strategy

In the beginning of 2010 the EU launched its Internal Security Strategy, which aims at the development of a 'larger consensus of the vision, values and objectives' which underpin European internal security.[28] As main objectives of the strategy a proactive, intelligence led approach is advocated that focuses on the prevention of criminal and terrorist acts before they can take place. Prevention and anticipation are emphasized, structured around analytical tools and early-warning systems. 'A comprehensive approach must be taken that is geared to constant detection and prevention of the threats and risks facing the EU in the various areas of internal security.' Further, the EU advocates a strategy of 'responsibilization': security policies must take a broad approach, involving not only law-enforcement agencies, but also 'institutions and professionals at both national and local levels', like schools, universities, the private sector and civil society organizations. One of the corner stones of the Internal Security Strategy is an accompanying Information Exchange Strategy, aimed at the timely access to 'as much data as possible'. The model will include all the different EU databases relevant for ensuring security in the EU so that there can be 'interaction between them' for the purpose of providing effective information exchange across the whole of the EU and 'maximizing the opportunities' presented by biometric and other technologies.

---

[27] For Rules applicable to Europol Analysis Files, see: <http://www.europol.europa.eu/legal/other/files/Rules_applicable_to_Europol_Analysis_Files_en.pdf>.

[28] Council of the European Union (2010) Note from Presidency to delegations. Draft Internal Security Strategy for the European Union: 'Towards a European Security Model', 5842/10 JAI 90, Brussels, 2 February 2010.

5. Conclusion: A Europe That Interlinks Polycentric Surveillance Practices

The expansion of the European surveillance society is intimately connected with the growing popularity of the precautionary principle (crime prevention, preventive intervention in fragile environments). While emphasizing that our sketch may be far from complete, we have looked into some European strategies in the area of internal security co-operation and we have identified these as indicative of the rapid introduction of new surveillance measures in the field of EU homeland security. Despite the fact that 'Big Brother' critiques have not managed to obtain much cultural and political purchase in the fact of the 'obvious' benefits of surveillance technology' (Loader 2007: 32), several concerns have been voiced about the all-encompassing surveillance society. A few years ago, Privacy International conducted a comparative international survey in 47 countries and found there had been an increase in surveillance and an erosion of privacy safeguards. Of the EU Member States that were included in the survey, the United Kingdom scored lowest (primarily because of its massive presence of CCTV cameras, the number of which in 2002 was estimated to be 4,2 million, and the sizeable police databases containing 5,5 million fingerprint records and 3,4 million DNA records).

Within the EU, the accumulation of surveillance measures is formidable, the speed with which measures have been adopted is impressive given their intrusive effect, the relative absence of controversy (public silence) is surprising, and the number of technological advances is hard to match with new data protection standards. Generally, however, one may argue that there has been a tidal shift in public opinion and checks and balances: governments have aggregated vast volumes of power and knowledge vis-à-vis their citizens. This process has been bolstered by the tidal concerns of the anxiety society in which organized crime and terrorism have been transformed into fluid and ungraspable demons. New legislation – in particular anti-terrorism legislation but also the development of administrative powers at local level[29] – has restricted (the access to) rights in the fields of due process and data protection.

So is large-scale surveillance, coupled with transnational security governance (Johnston 2006), effective in what it seeks to achieve? The answers provided by the law enforcement community are mostly positive, to the extent that e.g. the electronic identification of vehicle license plates amounts to stops, searches, successful 'hits' and arrests. The collection of electronic data may also assist in reconstructing the movements of criminals and illegal transports or money flows. For the time being, although there is a strong pragmatic and technocratic aspiration to interlink surveillance practices for the purpose of crime control, there are several political, organizational, cultural and technological obstacles which obscure the realization of a panopticon from our view. According to David Lyon (2006: 4), the more soft and subtle 'panoptic strategies', the more it produces the desired docile bodies, or worse, perhaps, the absence of social

[29] For a discussion in the British context, see House of Lords (2009: p. 41).

reflection on the emergence of surveillance practices. Future research will have to generate empirical data on whether surveillance contributes to early detection of deviance, marginalization or radicalization, and whether this proactive information stops future criminals and terrorists in their tracks in an effective, efficient and legitimate manner. Alternatively, crime control and surveillance measures can be regarded as colonizing speech acts, meant to expand the regulatory power of governmental authorities over 'deviant' minds.

References

Adviescommissie Informatiestromen Veiligheid (2007). *Data voor daadkracht. Gegevensbestanden voor veiligheid: observaties en analyse*. Den Haag.

American Civil Liberties Union (2004). *The Surveillance-Industrial Complex: How the American Government is Conscripting Business and Individuals in the Construction of a Surveillance Society*. Jay Stanley (author), New York. <http://www.aclu.org/FilesPDFs/surveillance_report.pdf>.

Akdeniz, Y., & Walker, C. (2003). Anti-Terrorism Laws and Data Retention: War is Over? *Northern Ireland Legal Quarterly, 54 (2)*, 159-182.

Balzacq, T, (2008). The Policy Tools of Securitization: Information Exchange, EU Foreign and Interior Policies. *Journal of Common Market Studies, 46 (1)*, 75-100.

Bendiek, A. (2006). *EU Strategy on Counter Terrorism: Steps towards a Coherent Network Policy*. SWP Research Paper 2006/RP 12.

Bigo, D. (1994). The European Internal Security Field: Stakes and Rivalries in a Newly Developing Area of Police Intervention. In M. Anderson, & M. den Boer (Eds.), *Policing Across National Boundaries*. London: Pinter Publications.

Borgers, M., & Van Sliedregt, E. (2009). The Meaning of the Precautionary Principle for the Assessment of Criminal Measures in the Fight Against Terrorism. *Erasmus Law Review, 2 (2)*, 171-195.

Born, H. (Ed.) (2003). *Parliamentary Oversight of the Security Sector. Principles, Mechanisms and Practices*. Geneva: Geneva Centre for the Democratic Control of Armed Forces.

Boutellier, H. (2002). *De Veiligheidsutopie*. Den Haag: Boom Juridische uitgevers.

Brodeur, J.P. (1983/1996). High and Low Policing: Remarks about The Policing of Political Activities. *Social Problems* (1983/1996) 30/5:507–521. (reprinted in R. Reiner (Ed.) (1996). *Police Discretion and Accountability, Policing Vol. II*. Aldershot (UK): Dartmouth Pub, 261–274).

Deleuze, G., & Guattari, F. (1987). *A Thousand Plateaus: Capitalism and Schizophrenia*. Minneapolis, University of Minnesota Press.

Den Boer, M. (2010). Revolving Doors: Ethics in a Shifting Security Paradigm. In M. den Boer, & E. Kolthoff (Eds.) (2010), *Ethics & Security*. The Hague: Boom Juridische uitgevers.

Den Boer, M. (forthcoming). Go with the Flow and Undo the Knots: Policing Strategies in an Interconnected World. In F. Allum (Ed.), *Handbook on Transnational Organized Crime*. London: Routledge.

Den Boer, M., & Van Buuren, J. (forthcoming). *Door het oog van de staat*. Amsterdam: Boom.

Elden, S. (2003). Plague, Panopticon, Police. *Surveillance & Society 1 (3)*, 240-253.

Ericson, R. (2007). *Crime in an Insecure World*. Cambridge: Polity Press.

European Parliament (2008). *Working Document on Profiling, Notably on the Basis of Ethnicity and Race, in Counter-Terrorism, Law Enforcement, Immigration, Customs and Border Control*. Committee on Civil Liberties, Justice and Home Affairs, Sarah Ludford (rapporteur), 30 September 2008, DT\745085EN.doc.

European Parliament (2009). *A Review of the Increased Use of CCTV and Video-Surveillance for Crime Prevention Purposes in Europe*. Clive Norris (author), note for the European Parliament's Committee on Civil Liberties, Justice and Home Affairs, PE 419.588.

Foucault, M. (1995). *Discipline and Punish*. New York: Random House.

Gill, P. (2006). Not Just Joining the Dots But Crossing the Borders and Bridging the Voids: Constructing Security Networks after 11 September 2001. *Policing & Society, 16 (1)*, 27-49.

Guild, E. (2010). *Global Data Transfers: The Human Rights Implications*. Brussels: Centre for European Policy Studies. INEX Policy Brief No. 9 (www.inexproject.eu).

Haggerty, K.D., & Ericson, R.V. (2000). The Surveillant Assemblage. *British Journal of Sociology, 51 (4)*, 605-622.

Hempel, L., & Topfer, E. (2009). The Surveillance Consensus: Reviewing the Politics of CCTV in Three European Countries. *European Journal of Criminology, 6 (2)*, 157-177.

House of Lords (2009). *Surveillance: Citizens and the State*. House of Lords Select Committee on the Constitution, Volume I, HL Report 18-I.

Johnston, L. (2006). Transnational Security Governance. In J. Wood, & B. Dupont (Eds.), *Democracy, Society and the Governance of Security*. Cambridge: Cambridge University Press.

Johnston, L., & Shearing, C. (2003). *Governing Security, Explorations in Policing and Justice*. London: Routledge.

Koffijberg, J., Dekkers, S., Homburg, G., & Van den Berg, B. (2009). *Niets te verbergen en toch bang. Nederlandse burgers over het gebruik van hun gegevens in de glazen samenleving*. Regioplan, see: www.cpbweb.nl.

Kuipers, F. (2008). *No Dream Ticket to Security. PNR Data & Terrorism*. Clingendael Security Paper No. 5, The Hague.

Lewis, N. (2005). Expanding Surveillance: Connecting Biometric Information Systems to International Police Cooperation. In E. Zureik, & M. Salter (Eds.), *Global Surveillance and Policing: Borders, Security, Identity* (pp. 97-112). Devon: Willan Publishing.

Loader, I. (2007). The Cultural Lives of Security and Rights. In B. J. Goold, & L. Lazarus (Eds.), *Security and Human Rights*. Oxford and Portland: Hart Publishing.

Lyon, D. (2003). *Surveillance after September 11th*. Cambridge: Polity Press.

Lyon, D. (2006). The Search for Surveillance Theories. In D. Lyon (Ed.), *Theorizing Surveillance. The Panopticon and Beyond* (pp. 3-20). Collumpton: Willan Publishing.

MacVean, A. (2008). The Governance of Intelligence. In C. Harfield, A. MacVean, J. Grieve, & D. Phillips (Eds.), *The Handbook of Intelligent Policing. Consilience, Crime Control and Community Safety*. Oxford: Oxford University Press, 63-73.

Marx, G.T. (1998). An Ethics for the New Surveillance. *The Information Society, 14 (3)*, 171-186.

Rathenau Instituut (2007). *Van privacyparadijs tot controlestaat? Misdaad- en terreurbestrijding in Nederland aan het begin van de 21ste eeuw.* Studie 49, February, The Hague.

Ratzel, M.-P. (2007). Europol – das Europäische Polizeiamt, Teil 1: Geschichte, Organisation, Aufgaben, Zuständigkeiten und Rechtsgrundlage. *Kriminalistik 5/2007*, 284-291.

Sackers, H. (2010). *Herder, hoeder en handhaver. De burgemeester en het bestuurlijk sanctierecht.* Inaugural Speech, 15 januari, Radboud University Nijmegen.

Sheptycki, J. (2007). High Policing in the Security Control Society. *Policing, 1 (1)*, 70-79.

Trommel, W. (2009). *Gulzig Bestuur.* Inaugural Speech. VU University Amsterdam, 17 September 2009.

Van Linde, E. (2002). *Quick Scan of Post 9/11 National Counter-Terrorism Policymaking and Implementation in Selected European Countries.* RAND, Europe.

Van Buuren, J. (2009). *Security as a Commodity. Ethical Dilemmas of Private Security.* Brussels: INEX.

Van 't Hof, C. (2007). *RFID & Identity Management in Everyday Life. Striking the Balance between Convenience, Choice and Control.* The Hague: The Rathenau Institute.

Whitaker, R. (1999). *The End of Privacy. How Total Surveillance is Becoming a Reality.* New York: The New Press.

Whitaker, R. (2006). A Faustian Bargain? America and the Dream of Total Information Awareness. In R.V. Ericson, & K.D. Haggerty (Eds.), *The New Politics of Surveillance and Visibility* (pp. 141-171). Toronto: University of Toronto Press.

Zedner, L. (2006). The Concept of Security: An Agenda for Comparative Analysis. *Legal Studies, 23(1)*, 153-176.

Zureik, E., & Salter, M. (2005). Global Surveillance and Policing: Borders, Security, Identity – Introduction. In E. Zureik, & M. Salter (Eds.), *Global Surveillance and Policing: Borders, Security, Identity* (pp. 1-10). Devon: Willan Publishing.

13. The Limits of Numbers: Impact Assessments and Increased Uncertainty

Tobias Arnoldussen

1. Introduction

In the run-up to the Dutch Parliamentary election of 2010, anti-immigration and anti-Islam politician Geert Wilders created a stir with his insistence that the public should be made aware of how much immigration costs the Dutch State. He wanted to conduct an elaborate study to examine how much immigrants contributed to Dutch society, but more importantly he wanted to know what they cost the Dutch economy. The reason Wilders wanted to know this is because he is rigidly opposed to immigration, and thus hoped these numbers would win him votes. Moreover, they would make his sometimes extreme anti-immigration legislative proposals more easily accepted among the public.

He timed his proposal to coincide with the controversy over proposed budget cuts. With the figures in hand, he was also able to show what the curtailing of immigration would deliver in terms of economic benefits in 2015 or 2020. Politicians from the left-leaning parties were angry because they saw the quantification of people as immoral. Nonetheless, Wilders did find a consultancy agency willing to draft such a report,[1] and Elsevier published an article about the conclusions: 'Mass immigration costs the Netherlands 7 billion euro per year'.[2] In the article, Wilders was quoted as saying: 'Billions of euros are there for the taking', and he linked this to the extensive budget cuts.

The article did not go deeply into the way the report was drafted. A link to the conclusions suffices. The readers do not know whether these immigration costs are deduced before or after the benefits have been deducted. They also will not read whether we need immigrants to keep the workforce intact at a time that the population is aging. Furthermore, it is not clear what the consequences for the job market would be if immigrants were to be expelled. In other words, only a number of 7 billion is given and a number is used in a political campaign. The number may be applied to argue for budget cuts on facilities for immigrants or to establish a more stringent immigration policy.

The left may be upset and invoke the moral principle that we do not calculate the worth of human beings, but strictly speaking that is not true. We do calculate

1 Nyfer, Budgettaire effecten van immigratie van niet-westerse allochtonen, May 2010.
2 http://www.elsevier.nl/web/Nieuws/Politiek/266116/Massaimmigratie-kost-Nederland-7-miljard-euro-per-jaar.htm.

the value of a human life: for instance, by using a VOSL method (value of a statistical life). This is common for example in analyses of the costs and benefits of road safety measures. According to a research memorandum drafted at the VU University Amsterdam, a literature review indicates that a human life may well be worth around 4.4 million dollars (De Blaeij 2003).

In this article, I will argue that Wilders' demand to calculate the costs of immigration is the outcome of a trend towards monetarisation and calculation in many policy fields. In this case, it leads to undesirable outcomes. Wilders' demand does not merely aim at presenting an innocuous piece of information to the public: this information can rouse the public and aid in pressing certain legislation. Wilders intends to use it to argue for strict regulations on immigration and for general anti-immigration policies.

I will use a Foucaultian perspective to analyse this discursive trend towards monetarisation and calculation. In my opinion, it became a 'technology of governance' with which legislators sought to add legitimacy to their proposals by presenting them within a scientific framework. Through this technology, the State could expand its regulatory competence and gain acceptance it would not otherwise have had for taking costly measures. Moreover, it could instil in the public a belief that preventing harm and increasing safety would ultimately pay off. This would mean an increase in efficiency.

However, this discourse upholds a claim to objectivity that it in fact can never live up to by using instruments like risk assessments and cost benefit analyses[3]. An artificial reality is created in which the models and the presumption embedded in them decide the outcome. The public thinks that it is dealing with facts, while it is actually dealing with models. The public generally lacks the expertise to check the underlying assumptions of these models, if it has access to them at all. This technocratic way of policy making impoverishes public debate, and instead of enhancing our feelings of security and certainty it will ultimately undermine them. In addition, it may conflict with fields that traditionally resist quantification and monetarisation, such as human rights and criminal law.

I will argue for this conclusion by showing the developments in environmental policy making. A comparison with environmental policy making is useful, because in the sphere of the environment and public health, policies based on such ex ante evaluations are very common.

---

3 I am aware that risk assessments, impact assessments, and cost benefit analyses are considerably different exercises. However, I consider them to be parts of the same actuarial discourse. They are all imbued with an actuarial outlook, and all present their findings in detailed graphics and numerical tables. Hence, I feel justified in discussing them together in this paper, and not entering into detailing their differences.

2. Cost Benefit Analyses and Risk Assessments

When cost benefit analyses are intended to be used for predicting future costs and benefits, they operate with the notion of risk. A risk may be considered to be an estimate of the chance a given unwanted situation will occur. In the Wilders example, crime rates are higher among immigrant groups. This means that immigrants run a higher risk of committing a crime. How high this risk is and how high the risks for second-generation immigrants are may be calculated by using risk assessment, which is devised in the context of the rise of insurance. Insurance operates with the notion of risk: namely, that a possible threat might become actual in the future. That event is by no means certain, but if it occurs it will result in great loss. Since the loss may well be too great to bear, the rational thing to do is to insure oneself against this occurrence. In essence, insurance is nothing but a pulling together of resources in order to compensate the person who happens to be unfortunate enough to incur this loss. To establish the premium, however, an insurer must have a good insight into the risks that are actually taken. Let us assume I would like to insure myself against the materialisation of a threat to my health. The insurer will ask me to pay a premium, but he will not simply propose a figure at random; he will make an assessment based on my prior health conditions, on my use of medicine and alcohol, and on hereditary conditions. In the same way that I calculate the risk to my health, the insurer needs to calculate his risk in insuring me and determining what kind of compensation is profitable for him to carry that risk. To this end, technologies have been devised to facilitate insurers to make these calculations such as risk assessments. On the basis of these assessments, further cost benefit analyses can be made by insurers or investors.

Various criminologists warn against the intrusion of such instruments in the context of criminal law and penal policies (Feely and Simon 1994; Garland 1996; Moerings 2003). They see this type of 'actuarial justice' conflicting with classical principles of criminal law. It is clear to see why the use of actuarial instruments is attractive for the regulator. Ex ante risk assessments could point out categories of people who are more prone to commit crime. Regulators may then focus their resources on these groups, and this would promise a more cost-effective and efficient allocation of means to fight crime. Ideally, such assessments may also help to prevent crime. If we can identify 'perpetrators' before they commit crimes, we have also reduced the number of victims. Such risk calculations are now made on a daily basis at airports, and individuals deemed high risk on account of terrorist activity or drug trafficking may be prevented from flying (Moerings 2003: 2).

In other fields, such actuarial thinking is much more advanced. It has been in use since at least the 1980s in environmental regulation (Winsemius 1986), and impact assessments are used to map the environment-related risks that certain undertakings cause. Making an environmental impact assessment has been mandatory for certain decisions since 1985.[4]

3. Framing Risks and Hazards in Numerical Terms

It should not be surprising that this type of ex ante evaluation for policy making has progressed furthest in the environmental domain. In environmental policy, one is always dealing with risks. Environmental and public health policies are currently dealing far more with future threats like climate change or loss of biodiversity than with local environmental concerns; hence, an account of their level of dangerousness is needed to counter future threats. In the environmental impact assessment approach and the risk approach, one of the founders of Dutch environmental policy, Pieter Winsemius, saw tools that could be used to set priorities for action (Winsemius 1986). In the US, policy makers were already more advanced in experimenting with these strategies for risk management. Moreover, risk assessments could be used to anticipate threats, which caused environmental regulation to shift from curative policies – ones that 'cleaned up' the environment after damage had been done – to preventative ones. These new actuarial approaches proved to be emancipating for environmental policy.

The environment was not an issue that dyed-in-the-wool economists and policy makers were much concerned about; or at least not until environmental policy makers learned to frame in monetary terms the degradation of the environment, its clean-up costs, and the benefits of preventative policy. Maarten Hajer describes how in the Netherlands and in Great Britain a type of environmental discourse has taken over, and is defined by its framing of environmental questions in monetary and natural science terms (Hajer 1995). This discourse and in tandem this political strategy known as 'ecological modernisation' (Hajer 1995; Mol, Sonneveld and Spaargaren 2009) emphasised the cost efficiency of progressive environmental policy, and even portrayed it as an area in which economic gains could be made by inculcating the need for innovation and technology to curb threats to the environment.

This mode of presentation made it much easier to present the problems of environmental degradation to a sceptical audience of industrial, agricultural, and transport sectors, and to convince other policy-making departments to include care for the environment in their own policies. It was clear to Winsemius that considerably more acceptance could be gained among the public when policy-relevant information was dispersed to it.[5] In this respect, monetary and natural

4 Directive on the assessment of the effects of certain public and private projects on the environment, Council Directive 85/337/EEC.

5 Tweede Kamer, vergaderjaar 1983-1984, 18 100 hoofdstuk I, nr. 7. Indicatief meerjarenprogramma ter bestrijding van de luchtverontreininginging 1984-1988 3.e IMP lucht.

science terms and frameworks were far more successful than the abstruse stories of marginalisation and equality with which the left-leaning environmental movement tried to persuade people to take care of their surroundings. Environmental risks could be made clear to the public by way of graphics and tables.

The success in the environmental field did not go unnoticed, and the type of ex ante assessment made headway in other related fields. The 2001 Strategy for Sustainable Development added another dimension to the increasing importance of environmental impact assessments. It called for '(...) mechanisms to ensure that all major legislative proposals include an assessment of the potential economic, environmental and social benefits and costs of action or lack of action, both inside and outside the EU'.[6] During the Laeken summit of 2002, the Mandelkern group presented a proposal to make a systematic impact assessment of major EU regulative projects obligatory (Meuwese 2009: 2). Because of this ongoing institutionalisation, Meuwese speaks of an 'impact assessment regime'.

4. Quantification as a Technology of Governance

What does such an 'impact assessment regime' mean for governance? Michel Foucault is one of the first theoreticians who emphasised the importance of science in the service of the government. He called this complex 'power/knowledge'.[7] Knowledge is never accepted for its own sake, but because of the power effects it may have. In the formation of modern society, technology functioned to make 'police' possible. This word carried a much broader meaning than it does now. Police or 'polizei wissenshaft' (police science) in Germany referred to the regulatory and preventative governance of internal order. In his collection of writings – 'Power/Knowledge' – Foucault describes police as follows:

> 'Down to the end of the ancient regime, the term "police" does not signify at least not exclusively the institution of police in the modern sense; 'police' is the ensemble of mechanisms serving to ensure order, the properly channeled growth of wealth and the conditions of preservation of health in general' (Foucault 1990).

Police ensured the orderly transportation of people, and shaped their morality, sexuality, and health. It emphasised the common good while at the same time expanding the power of the State over its subjects.

---

6 COM 2001 264 final A Sustainable Europe for a Better World: A European Union Strategy for Sustainable Development, p. 6.

7 Stanford encyclopedia of Philosophy, entry Michel Foucault < http://plato.stanford.edu/ entries/ Foucault>.

To be conducted successfully, police required certain technologies, and for the sovereign to implement police, the population needed to be mapped and investigated. Social sciences were an indispensable link in the chain of police and police governance. Of equal importance was the development of what Foucault calls optics. Optics encompasses all technologies by means of which subjects are made visible. This can be conducted through architecture, overseers, time clocks, and any other means of observation that seem insignificant, but work in unison to create environments in which people can always be watched.

Through the humanities and through optics, police made a certain mode of government possible, allowing the State to mobilise its subjects behind common goals and to create common identities. It functioned as a technique of normalisation, and created boundaries between the 'normals' and abnormal people, who could be identified and 'treated'. Ultimately, such technologies cause the subject to internalise the 'gaze' that is always upon him, and he will behave as if he is constantly under surveillance. Police as a technology of governance made the regimented modern State possible.

Can we understand risk assessment and, more broadly, 'quantification' as a technique of governance that makes a certain mode of governance possible? I think we can. Quantification of course was used early on as a police technology. The census, demographics, and statistics were all important tools in making the subjects visible to the sovereign. However, risk assessment and cost-benefit assessment work slightly differently. They are not essentially techniques that control how we see ourselves, but how we consider our surroundings. It made possible utilitarian consideration of the environment as an economic value. When quantification was used in the environmental domain, it facilitated a way of looking at the environment that made it an acceptable – even an important – field of policy from an economic point of view, as was discussed above.

Environmental protection turned from an activity that was considered to be inherently inimical to economic growth to a positive sum game (Hajer 1995). It is portrayed as a lucrative business. The first instances of this change of perception could be detected in the 1980s. The notion that pollution prevention pays became more dominant in Dutch policy plans:

> 'Protection of air quality also has beneficial effects for the economy and employment. Directly, because damage is avoided and preventative measures will be a lot cheaper than future cleaning, and also – from the point of view of employment – because we may profit from the production of environmental equipment and its export, the increase in knowledge, and the sales of "know-how". Indirectly economic activities are safeguarded for the long term.'[8]

[8] Tweede Kamer, vergaderjaar 1983-1984, 18 292, nrs. 1-2 Translation T.A.

Moreover, campaigns were run to provide transparency to the public in order to increase environmental awareness:

> '(...) with all groups targeted by policy, behaviour of the people determines the success of the measures proposed. By providing information with the aim of making available policy relevant data, providing insight into the policy-making process and the measures following from it, behavioural change is supervised and environmental awareness is increased.' [9]

The change of format from burden to industry to a positive sum game was accompanied by a change in discourse. Poor environmental management in the past was portrayed as 'a loan' that was entered into by the current generation, and which would have to be paid by succeeding generations (VROM 1989). Managerial terminology was now widely used to describe the environmental crisis. The widely publicised Stern Review called climate change the 'biggest market failure in the history of mankind'.[10] The notion of 'sustainable development' could be considered an end point in the effort to integrate economic, ecological, and social concerns. The label of sustainability could now be found everywhere, from sustainable banking practices to sustainable mobility programmes.

In the beginning, the results of scientific inquiry were presented in a sober fashion. Figure 1 (next page) indicating temperature change is taken from the NMP, the first Dutch national policy plan on the environment.[11]

---

9 Tweede Kamer, vergaderjaar 1984-1985, 18602, nrs. 1-2 Indicatief Meerjaren Programma Milieubeheer 1985-1989.

10 The complete Stern Review may be found here: http://webarchive.nationalarchives.gov.uk/+/http://www.hm-treasury.gov.uk/independent_reviews/stern_review_economics_climate_change/stern_review_report.cfm.

11 1988/1989 21 137 NR.2 Nationaal Milieubeleidsplan (NMP).

Figure 1 Expected sea level rise

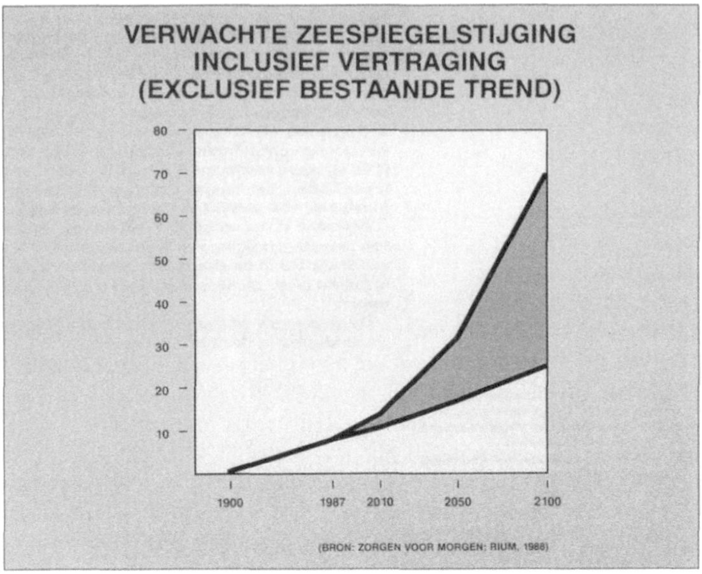

Over time, these graphics became more colourful and more elaborate. They showed more data on a single graphic, and were presented within more accessible reports.

Figure 2 Graph showing rising CO_2 levels, taken from *An Inconvenient Truth*

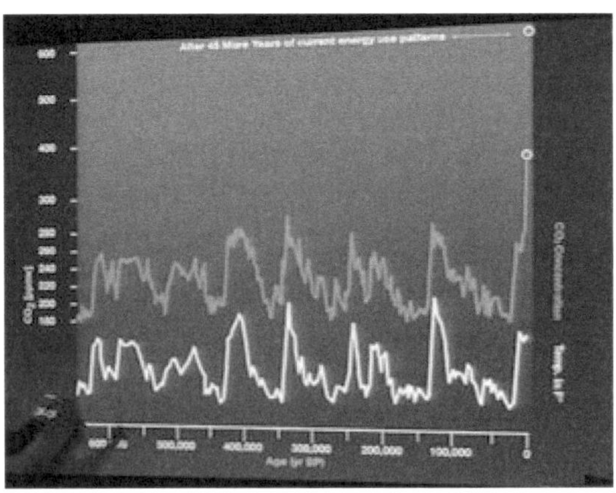

Contemporary displays are in general more elaborate and more dynamically presented than earlier ones. Figure 2 (page above) taken from the movie *An Inconvenient Truth* purports to show CO2 levels related to temperature rises, and the spike at the end allows for only one conclusion: bring your bathing gear.

Al Gore's film *An Inconvenient Truth* was successful in adding climate change to the Dutch political and social agenda (Breeman and Timmermans 2008). Though I have not specifically researched it, I have no reason to think it would be different in other countries.

The methods of compiling this graphical data also grew more advanced. In line with the ideas of pioneers of ecological modernisation, indicators were developed that could themselves be mapped and graphed to portray the effects of our life styles and economy on the environment (Von Prittwitz 1990). In this context, he spoke of a 'Querschnitt Strategie', the aim of which is to make people aware of environmental problems by including them in everyday economical statistics. The effects on the environment could be made calculable by satellite accounting, and real satellites were also used to make pictures of the earth's atmosphere in order to detect CO_2 levels, for instance, or air pollution. The aim of these indicators and concomitant graphic presentations is to embed the environment within other areas of governance. When we have the statistics and calculations, we can quickly see how much damage our energy policies do, or for how much air pollution our mobility policy is responsible. Such displays make acceptable often costly policies to clean up the environment or to curtail environmental risk. For example, *An Inconvenient Truth* led to a campaign demanding a 'climate law' (Breemans and Timmermans 2008).
For environmental protection, this type of presentation meant a leap forward on the political agenda, which tends to be dominated by economical concerns. By and large, the strategy of making the environment calculable did indeed result in heightened awareness. However, there is another side to the story. The presentation of environmental degradation in managerial terms and in natural science formats causes it to be considered a managerial problem. Maarten Hajer contends that the logic of ecological modernisation is utilitarian. Care of the environment is not portrayed as an end in itself, and appeals to ethics have a minor place, if at all, in the economically driven framework.

Quantification urges the subjects not to look at themselves in different ways, but to look at the environment and even at public health in a different way. They are urged to see these as economic goods. In this vein, the NMP urges us to 'look at the environment not as a free good to be exploited by anyone, but as a common good that has a limited carrying capacity'. The environment is still portrayed as a resource, but now one to be managed using economic acumen and scientific expertise. Attractive living conditions are not considered as ends in themselves, but as economically necessary.

The dynamic with the police science of old is the same: it provides the State with a rationale to intervene. Whereas the police science of old made intervention by the State possible to secure public order, quantification of environmental and health hazards – risks for short – also makes State intervention possible. They increase the range for State intervention significantly, because on the basis of quantification and statistics, risks that may materialise far into the future can be identified. The appeal within some administrative circles to mobilise resources for an ambitious construction programme involving dikes in the Netherlands is an example of the extent to which the State tries to prevent future threats.

However, when the discursive framework of quantification is pushed to the limits, it also engenders criticism of traditional arrangements, as I hope to show in the following sections.

5. The Impact of Quantification on Governance

I consider this emphasis on numerical valuations and prospective impact analyses to have two consequences. The first is that there will be a demand for increasingly more comprehensive models in many different fields, and for scientists to have a stronger foothold in politics. After all, they construct the model and sometimes are the only ones who understand the outcomes, as was the case in the comprehensive Gothenburg treaty on air pollution (Pleijel and Grennfelt 2007), and is also very much the case in the climate change debate. The second consequence is that when one frames policy questions this way, it is not surprising that pressure groups bring up their own 'counter assessments' or use the graphic displays provided in one area to further their own ends in wholly different areas. In this section, I will offer practical examples to illustrate these points.

A wide range of policy interventions is currently supported by calculating costs and benefits. A report on trends for obesity for instance did not hesitate to note that obesity was responsible for 500 million euros of added health costs in the Netherlands in 1999. In 2009, the Dutch Institute for Public Health and Environmental Hygiene (RIVM) pleaded for the introduction of more wide-ranging cost-effectiveness studies, incorporating a 'societal perspective':

> 'Because many preventative interventions have effects outside of the health sector and because the division of the health budget is a part of a more far-reaching question of division of means, we plead to present the results of cost-effectiveness assessments from a health perspective and a societal perspective. Switching to a societal perspective does have significant consequences, for the costs and effects that need to be incorporated as well as for the economic valuation of these costs and effects.' (Van Baal et al. 2009)

The increasing reliance on numbers has spawned a whole industry of model makers, consultants, NGOs, and state-aligned research agencies. As the indicators devised become more advanced, so do the models. A good example is the model used to conduct the Gothenburg protocol, RAINS, by the Austrian institute IIASA. Whereas environmental treaties used to consist of an agreement to reduce emission of a certain solution by a given percentage, the RAINS model made integrated assessments possible for reducing four pollutants at once. It calculates effects on rain and on soil, and calculates cost efficiency. Recently it has been updated to include greenhouse gasses and CO_2 in order to be a model for climate change. This example shows how the emphasis on justifying policy by the use of risk and cost-benefit assessments increases the demands for increasingly accurate models. This increases the need for expertise the State will have to rely on. In the case of the RAINS model and the Gothenburg protocol, a treaty was concluded in which 'only a few experts understand the mechanisms behind the distributions of the signatories' commitments' (Lidskog and Sundqvist 2007: 192).

Hence, while the State increases its scope for intervention and legitimises these interventions against resistance by the use of science, it also loses ground. Its policy makers become dependent on environmental scientists. While science is purported to be a neutral institution, there is ample evidence that suggests otherwise. Scientists may have personal motives or interests, and sub-groups of scientists may have these as well (Jasanoff 1990; Ravetz 1996). The locus of governance shifts towards the agenda of scientists and away from the State, while at the same time the State expands its legitimacy to publicly intervene.
With regard to the second point raised in this section, while scientists gain in power, the power of pressure groups to influence policy making does not seem to be diminished. Pressure groups may be pacified with this discourse initially, because they do not know the argumentative frameworks or possess the scientific know-how to produce them themselves. However, pressure groups do learn. When they adapted to this discursive format, it turned out that the graphical displays and economic vocabulary with which the administration first gained credibility could also be used to question the efficacy and commitments of the State itself. *An Inconvenient Truth* is an example of this. Gore used the graphical format to his advantage when he wanted to rouse the public into demanding measures against climate change. Such a mobilisation of public sentiment may for instance put pressure on the US government to sign the Kyoto protocol.

The emphasis on a natural science presentation of environmental conditions provides ample opportunities to influence public opinion. This became clear when satellite images appeared that showed the Netherlands to be a polluted country. In October 2004, Dutch newspapers printed this picture of the air quality situation in Europe (Figure 3). A dirty red smudge appeared where the

Netherlands should be. Air pollution had already hit the political agenda because of court cases postponing building projects due to bad air.

Figure 3 **NO_2 levels in Europe**

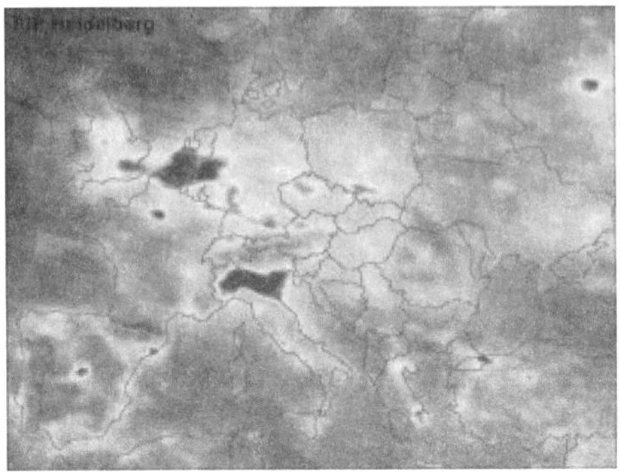

As the picture below shows, this image was subsequently used by the Dutch environmental pressure group Milieudefensie (Figure 4). It was used in a campaign to raise awareness about bad air quality and to urge people to go to court when the administration refused to remedy the situation.

Figure 4 **Hanging a campaign poster for Friends of the Earth Holland (Milieudefensie)**

Any nuance in the story about bad air quality was lost. In fact, the satellite images only show the amount of NO_2 in the upper layers of the atmosphere. NO_2 is itself practically harmless as a pollutant, and people do not live in the upper layers of the atmosphere, but on ground level. The details behind the pictures have decreased in importance; the presentation has taken over. The activities of the environmentalist groups saw Administrative Courts flooded with cancellation requests involving large projects due to air quality. Apparently the awareness-raising activities practiced in the Netherlands paid off; a critical public took to the courts, and this limited the power of the State.

But even when the data are backed up by a comprehensive cost-benefit analysis, which is considered best practice, one cannot be sure it will mitigate conflict. The EU emphasis on impact assessments has led to a number of highly detailed impact assessments containing a large number of variables. These assessments support large-scale, multi-billion euro environmental strategies. One of these is the CAFÉ (Clean Are For Europe) strategy, a programme to target air pollution caused by various different sectors such as agriculture, mobility, and industry. The cost-benefit assessment became a large-scale operation. More than 100 stakeholder meetings have taken place, a population consultation has been held, three different models have been used in the analysis work, and three separate DGs cooperate. Furthermore, the documents have been put on a website, the first page of which alone consists of over 60 papers, and there are further areas in the website where more documents can be obtained. The resulting impact assessment is a 170-page document.[12]

In her dissertation, Anne Meuwese states that impact assessment is considered an example of best practice (Meuwese 2009). On closer inspection, however, some oddities do surface. The explicit aim of an impact assessment is to justify the choices made by the Commission. Especially in this department it is flawed, as it does not justify the choice made. The Commission has studied three different reduction scenarios; it has opted for a cautious approach and has chosen a scenario between A and B for the reduction of air pollution under CAFÉ. The strategy adopted is envisaged to cost around 7.1 billion euro and to bring benefits of around 40 billion euro in the form of increased health and other such aspects. The additional more environmentally ambitious scenarios brought benefits that far outweigh the costs. The Commission chose a less ambitious policy because of intensive lobbying by the car and energy industry. EURELECTRIC, the association of European energy companies, complained that the ambition level is not cost effective, since the levels are set in the steeply rising part of the cost curve, where incremental costs outweigh incremental improvements in air quality.[13] According to the ENDS report, it was a concerted effort by the Business Association UNICE that caused the 40 percent cost reduction.[14] The Environmental Bureau EEB tried to argue for more far-reaching goals. Together with the NGO Secretariat on Acid Rain and Transport

12 SEC 2005 113 COMMISSION STAFF WORKING PAPER Annex to: The Communication on Thematic Strategy on Air Pollution and The Directive on 'Ambient Air Quality and Cleaner Air for Europe' Impact Assessment.

13 Eurelectric press release, December 2, 2005.

14 ENDS report 14 June 2005, '*EU air pollution strategy raises temperatures*'.

and Environment, it presented a position paper in which it argued that the costs were overestimated and the benefits underestimated.[15]

Despite the large body of literature and work on the impact assessment, which took years, it was not able to prevent conflict. Conflict arose with regard to the technicalities of cost effectiveness and the drafting of the assessment. Pressure groups come up with their own assessments and start questioning the official one. The arguments are all about overestimated and underestimated costs and benefits. This seems to be only a financial and technical matter, but the benefits in monetary terms actually represent lives saved, which have been quantified. Within the impact assessment, lives are measured against industrial opportunities. The conflict has not mitigated discussion, but has merely changed its form. The debate is cloaked in technical terms, and in language used by experts in finance and in the natural sciences, but it is ultimately about values. These values have been obscured, however, which makes it difficult to follow for an audience not specialised in this discourse of numbers.

The examples given above illustrate what may happen when a natural sciences framework comes to dominate policy questions. Initially the introduction of these frameworks increased the efficacy of the State in enacting legislation it deemed useful, contravening vested interests. It has been so effective that the European Union in particular considers it expedient to expand the scope of these actuarial assessments to other domains and other fields of policy making. However, this discourse demands increasingly detailed and expansive models. Every discourse produces legitimacy of power, but also creates possibilities for resistance. When participants have learned how to use the discursive frameworks, they will produce counter readings or counter discourses (Foucault 1990: 101). This is what we see happening here. When pressure groups of different kinds can use the scientific mode of presentation and understand the focal points of the arguments over numbers, they can undermine the legislator. I will explain in the following section why of necessity the use of actuarial frameworks will produce uncertainty instead of certainty, and rather than leading to the solution of problems, it will introduce new ones. These new problems may eventually threaten traditional discourse on human rights.

6. The Limits of Numbers

The impact assessment discussed above presents a conundrum. It is an integrated impact assessment, which means it should take into account a large body of data on the environmental, economic, and social effects of the clean air strategy. The scientists involved in the several working groups that drafted the

[15] EEB T&E, Swedish Secretariat on Acid Rain: Position Paper on the Thematic Strategy on Air Pollution, 31 Jan 2006.

impact assessment and the strategy itself did try to offer an assessment that is as complete as possible. Complete in this sense means that the scenarios considered are based on an analysis of prospective economic developments, on the predicted impact of other legislation, and on foreseen technological developments as well as the behaviours of pollutants. Three different models were used: the RAINS model discussed above; the PRIMES model, which predicts developments in energy markets; and the TREMOVE model, which predicts developments in transport and mobility. A great deal of time and effort was put into an assessment that has a high degree of completeness. Nevertheless, when we read the assessment we find caveats and warnings about how uncertain the findings are. Ultimately, this undermined the efficacy of the assessment, and it became vulnerable to criticisms from the industry and the environmental movement. The CAFÉ impact assessment is no exception. In a report sanctioned by the European Commission, we may find there is considerable mistrust of impact assessments.[16]

How is it possible that an instrument that is intended to reduce complexity and add legitimacy to decision making manages to do the opposite? I contend that the discourse – when pushed to the limits – will create uncertainty instead of resolving it. I consider it the dilemma of certainty and completeness. Actuarial instruments like impact assessments and cost benefit analyses should have a modicum of completeness, but uncertainty increases when completeness is pursued. Risk assessments, impact assessments, and models are expanded to encompass progressively more relevant variables. This gives the model a higher degree of completion, and leads to a greater chance that the model accurately depicts reality. A model that does not have a sufficient degree of completeness is useless, because of the possibility that variables not taken into account in the model have an impact. In a field like environmental science, in which the importance of a holistic vision is stressed, not being complete is a serious liability.

However, a more comprehensive analysis will contain data that is subject to often grave uncertainty. When one wishes to calculate the costs of pollution reduction, variables such as the development of the economy and the progress of technology must be included. This data can itself only be based on uncertain estimates. This undercuts the principal aim of such analysis: namely, to present a clear picture of the possibilities and scenarios relating to various policy alternatives. The two demands of completeness and a sufficient degree of certainty are at odds with one another. If more data are factored in, the chances of uncertainty increase, resulting in a conundrum. The analysis should be

[16] The Evaluation Partnership: Evaluation of the Commission's Impact Assessment System, final report April 2007.

complete as well as sufficiently certain in regard to its outcomes. However, the more complete the analysis, the more uncertain the findings become.

This problem is increasingly recognised In the field of risk sociology. Various important theorists like Ulrich Beck and Ortwin Renn move from a conception of risk to that of uncertainty (Pieterman, forthcoming). There is increased interest in decision making under conditions of uncertainty, such as the precautionary principle. In addition, some scholars argue that environmental policy making should aim at simplification (Oenema and Van der Kolk 2008). However, the general trend seems to be to look for increasingly sensitive models.

7. The Dangers of Numbers

In other policy fields, the discourse of numbers seems to be gaining ground, as the discussion on actuarial justice signifies. This trend may contain hidden dangers. The attraction of the discourse of quantification is that it promises a kind of objectivity. Simplistically put, the idea is that if we quantify everything and simply calculate the future outcomes of our choices, we can make the right policy decisions. The insistence on cost benefits analysis, impact assessments, and so on ensures the public that sound choices are made. At the same time, however, it teaches the public that this actuarial manner of making decisions is the appropriate way to conduct policy. In that light, the demand to calculate the cost of immigration fits the times. The problem politicians have in explaining that this is not a good comparison is understandable. In other situations, measurement and cost benefit analyses are the instruments of choice. Policy makers do not point out the grave uncertainties associated with these instruments, and so it is logical that a sizable part of the population thinks: 'Yes, why not; calculate the costs so that we know what an immigrant costs'.

The numerical presentation of data fans the flames as well. This map (Figure 5, next page) may be found in the Zorgatlas (www.zorgatlas.nl). It depicts the numbers of non-western immigrants living in the Netherlands in 2010.[17] It does so by showing a map of the Netherlands slowly coloring towards a deep purple.

The map published on the site is interactive. The map printed below is a depiction from 2010, but on the website one sees a map that runs the estimates from 2010 all the way up to 2025. Every five years the map displays larger areas of purple, meaning more residents of non-western descent. The map was reason enough for parliamentarian Rita Verdonk to ask the government questions about this 'shocking' demographic development and of course what it would cost the

[17] It may be found here: http://www.zorgatlas.nl/beinvloedende-factoren/demografie/etniciteit/niet-westerse-allochtonen-per-gemeente-2010-2025.

Dutch State.[18] Again, the presentation here is the key. We do not know what this trend means, and we do not know what assumptions are made in the future estimates. It may well be that people of non-western descent become better off financially and leave the crowded inner city areas for more quiet places in the countryside. On the contrary, the worst is immediately assumed and connected to costs. Qua presentation, the map closely resembles the maps of environmental risks depicted above. Dark spots are considered problematic. Like the satellite map, this map too can be used easily to mobilise the population to resist. This time it is not about resistance against scary issues like air pollution, but against scary people: immigrants.

Figure 5 **Non Western Immigrants 2010, 2015, 2020**

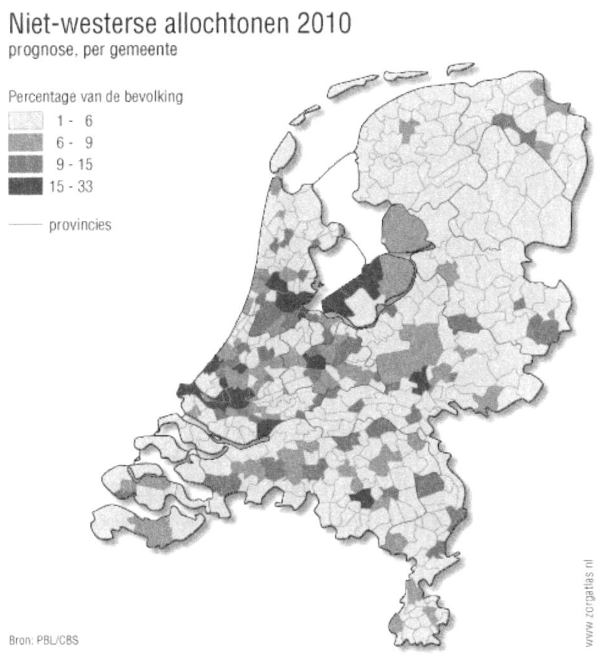

The way we deal with threatening things and the way we deal with threatening people is fortunately still very different. Policy makers do not like to make a cost benefit analysis about the costs related to groups of people, but a presentation using elements of the natural sciences is becoming increasingly common. The following map, depicting crime committed by young offenders,

[18] The questions to the Cabinet can be found on the website of TON, Ms Verdonk's political party: http://www.trotsopnederland.com/index.php?pageID=3&messageID=703.

can also be found in the Zorgatlas.[19] Notice how it is very similar to the map showing immigrant population densities.

Figure 6 Youth Crime Rate 2008

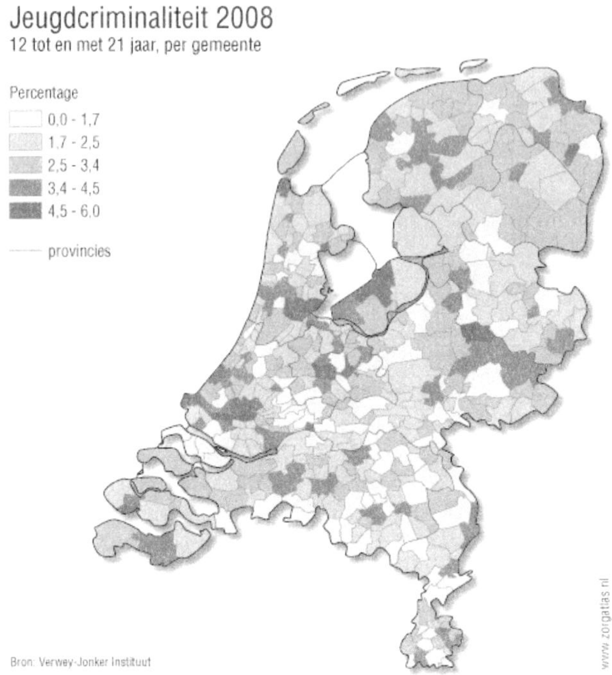

This kind of presentation will instil a type of thinking that is contrary to traditional criminal law. Criminal law is very much concerned with the rights of suspects, and reasoning by analogy for instance is forbidden, as is using repressive means against people simply because they are part of an ethnic group. In contrast, the discourse of numbers works in an opposite manner. It makes generalisations and reduces each special case to a monetary number, thus making a comparison. The introduction of an actuarial discourse will eventually undermine the rights of suspects and maybe even groups. A dramatic example of the former is the case of Lucia de Berk. In this high-profile case, a nurse was sentenced for murder solely on the basis of statistical data. The judges were not specialists in numbers and had to rely on the judgement of scientists. However, the statistical data proved wrong, although initially the judges could not argue against it.

19 http://www.zorgatlas.nl/beinvloedende-factoren/sociale-omgeving/veiligheid/jeugdcriminaliteit-per-gemeente-2008/

8. Conclusion 'Governance by Numbers'

Michel Foucault defines discursive practices as:

> '(…) characterised by the demarcation of a field of objects, by the definition of a legitimate perspective for a subject of knowledge, by the setting of norms for elaborating concepts and theories. Hence, each of them presupposes a play of prescriptions that govern exclusions and selections.'

The tendency to present policy by means of numbers and by recasting ethical or political dilemmas in managerial terms is just such a discursive practice. It defines a legitimate perspective for a subject of knowledge: namely, a numerical/managerial/scientific perspective. It sets the norms for elaborating concepts and theories by insisting on a numerical presentation supported by quantitative data. It governs exclusions by the numerical concept of risk and the question of economic cost and benefit. It allows for policy to be made that focuses on controlling people and things considered risky. This discourse seems to have expansionistic tendencies, since in terms of the definition above, the field of objects to which it is applied is increasing. Environment and public health were domains that fell early on to this managerial way of dealing with problems. The domains of public safety and crime control are about to be cast in this mold.

The reason for this expansionism is that the discourse of numbers seems to provide a sense of objectivity and certainty to the public. However, it will never be able to make good on that promise, because it has within itself an intrinsic limit. The most complete models to predict outcomes will be the most holistic ones, but the more holistic a model becomes, the more uncertain the eventual outcome will be. However, this objection is seldom raised. Ever since the actuarial method began to make headway, it has promised a means to control and to prevent future hazards: first in insurance, then in the way companies were run, and finally in the public domain.

This made the actuarial method a strong technology of governance in the hands of policy makers. The discursive and also oftentimes practical alliance between the State and science legitimised State intervention in important areas of human life, such as public health, mobility, environment, and spatial planning. Therefore it is no wonder that policy makers have embraced it. However, discourses cannot be picked up and used whenever we see fit. They are more powerful than that. In the end, they determine the way people think of solutions to problems. A discourse forms a horizon or backdrop against which some solutions appear while other approaches fade into obscurity. Discursive practices discipline their subjects into a certain way of thinking. The demand for a calculation of the costs and benefits of immigration is in line with this discursive practice, and therefore it is not surprising that this question arises. It emerges within a context in which almost everything else is cast in these terms, so why not immigration?

Foucault's point of looking at discourses is to determine why and how a certain economy of exclusion and marginalisation is made possible. In his books, he sides with the marginalised and with the 'abnormals', and tries to explain the mechanisations that incurred their predicament. The discourse of numbers has its own way of marginalisation that seems natural, but is in fact the product of a discourse. In the discourses Foucault describes – for instance, those on the birth of the prison or the history of sexuality – the marginalised are the 'abnormals', who do not conform to the drilling of discipline, or the 'mad' or 'perverted', who do not follow accepted sexual distinctions. The actuarial discourse produces marginalisation as well. These are the people or things deemed 'risky'. People or things that show indications of a possible future risk of danger or threat need to be disciplined, monitored, and in the last instance removed.

There is a debate in environmental law as to whether the precautionary principle does not needlessly stifle beneficial research and practices because of a possible risk (Pieterman 2008). Here the producers of technology are deemed risky, and face monitoring and increased protocols and research obligations. However, groups and individuals are marginalised or face increased State control as well. At airports, a person may be refused permission to board a plane if he has a certain profile that is considered risky. Children who exhibit behaviour that may indicate future problems involving crime may be monitored. Early intervention teams may enter houses of people who exhibit traits that may indicate there will be future problems.

The discourse of risk creates its own marginalised groups, because it is only a matter of time before the public demands 'transparency' and 'clarity' about the risks some segments of society entail and what each segment contributes to and costs society. That these figures cannot be provided with certainty will get lost in the discussion. The conflicts will be presented as managerial problems, and will be about the meaning of this or that variable in the impact assessment or risk analysis. When a discourse of numbers prevails within society, ethics will be utilitarian and people will inevitably become numbers as well.

Wilders may well succeed in his pleas to calculate the costs of immigration. The numbers will be used to stigmatise and further marginalise different groups of people, such as the Roma for instance. Health and police institutions will interfere more and more in people's lives on the basis of risk assessments concerning future behaviour. These interventions will be based on a discourse that has inherent limits of objectivity, but it will be some time before this is realised. In the meantime, public trust in numbers will even increase. Numbers are used in progressively more fields and are fed uncritically to an audience that will become used to a mode of discourse in which everything may be a subject for calculation, and its monetary value may be assessed. Foucault accused especially the humanities of complicity in marginalisation. It seems that the natural sciences can work as such an accomplice as well.

References

Baal, P.H.M. van, Feenstra, T.L., Polder, J.J., Tariq, L., Jama, W., & Berg, M. van den, (2009). *Kosteneffectiviteit van preventie, van gezondheidzorg-perspectief naar maatschappelijk perspectief.* Rapport 270091011/ 2009. Bilthoven: RIVM

Blaeij, A. de (2003). *De monetaire waarde van een menselijk leven in een verkeersveiligheidscontext.* Researchmemorandum 2003 20, Amsterdam: Vrije Universiteit.

Breeman, G.E., & Timmermans, A. (2008). *Politiek van de aandacht voor milieubeleid, een onderzoek naar maatschappelijke dynamiek, politieke agendavorming en prioriteiten in het Nederlandse milieubeleid.* WOT Rapport 77. Wageningen: Wageningen UR.

Feely, M.M., & Simon, J. (1994). Actuarial Justice, the Emerging New Criminal Law. In D. Nelkin (Ed.), *The Future of Criminology.* Thousand Oakes: Sage.

Foucault, M., & Gordon, C. (Eds.) (1980). *Power/Knowledge: Selected Interviews & Other Writings 1972-77.* New York: Pantheon Books.

Foucault, M. (1989). *Discipline, toezicht en straf, de geboorte van de gevangenis.* Groningen: Historische Uitgeverij.

Foucault, M. (1990). The History of Sexuality. New York: Vintage Books.

Garland, D. (1996). The Limits of the Sovereign State: Strategies of Crime Control. *Contemporary Society. British Journal of Criminology, 36(4),* 445-471.

Hajer, M. (1995). *The Politics of Environmental Discourse, Ecological Modernization and the Policy Process.* Oxford: Clarendon Press.

Jasanoff, S. (1990). *The Fifth Branch, Science Advisers and Policy Makers.* Cambridge MA: Harvard University Press.

Lidskog, R., & Sundqvist, G. (2007). Regulating European Air, Coproduction of Science and Policy. In H. Pleijel (Ed.), *Transboundary Air Pollution, Scientific Understanding and Environmental Policy in Europe.* Stockholm: Studentliteratur.

Meuwese, A. (2009). *Impact Assessment in EU Lawmaking.* The Hague: Kluwer Law International.

Moerings, M. (2003). *Straffen met het oog op veiligheid, een onderneming vol risico's.* Inaugurele Rede. Leiden: Universiteit Leiden.

Mol, A.P., Sonneveld, D.A., & Spaargaren, G. (2009). *The Ecological Modernisa-tion Reader. Environmental Reform in Theory and Practice.* London/New York: Routledge.

Oenema, O., Van der Kolk, J.W.H. (2008). *Moet het eenvoudiger? Een essay over de complexiteit van milieubeleid.* Wageningen: Wageningen UR.

Pieterman, R. (2008). *De voorzorgcultuur: streven naar veiligheid in een wereld vol risico en onzekerheid.* Den Haag: Boom Juridische uitgevers.

Pieterman, R. (forthcoming). *Fault, Risk and Precaution, Three Modern Ways of Dealing with Damage and Disgrace.*

Pleijel, H., & Grennfelt, P. (2007). European Air Pollution – The Historic Legacy. In H. Pleijel (Ed.), *Transboundary Air Pollution, Scientific Understanding and Environmental Policy in Europe*. Stockholm: Studentliteratur.

Prittwitz, V. (1990). *Das Katastrophenparadox. Elemente einer Theorie der Umweltpolitik*. Opladen: Leske+Budrich.

Ravetz, J. (1996). *Scientific Knowledge and Its Social Problems*. New Brunswick NJ: Transaction Publishers, edition 1996. Original edition (1971) Oxford: Clarendon Press.

Winsemius, P. (1986). *Gast in Eigen Huis*. Den Haag: Tjeenk Willink.

14. Between Proximity and Distance: Relationships between Police and Citizens in Amsterdam

Barbara van Caem

1. Introduction

During the last half of the former century all western countries have been confronted with the limits of its traditional criminal justice system and especially its limited potential to prevent crime. Ever rising crime rates under rapidly changing societal circumstances rather showed that the criminal justice system was inadequate as a sole measure to provide security. Furthermore, the idea of the public police as an effective crime fighter within this system proved to be no more than a myth. Contrary to the general belief, that the police was an institution occupied solely with law enforcement and catching criminals, researchers revealed another reality. Public police spend most of their time on peace keeping, moving from incident to incident, and only a very limited amount of time on crime fighting with very marginal results (Rumbaut and Bittner 1979; Bayley 1994). Additionally, research into the police revealed a rather closed group culture with a great deal of distrust towards citizens, resulting in a we versus them mentality and a police operating at a distance from citizens (Van der Torre 1999: 16).

The apparent inadequacy of and rising critique on the system led to an ongoing quest for seeking alternative ways to provide security. For the criminal justice system, such an alternative has been restorative justice, as described by the authors of the former paragraphs in this book. For the public police, the dominant alternative to traditional policing has been the introduction of community policing. Both alternatives strive to involve communities and are aimed at problem solving. Furthermore, both operate on a very local scale, restorative justice within a private community around offender and victim, community policing within a small neighbourhood community assigned to a community policing officer. But where restorative justice has a rather new and modest position in most western countries, at best complementary to the criminal justice system, community policing was adopted as alternative paradigm to the traditional policing model in the majority of western countries during the last half of the former century (Skogan 2006).

Unfortunately, different forms of community policing proofed difficult to fully implement in practice. Often only elements of community policing approaches were actually adopted. In addition, in the present century, among other factors, the new terroristic threat and new populist right wing orientated political winds led to a constant demand for harsher measures such as risk profiling and repression (Das, Huberts and Van Steden 2007). These are the kind of developments, that seem to cause a move towards a distant position to citizens within police strategies once again. The challenge for the community police officer (or neighbourhood coordinator; '*buurtregisseur*') now is how to deal with these, at first glance, contradictory and conflicting trends. On the one hand, he (or she), should promote trust and community involvement ('the police as your best friend'), on the other hand, he has to focus on order maintenance and law enforcement ('the police as crime fighter').

The changes mentioned above can be understood from a nodal governance perspective (Johnston and Shearing 2003). Nodal governance acknowledges governance by state, private, non-governmental and informal nodes coexist and cooperate, while neither of them holds a priority position. Johnston and Shearing (2003: 140/1) acknowledge that in such a system the common good might not be served, and propose a nodal governance model that combines a risk based approach with community involvement to ensure justice is served, next to security. Risk based approaches can cause distance in the relation between police and citizens, if they are primarily focussed on for instance high risk groups. Community involvement can enhance proximity in the relation between police and citizens, if it builds up citizens trust in the police, and by this their willingness to cooperate with the police.

This paper examines whether the Amsterdam neighbourhood coordination ('*buurtregie*'), a specific form of community policing, does reveal and connect proximity approaches linked to citizen participation to more distant approaches linked to more risk based methods. To that end, the paper first elaborates on the interdependent relation between police and citizens, a relation that always involves both proximity and distance. Second, the paper elaborates the concept of nodal governance and its relevance for the public police. Third, the paper presents the developed research model and method. Fourth, the results of a preliminary research on neighbourhood coordination in two Amsterdam neighbourhoods are presented. Finally the paper discusses to what extend neighbourhood coordination does reveal and connect proximity approaches to more distant approaches, and whether this can be understood as an illustration of a nodal orientation of public police.

2. Interdependence and Paradox

Before continuing about nodal governance, I need to elaborate on the specific nature of the relation between police and citizens, because this relation is characterized by mutual interdependence and internal paradox. Community involvement, one of the vital aspects of community policing, proved to be more or less inevitable, because police authority and legitimacy are derived from citizens and in addition police effectiveness is largely dependent on the functioning of citizens. Vice versa citizens expect help and protection from the police when in danger, and in addition, they are the most vital source of information for the police (Cachet and Versteegh 2007; Tyler 2006; Waddington 1999; Bayley 1994).

However, this relation also presents an internal paradox, because it is reciprocally characterized by a need for proximity as well as distance to each other. On the one hand, police need proximity to citizens to ensure public support. At the same time they need distance to citizens to be able to remain objective and guard the common good. On the other hand, citizens require connectedness to the police when they are in need of help and protection, but like to keep a distance when they are the subject of law enforcement or order maintenance by the police (Cachet 2007). Moreover, the need for protection of the police always coincides with the need for protection from the police. Police officers do not merely provide services, but they do also act against inadmissible conduct, what could hinder a relation of trust between police and citizens. In addition, a bond of trust between police and citizens could detain police officers from acting upon misconduct by these same citizens. In reverse, the police could also misuse information given to them by citizens in confidence (Waddington 1992: 21; Torre 1999: 192-198).

Next to community involvement community policing also requires a shift from reactive police surveillance and crime investigation to a problem solving orientation. Problem solving is about addressing the circumstances that have caused crime in the first place, and it can be approached in two ways. The first one focuses on patterns of common crime, determined by analysis of police registrations. The second one emphasizes community involvement at identifying and prioritizing a broad range of community problems. Police registration analysis is crime orientated and produces hotspot and repeat offender lists. Contrary, the problems citizens bring forward are usually not registered in police systems. They broaden the scope considerably by adding a diverse range of nuisance, disorder and liveability issues. To address these issues effectively, cooperation with citizens and many professional parties within society is inevitable (Skogan 2006). How do these complex networks of cooperation within governing security relate to the police in general and the neighbourhood coordinator specifically?

3. Police and Nodal Governance

The notion of nodal governance acknowledges that contemporary security governance is the result of a complex set of constantly changing and varying relationships between different governance nodes over time and place (Shearing and Wood 2003: 404). In this networked version of governance, state and public police are no longer considered to be the sole providers of security, but they are deemed to be just one governance node among many others, accompanied by for instance private and informal nodes (Johnston and Shearing 2003: 147). These nodes are more than a mere junction of information exchange within networks. According to the nodal governance perspective they are sites were the flow of information and communication is translated into action. Nodes are sites of governance where knowledge, capacity and resources are mobilized to achieve certain outcomes, like security (Burris, Drahos and Shearing 2005: 37).

The conditions underlying the nodal perspective drastically change the position of a former security key player: the public police. Although public police still are often regarded as the true defender of security, they also have had to recognize their own limits in their knowledge, capacity and resources. Consequently, public police have engaged in partnerships and safety networks with other auspices of security governance (Terpstra and Kouwenhoven 2004), and they have supported private and voluntary order maintenance. On these grounds, Wood and Shearing (2009: 11, 12) suggest that the public police should adopt a nodal orientation. The authors suggest the police should perceive itself as surrounded by rivalling nodes, that all strive to fulfil their own agendas. A nodal orientation indicates that the police has to acquire insight in the knowledge, capacity and resources of the other nodes, and reach an understanding of their way of thinking and acting. In this manner the police could engage in nodal assemblages in a way that promotes common good and safeguards public interest. (Wood and Shearing 2009: 15, 16).

However, the promotion of common good and public interest is not necessarily guaranteed by nodal security government. In fact, Johnston and Shearing (2003: 143) acknowledge that the diversity in the provision of security might give rise to a fragmented system. Such a system could suffer ineffectiveness due to lack of coordination and might cause injustice due to inequity in the distribution of services. Furthermore, a preoccupation with risk might lead to the emergence of an overly invasive form of security, especially when solely based on measures of actuarial justice.[1] Johnston and Shearing (2003: 140,141) propose a solution by suggesting a nodal governance model that should somehow integrate security and justice. In their view an optimal integration model of justice and security can best be effected through a future oriented risk based approach that is grounded on the mobilization of local knowledge and capacity.

Johnston et al. (2003: 22-30) used eight dimensions in their book *Governing Security* to describe this change from a past oriented and state centred way of governing security into a future oriented and nodal governance of security. Three of these dimensions are especially relevant to explore the relation between the neighbourhood coordinator and citizens in respect to the suggested nodal governance model that combines risk based approaches with community involvement. Risk based approaches indicate distance and community involvement indicates proximity. The first dimension, who makes the rules, is about which authority sets the standard about how things ought to be. Traditionally, defining order was supposed to be a prerogative of the state, but

1 The concept of actuarial justice by Feely and Simon (1994) is about a penal shift in attention towards controlling future criminal conduct: the tracing of people who might cause future damage and persons with a prior risk reputation because of previous committed crimes or inflicted damage.

currently there are several other authorities assuming this responsibility. For instance private companies providing their own security program in an amusement park for its employees and customers.

The second dimension, what is the nature of the rules, is about the intention of the norms. Whose interests do they serve, and do they apply equally to all members of a community or end up excluding one group from benefits another group gains? Curfew orders for youths for example, that means picking them up and returning them home in weekend nights to reduce disorder, can create a vast infringement of civil rights of movement of virtuous youths (Flint 2002: 256/7). The third dimension, modes of governance, is about how implementation is achieved. Traditionally, the public police was the primary institution to guard the peace. Nowadays, others are involved in guarding security as well. This can be citizens, united in neighbourhood watches or employees from the local housing corporation, whose job description holds security tasks.

4. Method

A Model on Proximity and Distance

In this paper the three selected dimensions of Johnston et al. (2003) were used to develop a model to explore the relation between neighbourhood coordinator and citizens. First, each dimension was translated into a dimension which was relevant for neighbourhood coordination in actual practice on the basis of academic literature, police policy documents, six inquiring interviews with key figures on neighbourhood coordination within Amsterdam police, and my own

Table 1: Dimensions of Neighbourhood Coordination

Proximity	Distance
1. Source of the approach	
Much input citizens	Few input citizens
Frontline led	Policy led
2. Intention of the approach	
Knowing and be known	Information led policing
Inclusion	Exclusion
5. Executing neighbourhood coordination	
Emphasis on citizen participation	Emphasis on supervision and enforcement
Citizen as partner	Citizen as ears and eyes

experience as a police officer there. Second, the most dominant factors for each dimension within police practice were traced, seeking two sides of one coin. Each police practical approach aimed at creating or causing proximity was complemented with one creating or causing distance. The model is presented in table 1.

The first dimension of neighbourhood coordination, the source of the approach, is about who determines which problems the neighbourhood coordinator will address. Citizens have either much or less input on the approach of the neighbourhood coordinator and his professional partners. This citizen input can vary from actual participation in the deliberation about which problems to address and how to solve them, to rhetoric consultation or even no consultation at all. Furthermore, there can be a frontline led approach, where the neighbourhood coordinator decides what to do in close consultation with his professional partners with or without citizens. However, there can also be a dominantly policy led approach, where regional police and municipal policy or the local neighbourhood police-chief mostly prescribe what the neighbourhood coordinator must do.

The second dimension of neighbourhood coordination, the intention of the approach, is about the purpose of the approach. For neighbourhood coordination an important element is 'knowing and be known' by the citizens in the community. The neighbourhood coordinator aims to be visible, approachable and available for citizens. On the other hand, he is also bound to work information led like all the other police officers from his neighbourhood police-team. To work information led in the Amsterdam-Amstelland police means to focus on certain objects and subjects of criminality problems on the basis of a local analysis and prioritization of police registration. The approach can either reach and include all residents of a neighbourhood, or exclude certain groups. If police focus exclusively on the groups most likely to cause trouble in the future, this might lead to undue attention of law enforcement on the basis of age or skin colour and cause exclusion. If the neighbourhood coordinator succeeds in providing his organization with knowledge about those crimes and disorder, that bother a community the most, joint policing efforts of surveillance and law enforcement might be directed towards the key issues that really deserve it without excluding certain communities within local residents (Innes, Abbott, Lowe and Roberts 2008).

The third dimension, executing neighbourhood coordination, is about how the neighbourhood coordinator actually conducts his work. He can guard the liveability and safety in his neighbourhood with emphasis on citizen participation, or he can do so by utilizing professional supervision and enforcement in his neighbourhood. Citizen participation means that citizens actually cooperate with the neighbourhood coordinator and fulfil some role of their own, like participating in a neighbourhood watch, or actually fulfilling a distinct role of their own in solving a neighbourhood problem (Caem 2008). The neighbourhood coordinator can also guard the peace in another way, he can organize extra police or municipal supervision and enforcement in the neighbourhood. Furthermore, when citizens participate, the neighbourhood coordinator can either treat them as real partners or more as ears and eyes. He can join forces with local residents, and approach them as equals. On the one hand he can value them for their specific local knowledge and use their potential capacity to suggest pragmatic solutions, decide in close collaboration and use their information, ideas and networks to find solutions and solve problems together. On the other hand the cooperation with citizens can be limited to acquire information from them and encourage them to report mischief in the neighbourhood.

Research Method

This paper reviews the results of a preliminary research phase of a larger research on the relation between police and citizens. The preliminary research is based on a limited number of interviews and observations of police officers only, and just two neighbourhoods. As such, for now, only police perceptions on the relation police and citizens are discussed. The total picture is still subject to ongoing research. It will involve twelve more neighbourhoods and interviews and discussions with groups of citizens from these researched neighbourhoods to trace their perception on the relation with the local police. Furthermore, for the larger research a model of proximity and distance on all eight dimensions was developed, for this paper only the developed three-dimension model is used.

In total ten interviews were held in the last three months of 2009. First, six open interviews were conducted with key officers within the Amsterdam police. These key officers were all involved with neighbourhood coordination on a central level, which assured insight and overview regarding neighbourhood coordination. Second, specified interview questions for a qualitative semi-structured interview were designed, based on the open interviews with the key officers and on the model of proximity and distance. Third, four semi-structured interviews were held of two neighbourhood coordinators and their chiefs in respectively Amsterdam north and Amsterdam south-east. In addition, both neighbourhood coordinators were observed during an entire shift. The interviews were taped, worked out integrally and were all approved by the respondents. The observations each resulted in a separate report, which were approved by the respondents as well. Finally, the results were analysed with the model to reveal whether neighbourhood coordination does connect proximity approaches to more distant approaches, and whether this can be understood as an illustration of a nodal orientation of public police.

5. The Amsterdam Neighbourhood Coordinator

In Amsterdam, the introduction of neighbourhood police-teams and abolition of beat constables in 1986, was succeeded by the introduction of a new style beat constable, that was named neighbourhood coordinator, in 2000. Today, the Amsterdam-Amstelland police has 230 neighbourhood coordinators, each responsible for the safety and security in their own neighbourhood of approximately 5.000 residents. They have a considerable higher rank than the beat constables from the '1970s'. Furthermore, all of them had to graduate in an extra two year education program, especially designed for Amsterdam neighbourhood coordination. As for beat constables, there focus is on proximity, a wide range of problems, preventive, proactive and repressive strategies and on cooperation with other parties including citizens (Terpstra 2008). The new element is that this neighbourhood coordinator is made responsible for the safety in his neighbourhood and is expected to coordinate cooperation with partners and citizens in the neighbourhood (Van Riessen 2007: 212), which also means being the most important link between the local neighbourhood team and the neighbourhood.

The Home-Base of the Neighbourhood Coordinator

The Amsterdam-Amstelland police region includes the city of Amsterdam and six surrounding smaller municipalities. The police region is divided into five police districts and consists of thirty-two fairly autonomous local neighbourhood police-teams, which consist of an average of sixty to eighty police officers. Most of them serve in uniform, a small part is occupied with handling minor common criminal investigations. At each neighbourhood policing-team on average seven neighbour-hood coordinators are stationed and nine police project-leaders. The neighbourhood coordinators are responsible for the safety and liveability in their specific neighbourhood. The nine project-leaders are responsible for projects on police-region priorities in the whole neighbourhood police-team ward and the daily steering of the neighbourhood police-team police-officers. Each neighbourhood police-team has a chief, who is responsible for the safety and security in the whole ward.

The police capacity is used flexibly, partly for providing emergency help and partly to supply capacity to projects or neighbourhoods within the ward or for regional projects and events. Project-leaders and neighbourhood coordinators can request for police capacity for problems within respectively their project or neighbourhood, making a formal work-request. The neighbourhood police-team management, consisting of the local police-chief, his substitute and an information-officer, will prioritize between the requests and other obligations on the base of their current information position. The scarce capacity will usually go to where it is deemed to be needed the most. The same goes for additional police and municipal surveillance capacity.

In the following, the practice of neighbourhood coordination in two neighbourhoods in respectively Amsterdam south-east and Amsterdam north is described. First the circumstances in the neighbourhoods will be described and subsequently how the neighbourhood coordinator and his chief perceive the relation between police and citizens in neighbourhood coordination on the dimensions source of the approach, intentions of the approach and executing neighbourhood coordination.

6. Amsterdam South-East: Reigersbos

The south-east area of Amsterdam consists of three neighbourhood police-teams. The Reigersbos neighbourhood is one of seven neighbourhoods in the neighbourhood police-team Remmerdenplein. The south-east area harbours many different nationalities. A number of neighbourhoods within the Remmerdenplein police-ward have numerous one-parent families, low incomes, mostly social housing and subordinate living circumstances. In short, an accumulation of risk factors that make the ward vulnerable for crime and disorder. In 2009, the whole south-east area was plagued by repeating shooting incidents between youth, causing three deaths. In response to the shooting incidents part of the area has been declared a security-risk area, including the neighbourhood Holendrecht that borders on Reigersbos. Here, the police has been given the power to undertake stop and search controls of all people present in the public domain. The neighbourhoods Holendrecht and Wisseloord both adjoin Reigersbos and both harbour a criminal youth-group, that causes crime and disorder.

Municipal surveys show that insecurity feelings within the Remmerdenplein police-ward have mounted since 2007, while they have been stable or declining in the rest of the city. In Reigersbos the majority of residents are immigrants, 58% non-western and 9% western. Native Dutch residents are in minority with 34%. The largest immigrant group are the Surinamers, 35% (www.os.amsterdam.nl). Reigersbos consists of mostly five- or six-layer social housing, arranged in courts that surround a shared open garden-space. The maintenance of the apartments and the public green is long overdue. The tardy pruning withdraws parking places and apartments from sight, creating opportunity for burglaries and other criminality and disorder. The neighbourhood also contains shopping-centre Reigersbos, a high school and a local community-centre.

Source of Neighbourhood Coordination Reigersbos

According to respondents, in Reigersbos residents hardly provide any coordinated input regarding which problems the neighbourhood coordinator should address. Respondents observe that residents in Reigersbos are hardly organized and don't report much to the police out of fear of reprisals, especially from criminal or disorderly youth. A residents meeting and survey among residents in Holendrecht showed that people are concerned. But they also lost confidence in the authorities and don't want to be known as a police informant and remain rather passive. The excessive media attention on Holendrecht, after a deadly shooting incident there in 2009, only increased this fear in the whole ward.

The situation appears to be too insecure to encourage active citizenship. The respondents state that police and their partners first have to deal with the criminal youth-groups, and that they must simultaneously convince citizens that their information and reports are indispensable to enable the authorities to act. The neighbourhood coordinator states furthermore, that people in Reigersbos are even afraid to talk themselves to disorderly youths about their conduct, because they will be threatened or receive a bold response. In his words: 'I wonder if people have a need for citizen participation at all, if they don't even dare to talk to the youths here'. There is emphasis on a policy led repressive strategy to tackle the youth problem, but the police-chief expects that after restoring order in joint cooperation with all partners, some increased input of residents will be feasible.

There is, however, more cooperation with local entrepreneurs from the Reigersbos shopping mall. They are organized in an entrepreneurs association, and on the initiative of, and with the neighbourhood coordinator, they strive for achieving the second star in the already earned municipal safety-mark 'safe entrepreneurship'. The chairman of this association is one of the neighbourhood coordinator's key-partners, as he is influential and respected by lay and professional members of the community and the municipality, and very persistent in making every party keep up to their part of the deal. During the observation we visited this chairman, and he illustrated his role immediately by reminding the neighbourhood coordinator that he had to deliver the required police-data on the shopping mall the next meeting.

The decisions about which problems the neighbourhood coordinator addresses are to some extent decided with for instance the housing cooperation. During the observation, we attended a meeting with the local housing-cooperation caretaker intended for the whole ward. Usually, at least one of the neighbourhood coordinators of the Remmerdenplein ward attends, and speaks for and informs the other neighbourhood coordinators. Here, a whole range of recent incidents were discussed and some possible ways of dealing with it, however, no real commitments were made. Furthermore, it was noticeable that most information on concrete incidents came from the caretaker and not from the neighbourhood coordinator.

Intention of Neighbourhood Coordination in Reigersbos

According to respondents, to realize a close connection with residents and knowing and be known, is difficult in Reigersbos. For instance, the few resident-associations present hardly contact the neighbourhood coordinator. The neighbourhood coordinator gives consultations in the local community centre once a week, and there at least some citizens attend. However, contacting the youths is even harder, there seems to be a stigma on contact with the police. The result is that the neighbourhood coordinator mostly works closely with professional partners, like with the housing cooperation caretaker.

Furthermore the neighbourhood coordinator mentions that, for knowing and be known, actually patrolling the neighbourhood is very important, but under pressure as he momentarily also attends the neighbourhood of a colleague and the special educational programme for neighbourhood coordinators. Still, according to the local police-chief, in a situation of distrust and low report rates a neighbourhood coordinator is vital to get information from the neighbourhood, because people will turn to him more easily, if they decide to approach police at all. And when serious incidents take place, the neighbourhood coordinator is the best equipped party to gauge the atmosphere and calm people down, as they do at least succeed in a deeper relationship with the local community than the other uniform police officers from the ward.

One way to reach the youths is frequently visiting the local secondary school in Reigersbos. The neighbourhood coordinator engages in regular contact with the school director and caretaker, and talks to youths if they somehow caused trouble on the school. In this respect he mentions that registering everything about the youths in police systems has the risk of stigmatising them, and sometimes makes his school director hesitant to report about the school children. 'Such a registration does not mean nothing en every child commits some tomfoolery sometimes'. However, the neighbourhood coordinator is satisfied with the information system in the ward, as it enables him to organise extra surveillance in Reigersbos, when needed. Mostly, he arranges this informally, as the system of formal requests is subject to a prioritization by the ward management and often denied, because the scarce capacity of the small police-team is needed in Holendrecht.

Lately, the concentrated focus on disorderly youths in the Holendrecht shopping mall and the installation of surveillance cameras in the Wisseloord shopping mall, cause the youths moving to Reigersbos shopping mall. These youths come with an attitude. According to the neighbourhood coordinator for now, the increased attention and repressive approach on these youths amplifies the agitation towards all uniforms. 'You do not talk to police officers in this neighbourhood and certainly not in public. If I greet these youths, they turn their back, ignore me and hawk up. I have never before encountered this behaviour in all my years in south-east Amsterdam, it makes me angry, and I would like to show my authority and drag them to the station. But that would only increase the boy's status.'

Executing Neighbourhood Coordination in Reigersbos

Respondents' view on executing neighbourhood coordination, about how the neighbourhood coordinator actually conducts his work, is as follows. Both chief and neighbourhood coordinator state that they predominantly work with professional supervision and enforcement and not with citizen participation, except for the cooperation with local entrepreneurs in shopping-centres Reigersbos and Wisseloord. Reigersbos also has some frequent complainers, mostly older, female and native Dutch women, who contact the neighbourhood coordinator regularly and do provide him with information when he asks for it. But obviously, emphasis is on supervision and enforcement. Except for with local entrepreneurs, there is no organised form of cooperation with citizens. Emphasis lies on attaining information from them and not on partnership.

The police ward information process enables the neighbourhood coordinator to arrange surveillance or extra police measures during his absence. The neighbourhood coordinator prefers to apply informally, as formal requests for police or other surveillance capacity, are often not granted due to worse problems elsewhere. The police ward concentrates its efforts on targeting the two criminal youths groups from Holendrecht and Wisseloord. They receive much extra, mostly repressive, attention, momentarily causing them to move their business into Reigersbos. Confronted with complaints from 'his' entrepreneurs, the neighbourhood coordinator has managed to frequently engage private and municipal supervisors to intervene in the shopping mall. 'If they are increasing pressure on the youths in Holendrecht and Wisseloord, they all come to Reigersbos. Consequently, the shopkeepers call me, and tell me that ten to twenty youths are hanging out in front of their store, that they are scared and will close their shop. Then, I engage the supervisors. They are experienced, and often have an immigrant background and are capable of talking to the boys. I stay in the background, in case things escalate. These supervisors are very important partners for me.'

7. Amsterdam North: Molenwijk

The north area of Amsterdam consists of two neighbourhood police-teams. The Molenwijk neighbourhood is one of nine neighbourhoods in the neighbourhood police-team Klimopweg. The respondents state, that the police-ward Amsterdam north can best be described as a ward combining a village character with big-city social problems. The original population is mostly working class and the area is traditionally fairly poor. Neighbourhood coordination seems to suit the neighbourhood well, because of the village character: residents prefer personal contact, which the neighbourhood coordinators do provide. Momentarily, the police-ward is in a phase of transition, with an expanding industry and harbour and new, more expensive housing. In addition the number of big events are increasing, which gives Amsterdam north an entertainment function and does claim an increasing part of the Klimopweg police-team capacity.

In Molenwijk the majority of residents, 58%, are native Dutch, furthermore there are 33% non-western immigrants and 9% western immigrants. The immigrant group counts numerous nationalities with no real dominant group in percentage (www.os.amsterdam.nl). Most native Dutch residents have lived there from the time the neighbourhood was build, around the late 1960s, and are of age, most newcomers are younger and often have larger families. The neighbourhood consist of fifteen high-rise condominiums and is in a phase of renovation. There is one criminal youth-group and there are disorder problems with youths. The disorder problems often involve drinking and drug abuse in the galleries and stare cases of the condominiums in the late evening and early night. There also is a shopping mall and two primary schools.

Source of Neighbourhood Coordination in Molenwijk

According to respondents, in Molenwijk, the neighbourhood coordinator involves residents in determining and tackling the problems he addresses. He has realized a strong cooperation with residents. He has told residents that he acknowledges the problems with the youths, but that he is incapable of solving all the problems on his own. So he requested their help. He has managed to inspire a local resident group of about forty residents to regularly meet with him and the housing-cooperation caretaker. These meetings resulted in several citizen initiatives. For instance, the residents arranged for a self defined version of sms-alert. Contrary to the official sms-alert, were the police informs citizens about an incident and asks for their help, this sms-alert means that the residents send an sms to other residents when in need of help because of trouble. In response, the other residents will come to assist the sms-sender. These sms-alerts are send to the neighbourhood coordinator as well, but in principle just to inform him. Only when residents cannot cope on their own, he will provide backup, simultaneously he stays informed directly about what is going on in Molenwijk. This neighbourhood coordinator is strongly involved with the people in his neighbourhood. 'The people that live here, they determine the atmosphere, they create the neighbourhood. I want to acknowledge that, and do something positive with that as a police officer (...) the challenge is to unite people.'

The Molenwijk neighbourhood coordinator has involved local shopkeepers as well. In the local shopping mall, the neighbourhood coordinator has managed to end a disorder problem with alcohol addicts by strict law enforcement actions. Subsequently, he has stimulated local entrepreneurs to join forces for the safety mark 'safe entrepreneurship'. To this end, he put considerable effort in mobilizing other professional partners, his own colleagues from program management and the municipality, and finally he has succeeded in motivating the local chairman and secretary of the shopping-mall association to become the driving force behind this initiative. This was the neighbourhood coordinator's intention in the first place, to return the responsibility for safety to where he thinks it belongs, in this case the shopping mall entrepreneurs.

In Molenwijk, both respondents state that the neighbourhood coordinator is granted much free space by his chief, how he arranges neighbourhood coordination is deemed his responsibility and new ideas are usually welcome. The chief states that 'the neighbourhood coordinator is a specialist. A good one knows what is going on on his turf and what is needed most. Like I feel responsible for the whole police-ward, they feel responsible for their part of the territory.' Nevertheless, sometimes the boarders of the neighbourhood coordinators freedom to act are in sight and subject of discussion with his chief.

Especially when incidents with a potentially great impact take place, the neighbourhood coordinator is expected to consult his chief about appropriate action. The chief states: 'Recently, a local pizzeria has been wrecked by some youths while it was open. Then I check with the neighbourhood coordinator whether he has taken stock of the situation, taken all necessary measures and what he can do and what I can do.'

Intention of Neighbourhood Coordination in Molenwijk

According to respondents, in Molenwijk one of the main purposes for neighbourhood coordination is knowing and be known. The Molenwijk neighbourhood coordinator states, that knowing and be known is a very important aspect for him and takes up a great deal of his time. During the observation, we met numerous residents and encountered a lot of youths. Most youths knew their neighbourhood coordinator by name and vice versa and he furthermore told me particular details about almost every single one. Quoting the neighbourhood coordinator about knowing and been known: 'I succeed when people say, 'that is my neighbourhood coordinator'. You can only reach that, if you care just as much about the neighbourhood as they do.' At the same time the neighbourhood coordinator repeats several times, 'Everybody in Molenwijk knows that I represent the law and if they break the law, I will enforce the law.' The Klimopweg chief stresses that the neighbourhood coordinator must know the neighbourhood and the people in it and needs to be as much in the neighbourhood as possible. But she acknowledges, that this is always under pressure. Many extra tasks have been delegated to neighbourhood coordinators, that require extra administrative work, like for instance advising the municipality about granting a permit. Likewise, the neighbourhood coordinators need to be selective which meetings they attend. Otherwise, they end up predominantly attending meetings.

The neighbourhood coordinator is convinced, that basically, he is able to reach all residents within his neighbourhood, but in some cases this is a negative kind of contact. Some multi-problem families are hard to reach. The neighbourhood coordinator always tries to help first, but if they don't change their behaviour and continue to cause mischief for other residents, they will be the object of vicious law enforcement and he will eventually aim at evicting them from their home, if the harassment of and nuisance for other residents does not end. Quoting, 'In one of the condominiums lives a family that causes disproportionate nuisance. I already succeeded in submitting the oldest son to a boarding school. Everybody wanted to move the family to another neighbourhood to get rid of them. I protested against that solution. In my opinion, it is not right to award such a family, that caused so much nuisance, by giving them a beautiful apartment in another neighbourhood. If nothing helps, than such a family should be evicted.' He adds, that before taking harsh measures, he always warns people and informs them about possible consequences when they do not change their behaviour.

According to respondents information led policing is still developing, and both respondents belief the right way to work intelligence led is by basing it on specific local knowledge. The police-chief states, 'Neighbourhood coordinators are the only police officers on the team, that have an information position, that enables them to make very specific work requests, that state what problem occurs when with whom. They are the only uniform police officers who can provide such information', but this still doesn't come through completely as intended. The chief deals with this problem by encouraging closer cooperation between project leaders and neighbourhood coordinators, with the aim to achieve more focussed work requests. The neighbourhood coordinator beliefs that 'if information led policing means a neighbourhood coordinator has to walk fixed routes on fixed schedules based on police data in figures, than I am against it. However, if the neighbourhood police-team is put into action based on information from residents, that they have given the neighbourhood coordinator, I am all for it.'

Executing Neighbourhood Coordination in Molenwijk

According to respondents, the Molenwijk neighbourhood coordinator predominantly works with residents and not with extra private security, although he strives to introduce structural extra municipal supervisors, who can aid him in the cooperation with the active citizen-group and also provide backup when he is not at work. He treats residents and local entrepreneurs more like partners than only ears and eyes, he aims to let them fulfil a distinct role of their own. Residents even arrested an offender shortly after the cooperation started and part of the local projects are complete citizen initiatives. The chief states, however, that the situation in Molenwijk even though it is desirable, is not representative for the rest of the police-ward, but rather an exceptional situation. 'We work mainly with private and municipal supervisors. These supervisors are well known within the team and mostly managed by the neighbourhood coordinators. Cooperating with citizens like in Molenwijk is relatively new and it raises questions about the limits of active citizenship.'

The primary focus of the approach in Molenwijk is the local criminal youth group similar to the south-east situation. The group is the dominant focus of police attention and subject to a strict approach. The only difference with the south-east situation is, that there is contact with the youths in numerous ways and citizens are involved as described before. The approach of the disorderly youths involves a warning and parent visit first. There the youth and parents have to engage in an agreement about no more disorderly behaviour and supervision by the parents. If the disorderly behaviour continues, the youth and his parents will be subjected to strict law enforcement aided with neighbourhood police-team capacity. Next to these repressive actions, citizens act on their own with the sms-alert system and during my observation I witnessed that the neighbourhood coordinator made a deal with a local youth-worker. The neighbourhood coordinator will arrange access for him to the condominiums, so that he can reach the youths causing trouble in the condominiums during the night, find out who they are and design an individual approach.

8. Conclusion

This paper explored whether the relation between police and citizens within Amsterdam neighbourhood coordination, can be understood from a nodal governance perspective and whether Amsterdam neighbourhood coordination does reveal and connect proximity approaches linked to citizen participation, to more distant approaches linked to more risk based methods. I will first discuss whether the relation between the neighbourhood coordinator and citizens, that is residents and entrepreneurs, can be understood from a nodal governance perspective. Then I will discuss to what extend proximity and distant approaches were found, and whether they are connected.

In both Reigersbos and Molenwijk the relation between neighbourhood coordinator and citizens revealed a somewhat unequal position of the neighbourhood coordinators and citizens in regard to security management. In Reigersbos residents were perceived as rather passive, any action was initiated by the neighbourhood coordinator and his partners. In Molenwijk however, the neighbourhood coordinator's explicit request for residents' help, led to a number of resident initiatives aimed at promoting safety and liveability in the neighbourhood. Concerning the relation to local entrepreneurs, entrepreneurs fulfilled their own role in security management, but in both cases only after considerable effort from the neighbourhood coordinator to make them join a safety-mark project.

The nodal governance perspective perceives the governance of security as a result of cooperation between different governing nodes, which should include citizen nodes. Specifically, this perspective denies hierarchy between the nodes. In contradiction to being one node amongst equals, in both Reigersbos and Molenwijk the neighbourhood coordinator had a prominent role in initiating safety initiatives involving entrepreneurs. In Molenwijk the neighbourhood coordinator had this prominent role in stimulating and enabling residents safety initiatives as well. Thus, the neighbourhood coordinators served as a catalyst to cooperation between different parties concerned with safety issues in both cases, although the cooperation with residents in Reigersbos was extremely limited. By expressing that the police should adopt a nodal orientation, and in that way could influence nodal assemblages to serve the common good, Shearing and Wood seem to acknowledge some distinct role for the police as well (Wood and Shearing 2009). So, even if the neighbourhood coordinator has a special role as catalyst, the relation between the neighbourhood coordinator and citizens can be understood from a nodal governance perspective in the light of the findings from both case studies.

Next to these citizen participation oriented proximity approaches both neighbourhoods showed a more distant approach linked to a risk based method.

The focus on criminal youths groups, although problem oriented, basically was risked based, because of its focus on repeat offenders. In Molenwijk, in addition to police registration data, the information about the youths was complemented by information from residents, who actually cooperated closely with the neighbourhood coordinator and employed their own actions. In Reigersbos the input of residents in this respect remained very limited. This caused emphasis on regional safety policy and police registration based deployment of police and other supervisors on the local youths, thus creating further distance between youths and authorities. This outcome indicates, that in Molenwijk both proximity and distant approaches are balanced and connected, while in Reigersbos the approach, in regard to the relation between police and residents, is rather distant and not connected to community involvement.

As stated before, citizens and police are interdependent. The Molenwijk case suggests, that increased community involvement is possible and can even help attune more focussed methods of policing to local needs and wishes. Within the Amsterdam police two pilots already try to improve community involvement and the connection between local input and more focussed, information led approaches. One pilot has the neighbourhood coordinator choose ten concrete local priority problems on which he will focus his attention and for which he will design a specific approach guideline for his colleagues (Meurs 2009). In the other pilot the neighbourhood coordinator is reinforced by another uniform officer and two municipal supervisors and explicitly instructed to consult residents about three concrete problems this safer neighbourhood team should focus on (Project team safer neighbourhood teams 2009).

The preliminary research provided a peek into the daily practice of neighbourhood coordinators and their connection to on the one hand the local residents and entrepreneurs and on the other hand the local police-team. It showed that it is possible for the neighbourhood coordinator to connect community policing proximity to more risk based approaches thriving on distance. This is, however, still rather an exception and certainly not easy to achieve and maintain in today's multicultural urban problem areas. Nonetheless, within ever changing societal circumstances community policing will remain valuable to reach and maintain a balance between proximity and distance in the police-citizen relation over and over again.

References

Bayley, D.H. (1994). *Police for the Future*. New York: Oxford University Press.

Burris, S., Drahos, P. & Shearing, C. (2005). Nodal Governance. *Australian Journal of Legal Philosophy, 30,* 30-57.

Caem, B. van (2008). *Verborgen kracht. Een onderzoek naar burgerparticipatie op het vlak van veiligheid*. Amsterdam: Vrije Universiteit.

Cachet, A., & Versteegh, P. (2007). Politie en samenleving. In C.J.C.F. Fijnaut, E.R. Muller, U. Rosenthal, & E.J. van der Torre (Eds.), *Politie. Studies over haar werking en organisatie*. Deventer: Kluwer.

Das, D., Huberts, L., & Van Steden, R. (2007). The Changing Soul of Dutch Policing: Responses to New Security Demands and the Relationship with Dutch Tradition. *Policing: An international Journal of Police Strategies & Management, 30 (3)*, 518-531.

Feeley, M., & Simon, J. (1994). Actuarial Justice: the Emerging New Criminal Law. In D. Nelken (Ed.), *The futures of criminology*. London: Sage.

Flint, J. (2002). Return of the Governors: Citizenship and the New Governance of Neighbourhood Disorder in the UK. *Citizenship studies, 6 (3)*, 245-264.

Innes, M., Abbott, L., Lowe, T., & Roberts, C. (2008). Seeing Like a Citizen: Field Experiments in Community Intelligence-led Policing. *Police Practice and Research, 1*, 1-16.

Johnston, L., & Shearing, C. (2003). *Governing Security. Explorations in Policing and Justice*. London and New York: Routledge.

Johnston, L., Shearing, C., & Stenning, P.C. (2003). Dimensions of Governance. In L. Johnston, & C. Shearing (Eds.), *Governing Security. Explorations in Policing and Justice*. London/New York: Routledge.

Meurs, T. (2009). *Prominenten aanpak*. Amsterdam: Politie Amsterdam-Amstelland (presentation).

Projectteam buurtveiligheidsteams (2009). *Leidraad buurtveiligheidsteams politie-regio Amsterdam-Amstelland. Een vijf-fasenmodel voor de aanpak van overlast*. Amsterdam: Politie Amsterdam-Amstelland.

Riessen, J. van (2007). *In naam der wet. Veertig jaar bij de Amsterdamse politie*. Amsterdam: Nieuw Amsterdam.

Rumbaut, R.G., & Bittner, E. (1979). Changing Conceptions of the Police Role: A Sociological Review. *Crime and Justice, 239*, 239-288.

Shearing, C., & Wood, J. (2003). Nodal Governance, Democracy and the New Denizens. *Journal of Law and Society, 30 (3)*, 400-419.

Skogan, W. (2006). Advocate: The Promise of Community Policing. In D. Weisburd, & A. Braga (Eds.), *Police Innovation. Contrasting Perspectives*. Cambridge: Cambridge University Press.

Terpstra, J. (2008). *Wijkagenten en hun dagelijks werk. Een onderzoek naar de uitvoering van gebiedsgebonden politiewerk*. Apeldoorn: Politie en Wetenschap.

Terpstra, J., & Kouwenhoven, R. (2004). *Samenwerking en netwerken in de lokale veiligheidszorg*.Twente: Politie en Wetenschap, IPIT Instituut voor Maatschappelijke Veiligheidsvraagstukken Universiteit Twente.

Torre, E.J. van der (1999). *Politiewerk. politiestijlen, community policing, professionalisme*. Alphen aan den Rijn: Samson.

Tyler, T. (2006). Psychological Perspectives on Legitimacy and Legitimation. *Annual Review Psychology, 57*, 375-400.

Waddington, P.A.J. (1999). *Policing Citizens: Authority and Rights*. London/New York: Routledge.

Wood, J., & Shearing, C. (2007). *Imagining Security*. Portland: Willan Publishing.

Wood, J., & Shearing, C. (2009). De nodale politiefunctie. *Justitiële Verkenningen, 35 (1)*, 11-28.

Internet

<http://www.os.amsterdam.nl/kerncijfers/15615/, consulted 21-01-2010>.

Biographies of the Authors

Tobias Arnoldussen is conducting PhD research on environmental regulation regarding air pollution in Europe and the Netherlands at the Erasmus University of Rotterdam. In his research he focuses on the interplay between local events and European legislation. Central themes of interest are the rise of sustainable development, the precautionary culture and the integration of environmental concerns in fields like public health, energy and transport. He studied law and philosophy at the University of Amsterdam.

John Blad is associate professor in the field of criminal law sciences at the Law Faculty of Erasmus University Rotterdam. His work is of a theoretical and integrative character, combining insights of the legal and the social sciences, especially sociology of law. He is involved in many restorative initiatives in the Netherlands, such as the foundation of the (Dutch) Forum for Restorative Justice and the (Dutch) Platform for Restorative detention. In 2008 General principles were published for the integration of restorative justice into the criminal justice system, produced by an ad hoc Platform for Mediation in Criminal Matters.
His most recent activities have been in China to help promote democratic rule of law and restorative justice.

Monica den Boer holds a Chair on comparative public administration at the VU University Amsterdam on behalf of the Police Academy of The Netherlands, with a focus on the internationalization of the police function. She obtained a PhD in 1990 from the European University Institute in Florence and before she joined the Police Academy, she worked at Edinburgh University, the Netherlands Study Centre for Crime and Law Enforcement in Leiden, the European Institute of Public Administration, Tilburg University, and the European Institute of Law Enforcement Co-operation. She is a Member of the Dutch Advisory Council on International Affairs, and served as a member of the Dutch Iraq Investigation Committee, as well as the Dutch Defence Future Survey Group. Currently she leads an EU-financed FP7 work package on value dilemma's of security professionals (INEX) and prepares a Police Ethics Handbook for the Asian European Foundation (ASEF). Her publications focus on (good) governance of 'internal' EU security co-operation, as well as European co-operation against organized crime and terrorism.

Jelle van Buuren is lecturer and researcher at the VU University Amsterdam at the Department of Public Governance. He worked for the EU-financed FP7 work package on value dilemma's of security professionals (INEX). His research and publications focus on European police cooperation, intelligence, counter-terrorism, border control, surveillance technologies and issues of good governance, like accountability and transparency. Prior to his academic career he worked as an investigative reporter on the same topics.

Barbara van Caem graduated at the University of Amsterdam with a master of laws degree in 1992 and has joined the Amsterdam-Amstelland foreign police in 1996. By completing the Netherlands Police Academy in 1999, she turned her police career around, changing from an administrative function to an executive one. By the end of 2007 she was posted at the VU University as researcher for the research chair safety, security & citizenship, a cooperation between VU University, the Amsterdam-Amstelland police and the municipality of Amsterdam. There she conducted research into safety related citizen participation in the Amsterdam-Amstelland region. Currently, she is combining a police job with PhD research at VU University. With the police she is a policy advisor within the project team safer neighbourhood teams. Her current PhD research concentrates on community policing within the Amsterdam police and specifically the relationship between police and citizens.

Christine Cleiren is Professor of Criminal Law and Criminal Procedural Law at the University of Leiden. She combines conducting research and teaching several criminal law courses with other responsibilities such as being head of the department of Criminal law and coordinating the inter-faculty research project 'Criminal Justice'. Her research focuses on the principles of criminal procedure in changing contexts. Besides academia, she is currently also active as a deputy judge in the Court of Appeals in Amsterdam and member of various committees related to legislation, criminal law, law enforcement and terrorism. Earlier on she worked as a Professor at the University of Rotterdam and was member of the UN-Commission which gathered and examined evidence of war crimes committed in the former Yugoslavia. From 1997 until 2000 Professor Cleiren worked as Director-General for Legislation, Administration of Justice, Law Enforcement and Legal Aid in the Ministry of Justice in the Netherlands.

Adam Crawford is Professor of Criminology and Criminal Justice and Director of the Centre for Criminal Justice Studies at the University of Leeds. His publications include *Crime Prevention Policies in Comparative Perspective* (2009), *Integrating Victims in Restorative Youth Justice* (2005); *Plural Policing* (2005), *Youth Offending and Restorative Justice* (with T. Newburn, 2003), *Crime and Insecurity* (ed. 2002), *Integrating Victims within Criminal Justice* (ed. 2000), *Crime Prevention and Community Safety* (1998) and *The Local Governance of Crime* (1997). He is completing an edited collection *International and Comparative Criminal Justice and Urban Governance* for Cambridge University Press. He is a member of the Scientific Committee of the Groupe Européen de Recherche sur les Normativités (GERN) and is co-organiser of the Worldwide Universities Network (WUN) *International and Comparative Criminal Justice Network*. From late 2010 he will assume the role of Editor in Chief of the journal *Criminology & Criminal Justice*.

Mireille Hildebrandt is Associate Professor of Jurisprudence at Erasmus University Rotterdam en senior researchter at Law Science Technology and

Society studies (LSTS), Vrije Universiteit Brussel. She publishes widely on the implications of future and emerging technologies for democracy and the rule of law. Together with Serge Gutwirth she edited Profiling the European Citizen. Cross-Disciplinary Perspectives (Springer, 2008) and with Antoinnette Rouvroy The Philosophy of Law meets the Philosophy of Technology: Autonomic Computing and Transformations of Human Agency (Routledge, forthcoming). She is Associate Editor of Criminal Law and Philosophy and of Identity in the Information Society and of Rechtsfilosofie & Rechtstheorie.

Hendrik Kaptein is senior university lecturer in philosophy of law and jurisprudence, Leyden University. Earlier on he taught at Nijmegen University and at the University of Amsterdam. His academic work focuses on legal ethics, criminal justice and argumentation theory. Publications include a doctoral dissertation on justification in normative thinking, a book on legal ethics and several edited books and articles on restorative justice, evidence and proof and other subjects.

Jean-Marc Piret (1960) is Associate Professor of Philosophy of Law at the University of Rotterdam Law School and at the Free University of Brussels. He publishes regularly on the history of ideas about public law, on law and religion in the public sphere, on liberty and security, and other issues of legal philosophy. Most recently he wrote articles about just war theory, the war on terrorism, and on the extraterritorial scope of the U.S. constitution after Boumediene v. Bush. In 2009 he also published a book in Dutch about Joseph de Maistre's, Marquis de Sade's and G.W.F. Hegel's relation to law, religion and history.

Abiola Makinwa is a researcher and PhD candidate with the Department of Private International and Comparative Law of the Faculty of Law, Erasmus University Rotterdam. Her research focuses on the use of the private law remedies and strategies in the fight against international corruption.

Klaas Rozemond is associate professor at the department of criminal law and criminology of the Vrije Universiteit Amsterdam. He is also a substitute judge at the District Court of Amsterdam. His main fields of research are European criminal law (the European Arrest Warrant), substantive criminal law (criminal responsibility), and the ethics and methodology of criminal law. His recent publications concern the surrender of nationals within the European Union, the casuistry of substantive criminal law, and judicial reasoning in criminal cases.

Ard Schoep took his law degree from the University of Leiden in the Netherlands and also defended there his doctoral thesis in Criminal Law in 2008. His thesis dealt with judicial policymaking in sentencing, in which he considered the question to what extent and under which conditions a form of policy can be pursued with regard to consistency in sentencing decisions. 2008 he was appointed to Associate Professor of Criminal Law and Criminal Procedure at the Institute for Criminal Law & Criminology at the University of Leiden. Since September 2007 he is also working as a part time judge at the District Court of Haarlem in the Netherlands.

Marc Schuilenburg teaches at the department of Criminology, VU University Amsterdam. Publications include articles on criminology, philosophy, law and popular culture. His most recently published books are Deleuze compendium (Boom, 2009) and Mediapolis. Popular Culture and the City (010-Publishers, 2007). He is currently working on a comparative study on the relation between security and assemblages. His website is www.marcschuilenburg.nl.

Philip Stenning has been a professor of Criminology at Keele University in the U.K. since the beginning of 2006. Before that he was Professor of Criminology and Director of the Institute of Criminology at Victoria University of Wellington, New Zealand, prior to which he had served in various positions at the Centre of Criminology at the University of Toronto in Canada. He obtained his doctorate in law (S.J.D.) from the University of Toronto in 1983. His principal areas of research have been policing (public and private), the prosecution process, the administration of criminal justice, and accountability for criminal justice. His most recently published book is The Modern Prosecution Process in New Zealand (Victoria University Press, 2008). In February 2011 he will take up a Chair in Criminology at Griffith University in Brisbane, Australia.

René van Swaaningen is Professor of International and Comparative Criminology at the Erasmus University Rotterdam (EUR) and scientific director of the inter-university Research School Safety and Justice, OMV. He has published mainly on risk-based justice, politics and crime control, comparative criminology, crime prevention and criminological theory.

Patrick Van Calster is professor of Criminology at the University of Groningen, the Netherlands. A criminologist and philosopher by training, his research interests include the interface between organizational criminology, policing, the regulatory state and complexity theory, as well as the cultural analysis of (representations of) crime and control. He has published prolifically on these issues in a wide variety of venues.